GROWTH AND TUR
CONTAINER/
BION'S CONTINUING LEGACY

Wilfred Bion remains the most cited author in psychoanalytic literature after Sigmund Freud. His formulation of alpha function, waking dream thoughts, his theory of thinking and of the container/contained have proven seminal for the elaboration of psychoanalytic theory and practice, as well as the exploration of psychic functioning and the primordial mind.

Growth and Turbulence in the Container/Contained: Bion's Continuing Legacy is based on papers presented at the 2009 International Bion Conference held in Boston, Massachusetts. It represents the state-of-the-art thinking of an outstanding international group of Bion scholars and experts. This book includes the most current trends in Bion scholarship, covering topics that range from the historical/biographical, to the clinical, the theoretical, the developmental, to the cultural and aesthetic.

Proving a vital stimulus to further creative explorations in the field, *Growth and Turbulence in the Container/Contained: Bion's Continuing Legacy* will be of particular interest to psychoanalytic practitioners, graduate psychoanalysts, analytic candidates, psychoanalytic therapists, advanced therapy trainees, and scholars of all schools.

Howard B. Levine works as a member of faculty at the Psychoanalytic Institute of New England East (PINE) and as a member of faculty and supervising analyst at Massachusetts Institute for Psychoanalysis (MIP). He is in private practice in Brookline, Massachusetts.

Lawrence J. Brown is a supervising child analyst at the Boston Psychoanalytic Institute (BPSI). He is a member of faculty at the BPSI as well as at MIP, where he is a supervising analyst. He is the author of *Intersubjective Processes and the Unconscious: An Integration of Freudian, Kleinian and Bionian Perspectives*, published in 2011 by Routledge (New Library of Psychoanalysis). He is in private practice in Newton Centre, Massachusetts.

PSYCHOANALYTIC INQUIRY BOOK SERIES
Joseph D. Lichtenberg
Series Editor

Like its counterpart, *Psychoanalytic Inquiry: A Topical Journal for Mental Health Professionals*, the Psychoanalytic Inquiry Book Series presents a diversity of subjects within a diversity of approaches to those subjects. Under the editorship of Joseph Lichtenberg, in collaboration with Melvin Bornstein and the editorial board of *Psychoanalytic Inquiry*, the volumes in this series strike a balance between research, theory, and clinical application. We are honored to have published the works of various innovators in psychoanalysis, such as Frank Lachmann, James Fosshage, Robert Stolorow, Donna Orange, Louis Sander, Léon Wurmser, James Grotstein, Joseph Jones, Doris Brothers, Fredric Busch, and Joseph D. Lichtenberg, among others.

The series includes books and monographs on mainline psychoanalytic topics, such as sexuality, narcissism, trauma, homosexuality, jealousy, envy, and varied aspects of analytic process and technique. In our efforts to broaden the field of analytic interest, the series has incorporated and embraced innovative discoveries in infant research, self psychology, intersubjectivity, motivational systems, affects as process, responses to cancer, borderline states, contextualism, postmodernism, attachment research and theory, medication, and mentalization. As further investigations in psychoanalysis come to fruition, we seek to present them in readable, easily comprehensible writing.

After 25 years, the core vision of this series remains the investigation, analysis and discussion of developments on the cutting edge of the psychoanalytic field, inspired by a boundless spirit of inquiry.

Vol. 41
Metaphor and Fields
Common Ground, Common Language and the Future of Psychoanalysis
S. Montana Katz (ed.)

Vol. 40
Growth and Turbulence in the Container/Contained: Bion's Continuing Legacy
Howard B. Levine & Lawrence J. Brown (eds.)

Vol. 39
Nothing Good Is Allowed to Stand
An Integrative View of the Negative Therapeutic Reaction
Léon Wurmser & Heidrun Jarass (eds.)

Vol. 38
Self Experiences in Group, Revisited
Affective Attachments, Intersubjective Regulations, and Human Understanding
Irene Harwood, Walter Stone, & Malcolm Pines (eds.)

Vol. 37
The Abyss of Madness
George E. Atwood

Vol. 36
Manual of Panic Focused Psychodynamic Psychotherapy – eXtended Range
Fredric N. Busch, Barbara L. Milrod, Meriamne B. Singer, & Andrew C. Aronson

Vol. 35
World, Affectivity, Trauma
Heidegger and Post-Cartesian Psychoanalysis
Robert D. Stolorow

Vol. 34
Change in Psychoanalysis
An Analyst's Reflections on the Therapeutic Relationship
Chris Jaenicke

Vol. 33
Psychoanalysis and Motivational Systems
A New Look
Joseph D. Lichtenberg, Frank M. Lachmann,& James L. Fosshage

Vol. 32
Persons in Context
The Challenge of Individuality in Theory and Practice
Roger Frie & William J. Coburn (eds.)

Vol. 31
Toward an Emancipatory Psychoanalysis
Brandchaft's Intersubjective Vision
Bernard Brandchaft, Shelley Doctors, & Dorienne Sorter

Vol. 30
From Psychoanalytic Narrative to Empirical Single Case Research
Implications for Psychoanalytic Practice
Horst Kächele, Joseph Schachter, Helmut Thomä & the Ulm Psychoanalytic Process Research Study Group

Vol. 29
Mentalization
Theoretical Considerations, Research Findings, and Clinical Implications
Fredric N. Busch (ed.)

Vol. 28
Transforming Narcissism
Reflections on Empathy, Humor, and Expectations
Frank M. Lachmann

Vol. 27
Toward a Psychology of Uncertainty
Trauma-Centered Psychoanalysis
Doris Brothers

Vol. 26
Living Systems, Evolving Consciousness, and the Emerging Person
A Selection of Papers from the Life Work of Louis Sander
Gherardo Amadei & Ilaria Bianchi (eds.)

Vol. 25
Sensuality and Sexuality across the Divide of Shame
Joseph D. Lichtenberg

Vol. 24
Jealousy and Envy
New Views about Two Powerful Feelings
Léon Wurmser & Heidrun Jarass (eds.)

Vol. 23
Trauma and Human Existence
Autobiographical, Psychoanalytic, and Philosophical Reflections
Robert D. Stolorow

Vol. 22
Psychotherapy and Medication
The Challenge of Integration
Fredric N. Busch & Larry S. Sandberg

Vol. 21
Attachment and Sexuality
Diana Diamond, Sidney J. Blatt, & Joseph D. Lichtenberg (eds.)

Vol. 20
Craft and Spirit
A Guide to Exploratory Psychotherapies
Joseph D. Lichtenberg

Vol. 19
A Spirit of Inquiry
Communication in Psychoanalysis
Joseph D. Lichtenberg, Frank M. Lachmann, & James L. Fosshage

Vol. 18
Kohut, Loewald, and the Postmoderns
A Comparative Study of Self and Relationship
Judith Guss Teicholz

Vol. 17
Working Intersubjectively
Contextualism in Psychoanalytic Practice
Donna M. Orange, George E. Atwood, & Robert D. Stolorow

Vol. 16
The Clinical Exchange
Techniques Derived from Self and Motivational Systems
Joseph D. Lichtenberg, Frank M. Lachmann, & James L. Fosshage

Vol. 14
Affects as Process
An Inquiry into the Centrality of Affect in Psychological Life
Joseph M. Jones

Vol. 13
Self and Motivational Systems
Toward a Theory of Psychoanalytic Technique
Joseph D. Lichtenberg, Frank M. Lachmann, & James L. Fosshage

Vol. 12
Contexts of Being
The Intersubjective Foundations of Psychological Life
Robert D. Stolorow & George E. Atwood

Vol. 10
Psychoanalysis and Motivation
Joseph D. Lichtenberg

Vol. 8
Psychoanalytic Treatment
An Intersubjective Approach
Robert D. Stolorow, Bernard Brandchaft, & George E. Atwood

Vol. 2
Psychoanalysis and Infant Research
Joseph D. Lichtenberg

Out of Print Titles in the PI Series

Vol. 15
Understanding Therapeutic Action
Psychodynamic Concepts of Cure
Lawrence E. Lifson (ed.)

Vol. 11
Cancer Stories
Creativity and Self-Repair
Esther Dreifuss-Kattan

Vol. 9
Female Homosexuality
Choice without Volition
Elaine V. Siegel

Vol. 7
The Borderline Patient
Emerging Concepts in Diagnosis, Psychodynamics, and Treatment, Vol. 2
James S. Grotstein, Marion F. Solomon, & Joan A. Lang (eds.)

Vol. 6
The Borderline Patient
Emerging Concepts in Diagnosis, Psychodynamics, and Treatment, Vol. 1
James S. Grotstein, Marion F. Solomon, & Joan A. Lang (eds.)

Vol. 5
Toward a Comprehensive Model for Schizophrenic Disorders
Psychoanalytic Essays in Memory of Ping-Nie Pao
David B. Feinsilver

Vol. 4
Structures of Subjectivity
Explorations in Psychoanalytic Phenomenology
George E. Atwood & Robert D. Stolorow

Vol. 3
Empathy, Volumes I & II
Joseph D. Lichtenberg, Melvin Bornstein, & Donald Silver (eds.)

Vol. 1
Reflections on Self Psychology
Joseph D. Lichtenberg & Samuel Kaplan (eds.)

GROWTH AND TURBULENCE IN THE CONTAINER/CONTAINED: BION'S CONTINUING LEGACY

Edited by
Howard B. Levine and
Lawrence J. Brown

Routledge
Taylor & Francis Group
LONDON AND NEW YORK

First published 2013
by Routledge
27 Church Road, Hove, East Sussex BN3 2FA

Simultaneously published in the USA and Canada
by Routledge
711 Third Avenue, New York, NY 10017

Routledge is an imprint of the Taylor & Francis Group, an informa business

British Library Cataloguing in Publication Data
A catalogue record for this book is available from the British Library

Library of Congress Cataloging in Publication Data
Growth and turbulence in the container/contained : Bion's continuing legacy / edited by Howard B. Levine and Lawrence J. Brown.
p. cm.
ISBN 978-0-415-61740-6 (978-0-415-61741-3) 1. Bion, Wilfred R. (Wilfred Ruprecht), 1897-1979. 2. Psychoanalysis. I. Levine, Howard B. II. Brown, Lawrence J., 1946–
BF109.B54G76 2012 150.19'5092--dc23
2012027247

ISBN: 978–0–415–61740–6 (hbk)
ISBN: 978–0–415–61741–3 (pbk)
ISBN: 978–0–203–07329–2 (ebk)

Typeset in Garamond and Helvetica Neue
by Bookcraft Ltd, Stroud, Glos

CONTENTS

ACKNOWLEDGEMENTS

"The Traumatic Roots of Containment: The Evolution of Bion's Metapsychology," Dorit Szykierski. First published in © The Psychoanalytic Quarterly, 2010, *The Psychoanalytic Quarterly*, 79(4):935–968.

James Grotstein, "Dreaming as a 'Curtain of Illusion': Revisiting the 'Royal Road' with Bion as Our Guide," *International Journal of Psychoanalysis* (2009) 90:733–752, John Wiley & Sons.

Beatriz Priel (Tel Aviv), "The Power of Form: The Shoah in Contemporary Hebrew Literature." Extracts from *Badenheim 1939* by Aharon Appelfeld, translated from the Hebrew by Dalya Bilu, reprinted by permission of David R. Godine, Publisher, Inc. Copyright 1980 by Aharon Appelfeld, Translation copyright reproduced with kind permission from © 1980 by Dalya Bilu. All rights reserved.

Extracts taken from "The Broken Bowl" by James Merrill from Merrill, J. (1996) *Selected Poems*, Manchester: Carcanet Press have been granted permission for use in Margot Waddell, "Meaning and Form: The Containing Function of Art."

"The Broken Bowl" from *Collected Poems* by James Merrill, edited by J. D. McClatchy and Stephen Yenser, copyright © 2001 by the Literary Estate of James Merrill at Washington University. Used by permission of Alfred A. Knopf, a division of Random House, Inc.

Every effort has been made to contact copyright-holders. Please advise the publisher of any errors or omissions, and these will be corrected in subsequent editions.

CONTRIBUTORS

Joseph Aguayo, Ph.D. is a training and supervising analyst at the Psychoanalytic Center of California, and holds doctorates in both clinical psychology and European history from UCLA. In full-time private practice in west Los Angeles, and also a recipient of a number of International Psychoanalytic Association/Research Advisory Board Fellowships, he has merged his clinical and research interests by specializing in the history of Kleinian psychoanalysis. He is completing a book entitled: *The Kleinian Development in London: 1918–2010,* the first few chapters of which have appeared in the *International Journal of Psychoanalysis.*

João Carlos Braga, M.D. is a training and supervising analyst at the Brazilian Psychoanalytic Society of São Paulo, Brazil. Previously a psychiatrist and on the faculty at the Medical School of the University of Paraná, Brazil, he has been in private psychoanalytic practice in Curitiba, Brazil, since 1982.

Lawrence J. Brown is a graduate of the BPSI in both child and adult psychoanalysis and is a supervising child analyst there. He is on the faculty of BPSI as well as the MIP and is a clinical instructor in psychiatry at Harvard Medical School. He has been on the North American editorial board of the *International Journal of Psychoanalysis* and is now on the editorial board of the *Psychoanalytic Quartely*. Dr. Brown was co-chair of the Bion in Boston 2009 International Conference held in July, 2009. His book, *Intersubjective Processes and the Unconscious: An Integration of Freudian, Kleinian and Bionian Perspectives*, was recently published in the New Library of Psychoanalysis series by Routledge in early 2011.

Alessandro Bruni was born in 1951 and began his professional life as a molecular biologist. After completing his dissertation on "LSD and Altered States of Consciousness," he entered the field of individual and group psychoanalysis, where he has supervised and led therapeutic groups, taught seminars on Wilfred Bion's theories and worked in public health services with alcohol and drug addicts. At present, he is a member of the IPA, a training analyst of the Italian Psychoanalytic Society and a founding member of the Italian Institute of Group Psychoanalysis (European Federation for Psychoanalytic Psychotherapy component). He is also a founding member of "Synaptica," a research group working in the field of psychosomatic illnesses from a theoretical and clinical perspective. Since 1980, Dr. Bruni has worked in the private practice of individual and group psychoanalysis.

Roosevelt M. S. Cassorla, M.D., Ph.D. is a psychoanalyst in private practice in Campinas, Brazil and training analyst of the Brazilian Psychoanalytic Society of São Paulo. He has worked as full professor at the Psychological Medicine Department, State University of Campinas and the postgraduate course in Mental Health. He is a member of the editorial board of the *International Journal of Psychoanalysis*, has edited three books on suicide and death and is the author of a number of book chapters and papers on medical psychology and psychoanalysis. His recent papers refer to analytical technique and borderline configurations.

Cláudio Laks Eizirik is a training and supervising analyst, Porto Alegre Psychoanalytical Society, adjunct professor, Department of Psychiatry, Federal University of Rio Grande do Sul and former President of the IPA.

Antonino Ferro is a training and supervising analyst of the Italian Psychoanalytic Society and a member of the IPA and the American Psychoanalytic Association (APsaA). He is the author of many journal articles and books, the last two of which are *Mind Works* and *Avoiding Emotions, Living Emotions*, both published by Routledge. In 2007, he was the recipient of the Mary S. Sigourney Award.

James S. Grotstein, M.D. is clinical professor of psychiatry at the David Geffen School of Medicine, UCLA, and training and supervising analyst at the New Center for Psychoanalysis and the Psychoanalytic Center of California, Los Angeles. He is a member of the editorial board of the *International Journal of Psychoanalysis* and is past North American vice-president of the IPA. He has published over 250 papers and is the author of many books, including, *Who is the Dreamer Who Dreams the Dream: A Study of Psychic Presences* (2000) and *A Beam of Intense Darkness: Wilfred Bion's Legacy to Psychoanalysis* (Karnac 2007). His most recent book is a two-volume work on psychoanalytic technique, "… *But at the Same Time and on Another Level …* " *Psychoanalytic Technique in the Kleinian/Bionian Mode, Volumes I and II* (Karnac 2009). In 2011, the

IPA 47th Congress in Mexico City featured a presentation and panel honoring his life's work. He is in the private practice of psychoanalysis in west Los Angeles.

Raul Hartke is a psychiatrist and a training and supervising analyst for the Porto Alegre Psychoanalytic Society, where he was a former scientific director, president and director of the institute. He is professor and supervisor for psychoanalytical psychotherapy at the Psychiatry Department, Medical School of the Federal University of Rio Grande do Sul.

Howard B. Levine is a member of the faculty and a supervising analyst at the Massachusetts Institute for Psychoanalysis (MIP), a member of the faculty at the Psychoanalytic Institute of New England East (PINE) and is in private practice in Brookline, Massachusetts. He is a member of the APsaA and the IPA, a founding member of the Group for the Study of Psychoanalytic Process (GSPP) and the Boston Group for Psychoanalytic Studies, Inc. (BGPS) and was co-chair of the 2009 International Bion Conference held in Boston, Massachusetts. Dr. Levine has served on the editorial boards of the *International Journal of Psycho-Analysis*, the *Journal of the American Psychoanalytic Association and Psychoanalytic Inquiry*, is a fellow of the College of the International Journal of Psycho-Analysis, and currently serves as North American representative to the board of the IPA. He has edited *Adult Analysis and Childhood Sexual Abuse* (Analytic Press 1990), co-edited *The Psychology of the Nuclear Threat* (Analytic Press 1986) and has authored numerous articles, book chapters and reviews on various subjects related to psychoanalytic process and technique, intersubjectivity, comparative psychoanalytic studies, the treatment of primitive personality disorders and the consequences and treatment of early trauma and childhood sexual abuse.

José Américo Junqueira de Mattos is a full member of the Brazilian Society of Psycho-Analysis of Sao Paulo and the Brazilian Society of Psycho-Analysis of Ribeirao Preto and the author of numerous articles. Dr. Junqueira de Mattos' ideas are influenced by those of W. R. Bion and follow the line of development of his thoughts.

Beatriz Priel is a founding member at the Tel Aviv Institute of Contemporary Psychoanalysis, and is actively involved in the training and supervising of mental health professionals in Israel. She is an emerita professor of psychology, Department of Psychology, Ben Gurion University of the Negev, where she chaired the clinical graduate program. In addition to clinical papers, her publications include studies on Agnon, Cervantes, Saramago, and especially Borges. She has a particular interest in the study of aesthetic experiences and on the implications of literature in psychoanalytical theory and praxis.

Marianne Robinson, Ph.D., MSW, FIPA is a training and supervising psychoanalyst in private practice in Seattle. She is a founding member of the Northwestern Psychoanalytic Society and a full member of the Psychoanalytic Center of California. She has led a number of infant observation groups and has written and presented on the value of infant observation in psychoanalytic training. Her research and writing have focused on the potential for growth that emerges when noting, investigating, analyzing and understanding the vestiges of early physical, emotional and mental experiences, as they manifest within the analytic relationship.

Angelika Staehle holds university diplomas in political science, economics and psychology, practices adult, child, and adolescent psychoanalysis (DPV [German Psychoanalytical Association]/IPA), and group psychoanalysis (DAGG [German Association of Group Psychotherapy and Group Dynamics], Group Analytic Society—London), is a training analyst and supervisor in child and adult psychoanalysis (DPV/IPA), and supervises group analysis. For many years, she was a member of the executive board and president of the Central Training Committee of the DPV. Currently, she holds the positions of director of training for child and adolescent psychoanalysis (DPV/IPA) and director of the scientific program committee. She is working in full private practice with children, adolescents and adults, individually and in groups. She has had numerous publications, many of which reflect her special interest in psychoanalytic technique, especially disturbances of symbolization in children, adolescents and adults.

Dorit Szykierski is a senior clinical psychologist in private practice in Tel Aviv-Yafo, Israel. She is a member of OFEK—the Israeli association for the study of group and organizational processes. She studies the evolution of Bion's ideas, and is particularly interested in the application of his theory to research on social and cultural phenomena.

Renato Trachtenberg is a psychiatrist, full member, training and supervising analyst for the Brazilian Psychoanalysis Society of Porto Alegre, where he was a former scientific director, secretary and secretary of the institute. He is full member of the Buenos Aires Psychoanalytic Association, a full member of the Psychoanalytical Studies Center of Porto Alegre, co-author of the book *The Seven Capital Envies* (with Arnaldo Chuster) and the author of many articles and papers for various psychoanalytical books, magazines and journals.

Margot Waddell is a member of the British Psychoanalytical Society and a child analyst. She has worked for over 30 years as a consultant child and adolescent psychotherapist at the Tavistock Clinic, London, is a widely published author and has taught both nationally and internationally for many years. Evident in her publications is a life-long interest in the relationship between the internal and the external world, between being an individual and at the same time a group animal. She has edited the Tavistock Clinic book series since its inception in 1998. An extended edition of her book, *Inside Lives; Psychoanalysis and the Growth of the Personality* was published by Karnac in 2002, *Understanding 12–14-year-olds* was published by Jessica Kingsley in 2005.

Heinz Weiss, Prof. M.D., DPV, DGPT is director of the Department of Psychosomatic Medicine, Robert-Bosch-Krankenhaus, Stuttgart, Germany, and a guest member of the British Psychoanalytical Society. He teaches at the University of Tübingen and has published a number of papers and books on various aspects of the history, theory and clinical aspects of psychoanalysis. His most recent book publication is *Das Labyrinth der Borderline-Kommunikation. Klinische Zugänge zum Erleben von Raum und Zeit* [The Labyrinth of Borderline Communication. Clinical Explorations into the Experience of Time and Space], published in 2009 by Klett-Cotta (Stuttgart).

Part 1

INTRODUCTION AND HISTORICAL OVERVIEW

INTRODUCTION

Cláudio Laks Eizirik

The concept of container/contained, built upon the elaboration of the communicative dimension of Melanie Klein's original description of projective identification, is central to the work of Bion. It is usually acknowledged that Bion developed and expanded Klein's original groundbreaking idea, in such a new and far reaching way that we currently can see how useful this notion can be for the understanding of so many different dimensions, such as the emotional contact of the infant with the mother, the analyst with the patient, the student with the teacher, the members of a group with the group structure, the two partners of a couple, parts of the self, the artist with his or her audience, and so on.

From a historical perspective, we can see Bion, who was in analysis with Klein from 1943 to 1953, today as one of the main members of the second generation of Kleinian analysts, together with his contemporaries Herbert Rosenfeld, Hanna Segal, Betty Joseph, all of whom were also influenced by his own work; or we can see him as someone unique, apart from his roots and influences. This is of course one of the many controversies that surround his creative contributions. In my own view, however, Bion continued the work of Klein, as she continued the work of Freud, as Ferro, Grotstein and the other contributors to this volume, and many others, continue the work of Bion, and so on.

At the same time, it cannot be denied that his own theoretical and clinical development grew up after Klein's death and he became more and more a reference and a decisive influence for the analytic thinking and clinical practice of many analysts from different countries.

The idea of projective identification as communication in the process of container/contained, in the way we understand it nowadays, can be found very early in Bion's writings in one of his most quoted descriptions:

> Throughout the analysis the patient resorted to projective identification with a persistence suggesting it was a mechanism of which he had never been able sufficiently to avail himself; the analysis afforded

> him the opportunity for the exercise of a mechanism of which he had been cheated … there were elements which indicate that the patient felt that parts of his personality that he wished to repose in me were refused entry by me …. When the patient strove to rid himself of fears of death which were felt to be too powerful for his personality to contain he split off his fears and put them into me , the idea apparently being that if they were allowed to repose there long enough they would undergo modification by my psyche and could then be safely reintrojected. On the occasion I have in mind the patient had felt … that I evacuated them so quickly that the feelings were not modified but had become more painful … he strove to force them into me with increased desperation and violence …. The more violent his fantasies of projective identification, the more frightened he became of me …. The analytic situation built up in my mind a sense of witnessing an extremely early scene. I felt that the patient had witnessed in infancy a mother who dutifully responded to the infant's emotional displays. The dutiful response had in it an element of impatience "I don't know what's the matter with the child." My deduction was that in order to understand what the child wanted the mother should have treated the infant's cry as more than a demand for her presence. From the infant's point of view she should have taken into her, and thus experienced, the fear that the child was dying. It was this fear that the child could not contain. He strove to split it off together with the part of the personality in which it lay and project it into the mother. An understanding mother is able to experience the feeling of dread that this baby was striving to deal with by projective identification, and yet retain a balanced outlook.
>
> (Bion, 1959, pp. 103–4)

In my view, here we can see the main features of an intimate relationship, and how it can work in terms of containing or not, and this is equally true for the relation between a mother and her baby or the analytic relation or any intimate and fertile relation, as mentioned above.

Several years later, Bion described three forms of the container/contained relationship: parasitic, symbiotic and commensal, in these terms:

> By commensal I mean a relationship in which two objects share a third to the advantage of all three. By symbiotic I understand a relationship in which one depends on another to mutual advantage. By parasitic I mean to represent a relationship in which one depends on another to produce a third which is destructive of all three.
>
> (Bion, 1970, p. 95)

Judging from the above, it is clear that there is a natural connection between the notion of container/contained, turbulence and growth. In his paper on emotional turbulence, Bion (1977), noting that turbulence usually goes hand in hand with great changes in life, as birth, adolescence, old age and so on, suggested that when a child who looks calm and cooperative becomes agitated, disturbed and angry, this fact is usually understood as pathology, but it can instead represent a necessary change from one mental state to another. Similarly, the analytic process requires a regressive return to an earlier mental state, which is accompanied by a clinical manifestation of emotional turbulence in the patient as well as in the analyst.

Departing from Klein's theories of infantile fantasy, Bion developed his theory of thinking. He used as a starting point the analytic hour, stressing the two principles of the emergence of truth and mental growth. According to him, the mind grows through exposure to truth, and the foundation for both mental development and truth is emotional experience (Bion, 1962).

The notion of container/contained is central for Bion's theory of thinking, which consists of the mating of a pre-conception and a realization, which leads to a conception and a step in the building of thought and theories.

What the reader will find in this book is a series of papers from authors from different regions, in which the articulations of the notions of growth, turbulence and the container/contained are pursued and illustrated in a very stimulating way, with lively material drawn from the clinical setting, normal development and cultural and aesthetic experience that aptly shows how Bion's thinking opens different vertices with which to observe and develop new ideas.

The International Bion Conferences originated in the 1990s as several devoted readers of Bion began to join in the congresses of the International Psychoanalytical Association (IPA) to exchange views and ideas and share concerns, doubts and the mutual experience of working with Bion's ideas. This group of Bionian analysts eventually decided to organize a specific conference on his theory and practice that was held in Turin, in 1997. In the following years, similar meetings were held in Buenos Aires, Los Angeles, São Paulo, Rome, then in 2009 in Boston, with the next one scheduled for 2011, in Porto Alegre. Each one of these meetings had its own features and focus, but shared in the common purpose of reflecting on Bion's ideas and way of analyzing, with great emphasis on discussions in small groups and wide space for the informal exchange of emotional experiences (Trachtenberg, 2011).

At the same time, in recent decades, the psychoanalytic community continues to have the opportunity of taking part in similar kinds of meetings devoted to the study of the work and influence of other authors, such as Ferenczi, Winnicott, Lacan, as well as the well attended French-speaking analysts' conferences. If we consider that each two years we have an IPA congress, as well as conferences from the three regional federations, and the national congresses, and many others, we might imagine that the psychoanalytic movement is in a state of fragmentation.

In my view, however, these facts of psychoanalytic development offer us still another good example of growth and turbulence in the container/contained. Each institution and congress, in its own way and tradition, provides the containment for the mating of different ideas; each meeting has its peculiar form of turbulence that eventually leads to mental growth.

The current scene—of which this volume is a component—attests to the vitality of psychoanalytic thinking and the several ways of being an analyst and of training new analysts. What is at stake now is our need to develop the capacity to listen to each other and not to get closed in specific small theoretical villages; in this sense, the Bion conferences offer a model for meetings devoted to listening and exchanging experiences across the various schools and regions of international psychoanalysis; they are not closed to a small group of selected guests, but rather open and stimulating free discussions.

In recent years, initiatives like the CAPSA program (analytic practice and scientific activities committee) of the IPA, that fosters clinical and theoretical exchanges among different regions and perspectives, similarly serve as tools for avoiding parochialism and stressing the need for open and objective discussions of our convergences and divergences (Eizirik, 2010).

Thanks to the stimulating and tireless effort of Larry Brown, Howard Levine and their colleagues, we had in Boston in 2009 a rewarding emotional experience, with all the elements I just mentioned. I am sure that the reader of this book will be able to feel something of that atmosphere and see how the thinking of Bion is stimulating new and talented analysts, who are not only careful readers of the maestro but who also dare to disturb the universe of the already known in his seminal work. I invite readers to join us and share in that experience.

References

Bion, W. R. (1959) Attacks on linking. *International Journal of Psychoanalysis*, 40:308–15.

Bion, W. R. (1962) A theory of thinking. *International Journal of Psychoanalysis*, 43:306–10.

Bion, W. R. (1970) *Attention and Interpretation*. London, Tavistock.

Bion, W. R. (1977) Emotional disturbance. In Hartocolis, P. *Borderline Personality Disorders*, New York: International Universities Press.

Eizirik, C. L. (2010) Analytic practice: convergences and divergences. *International Journal of Psychoanalysis*, 91:371–5.

Trachtenberg, R. (2011) Personal communication.

1

THE DEVELOPMENT OF BION'S CONCEPT OF CONTAINER AND CONTAINED

Lawrence J. Brown

This book is a collection of papers that deal with one of Bion's most generative concepts—the notion of the container/contained relationship. The reader will discover a wide range of contributions from international writers who have given considerable thought to the many implications of Bion's theory of the container/contained. As editors of this volume, Howard Levine and I have chosen papers that range across a broad swath of topics including, but not limited to, the impact of Bion's personal history on his ideas, aesthetic applications and clinical implications. Of particular interest are studies of the *turbulence* that may arise in the container/contained relationship, how this may be understood and worked with in the analytic encounter, in the nursery, and in artistic productions. We believe the reader will find these chapters stimulating new ways of thinking that illuminate the richness of Bion's concept.

But what is a container or the contained and what do we mean by the container/contained relationship? Where does the theory of container/contained fall within the accumulated oeuvre of Bion's thinking? This introduction will explore the development of the container/contained concept, its roots in his personal life and the place it occupies in the evolution of his major theories. We will see that this proposition, which was first introduced in his brief (1962a) paper, "A theory of thinking," developed from his notion of *alpha function* that was formulated during a very creative period from 1958 through 1960. So we shall turn our attention first to a consideration of the nature of alpha function.

The Concept of Alpha Function

Alpha function, of which the container/contained theory is a factor, has its beginnings in Bion's quest to understand the nature of thinking and its disturbances, a question that frames the bulk of his analytic writings. Indeed, his first publication in 1940, "The 'war of nerves': Civilian reaction, morale and prophylaxis," addressed how the experience of battle can disarticulate the soldier's capacity to think clearly. Bion noted that one unexpressed aim of battle is to evoke a state of confusion in the individual soldier that has the effect of stirring the most elemental unconscious phantasies, beclouding judgment and rendering the enemy unable to think clearly (Bion, 1940). Mind-numbing fear, created by the incessant bombing before a battle, disorients the fighters such that terrifying unconscious phantasies take over cognitive functioning, thereby enveloping them in the "fog of war" that ensues when conscious thought is attacked.

The impact of Bion's World War I experiences on his psychoanalytic theories has been the subject of recent studies (Brown, 2011b, in press; Souter, 2009; Symington, 1996; Szykierski, 2010, this volume). These are based upon his personal journals (1982, 1985, 1990, 1997) published after his death in which Bion's military experiences are recounted in often graphic and harrowing detail. Paradoxically, his war experiences chronicled in the diaries are rarely, if ever, directly mentioned in his "professional" writings, which make only oblique references to these experiences, if at all. Nevertheless, it was Francesca Bion (1997) herself who succinctly stated that Bion's war actions "all formed part of the real personal emotional experience on which his theories lie" (p. 311). For example, in his last paper, "Making the best of a bad job," Bion (1979) compares engagement with some patients to combat:

> In war the enemy's object is so to terrify you that you cannot think clearly, while your object is to continue to think clearly no matter how adverse or frightening the situation.
>
> (p. 322)

References to his war experiences are a constant underpinning to many of his writings, though rarely mentioned directly; thus, his last published sentence in his final paper, "Making the best of a bad job," is "That war has not ceased yet" (p. 331). Thus, one tributary to Bion's theory of alpha function was his first-hand experience in war that provided him an *in vivo* lesson of not being able to think, a paralyzing feeling he recalls in his diary of the 1918 Battle of Amiens written forty years later when he revisited the battle site with his wife, Francesca: "Bion felt sick. He wanted to think … He tried to think … He tried to think" (1997, p. 254).

A second tributary to the discovery of alpha function was his clinical experience with psychotic and borderline patients in whom he confronted a different kind of thinking disturbance than he witnessed in the battlefield "war of nerves." Nevertheless, the terrifying enemy bombardments which lit the sky with deadly meteorites of exploding shell splinters seem to have served as a template for Bion's (1957/1967) description of one aspect of the psychotic state of mind when he said "the patient feels surrounded by minute links which, being impregnated now with cruelty, link objects together cruelly" (p. 50). In addition, Bion (1959) noted that the psychotic part of the mind will attack links that hold things together, including the link between analyst and patient as well as the links that connect words to each other. He also observed that this "attack on linking" similarly desiccated his own thinking abilities, leaving him stranded in a dry concrete world of meaningless events.

Bion's (1957) analytic work with the psychotic part of the personality also brought him in contact with a near absence of what he termed *reverie*, which is the healthy mind's capacity for imaginative conjecture as opposed to the psychotic's entrapment in a concrete terrain. This observation seems to have led him to wonder about the origin of reverie, the factors that lead to its failures as well as to how it may be repaired. In a paper the next year, "On arrogance," Bion (1958) introduced the notion that the analyst must be able to accept the patient's projective identifications and allow them to "sojourn" in his psyche in order for that projection to be modified, thereby rendering it more readily tolerated by the projecting mind. Though he does not refer in this later paper to "reverie," it appears that Bion is starting to reflect on the role of the analyst's mind in helping the disturbed patient to strengthen, or perhaps develop for the first time, a capacity for reverie.

A third tributary leading to the formulation of alpha function derives from an especially creative period in Bion's personal and professional life that took place from 1958 through 1960. As mentioned above, he began writing the diary of the Battle of Amiens in 1958 and continued this until some point in 1960 when he stopped this account mid-sentence. Simultaneously with writing the diary, Bion (1992) embarked on writing numerous entries in *Cogitations*, his notebook of unpublished thoughts relating to psychoanalytic theory and practice. In my view, his articulation of alpha function was the crowning achievement of these two concurrent endeavors:

> Bion's discovery of alpha function was a milestone reached by having traveled the dual carriageway of the *Amiens* diary and *Cogitations*, an achievement that opened up new creative avenues that led to crafting the invaluable theories of thinking, the container and the contained, etc., that began with *Learning from Experience* in 1962.
>
> (Brown, 2011b)

Thus, the emotional "work" undertaken in the diary gave Bion grist for his conjectural deliberations in *Cogitations*, which, in turn, provided him with the theoretical scaffolding that continued to bolster working through the World War I trauma.

It was during this period of 1959–60 that Bion developed in *Cogitations* his own theory of dreaming that began first as an extension of Freud's ideas and eventuated in his proposal of alpha function. I suggest that beginning to revisit the horrors of World War I in 1958 through writing the Amiens diary, forty years after their occurrence, must have raised the question of how anyone can mentally survive the onslaught of such unrelenting and unbearable experience. In "Differentiation of the psychotic from the non-psychotic personalities" (1957) and "On arrogance" (1958), Bion had underscored the importance of two central factors of the healthy mind in dealing with reality: the capacity for *reverie* and the ability to tolerate projective identifications by allowing their mollifying *sojourn* within the analyst's psyche. These elements—*reverie* and a mollifying *sojourn*—pointed to some sort of transformational process that occurs within the analyst's mind and one which is lacking in the disturbed mind of the patient. These reflections brought Bion to a reconsideration of the nature of dreaming.

Bion's (1992) continued entries in *Cogitations* led him to the realization that dreaming also served what he termed a "mental digestive process" (p. 42) in giving personalized, emotional meaning to the reality events of one's life, a process which Grotstein (2000) likens to an "information processing" model. Freud (1900), of course, considered dreaming as occurring under the aegis of the *pleasure principle*: that dreams are constructed through *dream-work* that disguises unconscious wishes so that these might pass unnoticed by the censor which bars them from consciousness. However, Bion's view that dreaming was a "mental digestive process" gave prominence to dreams as operating within the framework of the reality principle and he borrowed Freud's term, *dream-work*, to describe this process. Bion expanded Freud's concept of dream-work to account for a process by which conscious *emotional* experience is absorbed by the psyche in order to become part of our unconscious, personalized record that is repressed. Unless this process "works on" raw emotional experiences these remain "undigested facts." Bion's widened application of dream work accounted for the transformative procedure by which these undigested facts were turned into memories which could be linked with other memories in an individual's self-narrative. Bion broadened the "domain of the dream" (p. 45) to include this metamorphosing process by which conscious emotional experience becomes personally represented within one's individual psyche, a never-ending progression forged by dream-work that operates while we are awake and asleep.

Thus, Bion's extension of Freud's dream-work helped him to begin to understand a very complex process of the mind by which reality experiences, especially painful ones, can be made more bearable and therefore absorbed by that mind, i.e., through dream-work. But starting in early 1960, Bion's *Cogitations* entries took an important step forward when he amended Freud's definition of dream-work by proposing *dream-work-α*, which denoted *the capacity to dream* rather than the process by which a dream disguises an unconscious wish. In adding "-α" to "dream-work" Bion was attempting to account for that psychic process by which undigested facts (conscious experience) are transformed into "emotional thoughts" (α elements) that may be linked together in a dream narrative. It was as though Bion were saying to Freud, "Herr Professor, in order for the sleeping mind to construct a dream through dream-work there needs to be a more basic process occurring, which is the production of dream (α) elements with which to construct that dream. My use of 'dream-work-α' accounts for how that happens."

Sometime later in 1960 (undated entry) Bion replaced dream-work-α with simply *alpha function*, therefore breaking further with Freud's theory and establishing his own viewpoint detached from Freud's original concept.[1] He had achieved much during this impressively fertile time from 1958 through 1960: Bion revisited the Battle of Amiens and digested its emotional impact further; he continued to learn from clinical experience with the psychotic mind about the factors which preclude the capacity to digest painful realities; and he creatively extended Freud's theory of dreaming to explain how the mind processes reality to make it more bearable so that we may learn from experience. This brings us to the threshold of Bion's introduction of his model of the *container/contained* that was introduced after this creative period when he wrote the Amiens diary and developed the theory of alpha function in *Cogitations*.

I would like to close this portion with my own theory of why Bion ended the Amiens diary in mid-sentence. The sentence follows Bion's recollection of a conversation with a colleague about a fellow officer who had "cracked up" under pressure. The colleague commented that Bion appeared steady and intact and Bion (1997) stated that "Bion did not believe him. He felt that people who cracked up were merely those who did not allow the rest of the world to … " (p. 308).

Francesca Bion (1997) believes that this sentence was never finished because he had moved on and "other more pressing commitments intervened" (p. 214), especially writing *Learning from Experience*. However, Szykierski (2010) opines that it seemed Bion was "about to formulate the great unknown of mental catastrophe, but could not find the words" (p. 959). Souter (2009), on the other hand, questions whether we should even attempt to complete this sentence, suggesting that we instead leave it open and tolerate the "demand that the bloodied gap be closed" (p. 806).

From my point of view, it seems more than coincidental that he would end the diary at the same time his speculations in *Cogitations* led him to introduce the concept of alpha function. Having discovered the vital role of dream-work-α (later, simply *alpha*) in processing and making more manageable overpowering emotional experience in reality, Bion had begun to understand some of the factors that could inoculate a soldier against "cracking up." This formulation also signaled Bion's final movement away from Freud's theory of dreaming (by abandoning any reference to Freud's "dream-work") and represents a quantum step forward in his independence as a psychoanalytic thinker. Therefore, it may be that he stopped writing in the diary because his intellectual labors in *Cogitations* and the emotional work in the diary brought the realization that had found the words "to formulate the great unknown of mental catastrophe" (Szykierski, 2010) and those words were "alpha function."

Alpha Function and the Container and the Contained[2]

Bion's gradual refinement of the concept of alpha function preceded his development of the theory of container and contained. Alpha function, which may be considered a part of the unconscious ego (Brown, 2009, 2011a), describes a psychic process, and the agency responsible for its operation, by which affective experience is transformed from its conscious sensory registration to an emotional thought; that is, from existing as an undigested fact to becoming a memory. We have seen how Bion's ideas about alpha function slowly evolved: first, as a borrowed term (dream-work) from Freud (1900); then gradually advancing into a distinctly unique and creative proposition. However, tracing the growth of the concept of alpha function still leaves unanswered the question of how it develops in the psyche of an individual and this query brings us to Bion's formulation of the container and the contained.

We have discussed how Bion's working through his World War I trauma by writing in the Amiens diary and in *Cogitations* as well as his clinical experience with psychotic thinking eventuated in his discovery of alpha function of which the theory of container and contained is a constituent. Szykierski (2010) links Bion's use of the word "containment" with its military implication, as in "containing" the enemy, and sees its roots in his war experiences. However, we should not discount the importance of Bion's therapeutic work in shaping his ideas about what it means to "contain."As early as 1956, in the paper "Development of schizophrenic thought," Bion described the psychotic's projection of "expelled particles of ego" (p. 39) into objects which are then experienced as "containing," and possibly being taken over, by the projection. In the following year, he (Bion, 1957) noted that the analyst's attempt to put back the projection into the patient through an interpretation made "the patient feel intruded upon, assaulted, and tortured by this re-entry even if willed by himself" (pp. 62–3).

Bion appears to have given considerable thought to the dilemma of how the analyst should manage what the patient has projected into him since interpreting the projection often served to increase the analysand's sense of persecution. And in "On arrogance," Bion (1958) stated that in analysis the patient and analyst were "required to pursue the truth, and in particular a capacity to tolerate the stresses associated with the introjections of another person's projective identification" (p. 88). In essence, then, Bion had learned that he must "tolerate the stress" that could allow for some "modification" of the patient's "bad feelings," though the process by which that metamorphosis is achieved awaited further explanation and anticipated his soon-to-arrive thoughts about the *container* and *contained.*

Bion's (1962a) brief paper, "The psycho-analytic study of thinking," introduces a specific kind of interaction between a mother and her infant which is then further explored in *Learning from Experience* (1962b) in the same year. In the paper on thinking, he links alpha function for the first time with a process "between mother and infant, a relationship in which normal projective identification is possible" (p. 115) and it is through this process that sense data are converted into alpha elements. Thus, he is starting to investigate the connection between alpha function and some as yet unspecified interaction occurring between a mother and her baby in which maternal receptivity plays a central role: "The mother's capacity for reverie[3] is the *receptor organ*[4] for the infant's harvest of self-sensation gained by its conscious" (1962a, p. 116) [italics in the original].

The infant needs a mother who is *receptive* to its projective identifications and through her capacity for *reverie* transforms the baby's overwhelming emotional experiences into manageable psychic events (α elements). Thus, this short paper on the nature of thinking offers a gateway to his extensive elaboration of the theory of alpha function by postulating an essential connection between the object relations of very early development and the emergence of a capacity for thinking, dreaming and managing affect.

At this point we must return to Bion's personal life to foster a better understanding of the factors contributing to development of the theory of container and contained, namely his marriage to Francesca Bion in the early 1950s.[5] Although he wrote about his war experiences in letters to his parents from 1917–19, these trauma remained "carried over almost unchewed and apparently undigested" (Bion, 1997, p. 309) until he returned to the site of the Battle of Amiens forty years later, an event which prompted him to write the Amiens diary. Francesca Bion reports that he rarely spoke to others about the war, yet on their first date he talked movingly about those horrible times. Although Bion's earlier recollections of the war convey the gruesomeness of battle, Souter (2009) observes that in the Amiens diary his descriptions especially delivered "his horror and repulsion very fully" (p. 802); therefore, he surely found in Francesca a containing figure with whom he felt safe enough to unburden the full load of his past trauma. Thus, Bion gleaned from his own invaluable experience the vital importance of having a trusted partner who could take in one's most anguished feelings, tolerate them and transform them into bearable emotions that stimulate personal growth.

In *Learning from Experience*, Bion (1962b) fleshes out "alpha function" which had only been briefly touched upon in the paper on thinking. In *Learning* we are introduced to alpha function as an overarching concept that is composed of various *factors*[6] that comprise it, especially reverie which "is a factor of the mother's alpha function" (p. 36) and is an expression of love for her baby through her "reception of the infant's projective identifications whether they are felt by the infant to be good or bad" (p. 36). From this perspective, this is a "*digestive model*"[7] (p. 42) of alpha function since "the alimentary system [is used] as a model for the processes of thought" (p. 62). From this perspective, the infant's immature psychic state which cannot process emotions is likened to the developing alimentary system that is unable to digest complex foods. The mother, like the mother of newly hatched chicks, must pre-masticate emotional experience through the factor of her reverie so that the internal and external stimuli affecting the baby are made into mentally "digestible" morsels (α elements) that the infant's nascent psyche can incorporate without undue frustration. Maternal reverie serves different purposes for the baby as psychological growth occurs; thus, the infant comes to rely on its mother in the *depressive position* for her capacity to link emotional experiences together into simple narratives that gradually achieve greater complexity. In Bion's digestive model of alpha function, the infant introjects its mother's alpha function, and the associated capacity for reverie, which forms the core of its own developing[8] ability to metabolize experience.

The concepts of container and contained are not introduced until the final pages of *Learning from Experience*. These are among the best known of his ideas and I want to emphasize that, in my opinion, the introduction of the container and contained moves Bion's thinking in a decidedly *intersubjective* direction (Brown, 2009, 2011b), which I have termed a *procreative* model and Sandler (2000) has called the "reproductive" point of view. By using the sign "♀" to denote the container and "♂" for the contained, Bion is implying a sexual connotation[9] about which he comments in *Attention and Interpretation* (1970) "The use of the male and female symbols is deliberate but must not be taken to mean that other than sexual implications are excluded ... [but is simultaneously] the sexual relationship ♀♂" (pp. 106–7). In addition, the intersubjective element is further emphasized when Bion describes the normal, developmentally facilitating interaction between the mother as container and the baby as contained as *commensal* which means that "the mother derives benefit and achieves mental growth from the experience: the infant likewise extracts benefit and achieves growth" (p. 910). And, most importantly "*The activity that I have here described as shared by two individuals becomes introjected by the infant so that the ♀♂ apparatus becomes installed in the infant* as part of the apparatus of alpha-function" (p. 91) [italics added].

Thus, alpha function becomes installed in the infant in two ways: first by the introjection of mother's reverie/alpha function and, second, by the introjection of the mother/infant pair "thinking" together. The capacity for emotional growth in the container/contained (♀♂) depends upon a milieu of *tolerated doubt* between mother and infant that establishes a receptive climate in which the selected fact may emerge and that, finally, this "Growing ♂♀ provides the basis of an apparatus for learning by experience" (p. 92).

To recapitulate: Bion formulated his theory of alpha function during an especially fertile period from 1958–60, but his ideas were primarily descriptive in nature and required further advancement to account for its development in the individual. He had become aware of the need for very troubled patients to deposit unendurable experiences into the analyst where these were to be modified by some unspecified process during their sojourn in the therapist's psyche. His continued exploration of the means by which this metabolizing operation occurred led Bion to appreciate the vital role of the mother's capacity to withstand taking in her baby's projections and subject these to her reverie, which he viewed as a factor of alpha function. Bion first considered this process from a digestive model in which the "infant depends on the Mother to act as its α-function" (Bion, 1963, p. 27); in effect pre-masticating experience for the baby, so that feeding may be successful. But he also outlined an intersubjective framework when he (Bion, 1962b) introduced the notion of the container (♀) and the contained (♂). The ♀♂ is a couple, mother and infant,[10] who grow together through the ability to tolerate doubt until some meaning is ascribed to unprocessed emotions, and this collective activity is introjected as the "apparatus for thinking" (Bion, 1963, p. 31) thoughts that is a major component of alpha function by which we are able to learn from experience. Thus, alpha function is the overarching concept of which reverie and the container/contained (♀♂) are factors. In a somewhat confusing way, Bion uses the sign ♀♂ to refer to two phenomena: the container/contained relationship between mother and infant and also to denote the "apparatus for thinking." While blurring the boundaries between these two central concepts, he is also implying an intricate linkage between the early mother/baby relationship and the capacity for thinking, both of which are constituents of alpha function.

Bion began to shift the emphasis in his writings away from alpha function per se to concentrate on the factors that comprised it, which he had already begun at the end of *Learning from Experience* when he launched the study of the container/contained. In *Elements of Psychoanalysis* (1963) he listed the "dynamic relationship between container and contained" (p. 3) as the first element, thereby according a primacy to the analytic dyad, its link to the early mother/infant dialogue and the development of the apparatus for thinking. To these phenomena he added a second element, the Ps↔D balance that refers to the oscillation between moments of coherence (D signifying the depressive position) and of relative disintegration (Ps standing for the paranoid-schizoid position). Bion links the concepts of Ps↔D and ♀♂ by stating that essentially each works in tandem with the other: that in order for coherence (D) to emerge out of fragmentation (Ps) the presence of a container that gathers up the psychic bits to offer a unifying selected fact is necessary. As a corollary, the ♀♂ depends upon the mind's capacity to tolerate swings in the Ps↔D balance[11] (tolerated doubt) and Bion states that these are "mechanisms each of which can at need assume the characteristics of the other" (p. 44).

I suggest that the connections and redundancies of these various factors may be gathered together under the rubric (schematized here)[12] of a *Constellation for Thinking*, all of which are subsumed by the super-ordinate concept of alpha function, which is the engine that drives transformations (see next section below):

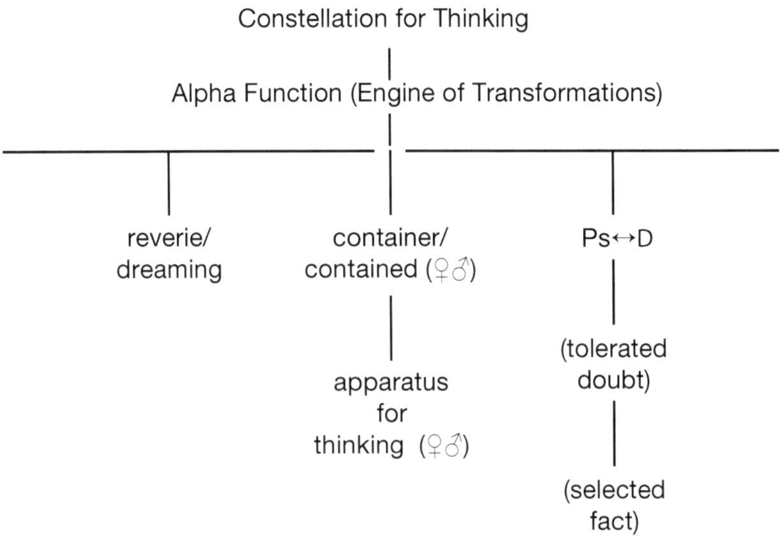

The three columns map the growth of the concept of alpha function as we move from the left to the right. Alpha function initially sprouted from Bion's observations about the hobbling of thinking/reverie in the psychotic part of the mind and from there to his augmentation of Freud's view of dreaming. Furthermore, he needed a theory about how the capacity to dream (as an act of transforming experience) developed in the individual psyche, which brought him to propose the model of the container/contained and an understanding of the role of very early object relations in the maturation of the "apparatus for thinking." Additional exploration of the elements of alpha function led Bion to broaden the definition of Klein's paranoid-schizoid and depressive positions as states of relative disintegration oscillating with experiences of integration, i.e., the Ps↔D balance. Finally, and most importantly, emotional growth in both the patient and analyst depended on being able to tolerate the doubt and turbulence (Ps) of not knowing until some selected fact appeared (D) to bring coherence to what had been disjointed and incomprehensible.

Alpha Function, the Container/Contained and Transformations

It is interesting that Bion's (1965) next major work, *Transformations*, rarely mentions alpha function or the container/contained yet, paradoxically, it represents a furthering of these basic concepts. However, just as the formulation of container/contained was necessary to explain the development of alpha function, so the theory of *transformations* described the inner functioning of the mind as it "worked on" unrepresented experience to transcribe it into the language of one's storehouse of personal meanings. Indeed, Bion's theories have always been about transformation: how the mind turns undigested facts (β) into emotional thoughts (α elements); the necessity of having internalized a fertile and resilient ♀♂ relationship; the capacity for dreaming/reverie; and the ability to tolerate the doubt associated with fluctuations between Ps↔D. Put another way, alpha function and its constituent factors are the mental machinery by which transformations are effected (see diagram of Constellation for Thinking above). Bion explores this territory with the keen focus of a scientist's eye and the searching soul of a poet.

Transformations is a very complex work and explicating all its suppositions goes beyond the scope of this paper, but I want to draw our attention to two main conceptual contributions: Bion's introduction of "O" and its transformation and, secondly, the aesthetic implications of O. I will start with the aesthetic aspects first because it is here that Bion begins the book. He opens by speaking about an artist's depiction of a landscape and the gap between the rendering of the scene and the sensory essence, what Bion calls the *invariant*, of that which the painter is portraying. While there may be a huge difference between the painting, especially if it is very abstract, and the invariant qualities of the actual scenery, we may say that the artistic work "contains" in some form the essential characteristics of the model upon which the painting is based. In other words, the painter has *transformed* the invariant features of the background into a personal vision in which the essence of that background is contained. Bion uses the letter "O"[13] as shorthand for the invariant qualities of an object: what may be termed the Absolute Truth or, following Kant, "the thing itself."[14] Even a still photograph of the painter's subject does not truly capture the O of the landscape because of variations in lighting, the photographer's angle, the various settings of the camera, etc; therefore, the scene's invariant essence, O, may only be apprehended asymptotically but never really completely grasped.

Where earlier in his writings Bion spoke of the difficulty in introjecting the analysand's projection, he now speaks in *Transformations* of the necessity of the analyst *becoming* the disowned O of the patient. What does this mean? Bion seems to be saying that the analyst must be receptive to the patient's projective identifications and that these must be free to penetrate into the therapist's inner object world. He uses the term (in *Attention and Interpretation*, 1970) of the analyst being at *one-ment* with the analysand which seems to indicate a special kind of identification, achieved through his reverie capacity, i.e., "the mother's capacity for reverie is the *receptor organ*" (1962a, p. 116), and through this reception the analyst identifies (unconsciously at first) with aspects in him that are resonant with what the patient cannot tolerate in himself (Brown, 2010, 2011a; Grotstein, 2005). Bion (1965) distinguishes transformations of O, which are "related to *becoming* or being O" (p. 163), from transformations of K (knowledge) which are "akin to *knowing about* something" (p. 163). In the analytic setting, the patient (as well as the analyst) may defend against becoming, i.e., truly feeling the emotional reality of, what is too frightening to experience by focusing instead on "knowing about" this intellectually (transformation in K) to spare himself from becoming emotionally immersed (transformation in O) in what he so greatly fears. Thus, Bion in *Transformations* has located the psychic coordinates of the analyst's containing function to operate somewhere in that dreamy "twilight zone" where analogous aspects of the analysand's and analyst's psyche intersect.

Bion (1970) deepens his exploration of the relationship between the container and the contained in *Attention and Interpretation* where he speaks poignantly about the difficulties of the analytic couple in confronting the "Truth."[15] Analyst and analysand together must "suffer," that is, bear and tolerate, the truth in order to achieve "the consolation which is drawn from the truth [which is] solid and durable" (p. 7, quoting a letter from Dr. Johnson to Bennet Langton).[16] If the transformation of O is a primary task of the analytic pair operating as a container/contained unit, as Bion states in *Transformations*, then the analyst's *intuition* becomes his chief tool in exploring a mental space that is unknowable. In this connection, Bion revisits his earlier (1967b) assertion that the analyst must eschew "memory and desire" to achieve a receptive state of mind, which he now relates to intuition: "For any who have been used to remembering what patients say and to desiring their welfare, it will be hard to entertain the harm to analytic intuition that is inseparable from *any* memories and *any* desires" (1970, p. 31) [italics in original]. However, relying upon intuition instead of one's memory and desire may leave the analyst feeling off balance, which must be met with *faith*: "faith that there is an ultimate reality and truth—the unknown, unknowable, 'formless infinite'" (p. 31).

What distinguishes the discussion of container/contained in *Attention and Interpretation* from previous accounts is Bion's frank depiction of the stresses on the analytic pair associated with the transformation of O as an intersubjective process. Bion states that patients "experience pain but not suffering … . The patient may say he suffers but this is only because he does not know what suffering is and mistakes pain for suffering it" (p. 19). Pain is a sensory experience which awaits a name that will then permit the patient to "suffer" it so that he may learn from experience. The analyst "can, and indeed must, suffer" (p. 19) the analysand's pain just as a mother intuitively attunes herself to her baby's inarticulate cries and through this process becomes the "O that is *common to analyst and analysand*"(p. 27) [italics added]. Meaningful psychic growth is, therefore, not easily achieved and depends upon the existence within the patient of a thinking apparatus (♀♂) that enables him to manage the trials of emotional life. However, when alpha function is disturbed (when the apparatus for thinking that is a distillate of the container/contained relationship is weakened or destroyed) the patient requires an analyst who can assist in containing and transforming painful experience. Over time, hopefully, this shared act of thinking together is introjected to strengthen the patient's inner capacities and build structures.

Conclusion

The evolution of Bion's concept of the container/contained has been traced from early contributions that began with his exploration of the nature of thinking and its disturbances. His traumatic experiences in World War I confronted him with horrific events that defied his capacity to absorb and think about them. Indeed, forty years passed between his initial writing about those experiences and the later writing of the Amiens diary. Together with his war exploits, his later analytic work with psychotic states of mind provided Bion with further exposure to disordered thinking, and the drive to understand both sets of experience spurred his discovery of alpha function during an extraordinarily productive period from 1958–60. Many of Bion's subsequent writings explored in greater detail the many elements which comprise alpha function, including the container/contained relationship, the apparatus for thinking, transformations, the Ps↔D balance and other factors that I have termed the *Constellation for Thinking*.

The excellent papers in this book represent a furthering of Bion's concept of the container/contained and its application to many different subject areas. Howard Levine and I hope that the reader finds in these pages many stimulating contributions that in themselves are fascinating studies and which also demonstrate the enduring creative genius of Wilfred Bion.

Notes

1 It is unclear whether Bion meant to completely replace Freud's theory of dreaming with his own or if his ideas were intended to augment Freud's. Grotstein (personal communication) believes that Freud's theory of dream-work best describes the neurotic mind at work, while Bion's concepts best explain how the psychotic (or badly traumatized) part of the mind fails to adequately "dream" the events of its actual life and therefore cannot learn from experience.

2 The subject of alpha function covers a wide range of phenomena including the differentiation of the conscious and unconscious, the nature of psychotic thinking, the relationship between dreaming and hallucination, to name a few. My focus here, however, is to investigate the development of Bion's theory of alpha function and his subsequent formulation of the container and contained as well as the interconnection between these concepts.

3 Bion (1957) had earlier referred to stunted capacity for *reverie*, i.e., an absence of freely imaginative thinking, in the psychotic part of the personality.

4 In Brown (in press) I note that "the use of this phrase, 'receptor organ,' seems to be a direct reference to Freud's (1912) statement that the analyst 'must turn his *own unconscious like a receptive organ* towards the transmitting unconscious of the patient'" (p. 115) [italics added]. Thus, Bion appears to be associating the capacity to tolerate the stress of accepting the patient's projections and the analyst's openness to reverie with Freud's description of unconscious communication (see also Brown, 2011a, chapter 4).

5 Their marriage is discussed in much greater depth in Brown (in press).

6 Bion (1962b) defines a *factor* as "the name for a mental activity operating in consort with other mental activities to constitute a function" (p. 2).

7 Bion also offers what I (Brown, 2009, 2011) call a "procreative model" of alpha function, which is discussed below.

8 Grotstein (2007) asserts that there is an inchoate alpha function at birth; thus, the introjection of maternal alpha function enables and strengthens this inborn capacity.

9 In the Commentary section of *Second Thoughts* Bion (1967) alludes to ♀♂ as a "sexual model" (p. 140), but does not elaborate this further.

10 Or, perhaps an analyst and patient, nor should we overlook any other couple relationship that provides this function.

11 Though Bion does not connect his earlier (1962b) concept of "tolerated doubt" with the Ps↔D balance (1963), it seems to me that these are nearly interchangeable ideas and that the latter replaced the earlier notion.

12 This schema is an expanded version of what I (Brown, 2011a) have previously proposed.

13 Bianchedi (2007) believes that Bion intended "O" to refer to the Origin of things.

14 The reader is referred to Grotstein's numerous writings (2004, 2007, 2009a,b,c) about O for a more in-depth discussion.

15 Bion seems to be restricting the notion of "truth" to refer to an emotional experience shared by the patient and analyst that is felt to "correctly" describe an affective event in which both are immersed.

16 Also see Levine's (2011) recent paper, "'The consolation which is drawn from truth': The analysis of a patient unable to suffer experience," which discusses this issue in greater depth. In: Mawson, C. (ed.) *Bion Today*. Hove, England and New York: Brunner-Routledge, 2011, pp. 188–211.

References

Bianchedi, E. (2007) Personal communication.

Bion, W. R. (1940) The "war of nerves": Civilian reaction, morale and prophylaxis. In *Neuroses in War*, E. Miller (ed.). New York: Macmillan & Co., 1945, pp. 180–200.

Bion, W. R. (1956) Development of schizophrenic thought. *International Journal of Psychoanalysis*, 37:344–6. Also in *Second Thoughts*.

Bion, W. R. (1957) Differentiation of the psychotic from the non-psychotic personalities. *International Journal of Psychoanalysis*, 38:266–75. Also in *Second Thoughts*, 43–63.

Bion, W. R. (1958) On arrogance. *International Journal of Psychoanalysis*, 39:144–6. Also in *Second Thoughts*, 86–92.

Bion, W. R. (1959) Attacks on linking. *International Journal of Psychoanalysis*, 40:308–15. Also in *Second Thoughts*, 93–109.

Bion, W. R. (1962a) A theory of thinking. *International Journal of Psychoanalysis*, 43:306–10.

Bion, W. R. (1962b) *Learning from Experience*. London: Heinemann.

Bion, W. R. (1963) *Elements of Psycho-Analysis*. London: Heinemann.

Bion, W. R. (1965) *Transformations*. London: Heinemann.

Bion, W. R. (1967a) *Second Thoughts*. NY: Jason Aronson.

Bion, W. R. (1967b) Notes on memory and desire. In Bion (1992) *Cogitations*. London: Karnac Books (extended 1994 version).

Bion, W. R. (1970) *Attention and Interpretation*. London: Heinemann.

Bion, W. R. (1973) Brazilian Lectures I. In *Brazilian Lectures*. London: Karnac, 1990.

Bion, W. R. (1977) Caesura. *Two Papers: The Grid and Caesura*. London: Karnac Books, 1989, pp. 35–56.

Bion, W. R. (1979) Making the best of a bad job. In *Clinical Seminars and Four Papers*. Oxford: Fleetwood Press, 1987.

Bion, W. R. (1982) *The Long Week-End, 1897–1919: Part of a Life*. Abington, UK: Fleetwood Press.

Bion, W. R. (1985). *All My Sins Remembered: Another Part of a Life and the Other Side of Genius: Family Letters*. London: Karnac.

Bion, W. R. (1991) *A Memoir of the Future: Books 1–3*. London: Karnac.

Bion, W. R. (1992) *Cogitations*. London: Karnac Books (extended 1994 version).

Bion, W. R. (1997) *War Memoirs: 1917–1919*, F. Bion (ed.) London: Karnac.

Brown, L. J. (2009) The ego psychology of Wilfred Bion: Implications for an intersubjective view of psychic structure. *Psychoanalytic Quarterly*, 78:27–55.

Brown, L. J. (2011a) *Intersubjective Processes and the Unconscious: An Integration of Freudian, Kleinian and Bionian Perspectives*. NY: Routledge.

Brown, L. J. (2010) Klein, Bion and intersubjectivity: Becoming, transforming and dreaming. *Psychoanalytic Dialogues*, 20:669–82.

Brown, L. J. (2011b) Working through war trauma: Bion's discover of alpha function 1958–1960. Paper given at the International Psychoanalytic Association meeting, Mexico City, July, 2011.

Brown, L. J. (in press) Bion's discovery of alpha function: Thinking under fire on the battle field and in the consulting room. *IJP.*

Freud, S. (1900) The interpretation of dreams. *Standard Edition*, 4–5.

Freud, S. (1912) Recommendations to physicians practising psycho-analysis. *Standard Edition*, 12:109–120.

Grotstein, J. S. (2000) *Who Is the Dreamer Who Dreams the Dream?* Hillsdale, NJ: Analytic Press.

Grotstein, J. S. (2004) The seventh servant: The implications of a truth drive in Bion's theory of "O." *International Journal of Psychoanalysis*, 85:1081–101.

Grotstein, J. S. (2005) "Projective transidentification": An extension of the concept of projective identification. *International Journal of Psychoanalysis*, 85:1051–69.

Grotstein, J. S. (2007) *A Beam of Intense Darkness: Wilfred Bion's Legacy to Psychoanalysis.* London: Karnac.

Grotstein, J. S. (2009a) Dreaming as a "curtain of illusion": Revisiting the "royal road" with Bion as our guide. *International Journal of Psychoanalysis*, 90:733–52.

Grotstein, J. S. (2009b) *" ... But at the Same Time and on Another Level ... ", Volume I. Psychoanalytic Theory and Technique in the Kleinian/Bionian Mode.* London: Karnac.

Grotstein, J. S. (2009c) *"... But at the Same Time and on Another Level ... ", Volume II. Clinical Applications in the Kleinian/Bionian Mode.* London: Karnac.

Levine, H. (2011) "The consolation which is drawn from truth": The analysis of a patient unable to suffer experience. In C. Mawson (Ed.) *Bion Today.* NY: Brunner-Routledge, 2011, pp. 188–211.

Sandler, P. (2000) What is thinking—an attempt at an integrated study of W. R. Bion's contributions to the processes of knowing. In P. Bion Talamo, F. Borgogno and S. Merciai (eds.) *W. R. Bion: Between Past and Future.* London: Karnac Books.

Souter, K. M. (2009) The *War Memoirs*: Some origins of the thought of W. R. Bion. *International Journal of Psychoanalysis*, 90:795–808.

Symington, J. and Symington, N. (1996). *The Clinical Thinking of Wilfred Bion.* New York, NY: Routledge.

Szykierski, D. (2010) The traumatic roots of containment: The evolution of Bion's metapsychology. *Psychoanalytic Quarterly*, 79:935–68.

EDITORS' INTRODUCTION

The Traumatic Roots of Containment: The Evolution of Bion's Metapsychology

Dorit Szykierski

A close reading of Bion's writings about his war experiences—*A Memoir of the Future*, the *War Memoirs*, *The Long Week-End*, *All My Sins Remembered*—illuminates the extent to which his subsequent psychoanalytic theories of thinking and container/contained reflect his lifelong struggles to metabolize the trauma of his personal experiences as a tank commander during World War I. Szykierski's conclusion, that Bion's theoretical formulations—culminating in the concept of container/contained—can be understood as a creative way of dealing with the arbitrariness of having physically and mentally survived World War I is both historically fascinating and a provocative contribution to our understanding of the origins of Bion's metapsychology and the vicissitudes of massive psychic trauma.

Rather than viewing Bion's war experiences as Bion himself did in his autobiographical works from the perspective of his metapsychology, Szykierski reverses perspective and views his metapsychology from the vantage point of his war experiences. In so doing, she proposes the latter as the source for his subsequent view that all experience is potentially overwhelming and traumatic and that if psychic survival is at all possible, it will come from whatever consolation might come from contact with reality and the truth that it contains. In order to bear that truth, however, Bion believed that each of us must face a potentially damaging existential reality in which our minds are "assaulted by sense impressions, forever oscillating between containing emotional experience and evading contact with reality."

Faced with the chaos and destruction of his war experience, Bion found that the only possible antidote to the horror of his war experience lay in the capacities to articulate, historicize and learn from his emotional experience. These capacities were, in turn, dependent upon his ability to tolerate contact with the most painful of realities and to remember and articulate an accurate sequence of events. Just as Freud took the structure of the dream as a model for his understanding of neurosis, so Bion created a theory of thinking and its development as a model for his understanding of psychosis, the development of the psyche and catastrophic change. Bion's questions about the mind's capacity to survive trauma "led him to elaborate on the complex process of containing emotional experience and ... address the lack of an elaborate theory of thinking in psychoanalytic metapsychology." Thus, he emphasized the processes of historicization—i.e. the transformation of "undigested facts" into memory, emotional experience into verbalizable thought, the conversion of beta-elements into alpha—as the model for all mental functioning.

As we follow Szykierski's careful study of Bion's war experience, we are left to wonder, to what extent Bion became numb in reaction to the trauma of war. Was this an overload phenomenon perhaps best described by the term "shellshock," or was he unconsciously and reflexively trying to defend himself from the horror, fear and unbearable pain of the war by shutting down his mind and senses? And if such defense was his last and only resort, did it go too far and become a state of extreme encapsulation that left a vital part of him isolated, blank and dehumanized? Szykierski persuasively argues that:

> while the harsh reality of [Bion's] physical vulnerability was barely understandable, [the] mental vulnerability was incomprehensible and left a trail of haunting questions, which drove Bion to create a theory of thinking as foundation for a metapsychology in which the concept of containment is a central organizing principle.

It is the latter that has proven so useful to so many analysts and we are grateful to Szykierski for allowing us this insight into its formative roots.

2

THE TRAUMATIC ROOTS OF CONTAINMENT

The Evolution of Bion's Metapsychology[1]

Dorit Szykierski

Bion's theoretical contribution can be conceived as a creative way of dealing with the arbitrariness of surviving the Great War, both physically and mentally. The concept of *containment* of these traumatic roots is the unique vision of a mind struggling to survive the devastating impact of internal and external reality by means of *learning from experience* (Bion, 1962).

In general, most of the discussion of Bion's concept of containment focuses on its clinical usefulness, and is concerned with nuanced intricacies of mental exchanges projected and introjected within human interaction. The delicate and complex images of a mother providing her baby with α-function that are sketched by this discourse stand in sharp contrast to the vast and desolate landscape of burning tanks and shallow trenches strewn with dead bodies of men and mules, conjured up by the observations in Bion's memoirs of his experiences in World War I. I argue that these diverse images are related to each other—the traumatic memories can be conceived as dreadful answers lying at the root of certain metapsychological questions, which in turn led him to conceptualize containment.

Although some authors have commented on the influence that Bion's war experiences had on his contribution (Bléandonu, 1994; Boris, 1986; López-Corvo, 2003; Meltzer, 1981; Sandler, 2003; Symington and Symington, 1996; Wisdom, 1987), these comments have not gone far beyond an intuitive delineation of a significant thread—linking these war experiences with certain clinical and conceptual aspects of Bion's work. Brown (2005; 2007), in an innovative discussion of the clinical and conceptual end of this thread, does explore the connection between Bion's war experiences and his theory of thinking. Brown offers a reading of the theory of thinking that accentuates the mind's reaction to traumatic experience and highlights the usefulness of this theory to clinical work with traumatized patients, an inference implicit in Bion's writings.

In this paper, I explore the other end of this thread, reading Bion's writings about his war experiences while highlighting hinted reflections and subtle echoes in order to demonstrate that his metapsychology in general, and the concept of containment (Bion, 1970) in particular, are the fruits of these traumatic roots. I will use a close reading of the many layers in Bion's writings regarding his war experiences to trace his metapsychological questions. I will suggest that particularly those questions regarding the ability of the mind to survive trauma led him to elaborate on the complex process of *containing* emotional experience. This process in turn inspired him to address the lack of an intricate theory of thinking in psychoanalytic metapsychology.

"A Questioning Attitude": Between Revisiting and Revisiting War Experiences

Bion served as a tank officer in France from June 26, 1917, to January 10, 1919. Three of his published works are autobiographical, all published posthumously (1982, 1985, 1997), and, together with significant parts of other works (1991, 1992), they deal with Bion's war experiences. These three works are:

- *War Memoirs, 1917–1919* (1997), which in turn contains three texts: the "Diary" Bion wrote for his parents soon after demobilization, when he went to Oxford (pp. 5–196); "Commentary," dated 1972, written after Bion read the typescript of the "Diary" (pp. 199–211); and "Amiens," written following a visit to France with his wife in August 1958, and abandoned in mid-sentence in 1960 (pp. 215–308).
- *The Long Week-End, 1897–1919: Part of a Life* (1982), in which 187 of a total of 287 pages are dedicated to war experiences (pp. 100–287).
- *All My Sins Remembered* (1985), significant sections of which deal with Bion's experiences in World War II; these are explicitly linked to his experiences in World War I.

Such an immense autobiographical effort can be seen as "a ceaseless struggle" to bear witness (Felman and Laub, 1992, p. 75). Bion attempted to decipher the meaning of these experiences through writing about them time and again from different vertices, using various literary styles—including the hybrid genre he created in the monumental *A Memoir of the Future* (1991).

The constant presence of these memories throughout Bion's life has been described by his wife, Francesca Bion (Bion, 1997), who wrote in parentheses, containing her testimony: "(It was clear that that war continued to occupy a prominent position in his mind when, during the first occasion we dined together, he spoke movingly of it as if compelled to communicate haunting memories)" (p. 2); and also by his daughter, Parthenope Bion Talamo (Bion, 1997), who noted that her father continued to buy books on war "right up till his death, as though the subject was never far from his mind, perhaps constituting ... a great unsolved puzzle" (p. 312). Parthenope Bion Talamo argues that in *A Memoir of the Future* (1991), Bion used some episodes "carried over almost unchewed and apparently undigested ... as though no further working-through were possible" (Bion, 1997, p. 310), to demonstrate the constant presence of regressive states of mind. Beyond this rhetorical function, I regard Bion's various forms of repeated reflection as aimed at historicization of a traumatic past (Brown, 2007).

Regarding Bion's question in Christmas 1917, "Had everyone gone mad?" (1997, p. 69), Parthenope Bion Talamo comments: "He gives it no immediate answer, but reading *War Memoirs* makes me wonder whether he did not perhaps spend a good portion of the rest of his life exploring the avenues of enquiry that it opened up" (1997, p. 309). As I argued elsewhere (Szykierski, 2008), Bion's war experiences lie at the foundation of his adherence to what he termed more than forty years later "a questioning attitude" (1961, p. 162), accounting for his ability to develop a radically innovative approach to work with groups.

Bion's recurrent emphasis on "a questioning attitude" is also expressed in the title of the published collection of his works, *Seven Servants* (1977). Here Bion borrows Rudyard Kipling's metaphor of the six servants—*What, Why, When, How, Where, Who* (Kipling, 1900, p. 85)—and adds another: the opinion "each individual has to arrive at for himself: his opinion and only *his*" (introduction to Bion, 1977, italics in original).

As part of her exhibition entitled "Attacks on Linking" at Tel-Aviv Museum of Art, the Israeli artist Michal Heiman (2008) presented a video of a lecture incorporating other video works that refer to Bion's term *attacks on linking* (Bion, 1959; 1967a). Suffused with uncanny premonition and saturated with anxiety, Heiman's video works decontextualize Bion's terminology from its theoretical universe and filter it through visual images expressing the artist's subjective experience of anguish, the anguish of witnessing human contact attacked—failing, falling, bleeding, or vanishing without a trace within spaces without witness. Questions stamped under the visual images undermine our habitual ways of seeing, and accentuate the anguish caught up in the images.

Contrary to terms like *attacks on linking*, in which there is a certain affinity between the connotations aroused and the clinical phenomena referred to, the word *containment* is defined in various contexts—some mundane, referring to the containing of inanimate or animate objects in a semiclosed space; but most of these definitions accentuate first and foremost the containment of dangers: from the political influence of a hostile nation, to radioactive fallout, to epidemics.[2] Hence, there is a significant gap between the commonplace function of the word and the penumbra of associations attached to the psychoanalytic usage of Bion's concept of containment (1970). Bion was aware of the military implication of the word, and chose it to convey a sense of "one force containing another" (p. 112); thus, a disciplined control of violence is at the root of a concept fundamental to the metapsychology Bion constructed.

However, in current psychoanalytic discourse, the concept of containment is usually discussed in the context of dyadic relations—either mother–baby or analyst–analysand—while disregarding its traumatic roots; thus it tends to be misconceived as a complex process crossing the conscious/unconscious, verbal/nonverbal, cognitive/emotional divisions. In a seminal paper, Ogden (2004) addressed a similar confusion between *containing* and *holding*. Such is the case, for example, when Langs (1981, p. 446) discusses Bion's concept of containment, Winnicott's concept of holding and Chan's concept of the maternal shield; Langs narrows significantly the meaning of the concept of containment, as he sees all these as metaphors for protective, non-interpretative aspects of the analyst's relationship with the analysand.

Heiman's work, in its sensitive following of her own subjective associations, throws light on a certain tension in Bion's conceptualization, motivated by his similar sensitivity to the restrictive effect of a penumbra of associations, which might compromise an open-minded exploration of clinical material. Along the lines of this consideration, a subtle tension can be detected in Bion's work between the creation of evocative terms such as *attacks on linking* and *containment,* both saturated with a threatening sense of danger, and the offer of "empty" concepts yet to be saturated by psychoanalytic inquiry (Bion, 1962, p. 3). This tension culminates in the formulation of Bion's Grid (1962), where β elements are to be transformed by α-function into α elements, and statements are contained by careful classification into precise categories.

The evolution of Bion's language did not stop at that. Bléandonu's (1994) formulation of an epistemological period in Bion's work, which includes the four works collected in *Seven Servants* (1977), blurs salient differences in structure and style yet to be explored between the first three books, on the one hand—*Learning from Experience* (1962), *Elements of Psychoanalysis* (1963), *Transformations* (1965)—and *Attention and Interpretation* (1970), on the other. For my purpose here, it is sufficient to note the difference, which for me signifies a move away from the deconstruction of the mind in an effort to create an "empty" scientific conceptual system, and toward an integration of individual and group, thought and emotion, leading to a decade of autobiographical writing and the creation of *A Memoir of the Future* (1991).

Bion's theoretical evolution is bound by two attempts on his part to write about his war experiences.[3] At one end is "Amiens," which was his first attempt to revisit the subject in writing, following a visit to France in 1958 with his wife—an attempt later relinquished in favor of "other, more pressing commitments" (1997, p. 214): the writing of the aforementioned four books during the 1960s. At the other end are "Commentary," the autobiographical writings, and *A Memoir of the Future*—all written during the 1970s.

Before discussing this evolution in the light of Bion's "ceaseless struggle" (Felman and Laub, 1992, p. 75) to bear witness, it is necessary to evaluate the function fulfilled by the "Diary" (1992) that Bion wrote for his parents after his demobilization.

"All Was Not Well" in No-Man's Land: Between Insignificance and Irrelevance

An awareness of psychological casualties in modern warfare, as well as the severe, long-term consequences they suffer, is the result of constant tension between an urgent need to address these clinical phenomena and a pressing wish to deny their political meaning and disavow their social significance.

The changing psychiatric terminology regarding psychological casualties of modern warfare reflects the constant tension between clinical needs and political interests. Bilu and Witztum (2000) describe the changing nosology in detail. During the American Civil War, it was designated *nostalgia* or *soldier's heart*, pointing to the idea that the breakdown was caused by homesickness. In World War I, the term *shell-shock* indicated that the etiological factor was neurological damage due to excessive exposure to shelling and bombing. After the Great War, the growing influence of psychoanalysis on psychiatry shifted the emphasis to unconscious conflicts as vulnerability-increasing factors, expressed in the term *war neurosis*. In 1943, during World War II, the term was modified into *combat exhaustion* or *combat fatigue*, conveying the notion that the psychological breakdown is reactive and transient rather than a manifestation of premorbid personality defect. In the same vein, the term *combat stress reaction* (CSR), prevalent in current psychiatric discourse, underscores the exposure to stress in combat as a critical factor. The long-term sequelae of CSR were termed in 1980 *post-traumatic stress disorder* (PTSD), as a result of effective lobbying by war veterans and mental health professionals in the aftermath of the Vietnam War to cast the crippling effects of CSR into a medical diagnosis (Bilu and Witztum, 2000, pp. 15–16).

Thus, the emergence of war-related PTSD as a psychiatric syndrome—indicating a common disturbance, chronic and severe, manifested in a wide range of symptoms and significant malfunctioning—followed from longitudinal studies concluding that approximately 50% of CSR casualties suffered from PTSD. Even more disconcerting were data indicating that, of a control group of soldiers who ostensibly survived the war without any psychic damage, 10 to 20% suffered from some form of PTSD a few years later (Bilu and Witztum, 2000, p. 22; Solomon, 1993). Hence, "certified" patients suffering from PTSD can be understood as located at the exposed end of an enclosed continuum, a space without witness containing numerous "uncertified" veterans dealing with hidden—and at times unacknowledged—psychic damage, to varying degrees.

Although Bion evidently did not suffer from CSR, there were consequences to his exposure to the horrors of the Great War. Francesca Bion (Bion, 1997) states that:

> He was catapulted, like millions of others, from schoolboy to combatant soldier in a few months. The horror of that war inflicted on such young men did not contribute to their maturity; it destroyed their youth and made them "old" before their time. Bion's remarkable physical survival against heavy odds concealed the emotional injury which left scars for many years to come.
>
> (p. 2)

In 1972, after reading the typescript of his "Diary" written in 1919, Bion wrote the "Commentary" in the form of a dialogue between MYSELF (that is, Bion at the time of writing the "Commentary") and BION (Bion at the time of writing the "Diary"). There, BION says that, while in Oxford, he was not able to work or to enjoy games (1997, p. 209), and MYSELF states that he "did not stand up to the rigours of war very well." BION replies:

> Of course we did not know that, though I was always afraid I would not. I think even the diary shows that as it goes on, though at Oxford I was still too ashamed to admit it, and very glad of the opportunity that Oxford gave me to be seduced into a more self-satisfied state of mind. But I never quite got rid of the sense that all was *not* well.
>
> (1997, p. 201, italics in original)

After which MYSELF concludes: "That ultimately drove me into psycho-analysis" (1997, p. 201).

So, what does the "Diary" show us as it goes on? The "Diary" is first and foremost a text Bion wrote to his parents. Francesca Bion (Bion, 1997) says that

> He would have been unable to express his very recent painful experiences, especially to his parents. But it is evident that he had them

> in mind throughout: detailed descriptions of tanks and equipment, explanations of battle strategy, photographs and diagrams were included for their benefit—and "bloody" became "b--y" in deference to their disapproval of swearing.
>
> (p. 2)

These detailed factual descriptions of external reality, as well as meticulous visual representations (Heiman, 2008, p. 147), are the most salient feature of Bion's effort to reach out to his parents, the witnesses to his testimony. Additionally, explicit references invoke the readers throughout the text, mostly through the use of the pronoun *you* (and the imperatives *note* or *imagine*). These references function as a repeated appeal for understanding as they insert the readers directly into the situation, inviting them to experience Bion's experience.[4]

Bion's intent to communicate his emotional experience to his parents is stated in the opening paragraph of the "Diary," in the first-person plural: "to give you our feelings at the time," etc. (1997, p. 5). It seems that Bion's difficulty in "express[ing] his very recent painful experiences, especially to his parents" (p. 2) led him to weave his experience into the common experience he inferred from observed group behavior. For example, he wrote: "We felt very miserable, as we had no idea what was going to happen, and really felt quite useless if the enemy did attack" (p. 59).

Still, the use of first-person plural pronouns does not blur the emotional experience Bion depicts, as in the following sentences:

> All our nerves were in an awful state, and we tried not to think of what was coming. The waiting was awful and seemed to be almost a physical pain—a sort of frightfully "heavy" feeling about one's limbs and body generally.
>
> (1997, p. 29)

Such hybrid statements exemplify Bion's ability to integrate observed group behavior with internal emotional experience composed of physical sensations and psychic impressions, in order to recount the complex event of anxious waiting saturated with psychic terror that is experienced as physical pain.

Moreover, Bion detects the detrimental effect anxiety has on thinking, further explored as the hybrid statements make way to increasing differentiation of Bion's internal experience from the group's expressed emotions, as formulated in the following statement written in regard to walking upright under a barrage: "I must have been very nearly mad to do it. But I never *thought* more clearly in my life" (1997, p. 106, italics in original). Bion notices that while terror arising from contact with a dreadful external reality inhibits thinking, severing this contact brings about a semblance of clear thought unimpeded by the facts. In contrast to the inhibition of thinking when he is within the group, when he is alone, trying to return to his men, thinking seems to be facilitated.

Thus, Bion becomes aware of the complex relation between unthinking group behavior and the thinking individual, shaping the constant conflict between individual and group; as noted by Eisold (2005, p. 366), Bion came to conceive himself "in his own terms" as "a group animal at war, both with the group and with those aspects of his personality that constitute his 'groupishness'" (Bion, 1961, p. 168).

Although the "Diary," as Francesca Bion (Bion, 1997) says, "has none of the nightmare quality he so vividly depicted in The Long Week-End [1982]" (p. 2), it is difficult to read, even more so than other autobiographical writings about the war. Contrary to these, the "Diary" is not divided into short chapters, focused and integrated, but is an ongoing, dense report conveying the sense of an endless war, referred to in *The Long Week-End* by quoting "catch phrases such as 'the first seven years are the worst'" (1982, p. 268). While the "Diary" is more about describing external reality than contemplating internal experience, much of Bion's state of mind is conveyed through his observations, accounting for the sense impressions that he had to historicize into a coherent sequence of events. Thus, the reader sees the battlefield through Bion's eyes: "All the enemy trenches were outlined in low-bursting shrapnel. It looked like clouds of white with golden rain in the bursts. It was very beautiful—and very deadly" (1997, p. 47).

The devastating impact war has on the land unfolds as Bion draws near the line:

> There were no trees with a leaf to be seen .... Old houses were simply mounds of bricks. Here and there guns were firing. The stench was terrible in places, and every now and then you came across dead horses and mules .... Everywhere the desolation was complete. You would see small parties of men hurrying over duckboard paths—no one loitered but tried to get out of the danger area as fast as possible.
> (1997, p. 22)

In this landscape, human behavior expresses the sense of imminent danger (see also 1997, p. 132).

In order to write the "Diary," Bion had to overcome various obstacles, some due to losses—external and internal—hindering his testimony. The first sentence discloses that this text is not the diary Bion wrote during the war, but a reconstruction of that diary, which he has lost: "In writing this, I cannot be absolutely accurate in some things, as I have lost my diary" (1997, p. 5). Not only the original diary was lost; other losses are mentioned, too. The loss of men is noted frequently (1997, pp. 89, 36, 138,

149, 186); on a few occasions, Bion states he himself was "hopelessly" or "thoroughly" lost (1997, pp. 28, 30, 91). But another loss that is gradually revealed in the "Diary" is the accumulating mental damage, the loss of mental faculties—either a temporary loss, as in "I had lost all sense of time now" (p. 95), or a persistent state of mind, as in:

> There was one thing that was becoming very clear—I had lost my nerve. Everything I did was difficult; in action I had to force myself to do my mere job. I became more or less paralysed at the thought of action, and my brain would *not* work.
>
> (p. 156, italics in original)

Bion describes a progressive deterioration in his functioning (1997, p. 120), and as he struggles to make sense of the crushing impact the war has on him, he is using the framework available to him then—a descriptive classification prevalent at the time:

> I seemed unable to shake off a kind of sluggishness and terror that threatened to crush all life out of me. I had reached the stage that many had reached before me—the B.E.F. [British Expeditionary Force] man who was "not as good as he had been."
>
> (1997, p. 156)

The sense of mental injury clarifies Bion's preoccupation with his inability to give an accurate report of external reality, although it is not material to communicating his internal experience. He says: "My dates of events out of the line cannot be accurate. Actions are, however, accurate as they are very clearly stamped on one's memory!" (p. 5).

But even his confidence in accuracy, at least in regard to actions, is undermined as the "Diary" unfolds. It seems Bion intuitively sensed that the ability to remember an accurate sequence of events is crucial to historicizing traumatic emotional experiences. Bion's preoccupation with accuracy also informs another preoccupation with the relation between uncertainty and knowledge: "Although now one sees how unfounded some of our fears were, yet at the time we could not tell, and it was just the uncertainty that made things difficult to judge and unpleasant to think about" (p. 5). Bion seeks accurate knowledge of external reality in order to remedy the detrimental effect of the anxiety flowing from uncertainty, since the space stretching between uncertainty and knowledge, between the "general scheme" and the particular action, is dominated by "terrific confusion" (p. 5).

Hence, I assume that the original diary that was lost served as an anchor meant to preserve Bion's contact with reality—external and internal—despite the "terrific confusion" from without and the physical wear compounded by psychic tearing from within. The function of the reconstructed "Diary" that was written after the war was to pin down the facts in a coherent sequence as accurately as possible, and thus to historicize emotional experiences by transforming traumatic, "undigested" facts into memories (Brown, 2007). In writing the "Diary," Bion essentially engendered a therapeutic process of transforming trauma into memory, emotional experience into verbal thought, as it is understood by Felman and Laub (1992):

> The survivors did not need to survive so that they could tell their story; they also needed to tell their story in order to survive. There is, in each survivor, an imperative need to *tell* and thus to come to *know* one's story, unimpeded by ghosts from the past against which one has to protect oneself. One has to know one's buried truth in order to be able to live one's life.
>
> (p. 76, italics in original)

However, the task of historicizing traumatic experiences was not accomplished effortlessly. Psychic erosion and physical exhaustion caused fragmentation of memory, as expressed in Bion's comment on going into action on August 8, 1918, sick with influenza:

> I am really at a loss to describe the rest of the action. I only remember incidents and can't remember how I got from one place to another. I think that the best thing I can do is simply to give you a series of incidents in the order in which they came (as far as I know).
>
> (1997, p. 147)

In *The Long Week-End* (1982), Bion concludes: "Though we did not realize it, we were men who had grown from insignificance to irrelevance in the passage of a few short years" (p. 286). In the no-man's land stretching between the insignificance of being mobilized as one of millions thrown out to be killed in trench warfare, and the irrelevance of being demobilized and thrown back into a society that ignored them and forgot them as quickly as possible, Bion returned home to discover that veterans just fade away: "I think to some extent we were depressed by the lack of welcome. No one took any notice of us, no one seemed to know we had been fighting and were glad to be back" (1997, p. 194).

Under these circumstances, Bion had to attend to repairing the internal damage he suffered. In the "Commentary" (1997), MYSELF notes that events left out from the historicization process in the writing of the "Diary"—"events that in retrospect seem utterly horrible, [like the] sickly, sweet stench of corpses" in a farmhouse, "when you were asleep on the stone floor"—continued to gnaw him from within:

> That was what was so awful. You were not even frightened. By the time you got to Oxford, you had "forgotten" it. *I* don't remember it, but my gut does. I was and am still scared. What about? I don't know—just scared. No, not even "just" scared. Scared.
>
> (1997, pp. 209–10, italics in original)

Although writing the "Diary" enabled Bion to counteract the avoidant tendency to ignore and forget, the therapeutic effect was incomplete, leaving haunting residues, so he continued to feel that "all was *not* well" (p. 201).

"A Thousand Sleepless Nights": Witnessing Shredded Bodies and Shattered Minds

Beyond the function of historicizing experiences and transforming them into memories, Bion's testimony can be conceived as explicit answers to implicit questions, some of these remaining open to further exploration as Bion became a psychoanalyst. A close reading of the "Diary" and other autobiographical writings allows one to trace the haunting questions that form the roots of the evolution of a unique metapsychology.

The Great War was a full-scale display of modern warfare's destructiveness on an unprecedented scale. Out of 70,000,000 soldiers mobilized, 15,000,000 were killed, 7,000,000 were permanently disabled, and 15,000,000 seriously injured. About 8,000,000 surrendered and were held in POW camps, with a much higher survival rate than their peers on the front. In addition to various contagious diseases claiming many lives, an influenza epidemic started in Western Europe in the last months of the war and spread rapidly, killing millions in Europe and 50,000,000 around the world. The war to end all wars exposed the vulnerability of body and mind, and is discussed here as it is represented in Bion's war memoirs.

Death was omnipresent, imminent (Bion 1997, pp. 36, 38; 1982, pp. 135, 176), and on occasion occurred without any warning, as reported by Bion in reference to a fighting comrade: "He said everything was going splendidly. A moment later a sniper got him through the head, and he died a bit later" (1997, p. 51; see also 1991, p. 454). On occasion, death was so sudden and swift that it was incomprehensible (1982, p. 283). Thus, upon receiving orders to attack at 10:30 a.m. without a smoke screen, Bion realized that these "were not orders," but "sentences of death;" the tank officers "tried the previous evening to insist to the divisional command that zero would have to be at dawn. When the mind will not receive the obvious there is nothing to be done" (1982, pp. 253–4). As a result, all tanks and crews were destroyed.

A serious injury might result in permanent mutilation and was no less terrifying than death, maybe more so (1997, pp. 147, 211, 240). Bion understood that "sooner or later my parents would be bound to have the telegram announcing my death; the war had only to go on long enough. Already I had exhausted my quota of chances of survival" (1997, p. 247).

While the number of casualties was generally high (roughly 1:10), the rate of casualties among the tank battalions was extremely high: "The proportion of killed to living remained one in three" (1982, p. 253). Bion realized that only promotion afforded greater chances of survival, but even these were slim:

> Some tank commanders escaped being killed long enough to be promoted to command sections. As section commanders their expectation of life was greater; they might accordingly survive to reach to the command or second in command of companies. For non-commissioned ranks it was virtually impossible to reach safety by promotion …. Slight wounds were so rare that the avenues of escape were restricted to chronic invalidism or forms of elaborate foot-dragging. After August 8 there were no senior officers with actual experience of tanks in action, and no junior officers who could reasonably suppose they had a chance of survival to higher rank.
>
> (1982, p. 268)

Uncertainty and arbitrariness saturated day-to-day survival, leading to fluctuations between fear and hope, and taking its toll in permanent anxiety (1997, pp. 241–2). Fear was difficult to evade while "being pushed into the unknown—into the terror all the inhabitants had been fleeing" (p. 79); nevertheless, Bion notes, "It is curious how one hoped for the best when one had the chance" (p. 108). Lack of control over one's fate accentuated the importance of luck (pp. 36, 38, 84, 132) and enhanced the spread of superstition (p. 135). Bion tried to maintain a rational view by turning to statistics:

> Only two out of every three who took part in the tank war survived to tell the tale within twenty-four hours of the start of the action. This was not a matter, then, for any optimism; it was not even a matter of fighting; it seemed to be simply a question of statistics and the laws of chance.
>
> (1997, p. 240; see also Bion 1985, pp. 181–2)

Hence, the unavoidable conclusion was that these laws indicated his inevitable death (1985, p. 43). Still, the mind resisted inescapable reality:

> "Oh my, I don't want to die, I want to go home," we used to sing. *That* was true; we hoped that the ugly reality would not penetrate the joke armour-plate. The armour-plate of a tank was penetrable; we were

> bewitched, bemused, "probability"-dazzled cowards. "Probably" we would not be killed.
>
> (1991, p. 396, italics in original)

Bion's fear was continuously stimulated by sense impressions of the dead, scattered about in grotesque postures and in various stages of decomposition (1982, pp. 138, 251). The arbitrary certainty of death and mutilation induced helplessness, which Bion resisted paradoxically by resigning himself to death. In the "Diary," Bion struggles against the anticipated misunderstanding of his parents, explaining how it was that wishing for death enabled him to survive emotionally:

> But the fact remains that life had now reached such a pitch that horrible mutilations or death could not conceivably be worse. I found myself looking forward to getting killed, as then, at least, one would be rid of this intolerable misery. These thoughts were uppermost with me then and excluded all others—and I think many were in the same state. After all, if you get a man and hunt him like an animal, in time he will become one. I am at a loss now to tell you of our life. Such worlds separate the ordinary human's point of view from mine at that time, that anything I can write will either be incomprehensible or will give a quite wrong impression. Briefly, I felt like this: I didn't care tuppence whether we held the "line" or not. Germany's victory or defeat was nothing. Nevertheless, I would do my job by my men as well as I could, as there was nothing else to do. I wasn't interested in religion or world politics or any rot like that. I was merely an insignificant scrap of humanity that was being intolerably persecuted by unknown powers, and I was going to score off those powers by dying. After all, a mouse must feel that it is one up on the playful cat when it dies without making any sport for its captor. With this new idea before me, I felt better. I didn't feel afraid anymore, and I walked about doing my job feeling as if I had scored off Providence.
>
> (1997, pp. 94–5)

A mouse's compliance with dying as its only means of defiance against a playful cat constitutes a paradoxical metaphor of Bion's emotional experience.[5] In *The Long Week-End* (1982), the mouse turned into a rat—maybe because the mouse was a euphemism for a rat, or maybe even as an ironic tribute to actual rats encountered: "There was one old chap, bald, bloated, corpse-fed, who sat on my chest one night—it made me laugh because his whiskers tickled my face" (p. 265). This metaphor is referred to several times, and "the cornered rat being clubbed to death all over again" accentuates the incomprehensible, persecuted-animal existence of one tortured indefinitely by anonymous powers that be (1982, p. 227; see also pp. 198, 209, 262; 1991, pp. 76, 77). Animal-like existence threatened to take over one's behavior:

> From under this crawled Osprey. Pale, watery-eyed, unshaven, he was "like things you find under a stone," but he *was* a thing under a stone! … Osprey agreed readily enough not to take shelter in that way again; so readily in fact that I was sure he was afraid of what that rat-like life had done to him.
>
> (1982, p. 210, italics in original)

The regression to animal existence damaged cognitive function: "Our questions had little to do with a thirst for information; it was a mindless activity, the individual becoming merged into a primitive brute, an army" (1982, p. 123). Bion points to the source of mindlessness in the unpredictability of events: "Could a shell fall short or over? It could—so I gave up thinking about it, thus taking shelter instinctively in mindlessness" (p. 130). Once questions become meaningless, what Bion later referred to as "a questioning attitude" (1961, p. 162) ceases to exist.

In *The Long Week-End* (1982), Bion describes Broome's repeated attempts to tell how he tripped into a shell hole filled with a "human soup" of body parts, blood, and mud, while his peers repeatedly refuse to listen to him—a refusal echoed in the omission of the incident from the "Diary" written to his parents (pp. 139–40). Contrary to such omissions, Bion wrote different versions of some events, the most salient of which is the fatal injury of his runner Sweeting who "had his thoracic wall blown out, exposing his heart" (1991, p. 256), while both were taking cover in a shell hole (1997, pp. 126–8, 254–5, 290; 1982, pp. 247–50, 264; 1991, p. 290).[6] Both omissions and repetitions are extreme opposite strategies for dealing with traumatic memories.

In retrospect, Bion noticed he was "surprised that these casualties had so little impact on us at the time …. We did not discuss the casualties; they had gone and that was that" (1982, p. 166). Silence enveloped the dead (p. 255), but not only loss was encapsulated by silence—all emotional experience was barred from conversation, as in the refusal to listen to Broome's tale. When Bion tries to tell another officer, Carter, how he feels before action, Carter reacts angrily: "Why the hell do you keep on talking about it then?"—adding that "I'm scared out of my wits. I'm not daft—you'd have to be daft or a nit-wit not to be scared. But why talk?" Bion sums up the brief conversation: "I was angry and felt no better for feeling he was right" (p. 233).

Elsewhere Bion elaborates on the mindless loneliness instigated by silencing emotional experience:

> The behaviour, facial expression, and poverty of conversation could give an impression of depression and even fear at the prospect of

> battle. Fear there certainly was; fear of fear was, I think, common to all—officers and men. The inability to admit it to anyone, as there was no one to admit it to without being guilty of spreading alarm and despondency, produced a curious sense of being entirely alone in company with a crowd of mindless robots—machines devoid of humanity. The loneliness was intense; I can still feel my skin drawn over the bones of my face as if it were the mask of a cadaver.
>
> (1997, p. 204)

The encapsulation of emotional experience probably enabled many men to withstand the strain of fighting at the cost of gradual mental deterioration and increasing mental vulnerability; it was crucial to keep the encapsulation intact, since its rupture was conceived as equivalent to mental breakdown. Bion describes one occasion when the silence, disguised as a matter-of-fact exchange, cracked when he was informed of the death of his second in command in the Battle of Amiens:

> Cook was back and drew me aside. "We found a bullet through his heart." I stared at him; he looked serious. I nearly said "Liar!"—what I meant was "Don't be a melodramatic ass!" what I said was "Oh." Then I burst into tears, wiped them off my face. "Sorry," I said, "I'm tired." Cook looked at me curiously. I hoped he wasn't going to suggest I had "shell-shock."
>
> (1982, p. 256)

Encapsulation was founded on clinging to the facts, leaving one with dreadful answers devoid of the muted questions about the meaning of it all—shredded bodies and shattered minds. For Bion, the *containment* of war experiences—a concept yet to be created by him—began with the rupture of encapsulation when writing the "Diary," which was only the beginning of an ongoing process, one that culminated in writing the autobiographical works. While the harsh reality of physical vulnerability was barely understandable, mental vulnerability was incomprehensible and left a trail of haunting questions, which may have contributed to Bion's creation of his theory of thinking as the foundation for a meta-psychology in which the concept of containment is a central organizing principle.

Bion was repeatedly exposed to a wide variety of manifestations of mental vulnerability (1997, pp. 36, 38, 48, 50, 51; 1982, pp. 137, 156, 169–70, 176–7, 186, 209–10), ranging from the officer Quainton's baffling hospitalization after driving a car into a ditch while on leave in England (1997, pp. 237, 299); to Gunner Allen's "dumb insolence" (1982, p. 236); to Gunner Harrison, who had "gone nuts" and started shooting at German prisoners of war (1997, p. 290). Thus Bion concludes:

> So; the officer had died of wounds—or was it shell-shock? Shell-shock was obviously complicated—from Quainton who, according to Clifford, was working his ticket, to the officer who did not bother about his wounds but thought that everyone from the Boche to his nurse was trying to murder him; all apparently had shell-shock.
>
> (1982, p. 193)

A confusing state of affairs, dealt with in pragmatic terms in relation to the army's task, fighting. As an officer, Bion had to recognize that when one was on the verge of shell-shock, "his nerves were too far gone for him to be any real use" (1997, p. 113; see also p. 62). Shell-shock presented a problem since it led to withdrawing the soldier from active duty and then invalidating him from service. Hence, the military addressed the problem of mental breakdown as malingering resulting from cowardice, i.e. as a means to the end of getting away from the battlefield (1997, pp. 228, 237). In *The Long Week-End* (1982), Bion reflects on this conception: "Nowadays I would not make such a simple diagnosis, but as it was I was impelled to prove my courage—the lack of it being, as I thought, my main defect. This erroneous idea was and still is, generally held" (p. 200).

Bion himself struggled with a sense of cowardice; he was acutely aware of his fear and attempted to hide it: "I knew only too well that if I relaxed my grim, determined jaw, my teeth would chatter" (1997, p. 205; see also pp. 224–5). It seems that reflective awareness regarding emotional experience protected Bion from a rupture of encapsulation, which would be tantamount to mental breakdown, but it also taxed him with agonizing self-consciousness:

> I was aware that *I* was not competent, particularly as I was so scared and that did not seem to fit in with being a soldier. I could not even be sure of what I was frightened. Death? No. Being terribly mutilated? Perhaps. I knew a bit more about the possibilities later. Going mad? No. whatever I thought of, it didn't seem to be right.
>
> (1997, p. 202, italics in original)

Even receiving the Distinguished Service Order (DSO) did not appease Bion's excruciating sense of cowardice:

> But … I had not reckoned with cowardice. I still felt just as ridiculous …. I felt I might with equal relevance have been recommended for a Court Martial. It depended on the direction which one took when one ran away.
>
> (1982, p. 278)

In the "Commentary" (1997), MYSELF remarks: "Incidentally, I think the VC could have toppled *you* into a 'breakdown.' You were lucky not to get it"[7] (p. 204, italics in original)—thus positioning cowardice and valor in a complex relation to mental breakdown. Commendation was supposed to mollify his sense of cowardice, but it did not. Instead, it enhanced two dangers—breakdown and death, both stemming from a desperate attempt to deserve it: "I suppose awards for valour do stimulate the impulse to be valorous. I think professional soldiers may be able to survive them unharmed better than people with fewer years of discipline" (1997, p. 205; see also 1982, p. 193, and 1991, pp. 149, 451).

Bion realized the importance of discipline, the value of adhering to the task at hand so as to maintain contact with reality, an understanding that would serve him well in years to come—as a psychiatrist in World War II, suggesting that disciplined activity can be a prophylactic and a cure (Bion, 1940; Bion, 1961, pp. 12–15; Szykierski, 2008). This was also true later, when he became a psychoanalyst advocating a discipline of no memory, no desire, no understanding, in order to enable containment (Bion, 1967b).

Discipline was necessary not only to withstand the strain of fighting, but also because of Bion's sense of duty regarding his role as an officer to his men. The latter was expressed in the "Diary" in two opposite directions: on the one hand, the only occasion he mentions that he was "very proud" of himself is when he managed to bring hot tea and boiling stew to his men (1997, p. 84); and on the other hand, he initiated what Parthenope Bion Talamo designated "a rough sort of 'behaviourist' group therapy" (1997, pp. 310–11) "by pretending … to enjoy action and to discourage in mess and elsewhere all talk of 'wind up,'" so as to enhance morale and create "a better fighting spirit" (pp. 89–90).

In retrospect, Bion comments regarding the behavior of some of the other officers: "They did not seem able to feel with their men and yet retain their awareness that although they were men like their men, they were paid to be gods, very minor gods perhaps, but gods" (1982, p. 236). Thus, the practices of his role as an officer left Bion sensitive to the politics of shell-shock, an obscure phenomenon encumbered with doubts:

> I was still suffering from the DSO that had been inflicted, with my collusion, on me: the Senior Psychiatrist was suffering from having to appoint officers to the Shell-shock (as it was called) Hospital. None of us knew what shell-shock was or even if it existed outside the imagination of soldiers like me and Sergeant O'Toole who had to cope with the "dumb insolence" of the little board-school slum-dweller, Allen, who had been considered to be just the stuff that heroes are made of, coming from a land fit to be loved by slum-dwellers who would want to die for it.
>
> (1985, p. 56)

Bion's skepticism about authority and leadership was consequent to a harsh disillusionment; as BION says in the "Commentary" (1997): "We could see for ourselves what our immediate seniors were" (p. 205). His attitude was transformed into a more complex position, even if a no less critical one, when he realized—as MYSELF asks—"Don't you think your immediate seniors had fears that likewise had to be masked? They too had seniors in rank and time." Young BION tenaciously holds his ground: "They died; we were killed" (p. 205). But later on, he comments: "At Oxford, when I wrote the account, we were not so critical ... because it was less awful to think all was well than to believe our bigger enemy was what you later called—," and MYSELF fills in, "the Establishment" (pp. 205–6). MYSELF adds, "But I do not blame the Establishment. It is us I blame—all of us. Victory seems to be regarded by us as desirable because it leads to an opportunity to sink into slumber again" (p. 207).

For Bion, sinking into slumber as a refuge was undermined by the residues of war. Already in the "Diary," Bion tried to explore the blurring of the boundary between dream and reality: "It was almost impossible to distinguish dream from reality .... The German machine-guns would chime in with your dream with uncanny effect, so that when you awoke you wondered whether you were dreaming" (1997, p. 94). The reality of war sneaked into one's dreams, but waking up did not guarantee peace of mind:

> For some time we had been unable to sleep except in full equipment .... The first time I did it I woke with an awful taste of blood in my mouth, and you can imagine the effect on a very sleepy man who had been dreaming action.
>
> (1997, p. 104)

While in the "Diary" Bion relates to the slide from realistic nightmare to nightmarish reality, in *The Long Week-End* (1982), he elaborates the evolution of a dream:

> The ground was hard, but I was tired. So I slept and I had a terrible dream. I awoke just as I was about to go into battle; it was unnerving to find that I was. The dream was grey, shapeless; horror and dread gripped me. I could not cry out, just as now, many years later, I can find no words. Then I had no words to find; I was awake to the relatively benign terrors of real war. Yet for a moment I wished it was only a dream. In the dream I must have wished it was only a war.
>
> (p. 237)

Bion traces the grey shapeless horror in the background of a recurrent nightmare he had at Oxford:

> The grey scene later formed an amalgam with the scene at the Steenbeck and became the backcloth of a dream I had at Oxford—"when the war was over." Night after night I found myself on my belly clinging by my toes and fingers to a glistening slope at the bottom of which was a raging torrent—the dirty trickle of the Steenbeck. Towards this I slithered. If I tried to arrest my progress by sticking my toes or fingers it accelerated the descent; if I desisted, it again accelerated my descent. I did not make a sound. I just woke up bathed in sweat.
>
> (1982, p. 211; see also 1997, pp. 207–8)[8]

It was difficult to acknowledge the damage done to him by the war, and yet it was impossible to deny it:

> Nevertheless, I did not see; I did not see that peacetime was no time for me. I was twenty-four; no good for war, no good for peace, and too old to change. It was truly terrifying. Sometimes it burst out in sleep. Terrified. What about? Nothing, nothing. Oh well, yes. I had a dream. I dug my nails into the steep and slippery walls of mud that fell sheer into the waters of a raging, foaming Steenbeck. Ridiculous! That dirty little trickle? If blood is thicker than water, what price the thickness of dreams? Suppose broad daylight was not thick enough to keep out the terror. Suppose I was so terrified that I ran away when it was really a battle. I woke up. Was I going crazy? Perhaps I *was* crazy.
>
> (1985, p. 16, italics in original)

Bion was awarded the Legion of Honour decoration for the action on August 8, 1918, and although "the citation had a curiously plausible resemblance to the 'facts,' yet I could not believe that the battle I had experienced and the one cited were the same" (1982, p. 273). Bion continued to reflect on the impact that particular action had on him: "I cannot imagine what was wrong, but I never recovered from the survival of the Battle of Amiens" (1997, p. 209). He concluded that "they have a way of making people look so life-like, but really we are dead. I? Oh yes, I died—on August 8, 1918" (1982, p. 265).[9] He says: "My feeling of guilt about my last battle in the war grew steadily for many years after" (1982, p. 276; see also 1991, pp. 450, 506).

These experiences furnished Bion's private hell with sleeping and waking nightmares (1982, p. 191). Haunted by his ghosts, Bion says: "I see them still in the watch fires of a thousand sleepless nights, for the soul goes marching on" (p. 128). He conceived himself as a witness to disaster—"nothing less than murder of the spirit of incomparable men. For me the disaster was to have survived and to undergo the mortification of being watched leaving the battle by men condemned to stay" (p. 212).

Bion had to deal with survivors' guilt not only in regard to the dead and the mutilated, but also to those who did not survive mentally, like Quainton. When Bion met him years later, he found that

> He was changed from a cheerful, frank fellow whom I had envied for his easy capacity for deep friendliness, into a timid, cautious and scared apology for a man .... Of course, I did not know that the Quainton I knew was only surviving as a physical representation of himself.
>
> (1997, p. 202)

While Bion's physical survival could be understood by him as an arbitrary result, his mental survival remained intriguing (1982, p. 105), and eventually he concluded: "No, I had not got shell-shock. What nonsense they were ready to talk! But, love had died. Love for anyone and anything" (1991, p. 150). Bion stayed sane, and made his way to the psychoanalytic study of the mind.

Bion's above-mentioned attempt in "Amiens" (published in 1997, though written in 1958) to revisit his war experiences was aborted in order to write what can be regarded as the three books that together form the core of his metapsychology (1962, 1963, 1965). Bion abandoned the writing of "Amiens" in mid-sentence: "He felt that people who cracked up were merely those who did not allow the rest of the world to ..." (1997, p. 308); it reads as though Bion were about to formulate the great unknown of mental catastrophe, but could not find the words, and went on an intellectual journey to find the elements and factors determining the transformations that determine whether a mind will *learn from experience* or "crack up."

A clue to Bion's view on the matter appears in his description of a particular soldier's fate, where he says that an ability to endure alone the horrible truth about the reality of war is crucial to mental survival:

> No, poor chap, he went sane long before the war was over; he couldn't bear the truth and being in a minority of one at the same time. It was pitiful—lying there in the ditch blubbing. He took to drink; even that couldn't save him from reality.
>
> (1991, p. 423; see also p. 515)

Containment of a "Cracked-Up," Postmodern Consciousness

Bléandonu (1994) argues that the war experiences are at the root of Bion's explorations of extreme unbearable emotions, and suggests that, in light of these experiences, Bion's "enigmatic concepts ... acquire extraordinary reality and depth" (p. 31). As a psychiatrist in World War

II and for a few years after its end in the Tavistock Clinic, Bion concentrated his work on the tensions between the individual and the group, and on the value of "a questioning attitude" for the empowerment of individuals caught in a web of group tensions (Szykierski, 2008). He turned to a psychoanalytic study of the psychotic mind, thus laying the foundations for a theory of thinking by exploring its most severe disorders (Bion, 1967a). The evolution of Bion's metapsychology in these contexts accentuates the influence of questions regarding his mental survival on the exploration of internal and external dangers to the functioning of the containing mind.

Wisdom (1987) considers Bion's war experiences to be of "inestimable importance" to his ability to "stay functional under stress" (p. 543). However, the impact of Bion's military service in World War I was far more fundamental and comprehensive. According to artist Michal Heiman (2008), "Bion, in his diary and in his entire theoretical work, both early and late—acts in the space of combative thought, the space of shell-shock, like one under attack" (p. 147).

In a similar vein, Meltzer analyzes Bion's response to questions presented to him in seminars, when "under pressure of the group," and suggests a military model describing Bion's mind at work:

> When confronted with a direct question, Bion's tactics seemed military indeed. He seemed to start off in a direction quite contrary to that of the question, as if in retreat from the aggressive intent, then made a wide sweep ending by taking the enemy, not even on its flank, but from the rear. During this excursion he would make little sallies at the question, trying one vertex after another, until one of them found a rather soft spot in the armour of the language in which the question had been phrased.
>
> (1981, p. 11)

An example that supports Meltzer's analysis regarding the impact of the war experiences on Bion's clinical thinking appears in one of Bion's discussions of his work with psychotic patients, written on May 16, 1959, wherein he states that the analyst's

> position is not unlike that of the soldier in war who is aware of his own troubles but not of his enemy's. It must therefore be borne in mind that the fundamental importance of our work demands that kind of fortitude and high morale which places the welfare of the analytic group and its work before the welfare of the individual analyst, and sometimes before the welfare even of a particular patient.
>
> (Bion 1992, p. 24)

So it seems that Bion's war experiences engendered a deep-seated strategy, applied to the study of mental phenomena, which he used in creating a theory of thinking only after making "a wide sweep" through the study of groups and the analysis of psychosis—thus not approaching his subject on the flank of PTSD, but from the rear of other regressive states of mind. Armed with a new understanding of the mind, Bion returned to his war experiences, "trying one vertex after another," so as to find "a soft spot in the armour" of opaque memories. As previously noted in this paper, Bion's metapsychology is viewed from the vertex of his war experiences—quite the opposite of reflecting on these war experiences from the vertex of metapsychology, as he himself did in his autobiographical works (1982; 1985; 1991).

"So—why write an autobiography?" asks Bion, and he answers, "Because it is interesting to me to review the life I have led in the universe in which I have lived" (1985, p. 22). In the "Commentary" (1997), BION says: "I forgot it as fast as I could" (p. 207), but half a century later, Bion reviews his testimony despite internal resistance and external silence (1982, pp. 124–5). These are the recurring obstacles to testimonies concerning horrors, as evident not only in the time gap before Bion's return to his World War I testimony during the 1970s (a gap of about a half century), but also in the gap between Felman and Laub's (1992) work regarding testimony and its subject—the Holocaust, and in the difficulties encountered in the group relations conferences entitled "Germans and Israelis—the Past in the Present" during the 1990s (Erlich et al., 2009).

Bion wrote a coherent and integrated chronological narrative about his life, while also writing down his fragmented and conflicted self in *A Memoir of the Future* (1991). A salient feature of his autobiographical works is the juxtaposition of various states of mind encompassing all objects contained in the simultaneous time and multidimensional space of internal reality, thus allowing for learning from experience by connecting diverse phenomena across time and space.[10] Although learning from experience is ruthless at times, Bion regards it as the only feasible method of mental survival (1982, p. 202).

From the vertex of war experiences, it seems that Bion's metapsychology evolved so as to resolve haunting questions regarding what determines one's mental growth or another's psychic death. Therefore, this metapsychology concentrates on the functioning of the mind when confronted with emotional experience, always oscillating between evading contact with reality and learning from experience. It is not surprising, then, that Bion found Freud's tragic vision of knowledge appealing, as suggested by Hamilton (1982, pp. 238–55). According to this tragic vision, the pursuit of knowledge originates from the absence of the object, and hence necessarily involves frustration and pain, and is motivated by survival.

Bion's comprehensive exploration of knowledge evolved from his war experiences and addressed the lack of an elaborate theory of thinking in psychoanalytic conceptualization.

In all his autobiographical works from the "Diary" onward, Bion is always concerned with knowledge—its inadequate sources in rumors (1982, p. 183; 1997, pp. 53, 130), its influence on one's state of mind (1997, pp. 37, 132, 137), its importance for one's survival (1982, pp. 126, 131; 1997, pp. 59, 72, 135), and the dangers (1982, pp. 40, 275) as well as the relief (1982, pp. 156, 163) inherent in ignorance.

Bion learned from experience that knowledge can be used defensively: "It is such a relief to know *exactly* where everyone is. When you have no idea whatever where you are yourself, it is, as I discovered, an admirable substitute" (1982, p. 208, italics in original). Although Bion regarded learning from experience as crucial for survival (1982, p. 201; 1997, pp. 89, 135), he was attentive to the defensive maneuvers undermining it by congealing knowledge in social institutions and political establishments:

> But how, in war, does one decide what is daft? The answer is that one does not, if one can help it, decide these things in war. They are decided in peace, formulated in training manuals, enforced by orders. Such is the perversity of the human animal that these prudent dispositions intended to protect against irresponsibility and uniformed improvisation are then erected into rigid barriers as a defence against thought .... When we learn, like the child walking, to act automatically without expenditure of thought we also learn how to avoid pain by economizing thought.
>
> (1982, p. 204)

Thus, in retrospect, Bion becomes aware of the absence of a critical attitude in the military system, as well as among his peers and within himself:

> Looking back now it amazes me that I do not remember any occasion when it occurred to me or any of my friends to debate the military wisdom of our procedures. It is the more surprising that a critical attitude was common enough but never took a constructive form. It did not occur to me, or any tank commander of whom I heard, to report that Ypres was unsuitable for tank warfare. The tank commanders who might have provided the initiative and knowledge were either killed in action or too stunned, stupefied, to contribute anything.
>
> (1982, pp. 268–9)[11]

Even when a critical attitude took a constructive form, as in the abovementioned event when the tank officers warned against an attack at

10:30 a.m. without a smoke screen, their advice was ignored and all the tanks destroyed (1982, pp. 253–4); only then was the event mentioned by Marshal Foch: "A short note advised that in future all general officers should take the advice offered by officers in command of technical units" (1997, p. 135). Learning from experience was achieved only after the fact, after the experience had taken its death toll.

Hence, when exploring the intricacies of knowledge, Bion remains alert to the dangers awaiting one while confronted with the choice between containing emotional experience so as to maintain contact with reality, and various defensive maneuvers intended to evade contact with reality and avoid learning from experience.

In *A Memoir of the Future* (1991), Bion introduces the metapsychology of the multilayered and multivoiced, fragmented self, informed by Freud's conflicted self and Klein's self-containing phantasized objects. As Parthenope Bion Talamo argues:

> This vision of the mind as a palimpsest with a continual potentiality for almost instantaneous regression can be seen to tie up to the theory of beta-elements, a continuous flow of unprocessed pre-mental sensory data, which then have to be subjected to alpha-function in order to be used for thinking at all.
>
> (Bion 1997, p. 310)

An overwhelming surplus of experience is Bion's point of origin (Boris, 1986, p. 160) when conceptualizing "the mind that is a too heavy load for the sensuous beast to carry" (Bion 1991, p. 38)—a mind that is constantly assaulted by sense impressions, forever oscillating between containing emotional experience and evading contact with reality. Note that while discussing the various functions of containment, Bion explicitly states that he is using "the word with its military implication of one force containing another" (1970, p. 112); thus military containment serves as a model for mental containment, a concept that gradually becomes essential to Bion's account of the ceaseless struggle of the human mind to survive reality. In the context of the mind's struggle to deal with the threat of overwhelming sense impressions and to contain experience, Bion's evocative term *nameless dread* (1962, p. 96) marks a common denominator of PTSD and psychosis, signifying both cause and effect of a serious impairment in contact with reality.

J. Symington and N. Symington (1996) conclude that Bion tried throughout his life to assimilate his appalling war experiences, and thus much of his theoretical work can be viewed as an effort to work through these traumatic experiences. As Brown (2007) argues, "From this perspective, therefore, Bion's theories of thinking and its disturbance devolve from both his personal experiences with trauma as well as his work with the psychotic portion of the mind" (p. 1571). Bion regarded analytic work in general and with psychosis in particular as analogous to war in its requirement for mental containment of dangerous states of mind (1991, pp. 516–17), when even physical containment fails from time to time:

> Psychiatrists try to restrain "illogical" systems physically within mental institutions. As often as not the guardians—doctors, nurses and others—fall to the assault of the systems they are supposed to "contain," like an army which, "containing" a besieged force, falls to an attack by the besieged. They call the psychiatric casualties "breakdowns."
>
> (1991, p. 266)

On occasion, Bion explicitly used the military implication of the term *containment* in order to create a *thick description* (Geertz, 1973) of nuanced subtleties of mental phenomena, as exemplified in his discussion of a stammerer:

> The man was trying to contain his experience in a form of words; he was trying to contain himself, as one sometimes says to someone about to lose control of himself; he was trying to "contain" his emotions within a form of words, as one might speak of a general attempting to "contain" enemy forces within a given zone. The words that should have represented the meaning the man wanted to express were fragmented by the emotional forces to which he wished to give only verbal expression. The verbal formulation could not "contain" his emotions, which broke through and dispersed it as enemy forces might break through the forces that strove to contain them. The stammerer, in his attempt to avoid the contingency I have described, resorted to modes of expression so boring that they failed to express the meaning he wished to convey; he was thus no nearer to his goal. His verbal formulation could be described as like to the military forces that are worn by the attrition to which they are subjected by the contained forces. The meaning he was striving to express was denuded of meaning.
>
> (Bion, 1970, p. 94)

Hence, the concept of containment as elaborated in *Attention and Interpretation* (1970) evolved into an organizing principle in Bion's metapsychology, as the different relations between container and contained can be applied in the study of all the arenas of function (or dysfunction) of the mind, while allowing for movement between distinct levels of functioning, including the political function of an individual or the dynamics of a social group. In this sense, *containment* is an elastic concept, describing both nuanced intricacies and gross maneuvers, since it is conceptualized as a complex process, determined by various relations between container and contained, and determining mental functions as well as social interactions and political phenomena.

Bion's metapsychology was configured by a modern war that was a ruthless capitalistic struggle for survival (Eisold, 2005), barely disguised by a veil of patriotism, and thus was the point of origin for postmodern consciousness that became embedded in Bion's vision of a mind struggling against fragmentation to contain emotional experience.

Notes

1 This chapter has been previously published in *The Psychoanalytic Quarterly*, 2010 Volume LXXIX, Number 4, pp. 935–68. We are grateful to the *Quarterly* for permission to reprint it here.

2 For example, we read of "a policy aimed at controlling the spread of communism around the world, developed in the administration of President Harry S. Truman. The formation of the North Atlantic Treaty Organization (NATO) in 1949 was an important step in the development of containment" (Hirsch and Kett, 2002, p. 283).

3 Bion's attempt to revisit his war experiences in "Amiens" happened on the boundary between the publications of his papers on psychosis in the 1950s (later collected and republished with his reviewing commentary in *Second Thoughts* [1967a]) and his theoretical publications of the 1960s.

4 These references appear in two forms: thirty-five occurrences (70%) occur in the context of describing external reality—both in the text and in captions for drawings, maps, diagrams or pictures; and fifteen occurrences (30%) occur in the context of explaining Bion's internal reality.

5 Curiously, the Greek bucolic poet Bion of Smyrna, who lived in about 100 BC, was said to have commented on cruelty to animals: "It was the saying of Bion that, though boys throw stones at frogs in sport, yet the frogs do not die in sport but in earnest" (Plutarch [c. AD 100], p. 170).

6 Souter (2009) argues that Bion's repeated explorations of this event crystallize the impact of Bion's war experiences on his insight into the nature of the mind and "the horrors of psychic abandonment," as well as "the absolute necessity of the presence of another mind for psychic survival" (p. 795).

7 Initially, Bion was recommended for the Victoria Cross (VC), Britain's highest award for conspicuous valor, but received the DSO.

8 One of the war's major conflicts, the Battle of Passchendaele, took place near the River Steenbeck between July and November 1917 (see also footnote 11).

9 The Battle of Amiens began on August 8, 1918, and was the opening phase of the Allied Hundred Days Offensive that led to the end of World War I. It was one of the first major battles involving armored warfare and marked the end of trench warfare on the Western Front. This quotation is one of several instances when Bion said that he had died on August 8.

10 *A Memoir of the Future* (1991) is constructed by means of a conversational juxtaposition of different experiences. Such connections appear in the "Diary" (1997, pp. 17, 103, 122). They are also prevalent in *The Long Week-End* (1982), moving forward and backward in time and space between childhood memories and war experiences (pp. 16, 20, 22, 29, 115, 202), as well as between distant and diverse experiences during the war (pp. 103–4, 113, 119, 120–1, 156, 160, 267, 272). In this latter work,

Bion points to forgotten meanings lost in time (pp. 124–5, 127, 142), reflects on the impact that some haunting residues of war had on his life (pp. 143, 191, 256), and reviews his war experiences (pp. 264, 276, 279).

11 The third battle of Ypres, or the Battle of Passchendaele (see footnote 8), was Bion's first battle during the war (see 1982, pp. 121–41; 1997, pp. 22–38), and has become known for attrition warfare fought in thick mud, since it took place on reclaimed marshland, swampy even without rain. The summer of 1917 was unusually cold and wet, and in addition, the preliminary heavy artillery bombardment of the Allied forces destroyed the surface of the land and the drainage system, exacerbating the problem. As a result, tanks bogged down in mud, and soldiers often drowned in it.

References

Bilu, Y. and Witztum, E. (2000) War-related loss and suffering in Israeli society: a historical perspective. *Israel Studies*, 5(2):1–31.

Bion, W. R. (1940) The "war of nerves": civilian reaction, morale and prophylaxis. In *The Neuroses in War*, E. Miller (ed.). New York: Macmillan & Co., 1945. pp. 180–200.

Bion, W. R. (1959) Attacks on linking. *The International Journal of Psychoanalysis*, 40:308–15.

Bion, W. R. (1961) *Experiences in Groups and Other Papers*. London: Tavistock.

Bion, W. R. (1962) *Learning from Experience*. London/New York: Karnac.

Bion, W. R. (1963) *Elements of Psychoanalysis*. London/New York: Karnac.

Bion, W. R. (1965) *Transformations: Changing from Learning to Growth*. New York: Basic Books.

Bion, W. R. (1967a) *Second Thoughts*. London/New York: Karnac.

Bion, W. R. (1967b) Notes on memory and desire. In *Melanie Klein Today, Vol. 2: Mainly Practice*, E. Spillius (ed.). London: Routledge, 1988.

Bion, W. R. (1970) *Attention and Interpretation*. London/New York: Karnac.

Bion, W. R. (1977) *Seven Servants*. New York: Jason Aronson.

Bion, W. R. (1982) *The Long Week-End, 1897–1919: Part of a Life*. Abingdon, UK: Fleetwood Press.

Bion, W. R. (1985) *All My Sins Remembered: Another Part of a Life and the Other Side of Genius: Family Letters*. London: Karnac.

Bion, W. R. (1991) *A Memoir of the Future*. London: Karnac.

Bion, W. R. (1992) *Cogitations*. London/New York: Karnac.

Bion, W. R. (1997) *War Memoirs: 1917–1919*. In F. Bion (ed.). London: Karnac.

Bléandonu, G. (1994) *Wilfred Bion: His Life and Works, 1897–1979*. London: Free Association.

Boris, H. N. (1986) Bion re-visited. *Contemporary Psychoanalysis*, 22:159–84.

Brown, L. J. (2005) The cognitive effects of trauma: reversal of alpha function and the formation of a beta screen. *The Psychoanalytic Quarterly*, 74:397–420.

Brown, L. J. (2007) Julie's museum: the evolution of thinking, dreaming and historicization in traumatized patients. *The International Journal of Psychoanalysis*, 87:1569–85.

Eisold, K. (2005) Using Bion. *Psychoanalytic Psychology*, 22:357–69.

Erlich, H. S., Erlich-Ginor, M. and Beland, H. (2009) *Fed with Tears—Poisoned with Milk: The "Nazareth" Group-Relations-Conferences: Germans and Israelis—The Past in the Present*. Gieben, Germany: Psychosocial-Verlag.

Felman, S. and Laub, D. (1992) *Testimony: Crisis of Witnessing in Literature, Psychoanalysis and History*. New York/London: Routledge.

Geertz, C. (1973) *The Interpretation of Cultures*. New York: Basic Books.

Hamilton, V. (1982) *Narcissus and Oedipus: The Children of Psychoanalysis.* London/Boston: Routledge/Kegan Paul.

Heiman, M. (2008) *Through the Visual: A Tale of Art that Attacks Linking, 1917–2008.* Catalogue published in conjunction with the 2008–09 exhibition "Attacks on Linking" at Tel-Aviv Museum of Art.

Hirsch, E. D. and Kett, J. F. (2002) *The New Dictionary of Cultural Literacy.* New York: Houghton Mifflin.

Kipling, R. (1900) I keep six honest serving-men. In *Just So Stories.* Garden City, NJ/New York: Doubleday & Co., 1965.

Langs, R. J. (1981) Some communicative properties of the bipersonal field. In *Do I Dare Disturb the Universe? A Memorial to Wilfred* R. *Bion,* J. S. Grotstein (ed.). London: Maresfield Reprints, pp. 441–87.

López-Corvo, R. E. (2003) *The Dictionary of the Work of W.* R. *Bion.* London/New York: Karnac.

Meltzer, D. (1981). Memorial meeting for Dr. Wilfred Bion held by the British Psycho-Analytical Society on 20 February 1980. *International Review of Psychoanalysis,* 8:3–14.

Ogden, T. H. (2004) On holding and containing, being and dreaming. *The International Journal of Psychoanalysis,* 85:1349–64.

Plutarch (c. AD 100) Which are the most crafty, water-animals or those creatures that breed upon the land? In *Plutarch's Morals,* rev. W. W. Goodwin. Boston, MA: Little, Brown & Co., 1874.

Sandler, P. C. (2003) Bion's war memoirs: a psychoanalytical commentary—living experiences and learning from them: some early roots of Bion's contributions to psychoanalysis. In *Building on Bion: Roots. Origins and Context of Bion's Contributions to Theory and Practice,* R. M. Lipgar and M. Pines (eds.). London/New York: Jessica Kingsley Publishers, pp. 59–84.

Solomon, Z. (1993) *Combat Stress Reactions: The Enduring Toll of War.* New York: Plenum Press.

Symington, J. and Symington, N. (1996) *The Clinical Thinking of Wilfred Bion.* London/New York: Routledge.

Szykierski, D. (2008) The Northfield experiment and the enigma of psychiatry without psychiatrists: exclusion by inclusion of the radical contribution of W. R. Bion. *Organisational and Social Dynamics,* 8(1):38–62.

Wisdom, J. O. (1987) Bion's place in the troika. *International Review of Psychoanalysis,* 14:541–51.

EDITORS' INTRODUCTION

Wilfred Bion's "Caesura": From Public Lecture to Published Text— (1975–1977)

Joseph Aguayo

This chapter deals with the evolution of the caesura concept, from a recently discovered audiotape of a lecture that Bion gave in Los Angeles in 1975—a transcript of which appears here for the first time in print—to its later published version in 1977. Bion adopted the term, "caesura," from a quote by Freud (1926): "there is much more continuity between intra-uterine life and earliest infancy than the impressive *caesura* of the act of birth allows us to suppose" (p. 138) and employed it as a metaphor "to describe that which unites and separates at the same time." Given the conflicts that existed between the ego psychologists and newly emerging, Bion-inspired Kleinians at the LA Institute at the time of Bion's talk, his focus on a phenomenon associated with birth may have (consciously or not) conveyed some reference to Otto Rank's theory of the birth trauma and his expulsion from Freud's "Secret Committee."

Aguayo leads readers through a careful textual analysis of Bion's work, enabling them to observe the differences between the original lecture and the later, published version. In the former, where Bion was talking to an audience of American analysts, many of whom were unfamiliar with his ideas, Bion appears to lean a bit more heavily on classical Freudian sensibilities, quoting Freud more frequently than was his custom, perhaps in an attempt to build a bridge to his audience and show that "if he could understand their dialect perhaps they could understand his." Bion also chose to omit mention of the presumably more controversial theological/mystical references (e.g. Martin Buber, St. John of the Cross), which would appear in the later published version. As Aguayo demonstrates, by the time the latter appears, Bion has clearly moved into his own creative territory with a radical new view of caesura and its manifestations in and implications for the clinical relationship. Choosing to lecture on the topic of caesura might also be thought of as Bion's way of metaphorically expressing his own break with the continuity of living in

London for many years, as well as addressing the process of transformation in the Los Angeles psychoanalytic scene of which he was a central figure.

The lecture starts by referencing Freud's work to an audience on intimate terms with the latter's theories, but then moves on from that beginning to introduce Bion's personal interpretations of Freud and, "by making the familiar strange and the strange familiar," captures the attention of his listeners. In one instance, Bion introduces the topic of "free association" with which all are familiar, but then abruptly offers an extension of that concept to include the non-verbal patient and asks, "is it possible to make any progress with a patient who doesn't say anything?" This query, of course, is rhetorical and leads Bion to outline his views of the communicative aspects of projective identification that help the analyst to listen to other than the analysand's verbal expressions. Thus, by anchoring the lecture in Freud's ideas, Bion essentially softened the impact of the caesura that he was creating "by making the familiar strange."

3

WILFRED BION'S "CAESURA"

From Public Lecture to Published Text—(1975–1977)

Joseph Aguayo

Introduction

In recent years, as the work of pioneering psychoanalysts has been the subject of careful, archival study, we have learned more about the creative processes reflected in the work of Sigmund Freud and Melanie Klein (Gay, 1988; Spillius, 2007; Frank, 2009). Researchers have examined the writings of analytic pioneers, available in the form of original drafts, re-workings of manuscripts in addition to published versions of their psychoanalytic work. It is altogether common for such analysts to have revised their original manuscripts in subsequent editions—and here, one can ask if there is something to be learned from making detailed comparisons between early and late drafts.

Over the years that I have practiced as a psychoanalyst in Los Angeles, I have also maintained an active research interest in this area of the history of psychoanalysis, specifically the history of Kleinian psychoanalysis at the British Society of Psychoanalysis (Aguayo, 2009). As a result of this interest, I have come in contact with other analysts, particularly members of the Psychoanalytic Center of California, who either had supervision or analytic treatment with Wilfred Bion during the time when he lived and practiced in Beverly Hills from 1968 to 1978. To date, I have collected both written and recorded materials for a potential local archive that would document Dr. Bion's life and work here in Los Angeles during the last phase of his prolific career. This chapter touches on a number of points, both contextual and clinical that relate to one such remnant of Bion's career in Los Angeles in the form of an audio-recording of a talk that Bion gave on the "Caesura" at the Los Angeles Psychoanalytic Society and Institute (LAPSI) in 1975.

The family of one of Bion's supervisees, Dr. Jarvin Heiman, who was then a member of the Southern California Psychoanalytic Institute, was kind enough to allow me the use of the recording, so that a typed transcription could be made. This public lecture appears here for the first time, as Wilfred Bion gave his lecture on the "Caesura" at the Los Angeles Psychoanalytic Institute, on June 4th, 1975. My aim in this chapter is to provide some immediate local context for Bion's work in Los Angeles, followed by the actual transcription of his lecture, and to conclude with some comparative remarks on how the public lecture throws an illuminating perspective on the written and final text of the paper Bion (1977) eventually published.

Starting with some orienting local context regarding the Los Angeles psychoanalytic scene in 1975, analytic participants in what came to be known as the "Freud–Klein Troubles" had passionate differences of opinion regarding a sort of "British Kleinian invasion," when in the early 1960s, prominent Kleinian analysts were invited to visit, lecture and supervise local analysts in Los Angeles (Kirsner, 2000, pp. 139–40). Psychoanalysts in Los Angeles, such as Bernard Brandschaft, James Grotstein, and Bernard Bail, amongst others, had developed a keen interest in Kleinian analysis, and as a result, invited practitioners such as Wilfred Bion, Herbert Rosenfeld and Hanna Segal to visit Los Angeles on a yearly basis for private small group gatherings in which they could teach and disseminate their clinical work. Out of their growing enthusiasm for Kleinian work throughout the 1960s, an invitation was extended to Wilfred Bion to immigrate to Los Angeles, an offer that he eventually accepted in 1968. The enthusiasm of local analysts for the work of these British Kleinians now began to encounter stiffening opposition from a powerful bastion of older Freudian analysts who resisted the growing Kleinian influence, especially amongst younger training analysts and psychoanalytic candidates who found themselves drawn to Bion's work (ibid., p. 172).

In all likelihood, Bion, as a prominent psychoanalyst in his own right, whose work was highly regarded by his peers at the British Psychoanalytical Society, might well have inherited Klein's mantle as the head of the Klein group in London after her death in 1960. But he chose instead to relocate to Los Angeles in 1968, where he thought he could more quietly pursue his analytic work, earn a decent living and most of all, write about psychoanalysis in relative peace undisturbed by the time-consuming administrative duties he had shouldered both as the president of the British Psychoanalytical Society and member of the Melanie Klein Trust. Yet his move to Los Angeles in 1968 also occasioned what became over the next few years, a great deal of animosity amongst local Freudian analysts towards the work of Melanie Klein and Kleinians, inadvertently polarizing an already fractious situation. By this time, independent of the ego psychologist–Klein conflicts, there already had existed long-standing bitter and competitive rivalries between well-known analysts such as Ralph Greenson and Leo Rangell at the Los Angeles Institute.

But more immediately troublesome for the English Kleinians in Los Angeles, Ralph Greenson had made it his personal mission to eliminate the influence and teaching of Klein at the Los Angeles Psychoanalytic Institute (Kirsner, 2000). He had made a quick study of the Kleinian method and concluded that it was wanting on a number of different levels. In a paper given at the IPA Congress in Paris in July 1973, "Transference: Freud or Klein," Greenson (1974) debated Herbert Rosenfeld on the liabilities of Kleinian clinical theory. In summary, Greenson (1974, 1975) criticized the Kleinians for not adhering to Freudian technique, and he recycled many of Anna Freud's earlier criticisms of Klein: he thought Kleinians were diagnostically indiscriminate insofar as they would seemingly analyze *any* type of patient, neurotic or psychotic, thus going against Freud's (1914) injunction against the unsuitability of the "narcissistic neuroses" for analytic treatment. Greenson also thought that Kleinians conducted "wild analysis" and made transference interpretations right from the beginning of treatment, often in an omniscient way. In short, in Greenson's view, there was too wide a gap for any meaningful dialogue between American Freudians and British Kleinians. For Greenson, it was as if the Controversial Discussions (1941–4) had never happened—and thus, the clinical theories of Freud and Klein remained fundamentally incompatible (King and Steiner, 1991).

Into this polarizing ferment came Wilfred Bion. When looking at the immediate context in which Bion lectured, he encountered enthusiasts, critics and the merely curious. The rancorous atmosphere that had pervaded the post-World War II theoretical rivalries amongst the three training groups at the British Society—the Kleinian, Freudian and Independents—now seemingly was reborn anew in the "Freud–Klein Troubles" during the Vietnam War era of the 1970s in Los Angeles. In listening to and studying Bion's "Caesura" lecture given at LAPSI in 1975, I have been struck by his rhetorical practices—with how he attempted to persuade his audience. From the sound of it, perhaps right down to his choice of an obscure passage from Freud's (1926) *Inhibitions, Symptoms and Anxiety*, he had an apparent keen appreciation of the local audience to whom he addressed his most recent ideas. In my view, his lecture to Freudian analysts in Los Angeles would not be quite the same one Bion might have given at a meeting of the British Society in London. For instance, in the public lecture, I noted the constant references to Freud's work, more plentiful than those that appeared in the final publication in 1977. Bion's overture here made practical sense because through his demonstration of a thorough understanding of Freudian ideas—and not mere caricatures of them—he forged a necessary link to the particular local analytic dialect of his audience. And so, if he could understand and articulate their Freudian dialect, perhaps they might understand his own. On the other hand, when he mentioned a number of Freud's ideas and papers in the public lecture, I noted also that he also tended not to include the quotations of mystic and religious thinkers that appeared in the published version of the "Caesura" in 1977. While it might have been difficult enough for an audience of Freudian analysts to be responsive to Bion's ideas, he might have frankly alienated these very analysts with quotations from theologians and religious thinkers, such as Martin Buber or St. John of the Cross. Bion demonstrated tact and restraint by not including these works in his 1975 lecture. Yet such quotations did however find their way into the published text of 1977.

So this is some of the local analytic context in which Bion gave his paper on the "Caesura" to a small group of American analysts in Beverly Hills on the night of June 4th 1975. After some light banter, where he discussed those patients who are rarely discussed in public meetings—those who come to consult the analyst and leave soon thereafter, never to be seen again—Bion got down to the business of the lecture. In *Symptoms, Inhibitions and Anxiety,* Freud (1926, p.138) wrote:

> for, just as the mother originally satisfied all the needs of the fetus through the apparatus of her own body, so now, after its birth, she continues to do so, though partly by other means. There is much more continuity between intra-uterine life and earliest infancy than the impressive *caesura* of the act of birth allows us to suppose. What happens is that the child's biological situation as a fetus is replaced for it by a psychical object-relation to its mother.

I am struck by the irony involved in Bion's selection of this small passage from Freud's 1926 monograph, in which one of Freud's primary aims was to mount an argument against Otto Rank's birth trauma theory, one of the final chapters in the "Secret Committee's" dismissal and banishment of someone they regarded as a "dissident" and heretical thinker. In thinking about Freud's "Secret Committee" its inception was designed to protect Freud's work from that of dissident and rival theories. In his lifetime, it was Freud who remained paramount in defining what the true boundaries of the psychoanalytic domain were—and also what went beyond the pale. I conjecture that this bit of history might have been at the back of Bion's mind as he discussed his recent ideas with Freudian analysts at LAPSI. After all, it was in the midst of contemporary charges made by Greenson that true psychoanalysis was to be restricted to the "transference neuroses" and thus, he could dismiss in a rather wholesale fashion the work done by the post-war Klein group on the feasibility of analyzing both psychotic and narcissistic states of mind (Rosenfeld, 1965). Bion's work had surely existed beyond the supposed orthodox pale patrolled by Greenson and other like-minded American Freudians.

Yet the hour was late: Bion was 71 years old and had left London because he no longer wanted to be involved in the small group politics that are endemic to any psychoanalytic institute. The struggle to establish a place for Kleinian theory in Los Angeles fell to younger men like Albert Mason, another analyst from the British Society, who had also been invited to relocate to Los Angeles from London and also attracted supervisees and analysands alike. In 1973, just after the IPA Congress in Paris in July, Mason also debated Greenson on September 20th, 1973 at Cedar's Sinai Hospital on the latter's caricatures of Kleinian theory and clinical work. In many respects, this meeting was a replay of Greenson's rancorous encounter with Rosenfeld in Paris (Kirsner, 2000, pp. 188–9). Others too had joined on behalf of the Kleinian cause, analysts like James Grotstein, Art Malin, Bernard Brandschaft and Bernard Berenson, locally known then as the "Four Horsemen of the Apocalypse."

But by this point, Bion was more the elder statesman of this young group, someone much more interested in developing and writing about his ideas than participating in psychoanalytic politics. So to the argument he made in "Caesura": the metaphor of *caesura*, which derives from the Latin word to cut, refers to a break or resting point in verse, such as "Loveliest of trees, the cherry now." Bion deployed this metaphor to describe that which unites and separates at the same time, a form of continuity through the experience of discontinuity. In both his public lecture and published text, he drew upon the *caesura* to examine disparate phenomena such as resistance, asking questions such as: what is it that prevents the patient from having a more far reaching conversation with some unclaimed part of himself? What separates and unites occidental and oriental cultures in terms of how ideas are thought about and conveyed in written form? What unites as well as separates the marital couple?

And of course, Bion had some interest (which he called "nonsense") in the concrete aspects of the *caesura* as well: in terms of the nascent field of infant observation and naturalistic studies, he also speculated about the literal connection between pre- and post-natal life—does the fetus think, see, feel or hear and do such experiences survive in post-natal life in the form of an "embryological intuition," either of the visual or auditory type? (Bion, 1977, p. 42).

As far ranging as these questions were, Bion rooted his talk in the clinical domain of his audience that night, yet he did it in his characteristic way by making the familiar strange and the strange familiar. Take the subtle points he made about free association in the lecture: starting with the more familiar notion of the analyst listening to his patient's associations until he could detect a pattern of meaningful connection between conscious and unconscious, past and present, deep and immediate, Bion was on familiar ground. But then, he abruptly (or so it seems to me) shifted the ground of the discussion by extending the definition of free association. He said:

> Now this brings me to another point: one gets an extraordinary amount of material—you get every sort of material from the patient who talks very freely, very easily, very coherently and articulately, to a patient who will go through a session without saying a word. Now that isn't what one ordinarily calls a free association, but I think one has to consider that it *is* a free association. The snag about it is that we don't know, or I don't know certainly and perhaps it is a matter that we here can do a research on—is it possible to make any progress with a patient who doesn't say anything?

Bion here referred to a more expansive definition of free association, namely in the direction of the communicative aspects of projective identification, when the patient's actions could be also understood as forming its own linking language—and words could be understood as actions as well. In short, this kind of clinical thinking was instrumental in moving Kleinian clinical technique into an area where the patient's enactments were rapidly becoming the focus of clinical work that helped to expand the parameters of psychoanalytic technique—again, beyond the pale of the Freud's "transference neuroses" into the realm of the "narcissistic neuroses." Elsewhere, I have noted that Bion's work was also fundamental in turning Betty Joseph's clinical technique more in the direction of the "difficult to treat" narcissistic patient (Aguayo, 2011). Following Bion's lead, Joseph marginalized the importance of the patient's early history, preferring to link it as the "past-in-the-present" transference occurring in the here and now. It was a purely Bion-inspired move for the analyst now to take up the "You and I" in the current existential moment.

The Text of Bion's "Caesura" Lecture

Bernard Hellinger, a psychiatrist and psychoanalyst who chaired a meeting at the Los Angeles Psychoanalytic Institute in 1975, (LAPSI) introduced Wilfred Bion to the LAPSI audience. At the point where the audiotape starts, Hellinger is in the middle of his introduction.

HELLINGER: I think that the size of the crowd is a little large for what he (Bion) had hoped for and in a way, I think he expected a dialogue with very few people, and this looks like a dialogue may develop here with an awful lot of people but in any case, I hopefully anticipate that this will simply be a "happening," so without a further ado, I'd like to turn this meeting over to Dr. Bion, and to yourselves and to me.

BION: It is a "happening" which is somewhat disconcerting, but after all, one is supposed to be used to that; but I find I never really do get used to it. I seem to make rather a rash problem when I said "anything," but the fact of the matter is that I find it somewhat intimidating to be expected to be talking about my concepts because I don't think I have any. I think it's a sort of state, which very easily arises because I don't think I have ever said anything original in my life. But, I think that what I say is probably unique simply just by definition, because we concern ourselves with the individual as being uniquely important. I think it is fair to say that psychoanalysts do in fact attach enormous importance to the individual person. I don't know if this was ever built into some sort of philosophy, or stated as if it were a philosophical prejudice or a philosophical point of view; but it seems to me that it is just what it is—that we are concerned with unique people and the uniqueness of the person.

Now, this raises a problem because in a sense, we are also concerned with the fact that the individual is a member of the human race (to put it at its vaguest and widest view). That is true and that is why it is interesting to consider what Freud regarded as being the hallmark, so to speak, of analysis—which means both the hallmark of the actual procedure and the hallmark of the subject which we investigate, which is the human individual. Now that part of the problem takes up very little of our time because, or so it seems to me, that for about three sessions, psychoanalytic theory is very useful because one has got nothing else to go on. One really knows nothing virtually about the person concerned. True, you have to fall back on theories and expectations, which you can entertain from such past experiences as you've got and from the literature. After that, if the analysis proceeds, then you are up against a unique situation; you are up against that unique individual.

John Rickman, whom I first went to for analysis for a long time, used to say that anybody could regard themselves as an analyst if they could see a patient for two sessions. He considered that to be a pretty considerable achievement. And I see what he means, because I have seen quite a lot of people, but never again. (Laughter). There are certain number though who somehow want to go on with the whole proceeding. And that is where you get into the real problem of what is psychoanalysis, from which I think that we could profit. But I also think we have achieved a discipline from which they could profit.

Now, I want now to change the subject rather: in his book on *Symptoms, Inhibitions and Anxiety*, Freud says there is much more continuity between intra-uterine life and earlier infancy than the impressive *caesura* of the act of birth allows us to suppose, to believe. I found that extremely illuminating, because in various ways, that peculiar little pattern seems to me to repeat itself over and over again—that you constantly find that the analysand says things, tells you something; and it seems to have a sort of reminiscence about it; it reminds you of something earlier, or what we call earlier. And indeed, the patient or the analysand seems to be repeating a sort of reminiscence.

Now, as you know, Freud hit on this scheme, by which he discovered that if people associated freely, then these apparently free associations were somehow connected with each other. Now this point was not and still is not obvious. One has to believe, as it were, that that is true and the next thing is that you have to believe it enough to go on listening to these free associations until there begins to emerge some sort of connection between them. Now this brings me again to another point: one gets an extraordinary amount of material—you get every sort of material from the patient who talks very freely, very easily, very coherently and articulately, to a patient who will go through a session without saying a word. Now that isn't what one ordinarily calls a free association, but I think one has to consider that it is a free association. The snag about it is that we don't know, or I don't know certainly and perhaps it is a matter that we here can do a research on—is it possible to make any progress with a patient who doesn't say anything?

Take another kind of patient, the kind of patient who would be quite prepared to play a musical instrument, if he thought that the analyst was capable of understanding music, but does not feel willing to talk and considers that the whole process of talking to be a very feeble form or method of investigation or communication even. And I have known a patient who is quite hostile to the idea of verbal communication, not just psychoanalysis, but verbal communication on the grounds that it is a ridiculous and incompetent method of communication.

I am reminded at this moment too of this odd fact that people even write differently. If you take, say a Chinaman, he does not write from left to right. Is there any difference between a person who writes from right to left or the person who writes from bottom upwards? Could one say they think like that? Certainly a lot of trouble was caused because for a long time, an attempt was made to understand Chinese on the grounds that it was like any other form of articulate speech, but it isn't, it is pictorial, and its constant use of what are in origins, at any rate, are little drawings, little pictures, although they have now lost their resemblance with what they are basically, fundamentally, supposed to represent.

Now amongst our patients, I think you get the same thing. The patient says he talks, shall we say, in quite an ordinary manner, just using ordinary articulate speech. But it's no good telling him back again that that is what he said—he knows that anyway. What then are we trying to tell him, or what then is it that we do want to draw attention to? Certainly, in analysis itself, one does get a sort of feeling that there is something important that the patient is trying to communicate. He doesn't come and waste his time and his money just about nothing, although he very often says so or even wants to make you believe that it is so. So one problem is: what is this pattern which we are trying to detect, or thinking that do we to detect other than what is communicated by the ordinary articulate communication?

Now, one reason I quoted this statement of Freud's is because it seems to me that there is, again, a peculiar oddity, a peculiar gap between what the patient is saying in his ordinary articulate speech, this is free association in short and what we think we would like to communicate if we knew what the interpretation was.

This is another quotation: "If one leads a happy spirited discussion with friends about currently debated topics to get down to the job of arranging introductory lectures on the subject for a large audience, one may be struck by a certain oddity—the two worlds seem to have no connection." Now that again seems to me to be peculiar and to be reminiscent of this *caesura*, which Freud speaks about, this thing which seems to be the impressive act of birth.

Well, there are plenty of these impressive things. The patient will often try to impress the analyst with this impressive fact. It is impossible to say what is bothering him, and so forth. There is any number of versions of the same thing. The difficulty is that one has to be receptive, not only about what is said, but what is not said, in this instance, of this kind of impressive *caesura*, the fact that there is this sort of gap. I don't think it is only a matter of being between pre-natal life and ante-, post-natal. But it is also to do with what we are usually quite familiar with as resistances. I am not at all sure that one won't really have to revise—this again is a medical research which all of us will have to concern ourselves with as to what is the nature of this resistance. Although a great deal has been done, and indeed has been formulated, I am sure that there is a great deal more that still has to be done, as usual with psychoanalysis. Every solved problem simply opens up a vast new area of unsolved problems.

Now, to come back to a point that seems to me to be very interesting, that is in the practice of psychoanalysis, as opposed to, well, this sort of discussion, or supervisions, or any ordinary conversation. And that is the vastness of the material which confronts us. I am including here the vastness of the experience when it includes silence, or as I supposed the musicians might say, rests, because in the totality of musical composition, at any rate, you have also these silences; they play a very big part in the composition and understanding of music. I don't think that we can neglect them because they are so important. And in fact, every now and then, you get some sort of curious event, like the person who, for some obscure reason, doesn't or won't listen to the music, but listens to something else. Like Freud, you don't listen to what the person is trying to communicate, but is listening to something else. And the next thing you know, you have this vast realm of psychoanalysis.

Now, our problem is this: not what to do because we know so little; that, of course we have and that will always be with us. That's one thing we can be certain of, but the other thing is the enormous fund of what has to be learned, partly because one can never get rid of one's ignorance and partly because the realm of what is not known, particularly to mere human beings, is simply terrific.

Now in practice, we are then confronted with the problem of choice: it is not a question so much of trying to think up of what interpretation to come up with because there are millions of them. It is a question of which one which in the very limited space of the time that is available to give. Taking it rather in slow motion, one could say that one problem is this problem of choice. Another problem is of getting the objects from which we are going to make our choice into some sort of order. One wants to decide which of these various alternatives to mention first. Now that involves what one could call, non-pathological splitting. After all, one is dealing with whole people, one is dealing with a whole universe, even if you talk about the universe of discussion—put a kind of barrier around what topics you want to talk about, even then, you've got this vast choice, and this problem which involves splitting this total mess into bits. What I say is non-pathological splitting. However, I think that all splitting has been non-pathological at some time. The infant and the child cannot really grasp the totality of the world in which they live. They have to split it; they have to split it into different little packets. And as I say, if one could take it in slow motion, one would then have to consider which order to put those packets into, and then which one of them to interpret, which one of them to formulate, and what words to formulate it in.

In his discussion in [*The Problem of*] *Lay Analysis*—I think I'm right—Freud mentions this fact—that there is this problem of what is one to teach anybody. Supposing one is concerned with teaching people to be analysts. Even if you take the very little bits that we already know, it involves things like philosophy, science, music, mathematics—you can multiply the lists straight away for yourselves, as fast as I could think of it even. So there again is this problem of choice: how is one to pick out of all that lot the most important things for the aspiring analyst to learn?

It's curious in mathematics that you seem to have more discussions of probability, which seem to me to be very much a discussion of something which analysts would know more about than most people because one is concerned with the probable and so on, but there doesn't seem to be much about the mathematics of choice, or it may simply be that I am purely ignorant about it. But anyhow, it is a matter that concerns us very much indeed and we might be able to throw some light on this, or produce some sort of material, which really capable mathematics might do something. The mathematicians may indeed be able to help us if only they knew a little bit about what we know—which might be again you see that it doesn't do for us to suppose that we have no contribution to make.

It is very difficult to combine this state of affairs, where it is constantly brought home to us how little we know—without losing sight of the fact that we know something—and that it might be worth communicating. But how is one to get across this gap, how is one to get across this *caesura*? As I say, I don't think we ought to be content in supposing this is solved or that the problem is a closed problem when one considers the theories of resistance—or any other psychoanalytic theory. One should give due weight, or faith, have great respect for what has been found, but not to the exclusion of what hasn't been found.

And this matter of resistance seems to be one of them, this impressive *caesura*, this impressive resistance, which may indeed hide from us, as much as it illuminates, how we are to get across that gap—not simply in this impressive act of birth, but in the birth of an idea. Supposing anybody comes across, or has an idea, how are they first of all to communicate it to themselves? That should seem to be extremely easy, but from my observation—I don't know why, it seems to require enormous courage. Patients have ideas—they won't express them. Sometimes it will be to a point where patients will go through session after session entirely silent, but then they do that to themselves; they won't write or they won't draw or paint, or try musical composition because they dare not, because they dare not communicate to themselves, say the musical composition because it will sound so horrible if they tried, but they've fed you other excuses or reasons for not doing it. Well, one wonders how many musicians have never existed for the simple reason that they never dared to be musicians.

But extend that to yourselves: how much are we actually dealing with people who are patients, or call themselves patients, or dare to come to a psychoanalyst, but who really need some sort of assistance which would enable them to penetrate their own resistance, or which would enable them to penetrate whatever this thing is which seems to get in between themselves and themselves. Of course, one does try to draw attention to a fact that they can't communicate to oneself. The resistance in the sense of something which exists between the analysand and the analyst—but in fact, that is only, as it were, a transitive experience, an experience which is in transit.

The process of interpreting what Freud described as the transference, is really a kind of a transitive activity, on the way to something else. My own impression is: it is on the way to their being able to communicate with themselves. All this, of course would be refuted by any non-analyst, who would say, "Well, of course, anybody would like to have an analysis—who wouldn't? Just talking about themselves, they would be absorbed with it and be delighted to do it." Yes, but it isn't so, and we as analysts have good reason to know that this isn't so. It is on or in an activity, which is supposedly to help them to talk about themselves; in fact, they seem they find the most intense difficulty in doing so; they seem to hate the process and as likely as not, hate you in the process.

I think in this way, I would now like to indulge in a bit of nonsense, probably more than usual I mean. If it is true that there is some sort of mental life in the fetus, what are we to do about that? Supposing you get a patient again in which you feel you could go on analyzing to the end of time and it wouldn't make any difference—because there seems to be such a gap between themselves and themselves that one doesn't seem to be able to penetrate it at all. Suppose a patient comes and complains that they have a headache or migraine. Then, the patient, after a time, it turns out they see what used to be known as "fortification patterns." Anyway, the headaches are apparently accompanied by apparently visual images. Does that start after birth, infancy or childhood? Or could it possibly be one of these things which are ante-natal and which nevertheless, as far as symptoms are concerned, at any rate penetrate the fact of birth, the *caesura*? Well, of course, one could go on with this, even to the point of making it ridiculous and say, all right then, when the optic pits are formed, what does the fetus see? When the auditory pits are formed, what does the fetus hear?

But the point would be something of this sort: is it possible to conceive of any psychology as existing before birth? Is it possible that some of what we see and hear in the office is a sort of vestige, something which is ante-natal, but which is nevertheless having a powerful influence, in the way that we know these things do, such as the unconscious idea has on conscious behavior?

Could it be possible for example, that the embryo doesn't see anything, but on the other hand, we do know that if we were to apply pressure to our eyeballs, one sees things, one sees lights and so forth.

If that is the case, why shouldn't the infant, or the embryo even, be subjected to pressures which translate themselves into sight and so forth, when in fact it is produced by pressure—not light, but pressure; and then, by analogy, is the conscious patient, the patient that we deal with, suffering from a reminiscence which has undergone that sort of transformation? I mention migraine because it is one of these things which is so often regarded as a sort of psychosomatic affair. But one wonders, you see, as to the extent to which we are dealing with transformed physical events, events which have been transformed into psychological events.

We are in the habit very often of talking about past events, and "you probably felt such and such when you were an infant or as a child … and so on." Well, that seems to me be extremely deceptive because in fact all that we really know, or all the patient really knows, is what they feel now in the present. But is there some present vestige of the thing, which was once conscious, or once current because the present in that case, you see, is simply the future of a past event?

But what we are dealing with the present event. One is dealing with the patient—man, woman or child patient that comes to us. Even now, I find this difficult to talk about because I don't think there is a language for it. There may be things for which we have found no language whatever, these things which may be residual effects, effects you see which are due to this continuity which Freud talks about, between intra-uterine life and earlier symptoms. But we are concerned with is what language are we to talk to them? How or what interpretation are you to give a patient who says that they have a headache or that they feel a physical symptom?

Dream? No, no dream, which may mean you see that they have had no articulate dreams—but why on earth does one have an articulate dream? Dreams are pretty fantastic anyway, even when they are articulated, verbalized and passed on to us. Why shouldn't there be dreams which are purely physical? It doesn't sound particularly important perhaps, but suppose you have a patient who cannot or won't lie on the couch and can produce any number of reasons for not doing so—and can even produce in you any number of reasons or rationalizations (I should prefer to say at this point) of why the patient doesn't lie down on the couch.

Now, when you go on giving interpretations with no effect whatsoever, it seems to me that one should consider that one's rational interpretations are really indistinguishable from rationalizations. If that is the case, one would have to reconsider altogether the nature of interpretations and what we have to deal with. As I say, one would have to consider the possibility that the patient cannot bear the pressure of the couch on his back side—or on his front side for that matter. But this seems to me to be again a matter which can only be decided in the consulting room, that this is the fascination in a sense of analysis. Of course, one has to dare to be ignorant and to hope that the patient also would dare to be ignorant.

It is such a bore when the patient says, "Yes, I know, yes I know, yes I know" to everything you say to them. One would like to say to them, "Oh for God's sake, be ignorant!" [Laughter.] But one can't. It is not one of these interpretations, which is in the book of works. [Laughter.] So there again, you see it is a problem. Do we know what analysts should do or be even? Of course, you can rapidly get a state you see in which the analyst himself turns into the most extraordinary sort of object who apparently has got no feelings, and is apparently able to stand anything. But I am not sure you see that that isn't putting forward a powerful interpretation. The patient can go by what the analyst is doing or saying.

So there is this problem again, what language are we to use? Once again, I take refuge in the fact that this is a research and therefore, I don't really feel under any particular pressure to try to answer these questions. But it seems to me to be rather important to try to indicate at least some of the questions that plague me. With a bit of luck, I might even hear an interpretation or two that might come in handy to myself. But the point is that it really is a perpetual research, this perpetual fact that in analysis, one is dealing with an open-ended question. The past, what is known, interpretations which are given and so on, those are very rapidly of no importance; the present and the future which hasn't happened yet, that is important. It's also very difficult because the future, which hasn't happened yet is as bad as a past that you can't remember—worse in fact.

Well, I think I would like to stop at this point, somewhat arbitrarily, but I know myself enough to know that I am prepared to talk for as long as my voice lasts, but I don't know that this is a particularly good idea.

[I include here as an excerpt a comment that Bion made in response to the program moderator, Dr. Hellinger.]

BERNARD HELLINGER: ... this speculation carries back to very early infancy to the early splitting process. It may be a natural process of the infant or child to organize the world.

DR. BION: What I feel sometimes is that the attempt to think of it in terms of the past or infancy or so on, becomes more of a liability than an asset because it hides the fact that one is dealing with a person, a mind, a character or a personality there in front of you. And it is curious you see if you start thinking of what the person may feel—while one is thinking about that, time passes and one is not able to listen to the patient or observe what is going on. That is why sometimes I have put this as getting rid of one's memories or one's desires because they act as a sort of barrier, because while you are wondering about the patient's past, the present goes on flying through; or while you are wondering either about what you are going to do, or what the patient is going to do or what is going to happen to the patient, something is happening and one fails to notice what is happening. Therefore, I don't really think of it in terms of what the patient felt, but rather in terms of there being various levels of the mind, which again is an artifact. I think it's most unlikely that there are levels of the mind anyhow—we couldn't see them or feel them or touch them or anything. It is just a sort of theory or a hunch that one puts forward to ease one's self, to make the comprehension easier, or at any rate to make one feel that one has understood the patient; that is the snag about it. And the whole time, there is reality, there are such things as facts, or so we think. One thinks that there is such a thing as character or personality. Either that or else we are crazy in spending our lives and time and everything such as psychoanalysis. The whole thing is based on the assumption that there is such a thing as mind that we are investigating. I think with very good reason. But it does lead to this difficulty about the immediate problem, where it seems to me that one could say about it that the patient is having a feeling which has got a very long history; it almost certainly existed at birth or before—and still does—that's the point. Now whether that is a true description or not, I have no idea. I think that the most one can hope for in a sense is that it might be illuminating.

I am reminded of Bacon's essay—what is truth?—suggesting that Pilate wouldn't wait for an answer. Well, we seem to think it is worthwhile waiting for an answer. And Freud you see suggests that there is a lot to be said for going on watching or listening to a pattern until whatever the patient is saying or doing, a pattern emerges—it seems to come out of it. I am tempted again there to say that it is rather like having to dare to use a sort of hallucination or a delusion on the off-chance that it may be, as it were, non-pathological. But of course, many patients are afraid of insanity and are therefore afraid of having thoughts or ideas, which could be described as irrational—and could be nipped in the bud straight away. After all, most patients have at varying times had very good ideas, but they have learned that it is very unwise to do so. So we are quite accustomed to this fact—that it is just as well that if one is going to say anything at all, to at least sound

> rational—if one is going to avoid getting locked up somewhere. But somebody's got to dare to be psychotic or crazy or idiot—or listen to the wrong thing, like people who won't listen to the music, but listen to the interference. The next thing you know is that you've got your radio and telescopes, and the rest of the apparatuses, doing nothing more than listening to the interference.

Commentary: From Public Lecture to Published Text

I proceed through some aspects of Bion's (1977) published text, calling attention to passages he added, leaving to one side what appeared in the 1975 public lecture that was actually repeated in the later text. Starting with the cited sources, Bion quoted from Western *as well as* Eastern thinkers—psychoanalysts, economists, theologians and mystics alike in the (1977) version—Freud, V. C. Walsh, Martin Buber, and St. John of the Cross. Given the local psychoanalytic context of Los Angeles, where many Freudian analysts considered themselves both scientific and atheistic, this would have seemed like a prudent rhetorical practice on Bion's part to leave out religious or mystical literature in the public lecture. The issue of local context as a "site of reception" is also relevant insofar as there have been so few studies on Bion's conceptual evolution that have focused on how this distinctive American cultural milieu may have affected Bion during the time he resided in Los Angeles. A small but telling example: in the public lecture, Dr. Hellinger introduced Bion's talk by calling it a "happening," an American vernacular or countercultural term for a "scene where exciting things can occur." One hears how distinctly awkward being the recipient of such a description appeared to be for Bion, as he in all likelihood felt uncomfortable with his colleagues in Los Angeles, as he had described earlier in *Cogitations* (entry of September, 1971):

> The relationship between myself and my colleagues here in Los Angeles could be accurately described as almost entirely unsuccessful. They are puzzled by, and cannot understand me—but have some respect for what they cannot understand. There is, if I am not mistaken, more fear than understanding or sympathy for my thoughts, personality or ideas. There is no question of the situation—the emotional situation—being any better anywhere else. I could say much the same for England. "The old order changeth, yielding place to new …."
>
> (Bion, 1992, p. 334)

In the contextual domain in which he set out the written text in 1977, Bion broadly introduced his topic as having relevance to both the physical and the social sciences as one might find in a university setting that is organized along departmental lines that emphasize the freedom of inquiry.

Within the context of the psychoanalytic consulting room however, the analyst nevertheless has to be concerned with the truth in the form of a serviceable interpretation, one selected from his understanding of the most pressing of the patient's anxieties hidden in the shadows. One is reminded of the aphorism that Bion often quoted, "There are no atheists in the foxhole," a reminder that the analyst has the responsibility to offer his best interpretation given all the data of direct evidence available to him "at the moment" in the form of the selected fact. As a counterpoint to Francis Bacon's (1626) depiction in his essay, "On Truth," of Pontius Pilate saying, "What is truth?, said jesting Pilate, and would not wait for an answer," the analyst does not have the luxury of inordinate time before he has to render as accurate a reading as possible of the patient's conflictual situation. Bion (1977, p. 41) noted here that the analyst may not be aware of what the truth is, but it is his inescapable preoccupation. Where the patient brings deceptions, evasions, fictions, phantasies, visions, hallucinations, the analyst answers with truth, truthfulness, accuracy, directness, factuality and verifiability—or at least always keeps these ends in mind.

It seemed important to Bion that the analyst also retain a sense of humility vis-à-vis the interpretations made to the patient. The analyst's classification of his interpretative material was best regarded as provisional, or transitive—it proceeded from one thought to another and was hardly permanent, "... not a halting spot at which the investigation is ended" (ibid., p. 43). Yes, the analyst could have "blind intuitions," when he had a sense of something without any corresponding concept, but the problem then became the matching of one's hunch with some formulation, some conceptual statement.

Of course, the analyst was also bound by the patient's limitations, such as those where the patient would rather sing than talk, or patients who do not want to lie down on the couch—or come along to their sessions and remain completely silent. Drawing upon the notion of projective identification as a means of communication, Bion here advocated complete phenomenological immersion in the patient's subjective experience, one that the analyst identified with via the mechanism of introjective identification. He also made it clear that diagnostic artifice merely served to lodge an impediment between the analyst's clear understanding and being able to communicate what he had learned back to his patient. In this quest, Bion made it clear that he didn't make much use of psychiatric diagnostic systems in the way favored by either German or American psychiatry:

> No terms—"autistic child"—"psychotic" or "borderline"—are of much use because the experience in an analysis is more subtle, detailed and difficult to divide up into these somewhat crude divisions available to us

> when we borrow from the practice of medicine, or existing philosophies, or other analytic theories.
>
> (ibid., p. 46)

He reiterated this point a bit further on when he wrote:

> The important thing is not that a patient is a borderline, psychotic, or a psychotic, or a neurotic, but that he is a total character minus … and then we have to inform our own judgment of what that patient is minus …
>
> (ibid., p. 52)

Bion also considered the transitive nature of free associations and interpretation. "Each free association and each interpretation represent the change in the situation which we psychoanalyze. Even the wrong interpretation causes change; misinformation in the form of the false—deliberately false—statements changes the situation" (ibid., p. 49). While mistakes could be made in analysis, the real test came with how quickly the analyst could recover from error. In this instance, Bion like Freud (1905) before him in the "Dora" case, had made public his own mistakes when he published his graduation paper on the "Imaginary Twin," where he made it clear that he had been caught up in a profound countertransference muddle for a long period of time. His analytic learning from experience came with how he tunneled out of this labyrinth of impasse (Bion, 1967). Melanie Klein herself had regarded interpretation as consisting of a series of successive approximations, when the analyst reduced the amount of error in interpretations, trying to apprehend as much as one can of the patient's psychical reality (Klein, 1927). This same process of successive approximation was referred to by Bion as a "sighting shot," deploying the military language of artillery fire, which zeroes in on the target via approximating and recalibration.

Bion concluded (1977, p. 56): "Investigate the caesura; not the analyst; not the analysand; not the unconscious; not the conscious; not the sanity; not the insanity. But the caesura, the link, the synapse, the (counter) transference, the transitive-intransitive mood." So in line with this exhortation, I close with a contemporary rendering of the concept of *caesura* in Bion's conceptual work (J. Grotstein, personal communication, 2010). As a clinical and conceptual metaphor, *caesura* relates to an *active selectively permeable* membrane that separates—and thereby insures the mutual operations of two mutually related sets of domains that interact oppositionally, collaboratively, and complementarily. Grotstein (1981) alludes to this concept by asking: Are the thumb and forefingers in opposition—or do they work in a complementary way to one another? So the *caesura* stands as a cognate of a "contact-barrier," that which separates conscious and unconscious, yet acts in a selective fashion, one that allows for the encoding of elements or stimuli either entering into or departing from either domain. In Freudian topographic language, perhaps the *caesura* can be thought of as the area of the "system preconscious" between the conscious and unconscious, a sort of "passport control" where mental contents travel from one direction towards another.

I close here with Bion's (1977, p. 50) own definition:

> Like birth, the caesura of marriage is dramatic; it may obscure the fact the events at the time of marriage and after are influenced by events which take place long before the marriage. As Freud put it with regard to birth, events ... in the patient's mind are greatly influenced by events which were in fact intra-uterine. Using this for theoretical purposes, events which are in the womb of time eventually show themselves in the conscious life of the person concerned who then has to act in the situation which has now become actual.

Acknowledgements

The author gratefully acknowledges the International Psychoanalytic Association's Research Advisory Board: through its support, a number of publications as well as research trips have been made possible to the archives of both the British Psychoanalytical Society and the Klein Archives at the Wellcome Institute in London. He also acknowledges the helpful comments from James Grotstein. The final responsibility for this manuscript is of course solely the author's.

References

Aguayo, J. (2009) On the Understanding of Projective Identification in Treatment of Psychotic States of Mind: The Publishing Cohort of H. Rosenfeld, H. Segal and W. R. Bion, 1946–1957, *The International Journal of Psychoanalysis*, 90:69–92.

Aguayo, J. (2011) The Role of the Patient's Remembered History and Unconscious Past in the Evolution of Betty Joseph's Clinical Technique, (1948–1989). *The International Journal of Psychoanalysis.*

Bacon, F. (1626) On Truth. *The Essays of Sir Francis Bacon.* New York: Norton.

Bion, W. R. (1967) *Second Thoughts: Selected Papers on Psycho-Analysis.* London: William Heinemann Medical Books.

Bion, W. R. (1977) *Two Papers: The Grid and Caesura.* London: Karnac.

Bion, W. R. (1992) *Cogitations.* London: Karnac.

Frank, C. (2009) *Melanie Klein in Berlin: Her First Psychoanalyses of Children.* London: Routledge.

Freud, S. (1905) Fragment of an Analysis of a Case of Hysteria. *Standard Edition,* 7:3–122.

Freud, S. (1914) On Narcissism: an Introduction. *Standard Edition,* 14:67–102. London: Hogarth Press.

Freud, S. (1926) Inhibitions, Symptoms and Anxiety. *S.E.*, 20:75–175. London: Hogarth Press.

Gay, P. (1988) *Freud: A Life for Our Time.* New York: Norton.

Greenson, R. (1974) Transference: Freud or Klein? *The International Journal of Psychoanalysis*, 55:37–48.

Greenson, R. (1975) Transference: Freud or Klein. A Reply to the Discussion by Herbert Rosenfeld. *The International Journal of Psychoanalysis*, 56:242–3.

Grotstein, J. S. (2010) personal communication.

King, P. and Steiner, R. (1991) *The Freud–Klein Controversies, 1941–1945.* London: Routledge.

Klein, M. (1927) Symposium on Child Analysis. *The International Journal of Psychoanalysis*, 8:339–70.

Kirsner, D. (2000) *Unfree Associations: Inside Psychoanalytic Institutes.* London: Process Press.

Rosenfeld, H. (1965) *Psychotic States: A Psychoanalytic Approach.* New York: International Universities Press.

Spillius, E. (2007) *Encounters with Melanie Klein: Selected Papers of Elizabeth Spillius.* London: Routledge.

Part 2

CLINICAL PROCESS

EDITORS' INTRODUCTION

Vicissitudes of the Container–Contained and Field Theory

Antonino Ferro

Antonino Ferro has been instrumental in integrating Bion's formulations with the field theory of Willy and Madeleine Baranger. In this chapter, derived from the plenary address he gave at the 2009 International Bion Conference, he continues to explore the implications of this synthesis, using multiple clinical examples with both adult and child patients to illustrate the process of "transformation by narration" (i.e. a mutual co-construction of narratives) and how it promotes the alpha-function of the analytic couple and their mutual capacity for containment. This, in turn, allows for a more robust and successful creation of *waking dream thoughts*, by both patient and analyst, as they psychically represent and metabolize raw, internal and external experience and create, strengthen and develop psychic structure and the capacity to think.

As Ferro demonstrates, analytic interaction and the narrative word play of analytic discourse are central to these processes. Rather than focusing upon the *uncovering* of hidden or repressed meanings, Ferro's work strives to create and strengthen meanings and to enhance the patient's abilities to dream, to feel and to think. What is required of the analyst in this process is a capacity to tolerate ambiguity ("negative capability") and an aptitude for creativity and play. Indeed, Ferro's sensibility as a child analyst and his deep appreciation of the work of Winnicott, especially the squiggle game, informs his understanding of the analytic process with adults as well as with children.

The resulting formulations offer us access to a broad, intermediary area of interventions that are in contrast to explicit ("saturated") interpretations and are especially useful when working with those patients and in those situations in which the patient's psyche is not yet ready to absorb, tolerate and think about traditional interpretations. Thus, Ferro describes how, in addition to the more usual type of transference interpretations (i.e. "interpretations *about* the transference"), his interventions reflect a "dual perspective," in which he is silently making comments that operate and function *within* the transference, while apparently engaging with the patient at the level of concrete "reality" (i.e. within the "dialect" of the patient's manifest discourse). The analogy here is to the child analyst, who can either communicate with a patient through action and words during their play or can step back from their game and make a summarizing interpretation about what he or she thinks the play is reflecting.

This chapter also illustrates how the appearance of each character in the patient's discourse functions as an "unconscious hologram" within the constant feedback system embedded in the field perspective. According to the latter, each response on the part of the patient to the analyst's interventions or actions reflects, comments upon and "bears witness ... to the oneiric level of functioning of the analytic couple, as well as to the fact that what a patient says after an interpretation is among other things a dream about the interpretation itself."

Overall, this essay represents an important step in Ferro's continuing attempts to shift our view of analysis from a process "concerned with contents and memories into one centered on the development of the instruments for dreaming, feeling and thinking;" and our view of the analyst to one "who trusts much more in the psychoanalytic method than in its contents."

4

VICISSITUDES OF THE CONTAINER–CONTAINED AND FIELD THEORY

Antonino Ferro

CAROLINE: Why won't you talk to the doctors?
LISBETH: Because they won't listen to what I say.

Introduction

This contribution is concerned mainly with the development of the container and the contained. What will of course remain implicit in my discussion are the continuous exchanges between projective identifications and reverie (or negative reverie in the case of a reversal of the flow of projective identifications, which may even lead to transformations in hallucinosis). The ongoing alphabetization of beta-elements in the direction of alpha-elements that occurs in a sufficiently well-functioning analytic field is likewise implicit. Ample clinical material will be presented in order to demonstrate the complexity of the phenomena involved and their simultaneity, which makes it a purely arbitrary decision to focus on a given aspect and leave others aside—not because the latter are inactive at the relevant time, but because they are deliberately not illuminated. In theory, the individual elements of the concept of container/contained are inseparable. However, in this paper, I shall "artificially" treat them as if separate, in order to better explicate certain movements in their development. In practice, we may observe that as the container develops, it will become immediately saturated by the contained. Fundamental to this process is, in my view, the analyst's ability to be in unison with the patient. In this connection, let me emphasize that the *narrative transformations* that permit sharing of the manifest text are a valuable working instrument (as opposed to excessive explicit, decoding interpretations, which often risk snapping the threads of the container instead of allowing them to develop).

Furthermore, *transformations in dreaming* constitute the maximum degree of transformation of any communication towards the oneiric plane, while the phenomena of *flash-type reverie* (*like a short film*) and *construction-type reverie* (*feature length films*) represent intermediate situations. *Transformation in dreaming* is an attitude, born of experience and negative capability, that enables us to precede every one of a patient's communications with a "magic filter," as I have called it, comprising the words "I had a dream in which … "—that is to say, a narrative deconstruction and de-concretization of the patient's communication, which is thereby stripped of any external-reality status and instead assumes that of psychoanalytic reality. The following clinical material will facilitate the reader's understanding of these concepts.

Fabrizio, a patient at an advanced stage of his analysis, begins a session by asking me if there are psychoanalytic societies in Sweden. He tells me he is reading two books by Stieg Larsson, *The Girl with the Dragon Tattoo*[1] and *The Girl Who Played with Fire*, which reveal some unexpected sides of Sweden, involving violence, prostitution, corruption, abuse and perversion. I tell him that there is more than one psychoanalytic society in Sweden and, giving an interpretation that from another perspective might be considered a kind of acting out because it entails a micro-self-disclosure, I respond to his mentioning the courtyard of the Nobel Building in Stockholm by commenting that, if one goes straight down the alley and turns left, one will reach the address of one of the Swedish societies. I add that they have many capable analysts, such as Salomonsson, Ferro-nsson, and so on. Having at first failed to grasp the meaning of my communication (which, however, seems obvious enough to me), he then understands it by himself; laughing, he says: "'Charles Bron-son' would also be fine as an analyst of my marginal, violent red-light areas, but I think the '-son' of Ferro could manage to steer a course even through these frontier areas."

This sequence basically reflects a number of facts: my showing him that I am familiar with the area where intelligence (Nobel prizes), violence (Stockholm nights) and the antidotes to violence (psychoanalytic societies) cohabit with each other, and, in particular, that I have faith in the functions of psychoanalysis (the analysts who are present), which can cope with these aspects too. All this takes place without interpretative caesuras and while sharing the apparently manifest meaning of Fabrizio's communication. The result is a narrative development, or transformation by narration—that is, a *narrative transformation* in the absence of an explicit, decoding interpretation on my part.

Giovanni, in the third year of his analysis, has to undergo some (medical!) "analyses," i.e. tests, because he and his young female partner are unable to have a child. The outcome of all his "analyses" is that he is producing a high percentage of "spermatozoa with monstrous abnormalities in their heads," and very few normal ones; echographic examination has also revealed areas of testicular calcification that suggest the risk of a "carcinoma in situ." However, the doctor has said that treatment is possible. From the psychoanalytic vertex (i.e. observational perspective), the patient's communication corresponds precisely to the state of our work in the consulting room. Giovanni is terrified by what is in "his" head, in his internal world: he does not know if the analysis will prove fertile or if he will be capable of producing only monstrous emotions (or proto-emotional states), and he is very frightened that he might have horrible tumorous lumps or hyper-proliferations inside him.

I feel that all this cannot for the time being be interpreted explicitly, because it is still "too raw," or "frozen," because too "real." We shall need two parallel rails, an explicit one that is apparently "real," and another, intrapsychic one of my own, with "silent interpretations" being the sleepers (ties) that will link the two levels which cannot for the moment be put together. However, the train represented by the emotions will be able to run over this track pending the activation of new meanings and transformations.

Giovanni now tells me that he is happy for his girlfriend, who has been awarded a study grant, to go away for two months (coinciding "of course" with my summer holiday), and adds that he wants to get himself a Labrador. Thinking of the Italian colloquial expression *labbra-d'or*,[2] which suggests something delicate, affectionate, but also ingratiating, I comment: "But what would a 'Flanders cattle dog' say if it found itself abandoned at a time like this by the very person with whom it wanted to create something?"

Without a moment's hesitation, he exclaims: "You filthy bitch, do you really think this is the right time to leave me all by myself?" "Yes," I say, "and why must you be the [pronouncing it syllable by syllable] *labbra-d'or*, the silver-tongued person who only ever lets affectionate comments pass his lips?" He answers: "It's because I feel I don't have a pen with a strong enough fence to contain Dobermans, wolves or mastiffs; mine has just enough strength for a Labrador." I comment: "So you need some iron [*ferro* in Italian, which is also my name] to reinforce the fence."

Of course, here too a large number of explicit interpretations would have been possible, and I had thought of quite a few, but I believe that, precisely because the patient feels that his view of things is shared, *transformational narration* can often facilitate the development of the container (♀♀♀♀), which will then be able to accommodate increasingly intense contents (or "containeds": (♂♂♂♂)).

However, what we have seen in both the above cases is not only the development of the container–contained; in particular, I have also made a quantitative leap from the binary concept of the container–contained to a new multi-group dimension that leads to the concept of the field. In the field, we have witnessed the appearance of various characters, some relating to each other, but each considered as masks concealing aspects and types of functioning both of myself and of the patient. In addition, my approach has been to use interpretative openings to help promote elaboration of the patients' narrative within the dialect of their own idiom and not saturated, decoding interpretations, which can tend for the moment to finalize or "complete" the patients' narratives and thereby create caesuras.[3]

Furthermore, narcissistic mortification of the patient (as often follows a "brilliant" interpretation) has been avoided, and, in Fabrizio's case, something new and unexpected has appeared: in particular, the "-son" that was not in either of our minds—namely, the patient's capacity to recognize a bond of affection and dependence as a "son." In Giovanni's case, the patient indicates that there are still "containeds" (e.g. "Dobermans, wolves and mastiffs") which are too violent to be made explicit without arousing excessive fear—that is, too violent to be contained—and that he still needs the help of the analysis and of myself (Ferro/*ferro* [iron]) to strengthen his containers.

Betta is a young woman patient who tells me one day that it is a long time since anybody has called her by her full name *Elisa-betta*. She began her analysis with a diagnosis of manic-depressive psychosis and a total lack of contact with her emotions. She seems to be telling me here that she has lost contact with *"Elisa,"* her emotional and affective part, which, while completely split off, must be re-found (or found for the first time? or invented?) in the analysis.

Elisa appears gradually, like the moon that causes high and low tides, but no connection is evidently made and retained. For Betta, there are only "facts," depression and mania, but no meaning, however ephemeral, attaches to them.

She would like to have children, but is afraid that if she does it will trigger a crisis: if she creates something living, if any emotion from Elisa makes its presence felt, she immediately fears it will make her ill. One day she tells me about a time when she was in hospital (which perhaps indicates what happens to her when she is "hospitalized" in her analyst's consulting room). She is beginning to put things together: "I realized that my fellow-patients [other split-off aspects?] were not mad as they had at first seemed; each of them had his own reasons for being ill and for being there." It is not a matter of madness: emotional states can have a meaning, causes, or a background of some kind.

In this way, Betta gradually gets in touch with the world of "Elisa"—even if, when contact with her emotions sometimes becomes too "hot," or contact with rage, despair and pain burns her excessively, she rushes forward like a novice in the art of walking on hot coals. When this happens one day in a session, she brings a dream where she is in a film from which she cannot easily escape; a fire breaks out and she manages to leap into her car, zooming off at high speed on the motorway as the flames spread. She then sees that the road is closed, and wakes up in hospital with all her bones broken, motionless and in an agony of pain.

Now at last the manic crisis is meaningful, when it occurs in one of her sessions: it proves to be an ever faster flight from intolerable emotions, until she eventually breaks a kind of sound barrier and plunges into depressive pain beyond the black hole in the parallel universe of suffering. But now there is a hospital, a Doctor Aiuti ["Help" in Italian], who appears in another dream and who can evidently supply the relief that has allowed Betta to re-own increasingly solid pieces of Elisa. The integration of Elisa can of course proceed until this aspect of herself can operate with a sufficient degree of well-being, which only Betta will be able to indicate.

I do not incidentally believe that the analyst must champion integration at all costs, but he must, from a given point on, also be aware of a possible request by a patient for "differentiating" between types of functioning in which he can recognize himself and others in which he cannot. Not all patients—and perhaps not all analysts—can accept for themselves the words the Latin poet Terence (165 BC) puts into the mouth of one of his characters: "*humani a me nil alienum puto*."[4] Differentiating between certain forms of functioning at a given point relieves the patient of parts of himself that he finds intolerable, which have to inhabit worlds of split-off potentiality—worlds that cannot all be mapped and regularly visited. Some possible worlds will have to remain purely potential, and the patient will—probably for ever—remain unaware of them.

We do not always sufficiently appreciate the defenses deployed by our species to survive the monstrosity represented by our imperfect minds. For its survival, the mind needs to evacuate, to become lethargic, to split and to project; it needs ideologies, fanaticisms and lies. A successful mixture of all these defense mechanisms (and of all other possible ones) puts us in the precarious state that we call adequate mental health. This state is guaranteed by the dreaming operations (the "dreaming ensemble" mentioned by Grotstein, 2007) that we succeed in performing; it is, on the other hand, seriously undermined by any excessive reversal of the oneiric functions.

It was Bion (2005) himself who noted that his concept of *waking dream thought* had been practically disregarded notwithstanding its theoretical and clinical implications. In my view, this concept revolutionizes not only theory, but also technique and the theory of technique. As I have said many times, I regard it as the strongest and most significant of his conceptualizations. Besides night dreams, by virtue of the alpha-function our minds constantly undertake the alphabetization of all sensory, proto-emotional stimuli that reach us. This operation eventually leads to the formation of alpha-elements which, when placed in sequence, give rise, precisely, to the waking dream state:

Stimuli (beta-elements) ↔ [(via) alpha-function] ↔ alpha-elements ↔ waking dream thought

My use of double-headed arrows is deliberate, because all these operations are reversible in certain situations—giving rise, for instance, to visual flashes, transformations in hallucinosis, hallucinations and the formation of bizarre objects. In these situations, the alpha-function itself is reversed and operates evacuatively. Of all these aspects, the phenomenon of transformation in hallucinosis (Bion, 1965) seems to me to be a particularly valuable insight, because it is encountered constantly, in terms of our theories as well as on the practical level, whenever we observe with certainty what we, as analysts, have unconsciously projected into our patients. Transformation in hallucinosis is the exact opposite of the reverie concept.

An interpretation may be followed by a broadening of the field, by a collapse of the field into a single point, or alternatively by the occurrence of evacuative phenomena, such as visual flashes in the patient, often in response to transformations in hallucinosis attributable to the analyst. To illustrate:

At an international meeting of analysts devoted to reviewing the range of possible psychoanalytic models, I invented the following imagined start to a fictitious session:

PATIENT 1: Yesterday I didn't like the food my mother gave me to eat; it's always the same old stuff.

ANALYST 1: The envy you feel when I tell you something stops you enjoying and accepting my interpretations.

PATIENT 1: Yesterday I saw a little boy nearly get run over by a tram (streetcar), but luckily he was able to get out of the way at the last minute.

ANALYST 1: The rage you felt at what I said to you nearly squashed you flat, but the memory of the work we have done together saved you from being run over by it.

I then suggested what might have happened in the same session with a hypothetical second analyst:

PATIENT 2: Yesterday I didn't like the food my mother gave me to eat; it's always the same old stuff.

ANALYST 2: I can understand that you were disappointed not to get what you wanted.

PATIENT 2: But my mother *does* try to understand what I like, if only I'm brave enough to tell her.

ANALYST 2: And then you can experience moments when you feel on the same wavelength as well as moments of disappointment.

The discussion then focused on the following questions: Can each session really be co-determined by the interaction of patient and analyst, and can what the patient says after an interpretation by the analyst be the *dream* the patient has had about the interpretation he has received? Can unsaturated interpretations also be regarded as interpretations of the transference, or at least *in* the transference,[5] without being presented in direct, explicit form, provided that the explicit conception is clearly present in the analyst's mind? Is the second analyst avoiding the transference and being "indulgent," or is he interpreting in the only way this patient can tolerate at this particular point in the analysis? And what is the analyst's aim with his interventions: to make what is not conscious conscious; to reveal the patient's unconscious fantasy; or to permit the expansion of the container and the strengthening and development of the patient's psyche through the experience of unison?

Stefano, a young boy, is in therapy for a selective "mutism" that began after his parents' separation and has gradually got worse. His mother abandoned the family and went to live with a new partner. After a short period when Stefano seemed to have adapted to the new situation, he first suffered from enuresis (here we see the theme of incontinence, or non-containment); after a while, he has completely stopped speaking at school (hyper-containment).

At his first meeting with the analyst, he does not say a word, his eyes are lifeless, and he seems to droop. The analyst has the idea of suggesting to Stefano that he whisper a few words to his father (who comes with Stefano to his session and remains present throughout); in this way, the father acts as a loudspeaker. Stefano whispers words to his father, who amplifies them and repeats them in audible form.

The first structured game to appear involves a zoo, in which tigers, lions and gorillas are locked up in extremely robust cages. In the second game, there is an exceedingly fierce dog that has to be muzzled. The analyst thinks of the story of Officer Starling and Hannibal Lecter, who is as it were muzzled to stop him biting people.[6] What lies behind this form of "mutism," or rather "setting the 'loudspeaker' volume to minimum," is manifestly the lack of containment, as is tellingly portrayed in Munch's painting *The Scream.*

It is not only his mother's abandonment but also her total absence of warmth and closeness that leaves Stefano wordless. When reflecting on Stefano's birth, his mother had commented: "He was always a burden and an obstacle to the career I had devoted my life to, and I just wanted to go on devoting my life to my career."

A few months into his therapy, Stefano is able to let his father leave the room and wait for him in the waiting room. As a development of his play, he eventually agrees to write down what his "characters" need to communicate at various stages of the game, while the analyst gives a voice to other characters.

It is in my view important to be aware of the defensive attitude of "hyper-containment" as an alternative to non-containment, because it then becomes possible to work on the deconstruction of the emotional tsunami, which is feared to be so devastating. This tsunami can be deconstructed into a number of different winds/emotions (the south-westerly *libeccio*, the northerly *tramontana*, the south-easterly *scirocco*, etc.), corresponding to an equivalent number of emotions that need to be deciphered, such as rage, jealousy or abandonment. To use another metaphor, it may from this point of view be useful to proceed by developing the container and the figure of a "tamer" of wild beasts in such a way as to ensure that ferocious animals (emotions and proto-emotions) can move about and be contained (not hyper-contained!) by this new function, thereby allowing them to be modulated.

A fine drawing in Federico Fellini's "book of dreams" (2007) shows exuberant, overflowing emotions at the top and, at the bottom, highly constrained, suffocated emotions in the form of a figure squashed between two gendarmes—the very essence of a claustrum (Meltzer, 1992).

Figure 1 Fellini

This pair of opposites (hyper-containment/non-containment) can of course be depicted as the alternating presence of the claustrum and of fragmentation of the container. If the container walls are thin and inelastic to over-intense containeds ("killer containeds"), they can only fragment, giving rise to the projection of fragmented containeds:

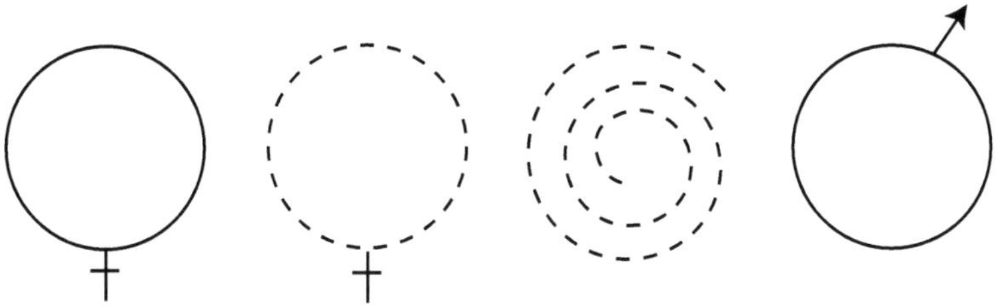

Figure 2 From the Container to Fragmented Containeds

The alternative is sclerotization of the container, with the claustrum as its outcome.

The situation with *Carlo* is very similar (although expressed in different symptoms). This adult patient presents himself as suffering from Asperger's syndrome (his own diagnosis). I shall report only one dream from his analysis: at a garage, he is having his car filled up with petrol (gasoline) by a woman, but then the fuel starts to leak out of the tank. The fuel is essential to the running of the car, but he is terrified in case it catches fire. In the second part of the dream, he has oral sex with the female attendant, but then discovers that she has a penis; this relieves him because he feels safe.

Carlo seems to be saying that he is aware that emotions are an essential fuel for living one's life, but that he is terrified in case they catch fire and become uncontainable (that is why he studied mathematics in spite of his passion for medicine); at the same time, he experiences the intimacy of the new analytic relationship (the oral sex), while, however, seeing his female analyst as a woman "with a prick" (with balls, reliable and strong), on whom, in other words, he can rely to contain his explosive side—a container capable of reception and intimacy, but also with sufficiently thick walls (the paternal function of limited extensibility of the container walls). So there is now a receptive, elastic container, which, however, cannot be stretched beyond a certain point—the recipe that can allow him to live without fear of fire and flooding (i.e. emotions); in other words, the ability of the analyst's mind to oscillate between elasticity and rigidity performs a modulating function.

Marina is in basically the same position. She bursts out laughing when I cough in her session. This, she says, is what has happened to her ever since her grandmother died of pulmonary edema in her presence: the grandmother coughed and coughed, and next thing she was dead. As if paralyzed, Marina sat for hours in terror beside the old woman's body.

After a few months of analysis, she dreams of a bowl filled with rice (in Italian, the same word, *riso*, means both "laugh" and "rice"), underneath which is a horrible mess of squashed insects that are quite indistinguishable from each other. So emotions that can be neither told apart nor alphabetized (i.e. transformed from beta- to alpha-elements) are hidden beneath a blanket of rice/laughter.

At the end of the second year of Marina's analysis, just before the summer holidays, she dreams that she is in a desert and has to survive without food on the water that collects on the leaves of a plant; then she hopes that her classmate will die so that he can't play with anyone else; and finally she is swimming in a swamp when a lion appears from the bottom and could bite her. I comment in terms of famine, the lack of water, jealousy and perhaps rage because her playmate is going away (this is of course an unsaturated transference interpretation). She responds that cats get disoriented if their whiskers are cut off. Yes, I say, because cats recognize spaces and places by using their whiskers, and it must be terrible to have to wait for the whiskers to regrow (I, of course, have whiskers!). All right, she says, but she is happy to know that her classmate and playmate will not die and that she will see him again in September, when school (and the analysis) resumes. The uncontainable, unrepresentable anxiety portrayed in the little beta-element creatures, has been transformed into decipherable, containable emotions.

It will now be clear that I regard the *container* as a function made up of emotional threads extending from analyst to patient and from patient to analyst, which can be enriched and strengthened by new emotional threads (or, alternatively, impoverished in the absence of unison or in situations of negative reverie (–R). It can be seen as a kind of safety net like those formerly used in circuses to protect trapeze artists. The difference is that it is in the form of a round angle (360 degrees). Its strength and elasticity determine the contents ("containeds") that can be accommodated in it—that is, in effect, the emotions that can dance or leap from one trapeze to another without fear of non-containment or of tearing the container.

The oscillation between non-saturation and saturation of interpretation also becomes the vehicle for this development of the container. When the container is sufficiently developed, the containeds are virtually swallowed up inside it, whereas premature interpretations of content or superego interpretations tear the container apart, giving rise to a haemorrhage of emotions or their fragmentation and non-containability. *Narrative transformations* (what the analyst cooks up in the kitchen department of his mind without making it explicit) are a vehicle for development of the container.

An interpretation often has to travel a very long way before it becomes a classical transference interpretation.

So far my approach has been to demonstrate clinical and technical concepts in the field. Now, however, I wish to introduce, if only briefly, some more theoretical considerations.

The Field and "Casting"

The field concept does not have a single, well-defined origin. Having started as a philosophical notion, it was rapidly adopted by psychoanalysis, especially in South America through the fundamental contributions of Willy and Madeleine Baranger (1961–2) and the same two authors with J. Mom (1983, 1988). In Italy, it gained currency through the work of Corrao (1986), whose contribution, while independent of the Barangers, had shared roots in Bion's work with groups and in his approach to non-saturation and to negative capability in the analytic session (Bion, 1962, 1963, 1970). The field differs from relationship or transference; it represents the formation of a new entity different from the sum of its parts (the minds of analyst and patient).

The concept came into being and was developed in a number of different ways, as described by Bezoari and Ferro (1992), Lewkowicz and Flechner (2005) and Ferro and Basile (2009). Originally a strong concept centered on the analyst's explicit interpretative activity in relation to the blind spot, or bulwark, represented by the intersecting projective identifications of analyst and patient, it became a constantly expanding *potential field* in which all possible worlds activated by the analytic encounter could body forth. What previously was conceptualized as belonging to a subject or to another person, could now be seen as belonging to the field; we can therefore think in terms of the alpha-function of the field, beta-elements or proto-emotional turbulences of the field, affective characters/holograms of the field, or the transformational and interpretative activity of the field. From the field perspective, the singularity of the voice of one or other of the participants is weakened, in favor of this new structure that anticipates and permits narrative transformations to come to life. The most significant transformations will be the development and growth (or indeed the very constitution) of the instruments for thinking thoughts—namely, the alpha-function, the container, and representable containeds. All the characters in the field will not be persons or internal objects or split-off parts, but concretizations, or rather syncretizations, of the functioning of places and of the field itself. What comes into being is a kind of three-dimensional film extending over 360 degrees and every level, of which the analyst becomes not only the guarantor but also the co-author.

In a recent contribution (Ferro and Basile, 2009), I wrote:

> The analytic field is inhabited by innumerable real and virtual presences in the process of aggregation, and a valid comparison might be with the universe as it is understood today. For the analytic field coincides with the unrepeatable "universe" that is born at the beginning of each session, only to be temporarily suspended when each session comes to an end. The field is inhabited by certain principal characters, who could be called the protagonists, as well as by supporting actors and, finally, by extras; moreover, all these presences can constantly change their roles. However, human characters (or even non-anthropomorphic ones) represent the most mature part of the field. They could be likened to the constellations discernible in a starry sky. The field is the locus of an infinite number of other phenomena, most of them unknown. An axiom of the field might be that the "Big Bang" occurs at the beginning of each session—and the "Big Crunch" at the end.
>
> Characters constitute the outcome of operations carried out further upstream. Their status is always complex and they do not correspond to the persons to whom they bear a superficial resemblance. The characters of the session are the fruit of mental operations performed by analyst and patient and reflect the mental functioning of both, as well as their proto-emotions, emotions and unknown aspects. In other words, they are holograms of the mental functioning of the analytic couple; but they also include kinds of functioning that would, in other languages, be said to be split off, or not yet accessible to thinkability. Characters enter and leave the session tangentially; others, having entered tangentially, become protagonists; while yet others immediately take essential parts. From this point of view, whatever the patient talks about, he or she is describing a form of functioning of the field.

The analyst's position here is very particular, swinging as it does between maximum asymmetry (for the responsibility is his) and maximum symmetry (the functioning of the field being co-determined by analyst and patient). What needs to be made explicit in my view are the links to Bion's thought and the technical implications of this concept. The aim of the field is transformation, once it has developed in a manner isomorphic with the patient's pathology—and in certain respects also with that of the analyst. The illness (or psychic dysfunction) must therefore enter the field, which will contract the same disease. The treatment of the field will coincide with that of the patient and the analyst. A patient who is unable to contain will sooner or later give rise to non-containment in a place in the field, where it may then be transformed (Ferro, 2006ab). As stated earlier, interpretations will be between the various characters of the field or, in addition, between the two special places in the field called the analyst and the patient. The field will be in a state of constant flux and transformation.

It seems to me that only clinical descriptions can fully immerse us in the climate of this operational concept, on which a huge potential for research remains to be tapped.

A Straight-Haired Blonde

Amanda is in the third year of her analysis; having agreed to four sessions a week, for various reasons she in fact comes just twice weekly. She is clever and attentive, but seems to live only half-heartedly, without expectations and lacking all passion. A romantic relationship in which she invested heavily has not worked out, and now she thinks herself incapable of any further relationships. She has a skilled job at a hospital, but is not motivated to invest in a career or start a private practice. She regularly spends her holidays (vacations) on a farm in Tuscany.

In my mind I start to call her "Miss Half Portion" because she seems to live life at half-speed. At some point, "a guy with black curls," whom she meets on the stairs and who she thinks is another of my patients, becomes a character of the sessions. At first, I do not pay any particular attention to this, but he appears again and again, and eventually she tells me that, while coming up the stairs, she has said hallo to the "guy with black curly hair" and then told him: "I bet we go to the same place."

At this stage, a picture suddenly comes into my mind: "Miss Half Portion," a straight-haired blonde woman (that is how she describes herself), has bumped into the "guy with black curly hair" (Yolanda, the daughter of the Black Pirate). I recall why I thought of calling her "Miss Half Portion": she has started to meet her other half. I am faced with the problem of how to use this fantasy of mine. I decide to share it with her by telling her the nickname I have given her and about the "half portion" of analysis she is having, her lack of verve and of plans for the future (she is 35 years old!), as well as her lack of ambition on the work front. I also comment that the "guy with black curly hair" seems to me to stand for her unexpressed potential—namely, the unknown, black "half portion" that could "turbocharge" her and give her some oomph. She asks me: "How so? Are you saying it's like I had a 1000 cc engine on board and the parts for an extra 1000 cc in my garage, so I could have a 2000 cc engine?" "Exactly," I reply. "Though I personally wouldn't worry so much about why, but instead about how to interpret the missing parts of the engine." A silence ensues. "On Monday there won't be a session: I'm going to a party given by my uncle and aunt from Germany. You know, they live in the Black Forest and eat frankfurters and wild boar." Only then do I realize that the patient's surname makes up half of the title of a famous book (the other half is missing).

In the following session, after complaining about her excessive workload and how her mother overfills her shopping trolley and then leaves it to the patient to put the shopping away, she brings three dreams. This is how she puts things together:

In the first dream she is in a square like Piazza San Babila. There are lots of crowded buses; then there is an explosion. At first it seems to be a very dangerous bomb, but then it turns out to be just a small blast. She decides to walk along Corso Venezia, which changes into Venice. Two friends—one who looks like a vagrant and the other a drug-addict—don't want to move on and stay there begging for money. In the second dream, a hospital consultant is trying to play a trick on a nurse by wrapping her in an electric blanket; he even wants to plug it in. In the third, she is leaving for Calabria to visit some people, perhaps relatives with double-barrelled surnames.

The patient does not know what to say, so I suggest that what I told her about the straight-haired blonde and the guy with the black curly hair at first seemed like a bomb and then led to a blast of emotions; and, if on the one hand there are new prospects (Corso Venezia → Venice), on the other there is some inertia against moving in that direction. But there are also other emotions: the fear that I want to trick her and take her for a ride, even though in the end she is leaving in search of double-barrelled surnames: the Blonde-Brunette family or the Dark-Haired-Blonde family. The session ends. As she gets up, we hear a terrible downpour outside. Only then do I realize that she is carrying two bags, a light one and a dark one with an umbrella. Glancing slyly at me, she says: "Luckily the brunette brought along an umbrella."

A concept strictly bound up with the foregoing is that of casting, which seems to me to be increasingly important in every analysis. In more classical analyses, we often have more or less the entire cast list from the beginning, as in an old-style whodunnit. In analyses with less capacity for symbolization, the development of a casting capability becomes one of the aims of the analysis. Mute, inexpressible areas become a matrix for the generation of characters, which may be animate or inanimate and exist in the present, as well as of stories that begin to confer meaning and make it possible to narrate what could previously not be expressed. The casting sometimes includes sets or places that will have to come alive later.

Faith in the method, reverie, intuition, negative capability and the capacity to listen to the pockets hidden in language are the fertilizers that will permit the growth of green shoots in former wilderness areas of the analyst and patient, or rather of the field. From this perspective, we are concerned with the development of the story (and the instruments for producing it), and not yet or primarily with the thing itself.

An underlying theme of these reflections is the untreatable disease of "conferring meaning" on, or "finding a meaning" in, even those things that often lack meaning. Whereas this activity is, considered from one angle, a vital peculiarity of our species, on the other hand it is also the disease of humanity, because seeking a meaning is one thing, while needing to find it or having found it is another. This attitude, whether inside or outside the analyst's consulting room, has given rise to dramatic situations, such as the outcomes of all kinds of fanaticism.

The facilitator of transformations of the indistinct and the meaningless into the possibility of weaving a fabric of stories, while, in particular, also allowing the introjection of the method, is the *alpha-function*, which is not only based on attention, receptivity and the capacity for reverie and re-dreaming, but also takes on this casting function in the film sets of the mind. Here we have a potential basis for an approach to the investigation of the mind and for the signing up of characters to undertake this work. Bion gives us a brilliant example of all this in his *Memoir of the Future* (1977). In the functioning of the field, the oscillation between grasping and casting is one of the factors of growth. Grasping at theories and the known provides us with the modicum of invariance that assures us of relative stability, whereas casting gives rise to micro-variations or macro-variations, or their precursors, which open the way to transformation and change. It seems to me that, the more the analyst works with narrative transformations or transformations in dreaming, the more significant casting will be; and transformations in dreaming allow for the highest possible degree of deconstruction and change.

In this context, proto-emotions could be thought of as swarms of bees that have been partially frozen in bags and then stratified, and have partially, given appropriate management, produced honey—that is, emotions—while other parts have been evacuated or isolated with various defense mechanisms. Analysis is a re-activator of these micro-swarms, which may sometimes be macro-swarms capable of assuming different narrative configurations.

A macro-swarm may for example present itself as the terrible chief physician who is one's boss or as a situation experienced as potentially persecutory (such as an examination). The work of analysis will be to deconstruct the character of the "gorilla" as it were.

The gorilla must then be "processed" into its sub-units, small aggregates of sub-swarms to be transformed into eventual new figures. The need is for the development of a "hive" or "beekeeper" function, to transform bees (beta-elements) into honey (alpha-elements). All metaphors of course have their limitations and are incapable of conveying the complexity of the problems at hand; they are like making a double bed with a single-bed sheet. This metaphor, in which proto-sensory inputs and proto-emotions are likened to bees or swarms and to their development towards liveability/thinkability (honey), perhaps complements another favorite of mine—namely, that of tomatoes seen as beta-elements and a tomato juicer as the alpha-function, the tomato juice being the liquid for depiction in pictograms, followed by chains of alpha-elements. Again, the figure reminds us that the specific form assumed by the proto-emotional swarm is unimportant. One composition is as good as any other, and it does not matter where in the field it comes to be accommodated.

Grotstein (2000, 2002, 2007) and Ogden (2003, 2005) have shown that mental suffering or health depend respectively on the absence or presence of dreaming functions. In my opinion, the field concept and, in particular, its most recent elaborations are one of the fundamental instruments for promoting the development that Grotstein, in his fine book *A Beam of Intense Darkness* (2007), calls the "dreaming ensemble." In accordance with the ideas developed by Ogden and Grotstein, it seems to me that our discipline is indeed changing from a psychoanalysis concerned with contents and memories into one centered on the development of the instruments for dreaming, feeling and thinking (Ferro, 2007).

From one point of view, the analytic field is the "unsaturated waiting room" in which emotions, proto-emotions, and characters are temporarily accommodated before it becomes possible to return them to their saturated destiny in the relationship or construction. Another approach is to see the field as made up of all the lines of force and all the proto-aggregates of proto-emotions, proto-characters and characters floating in the virtual space of the field, which gradually assume solidity, color and three-dimensionality. It is as if a large number of rubber bands, or possible narrative lines, were stretched between patient and analyst, and clips were gradually attached to them, representing the casting applied by the field to what was previously indeterminate. So it is that a climate suffused with pain, loss and relief gives way to narrations that convey these "characters" in more obvious, clearer form. These narrations and characters can be understood as the narrative derivatives generated by the waking dream of the field. What matters here is not the contained but the manner in which this form of functioning can lead to the development of the instruments for thinking thoughts. The development of the alpha-function and of the container becomes the aim of analytic work.

Of course, not all the clouds of sensoriality or proto-emotions can be transformed into pictograms; a certain proportion will inevitably be evacuated in the form of symptoms, acting out, quarrelling, phobias, paranoia, and so on, owing to the inadequacy of the alpha-function. The end point of analysis should be the development of the alpha-function in such a way that sense data/proto-emotions are evacuated to a lesser extent and instead transformed into alpha.

The field includes an unconscious part which is continually rendered thinkable by way of the phenomena of casting and transformation in dreaming. It is not easy to accept that the cornerstone of analysis is the development of the capacity to dream rather than working on repression or splits.

Let us now consider some events of the field.

The Patient as Indicator of the Movements of the Field

This process is of course the visible negative side (the "mould") of the functioning of the container and of the alpha-function (both seen as belonging to the patient or the analyst or, within a more complex vision, of the field). It follows that the patient constitutes the place in the field that bears witness (also) to the oneiric level of functioning of the analytic couple, as well as to the fact that what a patient says after an interpretation is among other things a dream about the interpretation itself; hence the characters that appear provide an indication of how the patient has heard the interpretation.

Let us see what happens—and how this is indicated by the field—when the analyst "goes offside" with regard to his responsibility for being the guardian of transformations in dreaming and instead becomes a factor in producing transformations in hallucinosis.

The field, then, is permeated by turbulences, by whirlwinds and sometimes by tsunamis of beta-elements which find, in the process of *transformation in dreaming* (Ferro, 2009), the transformational container that leads from disorganized potentialities to possible forms of representation. The field concept is rendered even more complex by all the virtualities at work in it—as it were, parallel worlds or universes that subsequently coalesce into narrations which come to life in accordance with the receptive capacity of the dreaming ensemble. Breaking down the latter, we encounter "night dreams," which become dreams of the field at the moment when they are narrated.

If the analyst's mind has turbulences of its own (or at least predominantly of its own) or participates in the turbulences of the field, that is not necessarily a disadvantage. Indeed, these ripples in the field offer an image in relief of the figures we might well have overlooked in a field lacking any undulation. This is the case provided that the analyst is aware that what happens in the field (in which he too is a participant) is co-determined.

Let us consider a clinical example.

The Little Girl and the Rubbish Dump

One Monday I thought I had had a good session with *Lucilla*. In the next session she brings a dream: she is in a desolate place, a kind of dump full of rubbish; walking in this refuse-filled space, she sees three ugly, dirty, witch-like women sadistically ill-treating a kitten. As she goes on through the darkness of the dump, more and more witches appear, arousing more and more anxiety. She is very afraid, but then a car full of "*virgili urbani*" [a slip of the tongue for *vigili urbani*: in Italian *vigili* are police, but the word is similar in sound to *Virgilio*, the Italian for the Latin poet and mentor figure Virgil] arrives and picks her up. The car is driven by a "fat policewoman" who seems not to take her story seriously; but although the patient is afraid of being "dumped" from the car too, the police keep her inside.

In a second dream, an established couple is, to her surprise, plunged into crisis; she takes their little girl in her arms, but the child slips out of her grasp and falls to the ground—though she seems not to have sustained a lethal injury.

I ponder over these dreams. I think of the time when I told her the dates of my holiday, even though that was several sessions ago, and realize only then that in the previous session I was preoccupied with a "personal" concern that had caused me to miss a few sentences pronounced by the patient, although I had, I thought, soon got back on her wavelength. I now ask her if anything had struck her about the last session. She immediately answers: "At one point I felt that you weren't listening to me."

This enables me to show her what happens when she experiences me as being less present in the session: she feels "dumped," and thinks she is worthless, no more than garbage to be got rid of in my eyes. Next she is progressively assailed by feelings of rage, pain and despair, which she fears are looming over her (the witches). But then she feels I am close to her once more, although unsure of my reliability; she is afraid of being dumped again, and when all this actually happens, a good couple—ourselves—is plunged into crisis, and trust (the little girl) falls to the ground, although no permanent damage has been done.

"You couldn't have summed up my feelings better than that," she says, adding: "Absolutely perfect; not a crease or blemish to be seen." "Yes," I reply, "it's not for nothing that my name means 'iron'."[7]

We are now able to start working on the roots of the "fear, and experience, of not being listened to," this time on another stage—that of her infancy and history.

But how are we to see this stage? It depends on the type of model one adopts. In one model, work in the here and now has afforded access to the world of infancy, of historical reconstruction. In another, the problem of not being listened to, which was throbbing away somewhere in the middle of the field, has now been "cooled down" and almost marginalized into a less manifest location, which nevertheless acts as a store of transformations. A third possibility is not to put the problem to oneself at all, but merely to regard some of the various bodies orbiting the field as more central and others as more peripheral, with continuous to-and-fro movements and with multiple possible screenplays and film sets in a constant state of flux.

Clearly, then, the patient is an important indicator of the analyst's mental dysfunction. Although not a new idea (Bion, 1985; Ferro, 1999, 2002ab; Ferro and Basile, 2004), it is good to have this listening vertex available rather than considering everything solely in terms of the patient's internal world or transference projections.

Plots and Narrations

Any case history can be summed up by a kind of graphic plot, which can then be narrated in various forms. For instance, the set of symbols reproduced below:

♂
♀
♂

could be used to represent the basic structures of the following clinical narration:

Giuseppina begins by enumerating the tumors that have always afflicted her family (from our vertex, and from ours only, we could think of a ♂♂♂♂♂—i.e. a proliferation of emotional proto-containeds). She then talks about her mother, who was abused by her own father (in this case the symbols might be a hypo-♀ faced with many hyper-♂♂♂s). She goes on to say that her father always flies into a violent rage unless everything turns out the way he wants. This, she adds, puts her in mind of the character Furio in the Carlo Verdone film, who plans everything down to the particular motorway restaurants where the children can stop en route for a pee. In other words, either the obsessional defense works or he explodes in furious rage.

In addition, the mother has a phobia of anyone belonging to a different ethnic group; this can be symbolized as follows:

Mother
♀ (too small a container) / Phobic barrier ♂
Unknown ethnic groups (too many contents)

That is to say, all emotional states that are not immediately recognizable are kept at a distance by means of the "defensive phobic barrier."

The patient then describes the first time she had sex: at the age of 24, she was virtually violated by her boyfriend (♂), who abused her, just as, she adds, Leila Bakita was abused in the Italian television soap *Incantesimo* ["The spell"]. Her thoroughly aroused boyfriend overwhelmed her. She was astonished and at the same time felt as if she had been raped.

This incipient narration basically offers a set of variations on a theme, concerning a container somehow inadequate to contain proto-emotional states that are in some way abusive by virtue of their intensity. A favorable aspect in my view is that, already at our first meeting, Giuseppina reaches out into the field of myth whenever she associates to a film or other contexts, as with her references to "Furio" or "Bakita." Such an example immediately makes us wonder which is more important: to engage in historical reconstruction, or to reinforce the instruments for containing and transforming emotions.

Prevalence of Hyper-Containeds

Luisa is described as a frightened fawn, very pretty and with tender eyes. She asks for analysis after being unexpectedly abandoned by her husband. Upon her first meeting with the analyst, she bursts into tears. She then tells of her separation from two previous partners, again in a tone of great affliction. Next she mentions a holiday at a Swiss *Kinderheim*, where she felt as if deported. After this, she mentions a sister, who is receiving chemotherapy for leukaemia.

Her account seems to be centered on separations and abandonments, which could be described as the "protagonists" and key points of her story. The narration continues with a description of a turbulent period of her life when she used drugs, attended venues where promiscuous behavior was the rule, went to orgy-like parties and visited gambling dens, associating with the criminals who frequented them.

Luisa is now obviously talking about the stimulating, anti-depressive defenses to which she resorted—and indeed still resorts—to protect herself from undigested, untransformed proto-emotions connected with abandonments. In a sequence, she then tells how she is beginning to recall instances when her grandfather "molested" and "abused" her, touching her improperly on many occasions. Next she reports a nightmare she had as a little girl, in which her mother was killed by a hail of bullets from a sub-machine gun. The proto-emotions connected with the abandonments—♂♂♂♂, or hyper-containeds which have remained untransformed and uncontained because they exceeded her capacity for metabolizing them—constantly "disturb," "abuse" and "improperly touch" her.

She goes on to recount how, after graduating, she was run over by a car, and a few months later suffered from an autoimmune condition that made her allergic to light. In a lighter tone, she now mentions a group of female friends whom she has been meeting for lunch for many years, like the protagonists of *Sex and the City*, saying that one of them stays as inconspicuous as possible, though she steals tidbits from the others' plates and never orders any food for herself.

At this point there clearly emerges a "presence," which we could call a tiger (a fawn)—Cecco Angiolieri (a very violent Italian mediaeval poet), who is allergic to light, who runs her over (she runs herself over), and who is in reality an extremely violent presence that would like to kill everyone with a machine gun. The presence survives by "taking tidbits" from other people's plates, but now needs to become visible; in other words, all the proto-emotional states that originated in the "abandonments and separations" constitute proto-containeds—hyper-beta-elements—that seek evacuation, looking for containers and transformation, even if the evacuation takes the form of "machine-gun fire."

The first session of Luisa's analysis undertakes the casting of these proto-emotions, in an initial attempt to name them; the story thus becomes that of a little girl in the patient's class, who has had a series of tumors and metastases. She tries to stay close to this girl, who has been admitted to a children's cancer ward where the doctors are very human and competent.

The patient's account includes on the one hand a "transformation in tumour" of the accumulated beta-elements—but also a transformation of these elements in dreaming at the time when they are narrated. So we have an "abandonoma" or a "separoma" awaiting further transformation, and the analysis is the cancer ward where it will—perhaps—be possible to treat these aggregates of beta-elements (or "betalomas"—cf. Barale and Ferro, 1992).

After the analyst's first, unsaturated interpretation—"Isn't it terrible that a little girl should be so ill"—Luisa mentions the girl's elder brother, who looks after her tenderly, and describes how the girl spends hour after hour stringing colored beads into necklaces. Immediately, then, there appears both a caring figure and a capacity to link things together and develop plans, session after session.

The first manifestation of aggregates of beta-elements is undifferentiated (abandonment and the associated proto-emotions). Then comes the more specific "presence" of rage, which, instead of remaining undifferentiated (for instance, in panic attacks), sets off on a path that lends itself more readily to narration—the presence, the sub-machine gun, the rage, and so on. In other words, we are witnessing a progressive shift from indistinct aggregates of beta-elements (indicative of trauma) to their alphabetization, which leads from differentiation to transformation into emotions and thoughts (on the path towards alpha).

From Proto-Sensoriality and the Proto-Emotional to the Image

At the beginning of many patients' analyses, fragments of proto-emotions are present; these could be called *proto-sememes*: - - - I ..:---| |…__
| _ ---| || ……...__--

These must be gathered in, organized, and transformed so as to generate *micro-sememes*:

G / --
A C – I I
Y- L – I
N – A – **I**
I – [F]
I **E** Γ **L**
O- I Z S

which must in turn be organized so as to create *basic sememes*—for example, JEALOUSY. This, either by itself or in combination with other basic sememes, must next be contextualized to accord with the manifest situation:

"Your friend gets jealous of X when … "

A further stage will be that of apparent *contextualization*, followed by explicit personification:

"At school you are jealous of X when … "

Finally, we have contextualization and explicit personification, which is often at first reversed:

"You're afraid I might be jealous when you … "

Last of all, we may reach the stage of contextualization with direct explicit personification:

"It seems to me that *you* are jealous when I … "

"School" or "your friend" will of course be thought of as locations in the present field; in other words, an interpretation in effect travels from an unsaturated interpretation in the field to an unsaturated interpretation of the field; then to an unsaturated interpretation in the transference; and finally to a saturated interpretation of the transference.

This suggests that patients are always talking (*inter alia*) about the oneiric level of the analytic couple's functioning, and, further, that what a patient says after an interpretation is also a dream he has had about that interpretation; hence the characters who appear also signify the way in which the patient heard the interpretation.

If a woman patient says that she suffers from vaginismus and cannot tolerate being penetrated by her husband, whatever else it may also refer to, from the field perspective this is very likely indicative of a ♀ ♂ configuration—or, in other words, of a mental situation that is insufficiently receptive and is not disposed to allow itself to be penetrated by the analyst's interpretations, which are experienced as intrusive, or is not prepared to admit split-off proto-emotional aspects of the patient's self.

What kind of analyst emerges, then, from these pages? In my imagination he is an analyst who travels light (let us say, with hand baggage only)—an analyst not weighed down or rendered rigid or inelastic by an excess of theories. He is an analyst who tolerates not knowing and is capable of waiting; an analyst who is not a truth fanatic, but seeks only the truth that is tolerable to his patient and himself. He is an analyst who is not afraid of lies, because these, as Grotstein (2007) bravely reminds us, reside in Column 2 of the Grid, the home of the lie, including the lie of dreams in comparison with O.[8] And he is an analyst who trusts much more in the psychoanalytic method than in its contents; an analyst who can regard theories as so much necessary scaffolding, which, however, can be dispensed with when they cease to be meaningful.

The analyst's mind is his main working instrument, and it is therefore "treated" and tested. The quality of its functioning is constantly signalled to us by the patient himself. This quality is itself a variable of the analytic field. In addition, our analyst will be more interested in what he does not know than in the reassuring celebration of what he does know. His mind is that of an explorer or navigator rather than of a tour guide.

Acknowledgement

This chapter was translated by Philip Slotkin, M.A. (Cantab.) MITI.

Notes

1 The Swedish (and Italian) title translates literally as "Men who hate women."

2 A Labrador is of course a particularly affectionate breed of dog. The Italian pronunciation is the same as *labbra d'or[o]*—literally "golden lips" [roughly equivalent to "silver-tongued" in English]. The Flanders cattle dog, or Bouvier des Flandres, is a very strong (and aggressive) breed used for herding and guarding.

3 Put in the language of Bion's Grid, we could say that the two of us, myself and the patient, have "played" along Row C (Dream Thoughts, Dreams and Myths).

4 "Nothing that is human is alien to me."
5 This is a common distinction in French analytic writing, but may not be familiar to Anglophone readers. "Interpretations *in* the transference" refer to all the analyst's interventions and behaviors when seen by the patient from the "vertex" (perspective) of the analyst as transference figure. "Interpretations *of* the transference" are statements that suggest or describe the ways in which the patient may be experiencing or feeling about the analyst *as if* he or she was similar or identical to an important internalized figure from the patient's past. The latter, interpretations of the transference, are what English-speaking readers commonly think of as "transference interpretations."
6 From the popular movie, *Silence of the Lambs.*
7 Translator's note: The Italian idiom in the patient's comment means literally "You don't make a crease," and the analyst's name (Ferro) means iron, so the allusion is to an iron that could smooth out the creases.
8 Bion (1970) described any transformation from O → K as a "lie," in the sense that it could only be an incomplete approximation of the "thing-in-itself."

References

Barale, F. and Ferro, A. (1992) Negative therapeutic reactions and microfractures in analytic communication. In: Nissim Momigliano, L., and Robutti, A. (eds.) *Shared Experience: The Psychoanalytic Dialogue.* London: Karnac.

Baranger, M. and Baranger, W. (1961–2) La situación analítica como campo dinámico [The analytic situation as a dynamic field]. *Revista Uruguaya de Psicoanálisis*, 4:3–54.

Baranger, M., Baranger, W. and Mom, J. (1983) Process and non-process in analytic work. *The International Journal of Psychoanalysis*, 64:1–15.

Baranger, M., Baranger, W. and Mom, J. (1988) The infantile psychic trauma from us to Freud: Pure trauma, retroactivity, and reconstruction. *The International Journal of Psychoanalysis*, 69:113–29.

Bezoari, M. and Ferro, A. (1992) From a play between "parts" to transformations in the couple. Psychoanalysis in a bipersonal field. In: Nissim Momigliano, L., and Robutti, A. (eds.) *Shared Experience: The Psychoanalytic Dialogue.* London: Karnac.

Bion, W. R. (1962) *Learning from Experience.* London: Tavistock.

Bion, W. R. (1963) *Elements of Psycho-Analysis.* London: Heinemann.

Bion, W. R. (1965) *Transformations.* London: Tavistock.

Bion, W. R. (1970) *Attention and Interpretation.* London: Tavistock.

Bion, W. R. (1977) The dawn of oblivion. In: *A Memoir of the Future Book 3.* Revised and corrected edition. London: Karnac, 1990.

Bion, W. R. (1985) *The Italian Seminars.* F. Bion (ed.), trans. P. Slotkin. London: Karnac, 2005.

Bion, W. R. (2005) *The Tavistock Seminars.* F. Bion (ed.). London: Karnac.

Corrao, F. (1986) Il concetto di campo come modello teorico [The field concept as a theoretical model]. *Gruppo e Funzione Analitica*, 7:9–21.

Fellini, F. (2007). *Il libro dei sogni* [The book of dreams]. Milan: Rizzoli.

Ferro, A. (1999) *Psychoanalysis as Therapy and Storytelling.* Trans. P. Slotkin. Hove: Routledge, 2006.

Ferro, A. (2002a) Some implications of Bion's thought: The waking dream and narrative derivatives. *The International Journal of Psychoanalysis*, 83:597–607.

Ferro, A. (2002b) *Seeds of Illness, Seeds of Recovery: The Genesis of Suffering and the Role of Psychoanalysis.* Trans. P. Slotkin. Hove: Brunner-Routledge, 2005.

Ferro, A. (2006a) Clinical implications of Bion's thought. *The International Journal of Psychoanalysis*, 87:989–1003.

Ferro, A. (2006b) *Mind Works. Technique and Creativity in Psychoanalysis.* Trans. P. Slotkin. Hove: Routledge, 2008.

Ferro, A. (2007) *Evitare le emozioni, vivere le emozioni* [Avoiding emotions, experiencing emotions]. Milan: Cortina.

Ferro, A. (2009) Transformations in dreaming and characters in the psychoanalytic field, *The International Journal of Psychoanalysis*, 90:209–30.

Ferro, A. and Basile, R. (2004) The psychoanalyst as individual: self-analysis and gradients of functioning. *The Psychoanalytic Quarterly*, 73:659–82.

Ferro, A. and Basile, R. (eds.) (2009) *The Analytic Field: A Clinical Concept.* Karnac London.

Grotstein, J. S. (2000) *Who is the Dreamer Who Dreams the Dream? A Study of Psychic Presences.* Hove: Routledge.

Grotstein, J. S. (2002) "We are such stuff as dreams are made of": Annotations on dreams and dreaming in Bion's works. In: Neri, C., Pines, M., and Friedman, R. (eds.) *Dreams in Group Psychotherapy: Theory and Technique.* London: Jessica Kingsley, pp. 110–45.

Grotstein, J. S. (2007) *A Beam of Intense Darkness: Wilfred Bion's Legacy to Psychoanalysis.* London: Karnac.

Larsson, S. (2006) *The Girl who Played with Fire.* Trans. R. Keeland. London: MacLehose Press, 2009.

Lewkowicz, S. and Flechner, S. (eds.) (2005) *Truth, Reality and the Psychoanalyst: Latin American Contributions to Psychoanalysis*. London: International Psychoanalytical Association.

Meltzer, D. (1992) *The Claustrum: An Investigation of Claustrophobic Phenomena.* London: Karnac.

Ogden, T. (2003) On not being able to dream. *The International Journal of Psychoanalysis*, 84:17–30.

Ogden, T. (2005) *This Art of Psychoanalysis: Dreaming Undreamt Dreams and Interrupted Cries.* Hove: Routledge.

Terence (Publius Terentius Afer) (165 BC) Heauton Timorumenos (The self-tormentor), I.1, v. 25. English in: *Terence: The Comedies.* Trans. P. Brown. Oxford: Oxford University Press, 2006.

EDITORS' INTRODUCTION

Dreaming as a "Curtain of Illusion": Revisiting the "Royal Road" with Bion as Our Guide

James S. Grotstein

In this chapter, which was the North American plenary address at the 2009 Bion in Boston conference, Grotstein masterfully compares and contrasts Bion's theory of dreaming with that of Freud, emphasizing Bion's idea that we are always dreaming while awake and asleep. Grotstein notes that while Freud focused upon the wish-fulfilling nature of the dream, Bion, who considered dreaming as the mind's way of giving meaning to emotional experience, emphasized the dream *process*. In Freud, the dream-work served to disguise discrete, unconscious wishes, allowing them partial expression, so that sleep could continue undisturbed. In contrast, Bion viewed dream-work as a continuous, ongoing, 24-hour/day unconscious activity by means of which the psyche created a *container* for raw affective experience (*beta* elements) and transformed the latter into the constituents of a personal narrative (*alpha* elements). Where Freud emphasized the conflict between conscious and unconscious sectors of the psyche and considered the taming of instinctual impulses to be the prime mover of dreams, Bion saw the conscious and unconscious sectors of the mind as mutually constitutive and proposed that the origin of dreaming lay in the mind's need to process *emotional truth*.

Building upon Bion's contribution, Grotstein posits a *dream ensemble* consisting of dream-work, alpha-function, container–contained, reverie, Ps↔D and unconscious waking thought, all of which are linked to the dreaming process. The end product of the work of this process is the containment and transformation of unmetabolized emotional experience through the creation of pictograms (alpha elements) that may be woven into the dream's narrative. Once constructed, the latter then functions as a soothing "curtain of illusion" to help the dreamer bear frightening emotions.

The considerably widened view of dreaming offered by Grotstein's elaboration of Bion's seminal thoughts provides a bedrock concept that permeates our understanding of psychopathology as well as the clinical encounter. From the perspective of the dream-work, then, psychopathology may be viewed as the consequence of "defective dreaming:" impairment of the capacity to dream (while awake or asleep) leads to unbridled exposure to powerful emotions that can overwhelm the psyche. In such situations, the mind is forced to resort to desperate maneuvers (ineffectual and/or primitive defenses), which mark the various pathological formations. Bion's and Grotstein's theory of dreaming encourages us to see the analytic relationship as an unconscious, collaborative, intersubjective process in which analyst and analysand are continuously and unconsciously engaged in creating, containing and transforming the unconscious phantasies of the field. Whether dealing with the nature of the unconscious, the exploration of trauma, art and cultural phenomena or the therapeutic process and relationship, Grotstein's adumbration of Bion's theory offers us a unifying, core concept with which to observe and explore their evolution.

5

DREAMING AS A "CURTAIN OF ILLUSION"

Revisiting the "Royal Road" with Bion as Our Guide

James S. Grotstein

In his sleep Vishnu dreamed the Universe.
(The Bhagavad-Gita)

All life is a dream, and the dreams are dreams from a dream.
(Calderón de la Barca)

What is man?
What is man not?
Man is but the dream's shadow.
(From the Eighth Pythian Ode of Pindar)

Introduction

Freud's discovery of the meaning of dreams continues to stand as a landmark in the evolution of psychoanalysis and to occupy a fundamental position in its episteme, but it was Bion more than any other who seems to have grabbed Freud's baton and run with it with extraordinary imaginative creativity. His extension of Freud's theory of dreaming constitutes one of the more significant paradigm changes that have taken place in psychoanalytic thinking, but his postulates about it are still not widely known nor appreciated. It was only recently that some authors have addressed his ideas on dreaming. They include Grotstein (2000, 2002), Ogden (2001, 2003, 2004, 2007, 2008), Brown (2006), and Burka et al. (2007). Bion's thinking about dreaming had been quietly germinating in his earlier works (Bion, 1953, 1962, 1963, 1965, 1967, and 1970) and emerged from his observations of psychotic patients, noting that they *hallucinate* (project) rather than *dream* (introject) their experiences (Bion, 1970, p. 16) and therefore cannot "learn from their emotional experiences." From this background he formulated the concept of alpha-function (Bion, 1962, p. 3) and implicated it as the instrument (model) that works on processing emotional experiences during sleep *and* waking life by producing alpha-elements which can be used for generating dream images for dream thoughts (p. 6) so as to render the emotional experiences *personally meaningful*. Insofar as dreaming is an agent of our personal subjectivity, it affects our uniqueness, our personal ways of looking at things, our subjectivity to the otherness of the object to appreciate its value and anticipate it and defuse its potential danger. Looked at in another way, it constitutes "*transference*" in its broadest sense.

Background

Bion's (1992) major work on dreaming was written in his private notebook, *Cogitations*. The concept of "dream-work-alpha" first saw the light of day in Bion's imaginative thinking in *Cogitations* in 1959 (p. 42) and ended, undated (on p. 253), certainly before 1968—but it appears nowhere else in his formal publications during his lifetime. He was later to separate dreaming (no longer using "dream-work") from alpha-function presumably because the former constituted a theory as well as an actual *in vivo* process, whereas the latter constituted an analogue model, a *virtual* function; thus, the two seemed to belong to different categories (Bion, 1992, p. 186; Sandler, 2005, pp. 231–56, and personal communication, 2007a). An intimate connection between dream-work, alpha-function, container↔contained, and the "contact-barrier," however, was implicit in his works from early on. Even though Bion did not neatly distinguish between dreaming and alpha-function after he stopped using "dream-work-alpha," he did once casually allude to a connection: "*the alpha-function of dream-work*" (Bion, 1992, p. 177). Thus, Bion tends to treat "dreaming" and "alpha-function" as being either identical, overlapping, and/or the latter's being a component of the former. *In what follows, I shall continue Bion's lead in using "dreaming" and "alpha-function" as virtually interchangeable as well as complementary processes.*

Bion's re-interpretation, reworking, and extension of Freud's postulates are of such range that I shall cite selected samples of them and then discuss them after first presenting the briefest epitome of Freud's theory of dreaming that is relevant to Bion's modifications. Further, I shall not present dream material because this contribution, like Bion's work, focuses strictly on *dreaming itself*.

Freud's Theory of Dream-Work: A Brief Epitome

The essentials of Freud's (1900, 1900–1) theory of dreaming as they interface with Bion's extensions and modifications are as follows:

i Dreams subserve the *pleasure principle* and disguise emotional problems *while one is asleep* (1900–1, p. 567).
ii Dreaming processes the day's residue of emotional conflicts and, through its dream-work, transforms it into a narrative which is conditioned by the *motive of wish-fulfillment sponsored by the pleasure principle* (1900–1, p. 567).
iii The ultimate purpose of dreaming is to guarantee sleep by *converting conflicts into wish-fulfillments* and thereby to keep the latent dream thoughts unconscious *so as to protect System Cs.* from them (1900–1, p. 615).
iv The manifest content of the dream is the result of dream-work, and the analytic task is to retranslate it so as *to be able to learn its latent content* (1900–01, pp. 652–61).
v Dream-work consists of *condensation, displacement, the creation of means of representations of the logical relations between the dismembered dream-thoughts by the dream-work, and considerations of representability*—including the use of symbols and sensory, mainly visual, images (1900–1, p. 445). To these we add *secondary revision* (1900–1, p. 449).
vi Freud states that dream-work *removes (disarticulates) the conjunctive links between thoughts* and then reverses the hierarchy of their importance by placing the more emotionally experienced ideas in the background and the less important ones in the foreground (1900–1, p. 445).

Freud's theory of dreaming postulates that dreaming occurs during sleep and that its motive is to employ the pleasure principle exclusively to create wish-fulfillment narratives to alter the day residue. The component operations of dreaming are identical to those Freud (1911) associates with the primary processes.

A Brief Summary of Bion's Assumptions about Dreaming: Caveat

Let me first epitomize Bion's overarching conception of dreaming so as to orient the reader to what follows. Bion (1992) states: "[T]hese events are *having something done to them* mentally, and *that which is being done to them I call being dreamed* … " (p. 39, italics mine).

Bion extends and modifies Freud's concept of dreaming as follows. He believes that:

i Sense impressions (imprints) of *emotional experience* (Bion, 1962, p. 26) constitute "first cause" in initiating dreaming; thus, dreaming accomplishes affect management.
ii Dreaming maintains the differentiation between sleep and wakefulness.
iii Dreaming continues throughout the day and night.
iv Thinking is not only dependent on dreaming—dreaming constitutes a component as well as a form of thinking.
v Dreaming acts as a contact-barrier (Bion, 1962, p. 17) and a veritable filter to differentiate and protect Systems Cs. and Ucs.
vi "Alpha-function or dreaming" unites the primary and secondary processes in a binary-oppositional structure (Lévi-Strauss, 1958, 1970).
vii Alpha-function (dreaming) exists on two levels, in System Ucs., where it functions under the hegemony of the pleasure principle, and in System Cs., where it functions under the hegemony of the reality principle.
viii Dreaming transforms unmentalized sense impressions of emotional experience into mentalizable alpha-elements—which means that one does something *mentally to (transforms) the sense impressions.*

[N.B. Bion never speaks of System *Pcs.*, but I believe that when he speaks of the locale of dreaming System *Pcs.* is really what he means. It is dreaming's "mixing room" (Grotstein, 2000, p. 33). Furthermore, I believe that the alpha-function (dreaming) that creates alpha-elements may be located at the border between Systems *Pcs.* and *Ucs.* and that it produces narratives at the border between Systems *Pcs.* and *Cs.*]

What is it, then, that the subject does to the sense impressions of the object that Bion qualifies as dreaming in the functions of *perception, observation, attention and thinking*? I believe that Bion means that what are added are:

i our *temperament* and its vicissitudes;
ii our conscious and unconscious experiences, i.e. *memory*; and
iii selected aspects of the Ideal Forms (Plato) and/or the noumena (things-in-themselves) (Kant), which act as inherent pre-conceptions, in addition to our acquired (experienced) pre-conceptions, so as to anticipate incoming stimuli, format the psyche for their arrival, and assign emotional significance to them as they matriculate through the transformational cycle from beta- to alpha-elements and finally to alpha-element narratives and feelings.

The mind, like the brain, functions to predict. Dreaming constitutes an integral aspect of the *patient's free associations* as well as the *analyst's observations and interpretations*. Patients are ill because of a failure in or incompleteness of dreaming their past and present ongoing experiences. *Dreams are imaginative fictions that preserve emotional truths*. Bion presents dreaming as a form of mentalization as well as emotional cognition and perception, and as an example of a "transformation in hallucinosis" (Bion, 1965, p. 133) because of the predominance of the visual sensory mode in dreaming. [N.B. Bion's (1962) use of "mentalization" is his way of accounting for the transformation via alpha-function of somatic stimuli (sense impression) to become useful for further "mental digestion." It differs from Fonagy's (2001) much later use of the term (pp. 165–67), which more approximates Klein's (1935, 1940) concept of the depressive position.]

Utmostly, dreaming first mediates the impingements of "*O*," the Absolute Truth about Ultimate (and Infinite) Reality, which presents as raw sense impressions (beta-elements) and becomes transformed by dreaming into mentalized alpha-elements. Thus, it functions as a *filter* for unmentalized infinite emotional Truth. Utmostly, Bion (1965) seems to suggest that dreaming consists of a "*curtain of illusion*" (p. 147) that circumscribes, envelops, and differentiates Systems *Cs.* and *Ucs.* so as to guarantee their separateness and independent function.

From my own reading of Bion, I hypothesize that dreaming constitutes:

- i a "membranous" "*curtain of illusion*" (Bion, 1965, p. 147) that defines and protects Systems *Cs.* and *Ucs.*, as stated earlier, and thereby constitutes a protective "contact-barrier" (Bion, 1962, p. 17) between and around the two Systems and their interface with the inexorable impingements of "O" (Bion, 1965, p. 17), the Absolute Truth about an Ultimate (and Infinite) Reality;
- ii as an extension of the previous speculation, the function of dreaming may be analogous to that of the of the amniotic sac for the fetus;
- iii the visual images produced by dreaming accumulate into pictograms or "narremes" which become organized into dream narrations by a more sophisticated alpha-function (Ferro, 1999, pp. 6, 38);
- iv dreaming constitutes "emotional thinking" (transformations) insofar as it mentalizes non-mental sense impressions (beta-elements) into alpha-elements, and in harvesting the latter to become narrative dreams and phantasies. Dreaming also *accompanies* cognitive thinking by processing its affective accompaniment. Thus dreaming constitutes "*affective attunement*."

What Is Dreaming? Dreaming as "Having Something Done To ... "

When Bion extended the function and expanded the landscape of dreaming, he not only suggested that dreaming occurs by day as well as by night; he also theorized that the act of dreaming consists of *adding something* or *having something done to the sense impressions* left by one's experience with objects. "Something-being-done-to" implicates the faculties of *thinking*, *perception*, *observation*, *attention*, *memory*, *free associations*, and *interpretation* (and even *playing*, *imagination*, and *reading*) as cognates, equivalents, or components of dreaming. Bion (1992) states: "[T]hese events are *having something done to them* mentally, and that which is being done to them I call being dreamed ..." (p. 39, italics mine).

We can infer that what are being "done to" the subject's raw experience of the object by the above-mentioned faculties are the projective attributions by the subject of unconsciously selected ingredients from his or her personality, those qualities that bespeak his or her individuality, uniqueness, and personal subjectivity—and are cast upon the sensory impressions of the incoming sensory stimulus and especially upon his or her unconscious connection with the Ideal Forms or noumena ("things-in-themselves") and Tomkins's (1962, 1963) inherent affect precursors. Dreaming, consequently, is "doing something" to the sense impressions as they become perceptions by day and visual images by night. What is it that is being done to the sense impression made by the sense impression (stimulus)?

It is my impression that, following Winnicott (1971), Damasio (1994, 1999), Barry (1997), Hoffman (1998), Grotstein (2000), and Llinás (2001) that the stimulus is being imaginatively and solipsistically re-created, i.e. *dreamed*, within the mind of the perceiving subject—fashioned creatively from the subject's internal building blocks, i.e. the Ideal Forms, the noumena (inherent pre-conceptions, "memoirs of the future"), and inherent affect potential which operate as formats for or anticipations of new events so as to be able to categorize them for recognition, accommodation, and assimilation (Piaget, 1951). Dreaming also re-signifies past object relations and thereby promotes psychic growth by this ability to reprocess earlier experiences.

Dreaming *personalizes* sensory impressions, which, in the first instance, may be *impersonal* O, even though the author of the impressions may be an intimate partner, mother, or analyst.

Dreaming, consequently, amounts to "emotional thinking" in the act of *editing*, which begins with *perception* with all its implications and referents, i.e. *observation*, *attention*, *translation*, *interpretation*, *association*, *transference*, *playing*, *reading*, *speaking* (and others), which act as formatting preconceptions (inherent and/or acquired) that are thrust upon one's sensory impression created by the stimulus—all in the service of anticipation and categorization of the new stimulus-object. The effect is to impart to it the quality of a *déjà-vu*, a strange-familiarity, "a memoir of the future" (Bion, 1992, p. 362), not unlike our immune system, whose antibodies anticipate the bacterial or viral antigen.

The Functions of Dreaming

(A) Dreaming helps preserve the distinction between sleep and wakefulness by modulating the level of emotional arousal or stimulus overload through the transformation or raw, impersonal proto-emotional stimuli (beta-elements) into tolerable, personally meaningful, and "mentally digestible" alpha-elements. Put another way, Freud (1900) believed that the purpose of dreaming (at night) was to preserve sleep (pp. 233–4). Bion (1962) also believed that we dream by day as well as by night and that dreaming by day helped us to remain awake (p. 6). Bion (1992) believes that the psychotic can neither sleep nor stay awake because he cannot sleep, thus he cannot protect the diurnal rhythm of sleep and wakefulness. Dreaming reinforces and maintains the function of the contact-barrier which constitutes a selectively permeable regulatory membrane between sleep and wakefulness as well as between Systems *Cs.* and *Ucs.*

(B) Dreaming effectively diminishes the subject's anxiety by supplying a soothing wishful narrative ("curtain of illusion"); and (C) by editing; thus, dreaming serves as an active ongoing: (D) *filter* (an "emotional immunity frontier," as it were) for sensory overload from internal as well as external stimuli. As such, it serves as: (E) a selective grid or grade to sort out and prioritize the data it processes; and (F) *escorts emotional Truth* through the sluices of transformation as a vehicle whose precious cargo is *Truth.* Further, dreaming is not only a form of thinking (mentation), but is *emotional thinking which* facilitates cognitive thinking.

Bion (1992) states:

> ... genuine "dream," ... this is an attempt to make a current emotional experience available for dream-thought; it is an ... attempt to make external reality and internal psychic reality available to thought, and ... *usher in an ability to learn from experience.*
>
> (p. 141, italics mine)

Dreaming uniquely *personalizes* impersonal experiences so as to make them one's own and thus serves the principle of: (G) *self-organization* (Schwalbe, 1991). In addition to modulation, (H) dreaming also attends to (pays *attention* to), perceives, anticipates, and formats oncoming *premonitory experiences.* A male patient who reported that he had just learned that his wife was pregnant, stated that it is taking him a long while to adjust to the fact—that his awareness of her pregnancy and its significance for him happen in stages. Dreaming arranges for the merciful dosage of awareness by postponement. (I) Dreaming, like thinking generally, constitutes "trial action" (Freud, 1911), i.e. the infant dreams the breast in its absence. Dreaming not only mentalizes and thinks; it also processes emotional events from memory but also for: (J) burial in the bins of repression.

Dreaming is not only the very essence of: (K) *transference* and *counter-transference* and also of the analysand's free associations as well as the analyst's interpretations; (L) dreaming ultimately is the function whereby we achieve *meaning* in context with our experiences. The *objective meaning* of events occurs atop a template of *personal, emotional meaning*. The two levels of meaning cannot do without each other.

Emotional Experience as "First Cause" for Dreaming

Bion emphasizes that:

i man cannot think if he cannot dream or phantasize;
ii emotional experience is first cause for the dreaming process, not wish-fulfillment, which is the defense;
iii the emotional experience, as a sensory impression (unmentalized beta-elements (Bion, 1962, p. 6), must, via alpha-function (Bion, 1962, p. 6), be transformed into mentalizable alpha-elements (Bion, 1962, p. 5), the fundamental building blocks for visual dream images that yield dream narrative thoughts).

With the production of dream thoughts the subject is able to stay awake by day and sleep by night because dreaming processes emotions by disencumbering the overflow from the day's residue. Thus Bion differs with Freud about the origin of the dream by stating that it is *emotional experience* not the *day residue* that produces the dream. In other words, Bion thinks that the experience of sense impressions of emotional experience, rather than the day residue *per se*, is the source of dreaming.

Bion (1962) states:

> To learn from experience alpha-function must operate on the awareness of the *emotional experience* [italics added]; alpha-elements are produced from the impressions [beta-elements] of the experience; these are thus made storable and available for dream-thoughts and for unconscious waking thinking.... *Alpha-function is needed for conscious thinking and reasoning and for the relegation of thinking to the unconscious when it is necessary to disencumber consciousness of the burden of thought by learning a skill.*
>
> (p. 8, italics mine)

> The sleeping man has an *emotional experience*, converts it into alpha-elements and so becomes capable of dream thoughts ... and therefore of *undisturbed consciousness*.
>
> (p. 15, italics mine)

Bion (1992) states further:

> If the patient cannot transform his emotional experiences into α-elements, he cannot dream … the patient who cannot dream cannot go to sleep and cannot wake up.
>
> (p. 7, italics mine)

> Freud assumed that the interpretation, the latent content, was the origin of the dream. I say that the origin is in an *emotional experience* [italics mine]—perhaps an experience that is emotional and nothing else—and that is worked on (rationalized?) to produce the dream, the manifest content as we know it, and that it is the *analyst* who then does the *interpretation* to produce the so-called latent content.
>
> (p. 135)

The Importance of Dreaming in Maintaining the Differentiation between Sleep and Wakefulness

Bion believes that wakefulness and sleep—and the differentiation between them—depend on the intervention of dreaming ("done to that something," as stated earlier) on the impinging sense impressions of emotional experience. He further believes that the *alpha-function of the dreaming* (Bion, 1992, p. 177) yields alpha-elements, one of whose functions is to reinforce the "contact barrier" (Bion, 1962, p. 27), which, as just stated above, functions in turn to serve as a selectively permeable boundary between Systems *Ucs.* and *Cs.* so as to guarantee their separate functioning—*so as, in turn, to allow thinking to take place.* I believe that dreaming seamlessly becomes the contact-barrier.

Bion (1992) states:

> Why cannot X wake up if he cannot "dream?" It must be for the same reason that you cannot let something become unconscious if α [dream-work α, i.e. "alpha-"] *is not done to that something.* The inability to have *visual images* of what is taking place means that the emotional experience cannot be preserved either in the conscious or the unconscious. (In this I have *equated* α *with having visual images* …)
>
> (pp. 139–40, italics mine)

Here Bion is also stating his belief that the two Systems function, not so much *conflictually*, as Freud (1915) theorized, but rather as *collaboratively oppositional* to one another so as to protect consciousness and the unconscious (by maintaining an effective barrier between them) while the subject is awake during the day and asleep at night. Further, by virtue of their joint action, the subject is able to differentiate sleep from wakefulness, according to Bion, unlike psychotics, who can neither be awake nor asleep because they cannot dream because they do not have an effective barrier between the two Systems. Put another way, dreaming, via the contact-barrier, makes consciousness unconscious and selective portions of the unconscious conscious.

Dreaming Throughout the Day and Night

As one can now conclude, the Ariadne's thread that runs through Bion's thinking about dreaming is a dialectical (collaborative binary-oppositional, e.g. night/day, sleep/wakefulness, System *Cs./Ucs*). Bion believes that dreaming functions continuously, by day as well as by night, and therefore constitutes a continuous daily/nightly function.

Bion (1992) states: "My belief is that the dependence of *waking life* on dreams has been overlooked and is even more important" (p. 47, italics mine). I take from these two ideas, first, that if *waking life*, like the preservation of sleep, is dependent on dreaming, then dreaming helps keep the individual focused while awake by simultaneously putting distracting or emotionally painful thoughts asleep. That Bion considers sleep's function during waking life is "even more important," strongly suggests that dreaming's relationship to mentalization, perception, and thinking is more important than its role in maintaining sleep (Freud's belief).

Dreaming as Unconscious Wakeful Thinking

Bion (1962, 1992), unlike Freud, believes that dreaming constitutes "unconscious wakeful thinking" (Bion, 1962, p. 8; Ferro, 1999, pp. 51–6). It is the "emotional thinking" that accompanies (parallels) and facilitates cognitive thinking. It includes the mentation of sense impressions (beta-elements) into alpha-elements. He also differs with Freud over the goals of displacement, i.e. dreaming seeks to modify, not evade, frustration by a protective distortion of the facts of reality—*so as secretly to preserve truth in fictive disguise*. He also believes that the "analyst must dream the (analytic) session" (Bion, 1992, p. 120). He associates dreaming the session with reverie (Bion, 1962, p. 36) as distinguished from countertransference. Bion (1992) states: "I suspect that Freud's displacement etc. is relevant; he took up only the negative attitude, dreams as 'concealing' something, not the way in which the *necessary* dream is constructed" (p. 33).

How does a dream evade frustration? By *distortion* of facts of reality, and by *displacement* of facts of reality. In short, by dream-work on the perception of facts—not, in this context, dream-work on the dream-thoughts except in so far as the dream-thoughts are thoughts portraying the facts. Freud attributes to dream-work the function of concealing the facts of internal mental life, the dream-thoughts, only. *I attribute to it the function of evading the frustration to which the dream-thoughts, and therefore the interpretation of dream-thoughts, would give rise if allowed to function properly—that is, as mechanisms associated with the legitimate tasks involved in real modification of frustration.* Consequently, since such legitimate tasks always carry an element of frustration, excessive intolerance short-sightedly leads to the attempt at evasion of the frustration intrinsic to the task of modification of frustration. "α [dream-work-alpha] *is concerned with, and is identical with, unconscious waking thinking* designed, as part of the *reality principle*, to aid in the task of real, as opposed to pathological, modification of frustration" (Bion, 1992, p. 54, italics mine).

Bion differs yet again with Freud on whether dreaming is an attempt to evade frustration (pleasure principle with no contribution from the reality principle) or an attempt to modify frustration and *thereby constitute unconscious thinking in the service of the reality principle*—all to preserve truth by modifying frustration, not to deny truth by wish-fulfillment. We can infer, furthermore, that Bion seems to suggest that a *direct correspondence and a reciprocal relationship exist between one's capacity to dream and one's tolerance of frustration.*

Alpha-Function, Dream-Work, and Narrative

Bion (1963) also mentions the importance of *visual images* as well as the narratives (p. 74) that employ them as the product of alpha-function, which seems to be a cognate for Bion's concept of dreaming. Ferro (1999) conceives that the visual images produced by dreaming accumulate into pictograms or "narremes" which become organized into dream narrations (pp. 6, 38) by a more sophisticated alpha-function (Grotstein, 2007b). For *whose eyes are these visual images and their narratives constructed*? (I shall return to this point later.) Emotional Truth is the latent content of the dream. The dream which emerges from dream-work must be experienced as a narrative that can be recorded and recalled. The narration, which can be expressed in dreams or phantasies, binds anxiety. Thus, emotional containment is a function of dreaming.

The Relationship between Dreaming, Thinking, and Emotional Experience and the Differentiation between Sleep and Wakefulness: Thinking is Dependent on Dreaming

Dreaming is necessary in order to be able to think by disencumbering consciousness of an excess of sense impressions of emotional experience, which are then transferred by alpha-function to System *Ucs.* for transformation into dream images (for further dreaming) and unconscious phantasies either to bury under repression or to move on to formal thinking and feeling. In other words, dreaming prepares the way for thinking and feeling by guarding and reinforcing the "contact-barrier" (Bion, 1962, p. 15) so that consciousness can be maintained by day and sleep by night by supplying alpha-elements for dream images (pictograms, narremes) so that "wakeful thinking" and thinking during sleep (mentalization of day residue sense impressions) can take place.

Bion (1953 [1967]) epitomizes the consummate importance of dreaming as follows: "It must mean that *without phantasies* and *without dreams* you have *not the means with which to think out your problem*" (p. 25, italics mine).

Bion thus believes that dreaming is not only a *form* of thinking; it is of utmost importance in allowing thinking to occur.

Dreaming (Alpha-Function) as a "Filter" to Protect Consciousness and Unconsciousness

Dreaming constitutes a "curtain of illusion" or "filter" (which I shall explicate later) that screens sense impressions so as to allow consciousness to take place by day and sleep by night in order for the alpha-function (which Bion loosely associates with dreaming) to produce the alpha-elements necessary for thinking by day and by night—all so that one can "*learn from experience*" (Bion, 1962).

Bion (1992) states:

> They [alpha-elements] have to be *retained*, if I am to *learn from experience*, by being converted through dream-work-α into α-elements, and these α-elements are combined according to certain rules to make them approximate to what in daytime wakefulness would be a *narrative* of the event in which I am participating and which I need to record …
>
> (p. 110, italics mine)

> [T]he dream work-α may have as its function the *exclusion of material that would otherwise distract from the main task in hand* – the actual conscious object … Dream work-α transforms … experience so that I can *store* it and *remember* it.
>
> (p. 140, italics mine)

> A comparison of the two levels suggests that some kind of approximation is being attempted between an awareness of an external event and an internal process of manipulation, "digestion," of the same event.
>
> (p. 149)

> One of the reasons why *sleep is essential* is to make possible, by *suspension of consciousness*, the emotional experiences that the personality

> would *not permit itself to have during conscious waking life*, and so to bring them *into reach of dream-work-α* ["alpha"] *for conversion into α-elements and a narrative form*, consecutive and dominated by a causation-theoretical outlook, *suitable for being worked on by conscious rational processes of thought. Dream-work-α, and its product of α-elements, is therefore an essential link between dream-thought and conscious rational thought, and the raw material on which both have to work.*
>
> (pp. 149–50, italics mine)

In the first citation Bion again refers to the consciousness-sparing function of dreaming. Implicit here and explicit elsewhere in his writings Bion propounds that dreaming functions by day as well as by night, differing from Freud's implicit views. In the second citation Bion alludes to another function of the alpha-elements produced by dreaming's alpha-function, their role in constituting and facilitating *memory*. In the third citation Bion theorizes that our capacity to "learn from experience" fundamentally depends on our being able to convert the raw emotional sense impressions (beta-elements) into mentalizable alpha-elements so as to produce dream images for dream thoughts. Dream thoughts allow us to *feel* (mentally) our bodily *emotions* (Damasio, 2003, p. 4), and thereby mentally grow and evolve from our acceptance of them and the truths about ourselves which emotions carry as their ballast. The dream thoughts constitute a *dream narrative*, an unconscious phantasy that parallels in the unconscious the corresponding objective thoughts in consciousness. The purpose of the narrative, according to Bion, is for the dreamer to be able to attribute *personal meaning* to the experience on one level and *objective meaning* on the other. ("As above, so below," Hermes Trismegistus, in Scully, 2003, p. 321.)

In the last citation Bion is stating that sleep is necessary to protect consciousness by allowing emotional experiences that cannot be sufficiently processed by alpha-function by day (dreaming under the hegemony of the reality principle) to become unconscious while the subject is conscious. Here is where Bion is alluding to his belief that the sense impressions of emotional experience that are intercepted by System *Cs.* must first be routed directly through the selectively-permeable contact-barrier into System *Ucs.* for waking dreaming to produce waking dream thoughts and then be *selectively returned to System* Cs. *for rational thought.* The conscious and unconscious Systems work harmoniously and complementarily.

Alpha-Function Unites the Primary and Secondary Processes

We have already seen how Bion united the actions of the pleasure and reality principles. One of his most radical departures from Freud was his uniting the primary and secondary processes into a collaboratively oppositional entity, alpha-function.

Bion (1962) states:

> The weakness of this theory of consciousness is manifest in the situation for which I have proposed the theory that alpha-function, by proliferating alpha-elements, is producing the contact-barrier, an entity that separates elements so that those on one side are, and form, the conscious and on the other side are, and form, the unconscious. The theory of consciousness is weak, not false, because by amending it to state that the conscious and the unconscious thus constantly produced together do function as if they were binocular therefore capable of correlation and self-regard.... For these reasons ... I find the theory of primary and secondary processes unsatisfactory. This theory is weak in the need to postulate two systems at the point where, in my theory of an alpha-function, an emotional experience is transformed into alpha-elements.
>
> (Bion, 1962, p. 54)

In this citation Bion reaffirms that Systems *Ucs.* and *Cs.* function binocularly. From this idea he then proceeds to conflate or unify the primary and secondary processes as a structure of "binary-opposition" (paradoxically collaborative as well as oppositional but not conflictual) under the supraordinate term, "*alpha-function.*" One of the consequences of this radical paradigm shift is the revelation of his belief that dreaming subserves the *reality principle* in collaboration with the *pleasure principle.*

The Two Levels of Alpha-Function or Dreaming

Apha-function or dreaming works both on the interface between Systems *Cs.* and *Ucs.* and between System *Cs.* and external reality. Thus, it functions on the lower level to produce alpha-elements for dreams and phantasy narratives (Ferro, 1999) and on the higher level to facilitate observation, attention, perception, and cognitive thinking.

Bion (1992) states: "A comparison of the two levels suggests that some kind of approximation is being attempted between an awareness of an external event and an internal process of manipulation, 'digestion', of the same event" (p. 149, italics mine). Here, Bion is elaborating on his dialectical ("binocular") conception that Systems *Cs.* and *Ucs.* function by combining conscious observation with a complementary dream narrative in the unconscious. Thus psychopathology would consist of a disharmony of this parallel but complementary relationship.

Discussion: Dreaming as a Protective and Imaginative "Curtain of Illusion" for Systems *Ucs.* and *Cs.*

Part One: Dreaming as a Protective and Imaginative "Curtain of Illusion"

Bion believes, as stated earlier, that alpha-function or dreaming operates on the initial sense impressions of emotional experience of consciousness as well as on the unconscious products of dreaming. *Alpha-function, consequently, occupies both Systems Ucs.* and *Cs.* I hypothesize, therefore, the following.

i Dreaming functions as a protective and imaginative (creative) "curtain of illusion" (Bion, 1965, p. 134) that rests between, as well as around, Systems *Cs.* and *Ucs.*, protecting their boundaries as well as their respective operations. Dreaming constitutes, consequently, a veritable affectively sensitive "filter" or "lens," an ongoing protective sentinel as well as mediator for our encounter with objects from inner and outer reality by *anticipating* them by virtue of their attributes based on our inherent pre-conceptions of them (the Ideal Forms) and the archive of our experiences (acquired pre-conceptions), treating the object as a prospective "antigen," as it were, for which one has an already formed a "memoir of the future" (Bion, 1991) which the object as "antigen" activates.

ii Dreaming or alpha-function comprises a gradient of cognitive as well as emotion-mediating functions or operations from the lowest (concrete) to the highest (abstract, symbolic) level. In other words, dreaming *mentalizes* concrete sense impressions (beta-elements) into ever more abstract alpha-elements.

iii Dreaming constitutes a binocular (dual-track) monitoring of the activities of Systems *Ucs.* and *Cs.*; and the "curtain of illusion," a virtual "membrane," which describes a figure-eight (or bi-spherical) pattern as it extends around both Systems, and arrives at the juncture of a point between each. That point represents the dream's "navel to the unknown" (Freud, 1900, p. 111) and constitutes dreaming's ultimate mystery, its exit into as well as emergence from its numinous origins.

iv The process of dreaming can be thought of as a "container" (Bion, 1962, p. 98) for sense impressions as well as a "holding object" (Winnicott, 1960, p. 40) or "background presence" (Grotstein, 1977) that facilitates the self's adapting to reality.

Conclusion

The acts of *perception* and *thinking* are intimately and perhaps indistinguishably linked with dreaming, which operates both in what Freud (1911) calls the primary and secondary processes. Dreaming functions or operates in Systems *Ucs.* and *Cs.* to seek to maintain awareness on a dual-track (binocular) perspective of external events *and* simultaneously of an internal process of "digestion" of the same event. Dreaming (as alpha-function) furnishes the emotional *vocabulary* (visual imagery or narremes) for dream thoughts to contain and utilize this emotional vocabulary to construct imaginative narratives, *truthful "archival fictions"* that transform and transduce the Absolute Truth about an *infinite*, cosmic, *impersonal* Ultimate Reality, O, into a tolerable, *finite*, and acceptable *personal* truth about one's own subjective relationship to one's objects in inner and outer reality. Dreaming is the protector, facilitator, conveyor, monitor, and mediator as well as dispenser of emotional Truth in the guise of fictive imagination. It is a constant security check for our cognitive and emotional life as it quietly and mysteriously triages, prioritizes, and mediates (edits) our continuing urgencies.

Part Two: The "Dreaming Ensemble"

In part one I dealt with the model of an all-encompassing protective membrane to describe the nature and functioning of dreaming. In part two I should like to reintroduce the idea that all Bion's major concepts on dreaming and alpha-function seem to perform many of the same functions from differing perspectives. The function of *transformation*, for instance, which we can correlate with the function *experience-editing* and *encoding*, seems to characterize the operations of dreaming and/or alpha-function generally, but we can see their operations in the contact-barrier, the Grid, in the container↔contained (♀♂), and in the interaction between the paranoid–schizoid and depressive positions (P–S↔D).

Dreaming as a Hologram

Put another way, Bion's theory of dreaming seems to hint at being a *hologram*, i.e. a three-dimensional image in which each pixel within the image comprises the whole image, like the chromosome located in each cell of the body. It seamlessly presumes the operation of:

i *alpha-function* (Bion, 1962, p. 6);
ii *container↔contained* (Bion, 1958, p. 69);
iii the *contact-barrier* (Bion, 1962, p. 17); and
iv the *Grid* (Bion, 1977), the latter of which acts as a cognitive sieve to grade, categorize, organize, and matriculate inchoate emotional elements into more developed thoughts and unconscious phantasies;
v the *caesura*, which divides fetal mental life from post-natal life and is also a metaphoric model used for all legitimate separations between varying aspects of the mind (Bion, 1977);

vi the theory of mental *transformations* that embraces all the above functions and operations (Bion, 1965); and
vii Bion's (1962) *binocular perspective* (p. 54) which allows for a dialectical, binary-oppositional, stereoscopic, non-linear model and a matrix for the use of dream-work in the act of dreaming.

I view each of these items as cognates, or even equivalents of each other as well as differing facets of a unified, composite function. I thus conceive of them from a *holographic* perspective, one in which each functions individually and at the same time comprises a seamless, indivisible whole, i.e. the very process of dreaming itself.

The Supraordinate Function of Dreaming

All the above dream operations comprise the supraordinating functions of:

i *creativity* or *imag(e)-ination* (creative generation of sensory (mainly visual) images),
ii narrative *editing* and/or *transformation* of beta-elements ultimately into meaningful clusters or accumulations of sophisticated alpha-elements that become visual images or narremes for narratives, and
iii a sensory–emotional filter between Systems *Ucs.* and *Cs.*

Each of the aforementioned dream functions seems to work simultaneously as well as in tandem. Alpha-function operating as an editing function includes grading (sifting, separating, differentiating, selecting) some aspects of the beta-elements, categorizing and evaluating them, and then encoding or encrypting them (mainly by the cooperative activity of the pleasure principle under the direction of the reality principle). The editing function emerges from the grading function and includes a deconstruction of the graded sense impressions (beta-elements) into their irreducible concrete *elements* and a *recombination* of them into a myriad of molecular, abstract, potential "alpha" and "meta-alpha" meanings, i.e. narratives (Ferro, 1999). Dreaming protectively obscures truth while it guards and vouchsafes its transmission as ballast within emotions. It is important to realize that Bion conflates dreaming with cognition by assuming that all thinking is ultimately inseparable from emotion.

Perception as Dreaming

Dreaming amounts to the act of *perception* with all its implications and referents, i.e. *observation, attention, interpretation, association, transference, playing, reading* (and others) which merge with the things-in-themselves (noumena) and Ideal Forms (inherent pre-conceptions) as well as acquired pre-conceptions, all of which anticipate what has been thrust upon one's sensory impressions by the stimulus—all in the service of the anticipation and categorization (formatting) of the new stimulus-object. The effect is to impart to it the quality of a *déjà-vu*, a strange-familiarity, "a memoir of the future" (Bion, 1992, p. 362).

In regard to perception Hoffman (1998), a cognitive scientist, states:

> Perhaps the most surprising insight that has emerged from vision research is this: Vision is not merely a matter of passive perception, it is an intelligent process of active construction. What you see is … what your visual intelligence constructs.
>
> (p. xii)

> Vision not only fabricates, it does so, at times, unconstrained by reality.
>
> (p. 4)

> Visual intelligence occupies almost half of your brain's cortex. … it is intimately connected to your emotional intelligence and your rational intelligence. It constructs the elaborate visual realities in which you live and move and interact. It forwards these constructions to your emotional and rational constructions.
>
> (p. 282)

Bion's (1965) concept of transformations in hallucinosis (p. 137) and reversibility of the operation of the sense organs (1958, p. 83) anticipated the current neurocognitive view that that we create (Bion would say "dream") the objects of reality as we discover them. *Furthermore, we may now hypothesize that internal objects are imaginatively created by dreaming.*

Attention as Dreaming

Attention for Bion constitutes an emotional as well as cognitive "searchlight" and a principal component of perception and therefore of dreaming. Bion (1992) states: "*How important is attention? And is it the same as I think it is, as 'dreaming' what is going on?*" (p. 139, italics mine)

Dreaming and Evasion versus Modification of Frustration

How does dreaming allow the individual to tolerate and thereby modify frustration—and the reverse, how does tolerating frustration enhance dreaming? My reading of Bion prompts the following. Central to Bion's episteme is the individual's capacity to tolerate and *modify* frustration as opposed to being intolerant and *evading* it. If the infant can tolerate frustration, it means that (s)he can effectively "dream" (hallucinate; Freud, 1911, p. 223) the image of the breast in its absence and thereby create and maintain a space (represent) for the absent breast to fill upon its return. If the infant cannot tolerate frustration, then the "no-breast" (Bion, 1965, p. 54) becomes concretized and reified as a negative, hateful object that precludes the formation and maintenance of the open mental space reserved for the return of the good breast. In this latter case the sense impressions that have accumulated, the beta-elements, must be evacuated through projective identification.

The capacity to think and dream depends, therefore, on the preservation of the open mental space.

The Use of Anagrams in Dreaming

Dreaming uses the model of the *anagram*. An anagram is: "A transposition of the letters of a word, noun, or phrase, whereby a new word or phrase is formed" (*Oxford English Dictionary*, 1971, p. 76). Dreaming likewise transposes sensory impressions into dream narratives, which, though in an altered form of the sense impressions, maintain their lowest common denominators (emotional truth) intact.

For Whose Eyes are Visual Images and Narratives Dreamed?

When one peruses Bion's work on dreaming in his various contributions, one becomes impressed by how often he alludes to the need for the dream to produce "*visual impressions.*" Why *is* dream-work concerned with means of representation and with considerations of representability? A possible answer would be to become visibly known to and retrieved, recognized, and "notarized" by an internal preternatural, numinous Intelligence or Presence within the unconscious. Bion (1992, p. 305) refers to "God" as a "demon" or "gnomon" in the mind. Bion (1970, p. 75) equates "God" with "*O*" (the Absolute Truth about Ultimate and Infinite Reality). It is my understanding that he conceives of God (as "godhead") both as a Platonic Ideal Form and also as *O*—but always non-religiously.

I nominate this God-demon as both the instigator of dreaming and, in another role, as the "audience" who receives its visual narrative results, i.e. the owner of the eyes (Grotstein, 2000). This suggests that the dream is a producer–director–playwright who must fashion the dream elements into a state of evocative visualizations so that the refashioned recombinations of alpha-elements can be visualized by an internal entity or organization that can then act upon them by relaying messages to other parts of the mental and physical self, like a "town-crier" or herald, stating that: "All is well. You may safely sleep" or "You may safely stay awake and think."

The Bimodal Nature of Dreaming

Whereas one aspect of dreaming supports the matriculation of the beta→alpha-elements into ever more developed cognitive pre-conceptions→conceptions, etc., an operation that mainly connotes the *secondary processing* aspect of alpha-function, another aspect of the dream's bimodal destiny, is one that is supported mainly by the *primary processing* aspect of alpha-function. Put another way, Systems *Ucs.* and *Cs.* support each other. *If this hypothesis is accurate, then Bion, perhaps without realizing it, is supporting the thesis that it is System Ucs., especially one's phantasy life, that constitutes the seat of psychopathology or mental health and that analytic therapeusis should preferentially be directed to the search for phantasies with the idea of recombining them with their conscious counterpart. Dreaming provides us with a story for every wound and a myth for every rite of passage.*

Bion (1992) suggests this when he states:

> α-[dream-work-α] destruction: One consequence is starvation of the psyche in its supply of reality. There is therefore *nothing that can be opposed to phantasy*. This is an additional reason for failure to wake up; there is not enough "up" to wake up to.
>
> (p. 96, italics mine)

I believe that this citation can be understood as being an affirmation of the dual, equal, and parallel roles of reality and phantasy but with the therapeutic accent being placed on the latter.

References

Barry, A. M. S. (1997) *Visual intelligence: Perception, image, and manipulation in visual communication.* Albany, NY: State U New York Press.

Bion, W. R. (1953) Notes on the theory of schizophrenia. In: *Second thoughts: Selected papers on psycho-analysis*, 23–35. London: Heinemann (1967).

Bion, W. R. (1958) On arrogance. *International Journal of Psychoanalysis*, 39(2):144–6.

Bion, W. R. (1962) *Learning from experience.* London: Heinemann.

Bion, W. R. (1963) *Elements of psycho-analysis.* New York: Basic Books.

Bion, W. R. (1965) *Transformations.* London: Heinemann.

Bion, W. R. (1967) *Second thoughts: Selected papers on psycho-analysis.* New York: Jason Aronson.

Bion, W. R. (1970) *Attention and interpretation.* London: Tavistock.

Bion, W. R. (1977) *Two papers: The grid and the caesura*, Salomao J. (ed.) Rio de Janeiro: Imago.

Bion, W. R. (1992) *Cogitations.* London: Karnac.

Brown, L. (2006) Julie's museum: The evolution of thinking, dreaming and historicization in the treatment of traumatized patients. *International Journal of Psychoanalysis*, 87:1569–85.

Burka, J., Sarnat, J. E., St John, C. (2007) Learning from experience in case conference: A Bionian approach to teaching and consulting. *International Journal of Psychoanalysis*, 88:981–1000.

Damasio, A. (1994) *Descartes' error: Emotion, reason, and the human brain.* New York: Grosset/Putnam.

Damasio, A. (1999) *The feeling of what happens: Body and emotion in the making of consciousness.* New York: Harcourt Brace.

Damasio, A. (2003) *Looking for Spinoza: Joy, sorrow, and the functioning brain.* New York: Harcourt Brace.

Ferro, A. (1999) *Psychoanalysis as storytelling,* Slotkin, P., Translator, London, New York: Routledge.

Fonagy, P. (2001) *Attachment theory and psychoanalysis.* New York: Other Press.

Freud, S. (1900) The interpretation of dreams. *Standard Edition,* 4.

Freud, S. (1900–1) The interpretation of dreams. *Standard Edition,* 5, 339–630.

Freud, S. (1911) Formulations on the two principles of mental functioning. *Standard Edition,* 12, 213–26.

Freud, S. (1915) The unconscious. *Standard Edition,* 14, 159–216.

Grotstein, J. S. (1977) The psychoanalytic concept of schizophrenia: I. The dilemma. *International Journal of Psychoanalysis,* 58:403–25.

Grotstein, J. S. (2000) *Who is the dreamer who understands the dream: The study of psychic presences.* Hillsdale, NJ: Analytic Press.

Grotstein, J. S. (2002) "We are such stuff as dreams are made on": Annotations on dreams and dreaming in Bion's works. In: Neri, C., Pines, M., Friedman, R. (eds.) *Dreams in group psychotherapy: Theory and technique,* 110–45. London: Kingsley.

Grotstein, J. S. (2007a) Personal communication.

Grotstein, J. S. (2007b) *A beam of intense darkness: Wilfred Bion's legacy to psychoanalysis.* London: Karnac.

Hoffman, D. D. (1998) *Visual intelligence: How we create what we see.* New York: Norton.

Klein, M. (1935) A contribution to the psychogenesis of manic-depressive states. *In: Contributions to psycho-analysis, 1921–1945,* 282–310. London: Hogarth (1950).

Klein, M. (1940) Mourning and its relation to manic-depressive states. In: *Contributions to psychoanalysis, 1921–1945,* 311–38. London: Hogarth (1950).

Lévi-Strauss, C. (1958) *Structural anthropology,* Jacobson, C., Grundfest, B., translators. London: Schoepf/Harmondsworth (Penguin, 1968).

Lévi-Strauss, C. (1970) *The elementary structures of kinship.* London: Tavistock.

Llinás, R. R. (2001) *I of the vortex: From neurons to self.* Cambridge, MA: MIT Press.

Ogden, T. (2001) *Conversations on the frontier of dreaming.* Northvale, NJ: Aronson.

Ogden, T. (2003) On not being able to dream. *International Journal of Psychoanalysis,* 84:17–30.

Ogden, T. (2004) On holding, containing, and being and dreaming. *International Journal of Psychoanalysis,* 85:1349–64.

Ogden, T. (2007) On talking-as-dreaming. *International Journal of Psychoanalysis,* 88:575–89.

Ogden, T. (2008) *Rediscovering psychoanalysis: Thinking and dreaming, learning and forgetting.* London: Routledge.

Piaget, J. (1951) *Play, dreams and imitation in childhood.* London: Routledge.

Sandler, P. (2005) *The language of Bion: A dictionary of concepts.* London: Karnac.

Schwalbe, M. L. (1991) The autogenesis of the self. *Journal for the Theory of Social Behavior,* 21(3):269–95.

Scully, N. (2003) *Alchemical healing: A guide to spiritual, physical and transformational medicine.* Rochester, NY: Bear and Co.

Tomkins, S. (1962) *Affects, imagery, consciousness*, vol. 1: The positive affects. New York: Springer.

Tomkins, S. (1963) *Affects, imagery, consciousness*, vol. 2: The negative affects. New York: Springer.

Winnicott, D. W. (1960) The theory of the parent–infant relationship. In: *The maturational processes and the facilitating environment*, 37–55. New York: International UP (1965).

Winnicott, D. W. (1971) The use of an object and relating through identifications. In: *Playing and reality*, 86–94. New York: Basic Books.

EDITORS' INTRODUCTION

Psychological Turbulence in the Analytic Situation

Raul Hartke

Hartke's paper, which was the plenary address from Latin America at the 2009 Bion in Boston conference, is a conceptual study of the unconscious and the emotional turbulence inherent in the analytic process that must be experienced, contained and transformed by both patient and analyst if psychic development is to occur. This turbulence, which Bion saw as an inevitable part of emotional growth, results from the need for the analytic dyad to come in contact with the "O" of the session. Hartke, following Bion, defines the latter as the "ultimate reality of the personality." In every analysis, there is a shared, powerful emotional experience that patient and analyst must face together and that touches inevitably upon areas of their individual personalities. The turbulence that follows from this individual and/or mutual evolution—and perhaps discovery—involves what Hartke calls "becoming what one is being" and produces "a sort of psychic vertigo" or existential encounter with what is truly alien and unknown in one's emotional experience and in one's self.

In order to explicate his views, Hartke traces the evolution of "O" in Bion's theory, beginning with Bion's use of Klein's emphasis upon our inherent wish to discover and know the truth, which she called the *epistemophilic instinct*. He outlines how Bion first shifted his own clinical and theoretical emphasis from a predominant concern with the vicissitudes of the drives within the body (Love and Hate, which Bion refers to as L and H links) to the role of knowledge—i.e. truth and learning from experience, which Bion called K links—in the evolution and functioning of the mind: "emotion is the kernel of psychic life ... and knowledge (K) is as primary and fundamental a link as love (L) and hate (H)."

However, as Hartke explains, Bion found that self-knowledge was always in transition and inevitably incomplete. Bion took seriously what Freud had noted in his 1915 paper on the unconscious and then again in 1923 in *The Ego and the Id*, that the repressed or dynamic unconscious was only a small portion of a larger unconscious totality that was unknowable and beyond full or immediate apprehension. It was this ineffable domain of "ultimate reality"—the "void and formless infinite, ... [that] contains the idea of *something essential that is unknowable and unlimited*"—that Bion, drawing upon the inspiration of poets, philosophers and mystics called "O."

As Hartke explains, for Bion, O

> refer[s] to everything that is outside the domain of the psyche, whether it be because it belongs to external reality—impossible to be known as such, in itself—or to the reality of the experiential self, which is distinct from the self grasped by the self-reflective thinking of the individual .... From a psychoanalytic vertex, O designates the ultimate reality of the personality, the "real" self, something central to emotional experience, a personal essence, which cannot be self-reflectively known, but, as Bion says, we can only "become."

It is this attempt to address the "transformation" or psychic movement of continual evolution and "becoming" rather than the search for hidden or otherwise disguised psychic contents that is behind Bion's insistence on an analytic listening stance that attempts to eschew memory and desire and an interpretive readiness to move via induction, inspiration and intuition beyond empiricism and sensorially-based deductive understanding. To further explicate his views, Hartke turns to chaos theory and the arts in search of approximations for the ineffable and offers a clinical illustration in a moving case vignette of a male patient who had lost his father and an examination of the reverberating impact of this loss upon both patient and analyst.

6

PSYCHOLOGICAL TURBULENCE IN THE ANALYTIC SITUATION

Raul Hartke

> The psycho-analytic problem is the problem of growth and its harmonious resolution in the relationship between the container and the contained, repeated in individual, pair, and finally group (intra and extra psychically).
>
> (Bion, 1970, pp. 15–16)

> Of all the hateful possibilities, growth and maturation are feared and detested most frequently.
>
> (Bion, 1970, p. 53)

> Mental evolution or growth is catastrophic and timeless.
>
> (Bion, 1970, p. 108)

In 1965, when Bion introduced the idea of "transformations in O" he provided us with the concepts needed to understand both the constant conjunction of elements bound together by the designation "psychological turbulence" and the conditions under which emotional growth may take place. His innovation presented us with a real "messianic [i.e. revolutionary] idea" (Bion, 1970), one that undoubtedly mobilizes turbulence in the reader and requires from each of us our own transformation in O, so that we can intuit and possibly accept what Bion is attempting to explicate for us. In other words, what is required to understand this concept is nothing less than an example of the very thing that is being examined! In this chapter, I shall attempt to explain, establish the foundation for and develop this proposition and summarize a few of the contributions and vicissitudes in Bion's thinking, which I find decisive for understanding the more specific and profound meaning of the concept of psychological turbulence.

From 1963 onwards, Bion's theory made explicit his view that emotion is the kernel of psychic life (Meltzer, 1983) and knowledge (K) is as primary and fundamental a link as love (L) and hate (H). In accordance with this view, several basic psychoanalytic concepts beginning with the theory of the "dream work alpha" (Bion, 1959) were modified or even reformulated from the perspective of K, rather than seen only or predominantly under the vertices of L and H, altering our understanding of the very purpose and technique of psychoanalysis. For example, the object, instead of being simply a "service object" (Meltzer, 1983), i.e. gratifying or frustrating the needs of the self, became a "provider of meanings"—originally a breast, which favors "understanding, experience and wisdom" (Bion, 1962, p. 11).

In Freud, the Oedipus complex involves the conflict generated by the child's *love* for one of its parents and the correlated *hatred* for the other. According to Bion (1957), the vertex of K "makes sexual crime a peripheral element of a story in which the main crime is Oedipus' arrogance when he swore that he would unveil the truth at any price" (p. 101). Thus, from the perspective of K, it is the arrogant investigation of truth towards an envied parental couple that gains prominence, and, in infantile fantasy, risks punishment in the form of mental confusion, madness and dementalization for this act of hubris (*Hybris*).

Additionally, from the K perspective, the unconscious may be seen to be more than a reservoir of erotic and destructive instincts. For many analysts, it becomes the domain of the as yet "undiscovered" or "unevolved," which does not necessarily originate in the individual himself (Bion, 1965, p. 171). Furthermore, in addition to the anxieties regarding loving and hateful desires classically described by Freud and Klein, the K vertex has allowed us to recognize and study what is possibly the most fundamental anxiety—the fear of a radical loss of meaning of emotional experience that can arise out of the helplessness of a human being as a thinking being—which Bion (1962) called "nameless dread."

With this new dimension in mind, the goal of analysis shifted and began to aim primarily at the expansion of the mental container, instead of seeking to work predominantly on uncovering the contained (i.e. its unconscious contents (Ferro, 1995)). With this shift, many interventions now explicitly aim to *create* the unconscious by incrementally strengthening the patient's alpha function.

Bion's postulates about O as "ultimate reality" (Bion, 1970) and the transformation in this ultimate reality that he called "transformations in O" constitute a radical step in his work, which I would consider equivalent to what, in Freud's thinking, many French analysts called "the turning point of the twenties." The latter referred to the introduction of the death instinct and the structural theory. For Bion, we might even call it the "turning point of 1965," shown and made explicit from chapter 10 of "Transformations" (1965) onwards. Metaphorically speaking, it is as though Bion had, until then courageously explored and ventured along the path of K—flanked by those of L and H—in order to suddenly see that path end abruptly, in the face of something unknown and impossible to understand with the tools available in the domains of K, L or H. And this, before having reached the desired goal!

But what is this unknowable something? In order to formulate and communicate it, i.e. in order to be able to present it to those who are still in the domain of K, Bion borrowed freely from the formulations of philosophers, poets and mystics. Particularly illuminating and evocative to me is the philosophic formulation of Kant concerning the thing-in-itself, as distinct from the phenomenon, together with the poetic expression of Milton, "void and formless infinite," because each contains the idea of *something essential that is unknowable and unlimited.* As I understand them, they refer to everything that is outside the domain of the psyche, whether it be because it belongs to external reality—impossible to be known as such, in itself—or to the reality of the experiential self, which is distinct from the self grasped by the self-reflective thinking of the individual. It is this "everything outside the domain of the psyche" that Bion (1965) refers to as the "ultimate unknowable reality," the "truth," and calls O.

From a psychoanalytic vertex, O designates the ultimate reality of the personality, the "real" self, something central to emotional experience, a personal essence, which cannot be self-reflectively known, but as Bion says, we can only "become."

Meltzer (1988) attempts to give a personal clinical meaning to O when, from an aesthetic, psychoanalytic vertex, he describes the essentially mysterious interior of the aesthetic object which may only be conceived by imaginative conjectures. This interior differs from the exterior, in that it is only the latter that is perceptible to the organs of the senses. Matte Blanco (1998) offers a related view from a mathematical psychoanalytic angle, with his postulates concerning the unconscious as "infinite sets."

I think that considering this angle of O at least helps us recognize and value the fact that in analysis our understandings (K) and interventions do not reveal unique and definitive truths. But this would only constitute its simplest implication.

Once Bion postulated O, his thinking in the consulting room turned to something that transcends emotional experience. Thus, he underlined the difference between *knowing "phenomena"* (such as the emotions, which can be objectified and named) and the *process of becoming a "reality,"* as, for instance, the reality of the self, or some aspect of it. Bion refers to this latter process as a change from K to O or K→O transformation, and describes it as the only kind of transformation that catalyzes the movement from the simple accumulation of knowledge about oneself to true emotional growth. This movement implies contact with a "multi-dimensional experience" (Bion, 1970, p. 71), with a "formlessness in which the potentiality for all distinctions exists" (Bion 1965, p. 167) and from which one or the other dimension may develop in the domain of K, thus enabling us to preserve it in the mind, and possibly, think it.

It is perhaps more appropriate to say that this is a process that enables one to "become what one is being," and not "what one is," due to the *ceaseless becoming* which characterizes life, countering the idea of a permanent and immutable being disguised as a God (Prigogine, 1993). I would also emphasize that the goal of "becoming what one is being" is distinct from the classical goal of "insight" (Richfield, 1954) insofar as it opens to the mystery of the thing-in-itself, instead of seeking to reveal an unconscious secret (Meltzer, 1988; Hartke, 2008).

Perhaps we can intuit something of the meaning and importance of this K→O transformation for personal development through an experience lived through and described by Rosalyn Tureck, the great American Chicago-born pianist, who is considered one of the greatest interpreters of Bach:

> Just before my 17th birthday I had an experience which changed my whole life. I had already learned many of the Preludes and Fugues of the Well-Tempered Clavier and was continuing to learn three each week, in order to complete the entire "48." I had begun work on the A minor Prelude and Fugue from Book I, when, having perceived its materials in its exposition section, I suddenly lost consciousness. I don't know for how long it was, but when I came to, I had a whole new insight into Bach's music. I suddenly understood that the realization of Bach's structures in performance required a whole new way of thinking about musical form and structure. I realized at that very same moment what this new concept consisted of, and also that a totally new performance technique had to be created to this concept of form and its detailed structures. I also perceived clearly at the same time what that technique entailed in the actual physical keyboard approach .... All this was so very different from the traditional approved ways, that it took me three days to learn only four lines. This new concept involved multi-leveled perceptions and their clear fulfillment in performance. These produced a profound change in my musical thinking and in my keyboard approach.
>
> (Tureck, 1999)

Did Tureck, in that transformative moment, intuit the O of Bach's music? Certainly, a simple hysterical dissociative episode could not have produced this intuition! If we can consider this experience as an example of a transformation in O, we must ask ourselves how often in our consulting rooms do we approach something with these characteristics and this dimension? Does each real psychic change, no matter how small, necessarily imply something analogous to this situation described by Tureck? Even without obviously involving a concrete loss of consciousness, such transformations imply an *essential discontinuity* in the usual way of apprehending the self and reality. Could it be for this reason that Bion (1975) compares the development of the personality to an onion—with layers of different skins—instead of to a piece of elastic, which is progressively stretched?

It is important to recall that O is not something exceptional or occasional. In the words of Bion (1970) it is the "central feature of every situation that the psycho-analyst has to meet" (p. 89). The rarest kind of experience involving O—in my view—is the K→O transformation, which he called "becoming O." Be that as it may, I consider that the acceptance and use of Bion's postulates regarding O and the K→O transformation as a basis for coming to personal maturity requires from analysts the same process of transformation: from only "knowing about" what it is to really "becoming" what it is.

But have we really apprehended and managed to use the dimension and depth of this proposition by Bion in our consulting rooms?

It is in the context of the postulate of O and the K→O transformation that we will encounter the meaning and importance of what Bion calls "psychological turbulence," which he presented in chapter 12 of *Transformations*, and took up again later in other of his writings (Bion, 1970, 1977a). In order to allow ourselves the possibility of being open to movements from K to O in the consulting room, according to Bion (1970) we need to renounce the ego functions that are habitually used and are essential in the domains of K—i.e. memory, desire, understanding and sensory perception. The active, disciplined exercise required in discarding these mental resources that are so precious and have been so laboriously achieved during the course of development, necessitates such a great belief in the existence of ultimate reality, such a disposition to receive and accept whatever is manifested during this state and such complete trust in our internal objects (Lópes Corvo, 2002) that Bion (1970) refers to this movement beyond K as an "act of faith" (p. 32).

What is required of the analyst may be experienced as a serious attack against the ego (Bion, 1970), and for this reason, from the vertex of K or, to continue the metaphor that has already been presented, observed from the abrupt end of K's path, may be perceived as a frightening abyss. In order to express the fear that this mobilizes, Bion (1965) borrows the metaphor of the three "dark nights of the soul" described in "Ascending Mount Carmel," by the Christian mystic, St. John of the Cross. It also recalls Pascal's phrase "*Le silence de ces espaces infinis m'effraie*" (The silence of these infinite spaces terrifies me), and also the drawings of turbulent whirlpools in the water and of untidy hair present in the *Sketches* of

Leonardo da Vinci. Thus, Bion states that turbulence is also a characteristic of O itself.

In *Attention and Interpretation* (1970) Bion compares the emotional state of this transformation in O to the dread that is aroused in Coleridge's poem, "The Ancient Mariner," by the feeling of the "frightful fiend" (p. 46) closely following the steps of a frightened traveler walking along a lonesome road. Bion explains that this terror is related both to the search for truth and to the defenses activated against it; and he distinguished this from the painful experiences generated by the unresolved conflicts of the analyst, i.e. the countertransference. For me it is in chapter 12 of *Transformations* (1965) and in this passage of *Attention and Interpretation* (1970) that the definition of psychological turbulence acquires its more radical, specific and profound meaning. I conceive of psychological turbulence as a sort of *psychic vertigo associated with the leap in the dark unknown towards* O *and to the contact itself with* O, which needs to be contained in order for the "change from learning to growth" to occur, as the subtitle of *Transformations* (1965) says.

I consider it essential to highlight and preserve this *denotative* kernel of the concept of psychological turbulence to avoid the risk of its dilution and banalization enabled by the different *connotative* aspects contained in the term, "turbulence." Thus, a hurried reading of the 1977 text of "Emotional Turbulence" may erroneously lead to its generalization, reducing it to the anxieties that can always be aroused by contact between people, because of the increase in libidinal (L) and destructive (H) instincts along the lines already described by classical psychoanalytical theory. In contrast, according to Bion (1965) the fundamental reason for all resistance is precisely the fear of psychological turbulence triggered by the threat of a transformation in O. It is for that very reason, that maturation is feared and hated.

As a defense against this fear, i.e. as a barrier against turbulence, recourse is taken to memory, desire, understanding and sensorialization in order to prematurely saturate our pre-conceptions, and avoid the K→O transformation. When these barriers are erected, analytic interpretations are accepted only within the scope of K, i.e. as an expansion of knowledge, and as a means to avoid becoming what one is being.[1]

The important thing to highlight for the present purposes is that, in terms of Bion a container–contained relationship will always be involved. Some transformations of O in the domain of K, perhaps at the limits of K appearing as a "messianic idea" (Bion, 1970), will have to be contained by a thinker. It should also be emphasized that, for Bion (1970), the messianic idea or new thought does not have to be of the individual himself who is about to contain it, as proposed by classical psychoanalytic theory. It can be a stray thought, without a thinker, a thought with the name of the author, but not yet thought by its host (such as Bion's postulate about O, for instance), or even a wild thought (Bion, 1977b).

In the analysand or in the analyst, i.e. intrapsychically, the container that will have to contain this idea will be the mind of each person, with its already existing dispositions or pre-conceptions, or, in yet other words, with its stable and constant aspects of personality, with the internal "establishment" (Bion, 1970). In the pair, patient and analyst will be able to function, each sometimes as contained, sometimes as container. In any case, for growth to occur it is necessary that the link between the new idea and thinker be symbiotic, in that it favors growth both for the contained and the container (Bion, 1970). And it is precisely when a symbiotic relationship approaches—in the individual or in the pair—i.e. when the "discovery" of the new idea by the thinker approaches, that a "critical situation" emerges (Bion, 1970, p. 118) along with the defenses against it. This "critical situation" is a configuration of phenomena which, in my view, contains some of the elements constituting the psychological turbulence and that are, at the same time, apprehensible in the consulting room. The defenses against this situation consist, ultimately in replacing the symbiotic link by another link that is commensal or parasitic, intra-psychically or between the analysand and the analyst.

Bion (1970) proposed that the individual needs to "be ready" to produce a "flash of genius" (p. 74) in the sense of generating and welcoming a really new idea about himself and his reality, even at the risk of giving rise to a catastrophic change (Bion, 1965). As such, the function of the analytic work is to favor the conditions for the emergence of the new idea, i.e. of this representation of O at the limits of K. This implies the capacity to contain the aforementioned "critical situation" that arises precisely at the time when this new idea is about to be "discovered."

According to Bion (1970) an important tool of an analysis (I would add the analysis of any theory or concept) is the correlation and confrontation of different vertexes. But this correlation and confrontation can only occur when the difference between the vertexes is not excessively small or overly large.

Bearing in mind this idea, I consider that the so-called thought of complexity (Morin, 2008) and many of the theories that can be related to it may constitute a rich source of metaphors to generate new vertexes to approach the issues discussed so far.

Thus, for instance, as regards the characteristics and conditions of the onset of the flash of genius, as well of the turbulence associated with it, I metaphorically use the notion of the "edge of chaos" proposed by the theoreticians of the so-called "complex adaptive systems" (Waldrop, 1992; Lewin, 1993; Kauffman, 1995). These systems consist of a very large number of independent agents with multiple possibilities of mutual interactions. They tend spontaneously to self-organization as an emerging property. They are adaptive, i.e. they record and use evolving events actively and advantageously. They can function in a stagnated form, i.e. in an order frozen by a point attractor, in a slightly more dynamic state influenced by periodic attractors, as well as in a chaotic condition, depending on the so-called strange attractors. But also, and characteristically, they tend to turn spontaneously to a level of functioning called the "edge of chaos" that finds a fine balance between stagnation and disordered turbulence, between frozen order and chaos. This is the point of maximum creativity and adaptability of the system, sustaining an optimized dynamic balance between stability and flexibility and permanently generating new, absolutely unpredictable forms. According to the fortunate expression of Atlan (1986), this point exists "between crystal and smoke." A crystallized state completely preserves information, but is not flexible. Smoke, in turn, unceasingly takes on new forms, but does not record or inscribe them in any way.

My conjecture (Hartke, 2004) consists of metaphorically dealing with the situation generated by the meeting of the analytic pair (as well as the mind of each of them) as a complex adaptive system, taking as its constituent agents for this purpose, the "assembly of internalized objects" described by Klein (Baranger, 1976, p. 68) or, in Minsky's terms (1985), each person's "society of the mind," interacting internally and with the other.

As such, under appropriate conditions, the relationship would present the intrinsic tendency to turn towards the edge of chaos, i.e. to the point of its maximum creativity. However, since we have a capacity for consciousness, i.e. of perceiving that we perceive, we become anxious at the proximity or the manifestations of chaos and turbulence. Furthermore, the characteristics of functioning of the conscious mind, essentially based on the logic of the secondary process, would make it impossible to apprehend our own mental functioning at the aforementioned edge of chaos. For these reasons, the analysand, the analyst and the pair that they constitute, or rather, the complex adaptive system that they generate, tend to remain defensively fixated, more or less this side of the edge of chaos, towards crystallization. In other words, the system tends to change from non-linear to linear. I think that Freud's psychoanalytic theories are best applied only to the latter situation, i.e. when the system is distant from the edge of chaos. But, the existential challenge to the ego, as Green also proposes (2005), is to "navigate between chaos and sclerosis" (p. 104).

Goodwin (2001), a biologist who uses the theory of complex adaptive systems in his research, suggests that the play of children described by Winnicott (1971) constitutes an example of creative functioning at the edge of chaos. And Winnicott (1971), in turn, considers psychoanalysis a specialized form of playing in the service of communication with oneself and with the other.

I consider that the basic instruments of the analytic technique tend to bring the functioning of the analysand, and, above all of the pair to the edge of chaos, although this is not usually conceptualized in this way. I refer to free association, free floating attention, and to Bion's proposition that analysts attempt to achieve a mental state without memory, desire, or understanding. I also include the emphasis given here to the use of open, non-saturated interpretations (Ferro, 1995) and to the "exploration" of dreams, distinct from their interpretation proper (Meltzer, 1983). Bearing in mind this same objective, I favor more and more what could be called, in analogy with the *squiggle game* proposed by Winnicott (1968), the "verbal squiggle game" with the analysand, and see the latter, along with the exercise in discarding memory, desire and understanding, as fundamental aspects of analytic technique. Besides, movement towards the desired limit of chaos in the analytic space is favored by Bion's conception that the objective of analysis is the asymptotic expansion of the mind towards O (the space probe model, Bion, 1970), instead of making explicit unconscious contents that would account for a given psychic phenomenon.

It is clear that this movement generates the anxieties that I have already mentioned, and therefore rouses defenses in the analysand, the analyst and the pair. It is at this point, in my opinion, that new ideas emerge, the flash of genius, in a characteristically unpredictable, random way. And it is thanks to these moments that changes and evolution arise in the relationship, which can then be introjected by the analysand (and by the analyst), in such a way as to promote internal change, and, above all, to expand the capacity to contain the anxieties generated by the approach of the edge of chaos.[2]

Turbulence, in this context, would involve both the need to denude ourselves of the logically ordered mind to be able to reach the edge of chaos, and the proximity, at this point, of the frightening chaotic whirlwind, i.e. the smoke in the beautiful metaphor proposed by Atlan (1986), which can be considered equal to madness in human beings.

Bion speaks of the need for constant oscillation between order and disorder, when he refers to the PS↔D oscillation, so essential for psychic development together with the container–contained operation. And the "selected fact" would emerge precisely in the transition from PS→D, favoring the appearance of the latter, i.e. of integration, until a new and necessary PS fragmentation occurs. But does this proposition highlight and favor the existence and crucial importance of the edge of chaos along the lines proposed by the model of complex adaptive systems? This and other issues, in my opinion, can be fruitfully raised and expanded with the help of the new vertexes mentioned above.

Curiously Poincaré, one of the great inspirations of Bion, took an interest in the study of turbulence at the end of his life (Ruelle, 1991). Besides the well-known idea of "selected fact," Bion bases his entire theory of transformations on the topological geometry discovered by the great French mathematician. But Poincaré had no way of building a theory of turbulence, because he did not yet have at his disposal the appropriate mathematical tools. They only appeared in the 1960s of last century, with chaos theory (Capra, 1996), which Bion does not appear to have used more consciously and consistently, and which is considered by many as a sort of subset of complexity (Lewin, 1993). Thus, when we use metaphors extracted from thinking about complexity, could we not perform a sort of *aggiornamento*[3] of some of Bion's ideas, in the light of this new epistemological horizon?

As regards the issue of the ultimate unknowable reality, I would use as a vertex for correlations and confrontations, the Santiago theory of cognition (Capra, 1996, 2002) proposed by the Chilean researchers Maturana and Varela (1984). It constitutes a hard blow to so-called "representationism," i.e. to the conception that knowledge involves a more or less faithful representation in the mind, of something that exists on the outside independent of the observer. According to Maturana and Varela (1984) we make a world appear through "acts of distinction," which depend absolutely on our self-organized and autopoetic structure. Could it have any repercussion as regards Bion's postulate of O?

I will now present a clinical situation. I would, however, like to underline that it is not a direct illustration of the Bionian ideas presented and discussed in this paper. It only represents the form and degree to which I have internalized them at this time. In terms of Bion (1965) himself, it is *my* transformation of his O. Furthermore, it certainly reflects the presence of my own psychic structure as well as the inspirational influence of important figures in my analytic training: my analyst, supervisors, teachers and several other psychoanalytic authors. Finally, I think that the situation is useful to present a moment in which—it seemed to me—I myself "became" what I was being. I do not have any way to assure that the same happened to the patient, although it seems to me that indeed it did, because of subsequent developments.

Mr. A is about sixty-five years old and has a long history of skin allergies, variously diagnosed and treated for many years, as well as frequent episodes of rhinitis. He sought treatment at the suggestion of relatives, but recognized that he had been feeling a lack of motivation for work and had become irritable at any small thing. After evaluation I proposed that we begin with two sessions a week, intending to eventually increase the frequency to three. Actually, after some time we had to reduce it to one session a week, because the patient said that he simply could not stand a greater frequency. I clearly felt that he would end treatment if I insisted on keeping up the previous rate, and thought that too frequent a meeting schedule would be inappropriate for his psychopathology, in which *operational functioning* as described by Marty (1990) predominated. For this reason, even though this report is not an example of a standard analytic process, I consider that it will serve my present purposes.

The sessions, which, in my opinion, are rather characteristic of this type of patient, were generally filled by factual reports of the week, and above all, by description of his symptoms. I would portray the treatment as initially feeling like a vast desert, with a few oases, in the sense of a vast majority of arid sessions dedicated to the laconic description of facts and clinical symptoms, with a scarce few others—like the one I will now report—that were emotionally richer. Often when I would open the door to receive Mr. A, I would find him pacing restlessly in the waiting room. On some occasions he asked to end the session before time was up. Very often, after the session began, a difficult situation would arise, as though we had nothing further to discuss, and we had arrived at a sort of *neutral* position. I would then feel pressured, or more likely, feel the need to ask a few questions about some topic discussed, trying to ask them as openly as possible. But the feeling has generally been like trying to get water from a stone. Retrospectively, I realize that on such occasions I was (and often at times still am) initially taken by a disagreeable feeling of risking a lack of motivation on my part, of switching off and losing interest in the session or even the patient. I feel as though I have to inject life and vitality into the relationship. It is at that moment that I mentally review the topics that Mr. A may have mentioned before, and ask for explanations or ask open questions (when I can). In short, I try somehow to get the relationship out of that neutral point. I even notice that my voice becomes more emphatic, more reactively alive.

Currently I think that on such occasions it is as though the signs of the *essential depression* described by Marty (1990), with its characteristic loss of libidinal tonus, of vital energy, without any positive economic counterpart, become manifest in our relationship. My reaction, in turn, consists in lending my own libido to the patient in order to try to inject some life into the relationship.

Gradually I have perceived that at certain times of greater emotional density during the sessions, or at least, when everything indicates that this density may occur, Mr. A often begins coughing.

During a session in the month of March, which ended up developing differently from usual, Mr. A entered the consulting room and, instead of sitting in the easy chair, as he usually does, went directly to the glass window right behind it, pointing and looking at an upside-down red triangle affixed there only a few days before. What is written there is: *Alternate exit. Use only with a firefighter's ladder.* He remarked that recently he was also required to affix the same kind of triangle in his office. Indeed, he added, the firefighter's inspector is always visiting his facilities, each time demanding some new preventative measure, equipment or architectural modification. He even thinks that sometimes the inspector wants to receive a bribe to ease up on the inspections, although this has never really happened. Mr. A made several remarks about this, and added that actually, when someone really needs the firefighters' service, the trucks are broken down, the hosepipes and pumps do not work and the ladders cannot be used. He wonders what is done with the tax money we pay. Slightly contaminated by his latter remarks I imagine myself needing to use that alternate exit, and not finding any ladder available. What would I do then? Jump? Fall flat on the ground four floors below?

As though following the same line of thought, Mr. A, mentions that if we really needed to use that exit, it is unlikely that we would be able to count on a firefighter's ladder to pick us up. Then I remember the recently ended summer vacation (in February), during which I did not see him. I think how much, deep inside, he may have felt abandoned by me. I know, in this sense, simply establishing connections, that these thoughts would not find any echo in Mr. A. Consequently, I just say that these kinds of things, i.e. paying taxes, undergoing frequent inspections, and even then not being sure of receiving appropriate help when necessary, usually make people angry. Mr. A agrees and then talks about other things that make him angry: the way that things are today in his field of work no one is really reliable, everyone wants things done, but they do not accept that someone would ask them to do what they should, and so on. I ask him and hear him talk about recent examples of situations of this kind. He then shows me how the allergies on his hands and legs are. I pay attention to what he is showing me, but when he shuts up, I tell him that earlier on he was talking to me about things that made him angry. He talks again about the firefighters, telling several of the things he was obliged to do recently. I listen attentively and even ask him to explain some of them. He then complains about an unfair lawsuit against him in labor law by an employee who stole from him. I continue listening and sometimes ask him about the subject that is being discussed. We talk about how important it is, and how one misses people whom one can really trust. Then, suddenly, he tells that he had a dream a few nights ago and reports the first dream since the treatment began more than six months ago.

"I dreamt"—he said—"that I was seeing my father wearing his usual hat in front of a pickup truck. It was the kind of truck he always loved having. My mother and my older brother were next to me. I point at him in surprise and tell them 'look at father, over there,' but they tell me that they could not see him."

I ask him whether this dream makes him think of anything else, but he peremptorily says no, that it is only a dream. His father died about ten years ago. It occurs to me, I don't know why, to ask him in what month that happened, and, a bit surprised, he answers that it was in March, but that he cannot remember the exact day. He then agrees with my remark that there might be some relationship between the dream and the month of his father's death. He recalls his mother's death at age ninety, which occurred a few months ago, after a long illness. I then remind him that he was concerned about the health of his older brother, and that, therefore, he appears to have dreamt of losses and fears of losses.

A long silence begins. Suddenly I feel a strong emotion inside myself, and remember that my own father died in March, a few years ago. I miss him, and vividly recall a few occasions in childhood shared with him that also involved cars. When I was still very small, for instance, at the approach to the garage behind our house, he used to put me on his lap and let me hold the steering wheel as though I were driving. It was an unforgettable feeling. My emotion increases and I begin to wish that the session will end soon, so that I can get out of this situation, because I fear that my feelings will become uncontrollably intense. This makes me think of the *window as alternate exit through which to escape in case of fire.*

Other memories come to my mind. Mr. A had already told me that his father had helped him at the beginning of his professional career. I recalled the support that I always received from my father, and the feeling of emotional security and protection that he offered. A curious thought then suddenly occurred to me: "Mr. A is not seeing these memories that I have of my father, just as in his dream the others did not see his father". Then intensively, clearly and at the same time in passing, ineffably, I felt something that seemed to lose all meaning and density when I now try to remember it and put it into words.

Although it is very difficult to describe, it was something like a totality that at the same time contained an infinity of dimensions and perspectives. I experienced myself as a son who had already lost his father, a father with daughters, a son and a married adult. I felt the reality of no longer having a father in the external world together with the depth and intimacy of keeping him in my mind. I was a son, father, analyst, and also the partner of my patient in the common feeling, intimately shared without being revealed. Solitude, internal company, loss and gratitude, freedom and responsibility: all of this at the same time. And I could continue, distinguishing and expressing an infinite number of other feelings, without managing to transmit the total experience of the moment. I hope that every reader will manage to evoke in himself some situation in which he has already had this experience. Could it be that Mr. A, in his deep silence, just then was experiencing something similar? I would never be able to know, but I had the impression that indeed he was.

I next became aware of sitting in the easy chair, which, at that time, seemed even more familiar and comfortable to me, an old acquaintance. And I also realized that I no longer felt the need for the alternate exit from the premature end of the session. What reliable lap or laps, such as those in childhood, were now supporting me internally, providing me with some security amidst such an intense situation? My former analyst? The supervisors and teachers I had? My family?

Finally, having slightly recovered emotionally, and bearing in mind all of these internal movements, I asked Mr. A: "Do you still miss him?" "Yes. Very much," he immediately answered. "How can that be, doctor? After so many years, one is already getting along in years and missing one's father. But I do miss him. And how!" I only say: "One does."

I realize that now we are using the term "one," as though sharing the same emotion, but I leave it at that, first of all because I had already verbalized it without noticing. But then also because I considered that it was an expression used colloquially, in the sense that it is what all people feel. We are in a dense silence; I would say a respectful, shared silence. Then I hear him say: "The strange thing is that in the dream, only I saw him. My mother and brother did not!" And I sort of hear myself answering him: "Maybe, Mr. A, because when the people we like die, we can keep them inside us, in our memory and in this place where only we see them." This is followed by a new, deep silence. "I understand," he says moved. And after being quiet for a few minutes he ends: "I agree with you."

And so we ended the session with the usual handshake, which, however, that day for some reason seemed to me more significant, more ... alive, and silently shared. This marked the beginning of a profound process of working through his grief at the loss of his father, with extensive positive repercussions in his life. It also involved analytic work with his ambivalences, oedipal competitions, etc., including interpretations of psychic defenses and contents, but these aspects go beyond my present aims.

Does the situation that occurred in the session I have reported really have something to do with O? Or, at least, with the unforeseeable and random emergence of something new, which could promote, metaphorically speaking, a "quantum leap" in the session and in the therapeutic process? In order to understand it, would we need these concepts of Bion? Does it at least illustrate the proposition that psychological turbulence is an inevitable concomitant of psychic growth in the contained and in the container? However we might try to formulate or describe the session, it constitutes an attempt to exemplify the form in which I try to work as much as possible without memory, desire and understanding, and with the game of "verbal squiggles." It should be emphasized that I consider the unexpected recall of my father's death in March as a *remembering*, instead of a *memory*. A remembrance that, for Bion (1970), constitutes something "essential for the evolution of the emotional reality of the session" (p. 107), as opposed to memory.

Finally, I wish to close with a passage from chapter 23 of *Moby-Dick* by Herman Melville, entitled "The Lee Shore." In this chapter Melville describes in an intensely evocative way the turbulence and terror that assail us when we seek the profound thought, the infinite and tempestuous ineffable truth.

> Wonderfullest things are ever the unmentionable; deep memories yield no epitaphs; this six-inch chapter is the stoneless grave of Bulkington. Let me only say that it fared with him as with the storm-tossed ship, that miserably drives along the leeward land. The port would fain give succor; the port is pitiful; in the port is safety, comfort, hearthstone, supper, warm blankets, friends, all that's kind to our mortalities. But in that gale, the port, the land, is that ship's direst jeopardy; she must fly all hospitality; one touch of land, though it but graze the keel, would make her shudder through and through. With all her might she crowds all sail off shore; in so doing, fights 'gainst the very winds that fain would blow her homeward; seeks all the lashed sea's landlessness again; for refuge's sake forlornly rushing into peril; her only friend her bitterest foe!
>
> Know ye now, Bulkington? Glimpses do ye seem to see of that mortally intolerable truth; that all deep, earnest thinking is but the intrepid effort of the soul to keep the open independence of her sea; while the wildest winds of heaven and earth conspire to cast her on the treacherous, slavish shore?
>
> But as in landlessness alone resides highest truth, shoreless, indefinite as God—so, better is it to perish in that howling infinite, than be ingloriously dashed upon the lee, even if that were safety! For worm-like, then, oh! Who would craven crawl to land! Terrors of the terrible! Is all this agony so vain?

Obviously the question remains of knowing whether in these turbulent situations, at these critical moments, we will founder, as Bulkington, and above all like Captain Ahab, obsessed by the exclusive desire for vengeance, i.e. by saturated memory and desire, or, whether on the contrary we will survive like Ishmael, managing to put our travels on the mysterious oceans of the mind into words.

Will all this turbulence be in vain?

Notes

1 In terms of the grid (Bion, 1963, 1971), the analysand and/or analyst make use of "concepts" (Row F) to utilize them as column two.

2 It is perhaps these moments that are related to what Stern et al. (2000) call "moments of meeting."

3 That is, updating.

References

Atlan, H. (1986) *Entre o cristal e a fumaça. Ensaio sobre a organização do ser vivo.* Rio de Janeiro: Jorge Zahar, 1992.

Baranger, W. (1976) *Posición y objeto em la obra de Melanie Klein.* Buenos Aires: Kargieman.

Bion, W. R. (1957) On arrogance. In: *Second Thoughts.* London: Heinemann, 1967.

Bion, W. R. (1959) Dream-work-α. In: W. R. Bion. *Cogitations.* London: Karnac, 1992.

Bion, W. R. (1962) Learning from experience. In: Bion, W. R. *Seven servants—Four works by Wilfred R. Bion.* New York: Jason Aronson, 1977.

Bion, W. R. (1963) Elements of psychoanalysis. In: Bion, W. R. *Seven servants—Four works by Wilfred R. Bion.* New York: Jason Aronson, 1977.

Bion, W. R. (1965) Transformations. In: Bion, W. R. *Seven servants—Four works by Wilfred R. Bion.* New York: Jason Aronson, 1977.

Bion, W. R. (1970) Attention and interpretation. In: Bion, W. R. *Seven servants—Four Works by Wilfred R. Bion.* New York: Jason Aronson, 1977.

Bion, W. R. (1971) The grid. In: *Two papers: The grid and caesura.* Rio de Janeiro: Imago, 1977.

Bion, W. R. (1975) Caesura. In: *Two papers: The grid and caesura.* Rio de Janeiro: Imago, 1977.

Bion, W. R. (1977a) Turbulência emocional. *Revista de Psicanálise da SPPA*, 7–3, dezembro 2000: 447–57.

Bion, W. R. (1977b) Untitled. In: *Taming wild thoughts.* London: Karnac, 1997.

Capra, F. (1996) *A teia da vida.* São Paulo: Cultrix, 1997.

Capra, F. (2002) *As conexões ocultas. Ciência para uma vida sustentável.* São Paulo: Cultrix, 2005.

Ferro, A. (1995) *A técnica na analise infantil.* Rio de Janeiro: Imago.

Freud, S. (1915). The unconscious. *Standard Edition,* 12.

Freud, S. (1923). The ego and the id. *Standard Edition,* 19.

Goodwin, B. (2001) *How the leopard changed its spots: the evolution of complexity.* Princeton: Princeton University Press.

Green, A. (2005) *Key ideas for a contemporary psychoanalysis.* London and New York: Routledge.

Hartke, R. (2004) Criatividade e expansão psíquica no limite do caos: a mente como um sistema adaptativo complexo. Trabalho apresentado no "Simpósio Bion" ocorrido em São Paulo, Brasil, 2004.

Hartke, R. (2008) A vida onírica e o trabalho analítico: entre o segredo e o mistério. Trabalho apresentado no Simpósio "O Pensamento vivo de Donald Meltzer," promovido pela Sociedade Brasileira de Psicanálise de São Paulo, 2008.

Kauffman, S. (1995) *At home in the universe: The search for the laws of self-organization and complexity.* New York: Oxford University Press.

Lewin, W. (1993) *Complexidade: a vida no limite do caos.* Rio de Janeiro: Editora Rocco, 1994.

Lópes Corvo, R. E. (2002) *Diccionario de la obra de Wilfred R. Bion.* Madrid: Biblioteca Nueva.

Marty, P. (1990) *La psicosomática del adulto.* Buenos Aires: Amorrortu, 1992.

Matte Blanco, I. (1998) *The unconscious as infinite sets. An essay in bi-logic.* London: Karnac.

Maturana, H. R. and Varela, F. J. (1984) *A árvore do conhecimento. As bases biológicas da compreensão humana.* São Paulo: Palas Athena, 2001

Meltzer, D. (1983) *Vida onírica: Una revisión de la teoria y de la técnica psicoanalítica*. Madrid: Tecnipublicaciones, 1987.
Meltzer, D. and Williams, M. H. (1988) *The apprehension of beauty*. Strath Tay: Clunie Press.
Melville, H. (1851) *Moby Dick ou, A baleia*. Tradução: Irene Hirsch e Alexandre Barbosa de Souza. São Paulo: Cosac Naify, 2008.
Minsky, M. C. (1985) *The society of mind*. New York: Simon & Schuster.
Morin, E. (2008) *Ciência com consciência*. Rio de Janeiro: Bertrand Brasil.
Prigogine, Y. (1993) *As leis do caos*. São Paulo: Editora da UNESP, 2002.
Richfield, J. (1954) An analysis of the concept of insight. *Psychoanalytic Quarterly*, 23: 398–408.
Ruelle, D. (1991) *Acaso e caos*. São Paulo: Editora UNESP, 1993.
Stern, D. N., Sander, L. W., Nahum, J. P., Harrison, A. M., Lyons-Ruth, K., Morgan, A. C., Bruschweilerstern, N. and Tronick, E. Z. (2000) Mecanismos não interpretativos na terapia psicanalítica. "Algo mais" além da interpretação. *Livro Anual de psicanálise*. XIV, 197–214.
Tureck, R. (1999) A portrait. Booklet of CD *Johann Sebastian Bach: Goldberg variations*. Hamburg: Deutsche Grammophon.
Waldrop, M. M. (1992) *Complexity: The emerging science at the edge of order and chaos*. New York: Simon & Schuster.
Winnicott, D. W. (1968) *O jogo do rabisco*. (Squiggle game). I: Winnicott, C., Shepherd, T., Davis, M. (eds.) Explorações psicanalíticas. Porto Alegre: Artes Médicas, 1994.
Winnicott, D. W. (1971) *O brincar e a realidade*. Rio de Janeiro: Imago, 1975.

EDITORS' INTRODUCTION

Reflections on Non-Dreams-for-Two, Enactment and the Analyst's Implicit Alpha-Function

Roosevelt M. S. Cassorla

This chapter, which won the Parthenope Bion Talamo award for best paper at the 2009 Bion in Boston conference, continues the author's (Cassorla 2005ab, 2008ab), earlier examination of the central role played by Bion's (1962ab) concepts of *waking dream thoughts* and *alpha-function* in the analytic transformation of unconscious phantasies. In the optimal clinical situation, a mutual, unconscious, intersubjective process develops between analyst and patient, in which each evokes waking dream thoughts in the other. This resonance, which Cassorla terms *dreams-for-two*, depends upon the analyst's intact alpha-function, is most evident in work with neurotics, lies at the heart of the analytic working relationship, guarantees that the analysand will be the analyst's "best colleague" (Bion, 1980) and is the engine of analytic progress.

In contrast, patients with significant psychotic areas of their personality, who possess a tendency towards massive and intense projective identification, often reveal pseudo-dream-like phenomena that Cassorla calls *non-dreams-for-two*. In the latter, although dream-like states may evolve, the analytic couple colludes unconsciously to evacuate painful experience rather than tolerate and transform it in the service of psychic growth. If the analyst is unaware of failing to dream a patient's evacuative non-dreams, enactments, unconsciously initiated by analysand, analyst or the pair may follow. These can become chronic, choking off any possibility of emotional growth.

Through careful clinical examples, Cassorla describes and illustrates how, by regaining contact with his *implicit alpha-function* that has been temporarily sidelined by the analysand's forceful projective identifications, the analyst's capacity to dream his patient may be restored.

7

REFLECTIONS ON NON-DREAMS-FOR-TWO, ENACTMENT AND THE ANALYST'S IMPLICIT ALPHA-FUNCTION

Roosevelt M. S. Cassorla

The objective of this paper is to go more deeply into reflections presented in previous articles (Cassorla, 1995, 2001, 2003, 2005ab, 2007, 2008abc) on the topics of dreams, dreams-for-two, non-dreams-for-two, enactments and the analyst's implicit alpha-function. Following Bion's theory of thinking (1962ab, 1963, 1992), it is expected that in an ideal analytic situation a *dream-for-two* will occur, where the term "dream" refers to waking dream-thoughts (the product of alpha-elements) that evidence transformations of primordial unconscious fantasies and beta-elements. This dream corresponds to Row C of Bion's grid (Bion, 1963, 1977), together with myths and night dreams.

When a patient is capable of dreaming, we are in the non-psychotic area of the patient's personality (Bion, 1957), an area that is capable of forming symbols. Dreams, then, present a plot or story that stimulate the analyst, who through his capacity for reverie and alpha-function, lets himself be led by the emotional expressivity of the scenes the patient describes and has his own dream in response. The analyst's dream, told back to the patient, re-molds and expands the symbolic net, giving rise to new meanings and revealing new currents, as the analyst points out, or undoes defenses that the patient was not aware of. The patient, who can be described as the analyst's "best colleague" (Bion, 1980; Ferro, 1996), in turn, by re-dreaming the dream told by the analyst, shows the analyst the effect of the analyst's work, and so on. In a well-functioning analytic process, both members of the analytic dyad dream and are dreamed in alternating sequence and at the same time.

Meltzer (1983) has described this process as follows:

> What seems to happen is that the analyst listens to the patient and watches the image that appears in his imagination. It might cogently be asserted that he allows the patient to evoke a dream in himself. Of course that is his dream and will be formed by the vicissitudes of his own personality. […] From this point of view one might imagine that every attempt to formulate an interpretation of a patient's dream could imply the tacit preamble, "While listening to your dream I had a dream which in my emotional life would mean the following, which I impart to you in the hope that it will throw some light on the meaning that your dream has for you."
>
> (p. 90)

Note that even though the analyst's dream is an attempt to dream the patient's dream, the dream clearly belongs to the analyst, since factors related to the real person of the analyst are involved, and they are all the more necessary to the extent that the patient's own capacity to symbolize is diminished. The less the patient is able to symbolize, the more will be required of the analyst.

Grotstein (2000, 2004) makes a similar point when he notes that the analyst is prompted, or called upon, to respond to the analysand's emotions and associations by means of his own personal emotions. Working in a state of reverie and employing alpha-function, the analyst uses his own emotions and experiences to resonate with the patient's emotional truth. In this way, the emotional truth of *both* participants become unconsciously identified and brought together, indicating the clinical truth of the moment as "common sense" (Bion, 1963).

Depending on the vertex of observation, dreams that take place between the members of the analytic dyad, can be considered as belonging to the patient, to the analyst, or to both. The concept of analytic field (Baranger and Baranger, 1961–2) indicates that nothing happens in one of the members of the dyad without the participation of the other and that what really matters is the emotional experience that takes place between the two persons and what is done with it (Bion, 1962b). Ogden's (1994ab) concept of analytic third and Ferro's (1992, 1996, 2009) notion of affective holography stress this perspective of the third, which co-exists in a dialectic relationship with the individual perspectives of the analyst and analysand. Thus, no matter what the perspective may be, we can state that both patient and analyst are involved in dreams-for-two.[1]

When the patient is unable to symbolize or does so inadequately, we are in the psychotic area of the personality (Bion, 1957). Here, patients find it impossible to dream and may evidence this mental state by discharges into acts, behavior, symptoms, speech, as well as by transformations in hallucinosis (hallucinations, omniscience, beliefs, fanaticism, delusions, etc.) (Bion, 1965). At such moments, the analyst listening to the patient may especially suffer the consequences of the patient's massive projective identifications in the form of mental pain, symptoms, difficulties in or blockages of thought, accompanied or not by pictograms (Barros 2000, 2002, 2005) or outlines of scenes. When such outlines exist, they are weak and without emotional resonance, and they may indicate contact with non-symbolic areas, glimpses of symbols, and sometimes symbolic equations, all of which pressure the analyst's mind to search for meaning. I suggest using the term *non-dreams* to refer to these evacuations.[2]

The analyst must let himself be invaded by these evacuations in order to allow himself to experience the patient's projected aspects. They induce the analyst towards exercise of his alpha-function, so that at the same time, or even later, he can separate himself from them and unmask them, thereby giving them meaning. This first happens through the creation of images (alpha-elements) that, in turn, pressure the analyst to create new and more complex forms of representation (narrative sequences), that especially rely upon the use of words.

In early stages, or even later, the analyst may not be able to find such representations. The scene continues in a search for meaning, while the analyst maintains his negative capability (Bion, 1970), waiting for verbal symbols to spontaneously arise. When they do, these, in turn, attract new symbols—be they images, sensory symbols or, most often, verbal symbols—which expand meaning. The mental landscape is thus broadened, opening up experience to new symbols, connections and meanings, with greater emotional development and richness of the work of the analytic dyad. Scenes and plots that occur on the analytic stage grow and become more sophisticated, in an endless process that generates meaning in a continuous expansion of the mind. Implied here is a process which Imbasciati (2001) calls *symbolopoese*, and which takes place in what Ferro (2009) referred to as a constantly expanding "oneiric holographic field." This process represents adequate functioning of the analyst's thinking apparatus, whose origins are the result of the dream-work-alpha (alpha-function).

Dreams and non-dreams are in fact extreme ideals on a continuum related to the capacity for mentalization,[3] symbolization and a functioning of the mind that may either encourage or attack this capacity. They are also related to the transformation of beta-elements ↔ alpha-elements and the PS↔D positions. Between these extremes, we find dreams that are reluctant to broaden their meanings, mixtures of dreams and non-dreams, dreams that are transformed into non-dreams, non-dreams that (in varying degrees) are almost dreamed, dreams that cover up non-dreams and vice-versa, non-dreams that emerge as nightmares, concrete non-dreams that simulate dreams, non-dreams that slipped by unnoticed in the past and that are recovered when the patient becomes able to symbolize, etc.

As noted above, the analyst must sustain the negative capability of not-knowing that is a part of non-dreaming, as he tries to achieve a new transformation via his dream-work. At times, this may not be possible due to failures of technique, limitations in alpha-function and/or because the patient's non-dream has mobilized some of the analyst's own areas that had not been sufficiently dreamed in his personal life (i.e. counter-transference). And, if these troublesome areas had already been dreamed, they could not bear being re-dreamed. Thus, the analyst's "indigestion" due to absorption of the patient's raw elements tends to involve aspects of both members of the dyad.

In these situations, not-knowing may be experienced as a persecutory internal object, leading the analyst to appeal to what is already known, such as memories, desires, theories and beliefs, not because they are "true," but to appease or escape from the persecutory object. This substitution of the unknown for the already known is also favored by the un-neutralized presence of the destructive superego from the psychotic part of the personality (Bion, 1959). The latter is moralistic and omniscient and prone to attack any not-knowing, by prematurely transforming it into the pseudo-knowledge of the already known. This process often resembles manic and obsessional reparative states that cover up melancholic and persecutory aspects. Another possibility that I shall discuss in detail below is that non-dreams-for-two may lead to unconscious collusions and enactments.

Clinical Considerations

The stimulus for this paper began with the observation of analytic situations that initially seemed to be progressing favorably, but were then abruptly and unexpectedly beset by unanticipated difficulties.[4] Upon reflection, the analyst came to realize that certain phenomena that at first appeared due to errors, were in fact related to the breakdown of an unconscious, obstructive collusion that had developed and that the phenomenon in question could be divided into three stages:

Phase 1. The analyst realized he had a difficult patient, but felt satisfied with the progress, even though he was dealing with strong obstacles to mental growth. Relying on his analytic function, he was certain that, with time, the obstacles would be understood and undone. So he continued working with positive expectations.

Moment M. Suddenly, the analyst found himself surprised at an intervention that he made and initially considered inopportune, an unthought-out discharge. He felt embarrassed and confused, frightened and guilty. He questioned his own sanity and felt as if he had been taken over by an unfamiliar force, had not been his usual self. Faced with the failure of his analytic function, he was concerned that he had harmed the patient and feared that the patient would retaliate in some way or even leave the analysis.

Phase 2. But nothing of the sort happened. On the contrary, after this intervention, the analytic process became more creative and the emergence of new material indicated an expansion of the symbolic net of thinking.

Upon retrospective study, the analyst realized that his initial impression—that the analytic process was going along well (Phase 1)—was incorrect. In fact, the analysis had become stagnated in several areas and in ways that he had failed to perceive. What then were the factors that blinded the dyad to the stagnation of the process in Phase 1? What were the origins of the untoward discharge (Moment M), and the subsequent events that made the analytic process productive (Phase 2)?

Initially, the most striking characteristic of this type of patient is an aggressive flood of complaints and lamentations. In contrast to patients who do not elaborate upon and associate to their suffering with specific ideas, these complaints describe scenes, stories and accounts in the analytic field in such a way as to allow the analyst to assume that he is dealing with both daydreams and night dreams. Past and present objects, fantasies, and situations come up in these "dreams" that are assumed to be responsible for the patient's suffering. At times, the analyst is manifestly included in the story and it is easy to assume that a vital analytic process is taking place.

But the process is soon disturbed by other manifestations that become predominant. The analyst realizes that his interpretations are being devitalized, denied or converted into persecutory aspects. He then assumes he has failed to understand, but was not sufficiently convinced of this fact. This type of patient cannot bear to enter into contact with facts of reality, and thus resorts to attacks on linking (Bion, 1959), and on the analyst's mind. Prior to this reassessment, the analyst may have felt comfortable and seemed sure that he was operating on familiar terrain. However, in retrospect, he recognizes that he has failed to notice the concomitant force of non-dreams in the patient. That is, primitive areas (non-dreams) that announce their presence through blocked off and repetitious discharges or themes that fail to instigate in him sufficiently creative images or ideas. As the analyst tries to dream these non-dreams of the patient, the patient attempts to turn the analyst's dreams back into non-dreams.

Dealing with this situation, the analyst feels unable to dream, and runs the risk of appealing to memories, desires, beliefs and theories. Since he can perceive this risk and has the power to prevent it, he feels certain that he can maintain his analytic capacity. He thus imagines he is working, simultaneously, with:

1 Dreams of the patient that, re-dreamed by the analyst, constitute dreams-for-two.
2 Dreams and non-dreams of the patient that, dreamed by the analyst, are attacked and transformed into non-dreams and are therefore worthless for thinking.
3 Non-dreams of the patient that the analyst is trying to dream without much success. He is aware of the risk of seeing his ability to analyze impaired.

Even though the work may seem sterile most of the time and the analyst may feel attacked in his analytic capacities, he continues to be interested in experiencing and understanding the patient's obstructive mechanisms. The feeling of being challenged also encourages the analyst. He feels that the analytic process is being as productive as possible and that obstacles are part of the difficulties encountered in areas where the patient's ability to dream and think are blocked. He is certain that, if he remains patient and maintains his negative capability (Bion, 1970), he will eventually undo the obstacles that he is encountering. This assurance is corroborated by other facts: the patient shows no desire to discontinue analysis, the analyst feels the patient emotionally close to him and there are phases when dreams-for-two do occur and make the work gratifying (i.e. some areas of productive work do occur).

During the latter phases, the analyst has the impression that mental expansion is going on, but he is sometimes surprised, as he wonders whether this is really the case. An outside observer, however, would probably say that he does not notice this progress and suggest that an obstructive collusion was occurring that had resulted from non-dreams-for-two (chronic enactment) that were not perceived by the analyst.

To illustrate, I will describe part of a session that took place at the beginning of the third year of analysis of a young woman, whom we will call L., who was living with her parents and was working with four sessions a week.

Phase 1

This particular session took place after a long weekend, during which, despite all of L.'s inhibitions, fears and phobias, she had gone on a trip. She seemed desperate as the session began, saying she had so much to tell about the trip and that the session would not be long enough. She was not doing well, not well at all—the trip had been terrible. She then began rattling off an endless litany of complaints in a tone of voice that emphasized their gravity and was obviously meant to convey to the analyst how much she was suffering. She said it had all been very tiring, hours of travel, very hot. She couldn't sleep, she felt very nervous before the trip and almost gave it up altogether. The hotel was horrible, the food was awful and she herself continued to feel unwell, checking her blood pressure hourly. She did not know how she managed to see anything, but when she did go out she felt isolated, and her fellow travelers were extremely unpleasant. She returned home from her trip in the wee hours of the morning on the day of the session. She was still sleepy and would never take another trip, and so on.

The analyst felt invaded by the patient's complaints. He tried not to become confused by the unpleasant, irritating feelings that took over the analytic field, but it was hard not to be overwhelmed. Various interpretations came to his mind, but he felt that they were all inadequate. They would be too theoretical, without resonance, and he discarded them as soon as they came up.

Then, a particular image came to his mind, of an instrument of torture that pulverizes everything into ashes. It was at this moment that he decided he had to put the brakes on. He interrupted L.'s complaints and pointed out that he had felt that an "instrument of torture," was in operation, and that it "ground everything up and transformed it into shit."

The patient was not pleased with this intervention, but then neither was the analyst. He felt that his tone of voice had sounded too angry and he was astonished to hear himself say "shit," since that was not his usual way of talking. L. complained vehemently that he was not letting her speak, that she was not being allowed to complain and even shouted at the analyst and accused him of shouting at her.

The analyst told L. that he thought she was shouting at him so she could continue to complain and that it would be better if they could think together about what was going on. In reply, L. said the analyst did not believe in her suffering, and detailed her complaints even further in order to convince him of the reality and intensity of her misfortunes.

The analyst then pointed out the patient's mistrust and her difficulty in seeing things positively. For example, despite all the difficulties, it had been her first trip in many years. (As he said this, the analyst realized he was trying to draw her attention to a "good side" in order to escape from the persecutory anxiety, and this made him feel even more inadequate.)

Apparently L. did not seem to hear the analyst, but he was nevertheless surprised at the emergence of new and somewhat different material. She recounted that when she arrived home from her trip that morning, she did not find her mother in the house and became alarmed. Without thinking about it consciously, the analyst heard himself say: "And did you think you'd killed her?" "Yes," she answered, that was exactly what she had thought. But then she went to take a shower, opened the bedroom door and saw her mother asleep in bed. "But she [the mother] pretended not to hear me," the patient added.

The analyst asked how she knew her mother had heard her. And she explained that she had made a lot of noise when she came into the house. L. took up her complaints again, and the session continued.

At the end of the session, the analyst silently realized he had survived, like the patient's mother, and that he would have to continue putting up with the "noise" until selected facts came up, without "pretending" not to hear her.

Moment M

Four months after the session described above, the following occurred:

L. transformed one of the analyst's interventions by distorting it, felt persecuted and, as a result, attacked him. She did not hear what he had to say and insisted stubbornly that he was accusing her unjustly and talking gibberish. She shouted at the analyst and he found himself awkwardly on the defensive, wanting to convince her that she was misconstruing him.

At that moment, without thinking, the analyst noisily hit the arm of his chair with his hand and interrupted L., shouting louder than she was. He complained that L. was not letting him speak and was not listening to him. L. suddenly stopped shouting and said, quite calmly and with an air of triumph and irony that the analyst had gotten upset with her and had shouted.

The analyst replied that she was right. He had really gotten quite angry. He was only human after all. He added, "It's just as well that I am able to get agitated, otherwise you'd just make me agree with everything you say and I'd be afraid of you. I'd be dominated, and you wouldn't have an analyst any longer." For the remainder of the session, both patient and analyst remained silent.

Afterwards, the analyst felt inept, embarrassed and guilty and was certain that he had not sustained his neutrality in the face of L.'s attacks due to shortcomings in his capacity to analyze. He was concerned about his lack of control and the repercussions it might have for L. He feared that he may have discharged unknown or reactivated mad parts of himself and wondered if he would be able to continue being a psychoanalyst. He imagined that L. suffered because of his actions, prepared himself for a terrible retaliation and feared she would discontinue the analysis.

Phase 2

Given what had happened, the analyst felt guilty and anxious, and was moved by a desire to mend things. Contrary to what the analyst expected, however, the patient neither left analysis nor retaliated and the analytic relationship seemed to become closer and more creative. There were fewer complaints and lamentations, L. seemed able to dream and think more consistently and the analyst felt listened to and respected.

Initially, he wondered if L. was sparing him, because she felt him weakened, and if the attacks would soon resume, but this was not the case. L. was not only less violent, but she came even closer to the analyst and showed a stronger capacity to observe what was happening to her and in the analytic situation. The same thing was true for the analyst. He realized that he was not being spared. The attacks continued, but his statements were listened to and they had an effect. Both members of the dyad could then dream together and the symbolic net of thinking was expanded.

The study of clinical situations of this type shows that the new recollections that patients often produce in Phase 2 refer back to traumatic situations experienced in early life, situations that had never been dreamed before, or at least not so clearly. Such situations can often be linked to situations experienced with the analyst that were being relived in the analytic relationship.

In the case of L., the analyst noted that the expansion of mind in Phase 2 went far beyond what, during Phase 1, he had imagined possible. She brought in new memories and night dreams related to situations of helplessness, including her mother's psychiatric hospitalizations and suicide attempts, as well as threats of separation from her parents. L. also described a traumatic childhood episode, which she had never brought up before, where she arrived home one day and could not find her mother anywhere in the house. She then imagined that her mother had died, and panicked. She could not breathe and called for medical assistance.

The analyst speculated that the patient had experienced a situation of this type during Moment M, and while L. agreed, she did not sound convincing. But, with time, new elements came up that made Moment M more understandable, as we will see below.

Reformulation (Reversal of Perspective)

In view of these new and unexpected facts, the analyst was obliged to modify his original hypotheses. Since the analytic process had become stronger after Moment M, with better expansion of the patient's capacity to think, the analyst realized that his initial perception that the process during Phase 1 had been productive was incorrect. He had been paralyzed and the dyad was involved in a sadomasochistic collusion, in which the patient was attacking the analyst, and the analyst, in an attempt to be tolerant, became a suffering victim.

This new, and opposite, perception made the analyst aware that he had been the victim of *reversed perspective* (Bion, 1963). What had appeared to be dreams of the patient being dreamed by the analyst were, in fact, *false dreams-for-two*. The patient's compliance served to devitalize the analyst's interpretations and unrecognized, defensive idealization had alternated with moments of violence. The analyst had been blind to this collusion, even though he had, at times, felt a certain discomfort. But the discomfort was not enough for him to "open his eyes."[5] Moment M, which seemed to be the result of the analyst's failings, proved to be just the opposite. The earlier collusion had been undone and the analyst was no longer being attacked or seduced by the patient. There had occurred what Symington (1983) referred to as "the analyst's act of freedom."

Enactments

Many contemporary authors (e.g. Jacobs, 1986; Ellman and Moskovitz, 1998; Bateman, 1998) refer to Moment M as an enactment. This term was coined in the United States in the late 1980s[6] to refer to abrupt action that involves both patient and analyst and opposes the work of the analysis. Enactment differs from acting out in that it always includes the analyst. In acting out, the analyst is a mere observer. In contrast, the analyst participates in enactment, subject to his own transference and blind spots.[7]

In another text (Cassorla, 2005a), I showed the analogy between enactment and concepts such as "actualization" (Sandler, 1976), "bastions" (Baranger and Baranger, 1961–2), "mutual effective recruiting" (Joseph, 1989) and "sterile container/contained relationships" (Bion, 1970). There, I suggested that enactment be understood on the basis of difficulties in the capacity to think. Obviously, this is a question of unconscious phenomena that are undone when they are replaced by thought.

I classify enactment as acute when the discharge is instantaneous and intense, as at Moment M, and chronic when discharges are maintained over time and weigh down the analytic process, as during Phase 1. Previously, I proposed that both were products of non-dreams-for-two, but I now see that *non-dreams-for-two occur mainly in chronic enactment*. This point will be taken up in greater detail below.

As was seen above, Phase 1 non-dreams-for-two (or chronic enactments) are expressed through unchanging scenes and situations that do not involve important visual components. On those occasions when a visual component is present, it is precarious or without movement. The material has no meaning; there is no space for connections, no emotional resonance for new connections and the analyst is swallowed up by the situation and unable to realize what is going on. These are situations where the relationship between container and contained is parasitic and sterile and the two members of the dyad annul one another.

Chronic enactment shows the strength of excessive projective identifications that induce the analyst to play certain roles that maintain the status quo and prevent psychic change, since any such change is felt by the patient as catastrophic. The analyst does not notice that his mind is being numbed, and takes as "real" what is actually the result of massive projective identifications. As Bion (1961) described,

> I can only call a temporary loss of insight, a sense of experiencing strong feelings and at the same time a belief that their existence is quite adequately justified by the objective situation without recourse to recondite explanation of their causation.
>
> (p. 149)

Subsequently, Bion (1962a) related these facts to the effect on the analyst of the patient's beta screen, which stirs up emotions in the analyst and nurtures the reaction that the patient unconsciously desires, thus destroying the analyst's ability to think.[8]

From the perspective of their potentiality, chronic enactments include clues that may show us the genesis of non-dreams, obstacles to the capacity to think, reversions of the alpha-function and the destructive functioning of the mind. In order to dream non-dreams, the analyst must identify within himself the obstacles that impede and sabotage his capacity to symbolize and think, since he is expected to live them out at-one-ment (Bion, 1970) with the patient.

Chronic enactment can only be undone when it is identified, and this identification takes place at the same time as the analyst recovers his ability to think. This happens in two situations: a) when the analyst detects a certain discomfort in other areas of his mind, a situation that leads him to propose a "second look" (Baranger et al., 1983) at what is happening; b) when the enactment becomes acute. We will examine this latter situation after presenting a second clinical example.

Patient T.

Patient T. was a young man, whose relationship with the analyst oscillated between phases when T. behaved in a violent, destructive and attacking manner and phases when he was cooperative, bringing forth rich material that allowed for fruitful work and amplification of his mental universe. The analyst identified at once a certain pattern: following phases of creative evolution, there would be a surge of attacks that attempted to ruin the achieved progress. During those phases, T. would try to show that he did not need analysis. The analyst did not feel knocked down by his destructiveness and understood those displays as evidence of borderline functioning. Work appeared to proceed in a productive fashion, forwards and backwards, in ways that were understandable within the transference. Sometimes, the analyst would surprise himself by eagerly awaiting T.'s arrival and regarding him as an "interesting" patient. Such feelings caused him to wonder occasionally whether the analytical process might not be going "too well" and if he was overlooking certain negative aspects.

Around the middle of the third year of analysis, the analyst moved his consulting room from his home to a building occupied exclusively by medical offices. T. had been informed of the move weeks in advance and they had been exploring fantasies regarding this subject. The analysis seemed to be progressing in an atmosphere that while turbulent, was felt to be just creative enough.

In the first session at the new consulting room, T. arrived looking upset and seemed almost psychotic, as he had been in the beginning of the analysis years before. The analyst felt beleaguered and frightened. T. would neither lie down nor sit in a chair. Standing up, he said in an aggressive manner that he was quitting the analysis. His confused and repetitive speech was jagged and impervious to all questioning. The analyst understood, with some difficulty, that T. was complaining of having been disrespected in regard to the change of the consulting room, but his reasons were unclear. The ferocity of T.'s resentment made the analyst fear that T. might assault him. Feeling very uncomfortable and with no idea of what was going on, the analyst stepped back towards a couple of chairs he used for interviews, and sat down in one of them. By doing that, he distanced himself from the couch and from his own chair. T. remained standing next to the door he had not bothered to close, protesting in challenging tones and threatening to leave. The analyst feared that T.'s shouting would be heard throughout the building.

Seizing a momentary break in the patient's flow of words, the analyst managed to tell T. that he did not understand why he was in such a state and asked him to explain his accusations. He had to raise his voice so that the patient would really listen to him. At once, T. walked away from the door and toward the second interview chair, and sat facing the analyst. Despite the latter's uneasiness, he was aware of being curious to make sense of the situation. The fear remained that the patient might suddenly get up and leave the room, not allowing him time to gather a few clues. While the patient was speaking, the analyst went to the door, shut it, and returned to the chair, where he sat again in front of the patient.

Gradually the analyst began to understand that the patient complained of having been misled, because he was not told that the new consulting room was in a medical building. The patient was disgusted by the "horrible and filthy building and by the sick children that amble through the hallways." He found that unbearable. Moreover, the receptionist was unfriendly and incompetent, the stairway was gloomy, etc. The patient complained that he should have been warned about "all this" by the analyst before the move.

In reply, the analyst tried to say that he had told T. that the new office was in a building, but T. interrupted him, saying, yes, he was told it was a building, but not that it was a private medical practitioners' building, which meant everyone there was just after the money. He went on criticizing the building (the ugly paint on the walls, the hideous plaque with the analyst's name on it, etc.), all the while insisting that he is done with the analysis. In response, the analyst began to feel that T. wished to leave, because the patient no longer trusted him.

Little by little, the analyst managed to formulate an intervention. After one or two attempts he was able to interrupt T. and tell him that he did not agree with the charge of deception. T. was now listening. The analyst proceeded, saying that T. was right about not having been told it was a medical building and he wished to know why T. was so upset by that fact. Was T. afraid of feeling very ill?

T. replied that it was not that. Luckily he did not know any of the doctors in the building, and, even if he did, he could always say that he was there to take part in a group study. T. then reiterated that he was disappointed with the analyst and was leaving. The session time ended and the analyst told T. that the matter remained unresolved and that he expected him to come to the following session. T. left crossly.

After the session, the analyst felt strained and guilty, knew that he made mistakes and feared that he was missing some blind spot due to countertransference problems. Initially, he concluded that he had missed something important regarding the communication of the change of address and that his mistake had made the patient suffer unnecessarily. He also fleetingly grasped that he felt bothered at having left his analyst's chair, behind the couch, for the interview chair.

To the analyst's surprise, however, in the sessions that followed, T. brought rich symbolic material, particularly dreams followed by fruitful associations. Contact was made with fantasies and memories and themes emerged of abandonment, separation, disappointment and intrusion, none of which had emerged with such abundance previously. T. recalled relocations that his family had been forced to make, due to his mother's job, and which entailed a constant separation from childhood friends. Behind each move was always his mother's ambition to make more money, and nobody was allowed to question her decisions. Those circumstances were being relived in the analysis by the analyst's change of address. T. felt forced to leave the analyst's home, where he imagined himself part of the family, for a place that was felt as unpleasant and hostile. He now described that he had never been able to rely on his mother, who was a strange and aloof woman. There arose also childhood memories, facts or fantasies, related to threats of sexual intrusion. It became possible, little by little, to reassign a meaning to these aspects, which then became part of the symbolic web of thought.[9]

Further Clinical Observations

Before the above digression on enactment, two reversed perspectives were described. In the first, during Phase 1, many of the supposed dreams and non-dreams that seemed to occur in the analytic field were in fact non-dreams-for-two, which we can correlate with and which express chronic enactments. The analyst's certainty that his forbearance with L. had always been beneficial was a mistaken belief, a transformation in hallucinosis (Bion, 1965). With T., the analyst realized there had been a seductive collusion that had made the analysis gratifying, but which also masked stagnation in certain areas.

The second reversed perspective took place when evaluating Moment M (acute enactment), which seemed to be the result of non-dreams. In fact, at this Moment M, the earlier collusion was being undone. The analyst simultaneously discriminated himself from the patient, recovered his ability to think and established a mind of his own (Caper, 1998).

In each clinical example, once the two reversed perspectives were undone, the analyst realized that even when disconcerted by Moment M, he had somehow been able to describe and interpret what had happened. In the case of L., when the analyst had shown himself to be a person who could get nervous, he also showed that his patience was not as omnipotent it had appeared to be. In addition, the patient realized that the analyst could take care of himself and not be destroyed, and so became more at ease with the violence of his destructiveness. The seductive collusion with T. was undone when the analyst was able to discuss fantasies related to the change in address. T. imagined himself as being part of the analyst's family, living symbiotically in his idealized home. This fantasy negated separation, exclusion and envy, until the change in the office location forced an abrupt disruption to an unconsciously imagined symbiotic attachment. Recognizing these sequences helped the analyst understand that acute enactments, while often causing immediate explosions in the analytic field, may also mark the prelude to useful interpretations.

The analyst's first impression had been that, at Moment M, he had been acutely and intensely involved in a non-dream, which then subsequently was turned into a dream. In fact, the apparent non-dream already had the components of a dream. It consisted of thought in action, which attracted other thoughts and was the reference for the analyst's subsequent interventions, broadening the symbolic net. This dream that occurred between patient and analyst also conveyed and concealed aspects of a non-dream, which, blending in with the dream, expressed its need to be dreamt. We can thus assert that acute enactment vividly expresses transformations in dreaming.[10]

Another fact that attracted the analyst's attention was that, after he understood the Moment M, the patients' associations led to the identification of real or imaginary situations of a traumatic nature, such as exclusion, disappointment, violence and intrusion. These facts and the transformation of chronic enactment into acute enactment led the analyst to formulate the hypothesis that if, during Moment M, a traumatic fact emerges, then this fact may have been silently present during the previous chronic collusion in Phase 1. In other words, if we take Moment M (acute enactment) as illustrative of catastrophic change, can the invariant elements of the pre-catastrophic (Bion, 1965, 1970) phase be identified?

Chronic Enactments and Traumatic Dreams

In both chronic enactments and traumatic dreams, one comes across the endless repetition of a scene, with no amplification of meaning, indicating a non-dream. The difference is that in traumatic dreams there is a manifestation of extreme anxiety, which does not occur during chronic enactment.

However, as has been pointed out, anxiety *does* underlie chronic enactment, although it does not manifest itself and goes unnoticed by both members of the analytic dyad. So might a function of chronic enactment be the bottling up of anxiety?

In one sense, traumatic dreams are frustrated searches for signal anxiety (Freud, 1926), a function, which, if it were not impaired by the traumatic situation, would activate defenses against the trauma. In fact, trauma (intense internal and/or external stimuli) constitutes itself as trauma precisely because the mind (the symbolic net of thought) is impaired to such an extent that it is rendered unable to set off the signal anxiety necessary to catalyze defensive protection. Without the latter, the mind may lose its capacity for representation and symbolization. A hole sets in, a terrifying non-mental void. Mental pain is experienced that mirrors the menace of nothingness, of the unnamable—annihilation anxiety or nameless dread (Bion, 1962b). Thus, we can say that a traumatic non-dream encompasses the repetition of the traumatic situation in a frustrated attempt to dream it. To the extent that the patient's mind (alpha-function) is disabled or injured, it is the analyst who must dream the non-dream.

We can thus regard chronic enactment as a non-dream-for-two with bottled up anxiety, in which the traumatic situation is "frozen" and unable to manifest itself openly. At some moment (M moment), the chronic enactment explodes and gives way to acute enactment. This shift indicates a reliving of the trauma, which had been frozen, and a release of the bottled up anxiety, and both abruptly take over the analytic field, where they become potentially available for analytic transformation. It is, therefore, via the shift from chronic to acute enactment (the realization of Moment M) that the analyst can come to realize that he has been involved in an obstructive collusion, a chronic enactment. The collusion that supported the chronic enactment encloses a set of phenomena related to traumas, such as terrifying affects born of annihilation anxiety, mnemonic traces of impact, samples of impaired mental functions, and defenses against the perception of these aspects,[11] which had become frozen. Acute enactment indicates that the frozen block has dissolved, allowing the trauma to be relived in an acute manner. The analytic field is intensely and violently overtaken by affective explosions involving detachment, abandonment, intrusion, separation, annihilation, etc. In other words, acute enactment is a sign of a psychological catastrophe where the trauma is relived in the analytic field.

This reliving, however, no longer needs be traumatic to the extent that, after Moment M, the analyst is able to understand, interpret and reassign meanings to the trauma, even when this process is not altogether conscious at the beginning. Phase 2 contains connections that can be noticed and thought and indicates that part of the patient's injured mind could be repaired, with restoration of the symbolic function and expansion of the patient's mental world.[12]

From this perspective, it now becomes clearer why the analyst feels guilty for his role in precipitating the acute enactments. He fears that his presumed faults have contributed to re-traumatizing the patient by breaking down the defenses against the trauma, which had been frozen into chronic enactment.

Implicit Alpha-Function during Chronic Enactment

During the phase of chronic enactment, the traumatized patient avoids being re-traumatized by "clinging" to the analyst and encouraging him to take part in the chronic enactment. This grip is similar to that of a drowning person toward his rescuer—so frantic that both are paralyzed. The immobilized analyst must not be intrusive, but neither should he give up on the patient, since these extremes are the two traumatic situations par excellence. When the patient paralyzes the analyst (and the analyst lets himself be paralyzed), the analytic process comes to a standstill.

The questions deserving further investigation at this point are:

1 What factors are responsible for the patient's and the analyst's sudden acquiring trust in the possibility of reliving the trauma and relinquishing of their holds?
2 Why does the trauma remain frozen as chronic enactment?

I believe that the trauma emerges through acute enactment, at a given moment (neither before nor after), when the analytic dyad unconsciously understands that enough mental function has been restored/achieved in the dyad and/or restored to the patient so that the latter may bear and handle the relived trauma. To further hypothesize how this recovery of mental functioning in traumatic areas occurs, we must examine in detail aspects of the analyst's work during chronic enactments. This will show us that, despite being blind to his involvement in the obstructive collusion, he nonetheless suspects that something is wrong and tries to grasp it.

For example, in the case of patient L., the analyst was aware of the violence, the envy and the attacks on his thinking capacity, which he attempted to describe and interpret. These interpretations were correct as regards both form and timing.

However, the patient would attack them or quickly devitalize them. The analyst believed he understood what was going on and that he should continue to patiently interpret, without giving in. He took seriously the Brazilian saying, "Soft dripping water will wear down solid rock."

In the case of patient T., the analyst sometimes wondered if the analytical process was not going too smoothly. He entertained the idea of discussing the material with his colleagues, but never actually did so. During Phase 1, T. would readily agree with transference interpretations concerning separation and exclusion. But only after Moment M did the analyst realize that this apparent smooth agreement was an unconscious way of devitalizing the process and thus hindering deeper probing.

One finds in these cases that part of the analyst's mind grasps the defenses against trauma and seeks to interpret them. But these interpretations do not work, or are devitalized, and obstructive collusion remains. This is not clear to the analyst. In other words, during chronic enactment, even though analyst and patient are, we might say, intertwined, the analyst retains a certain capacity for discrimination and thinking. That is, he is able to implicitly use his alpha-function in channels running parallel to the obstruction.[13] I suggest that this implicit alpha-function gradually restores the patient's mental functions. At some point, the unconscious intuition is that there has been enough restoration so that it becomes possible, and less dangerous, to face the reliving of the trauma. Such a confrontation is crucial for reassigning meaning. Defenses are relinquished and the trauma is relived as acute enactment.[14] However, what happens here is no longer a simple reliving, because the trauma has been dreamed. *What seems at first to be a destructive catastrophe is a catastrophic change consequent to the abrupt contact with reality*. The result is an attenuated trauma.

The hypothesis raised above, concerning the implicit alpha-function, leads us to presume the existence of deep unconscious communication between the two members of the analytic dyad. Could still another function of chronic enactment be to facilitate this unconscious communication?

During chronic enactment, when the patient clings to the analyst, thus covering up the traumatic injury, the analyst assumes the role of protective shield (Freud, 1920), the same protective shield that was missing in the traumatic situation.

Babies constantly test their mothers' ability to serve as protective shields, since all of life's situations are potentially traumatic. But in order to test its mother, a baby needs to grasp the mother's emotional states. Possibly, the more sensitive and vulnerable a baby is, the sharper this ability gets. As I see it, the patient does the same thing with his analyst's protective shield. The analyst, in turn, also unconsciously assesses his patient's mental functioning, while injecting in him implicit alpha-function. This process thus bears a resemblance to what Stern et al. (1998) called shared implicit relationship, an intersubjective rapport prior to symbolization.

During chronic enactment, even if the analyst seems incompetent, unable to understand, or even aggressive, the patient still feels that the re-traumatism in the present is less painful than the one in the past. The reason for this is twofold: 1) the patient fantasizes that he controls the analyst; 2) should the analyst fail to adequately deal with the re-traumatization, he continues to work on other areas of the patient's mind, trying to observe, investigate, and discriminate, without ever renouncing the wish to understand further. These facts are part of the analyst's implicit alpha-function, and the patient perceives this interest on the part of the analyst.

Unconscious Communication during Chronic Enactment

The observations and hypotheses raised above lead us to assume that, beneath the paralysis of chronic enactment, movements are taking place that rekindle early episodes of the mind's development, with its possibilities and hindrances, such as initial symbiosis and psychological birth (Tustin, 1981). Through projective identification and other mechanisms, the patient unconsciously scrutinizes his analyst as protective shield in order to assess his containing capacity. The analyst, on the other hand, microscopically attempts to examine the traumatized areas of the psyche and the defenses, which strive to protect it. Accordingly, he measures the amount of reality he is injecting into the patient, careful to avoid re-traumatization. The introjection of thought functions (alpha-function) by the patient is processed little by little. Elements of the traumatic situation thus gradually acquire the conditions for being thought. Using the model of trauma as a wound, one might say that the trauma heals from the symbolic periphery and moves toward the center of the traumatic nucleus (Levy, 2005).

As the analyst accompanies the patient's movements—his difficulties, blocks, obstructions and relapses—when the patient refuses to give the analyst's hypotheses a thought, or devitalizes them, the analyst assumes unconsciously that the injured area has not recovered enough to tolerate reality and that further work is required. On the other hand, by not recognizing clearly the devitalization of the process and his having been recruited by the patient's obstructive aspects, the analyst also may contribute to the paralyzing collusion.

Part of the analyst's implicit alpha-function is the capacity to patiently tolerate the obstructive movements brought about by the traumatic injury and hindrances to recovering from it, without giving up the quest for new approaches to what is taking place. Patience is necessary; the process is close to what we might call normal masochism.[15]

Chronic enactment ceases when, at some point, it is intuited by the dyad that the traumatic fabric has recovered enough for the defenses to be surrendered. The analyst no longer needs to act as a protective shield, an M moment then occurs and the traumatic situation is relived as acute enactment. If the recovery of the traumatic fabric is insufficient, the reliving of the trauma is aborted and the defenses are once again raised. This is probably a frequent occurrence with chronic enactments.

The process described above may be seen as a working through of the trauma, similar to the mourning process, in which each aspect of the trauma has to be meticulously worked through. And yet, is not this description at odds with the observation of the analyst who is paralyzed by the obstructive collusion in chronic enactment?

As was pointed out, the analyst's mind works simultaneously along two channels: in one of them he contributes to the paralysis. His function is obstructed and he operates under the sway of pathological masochism or manic defenses. In the other channel, he surrenders, and that surrender takes the form of normal masochism, necessary for obstructive collusion. The analyst becomes involved in the process due to his need to go deeply into the traumatically injured area. He must live it through, put its vulnerability to the test and carefully contribute to its recovery by bearing pain and suffering. In short, the analyst experiences inside himself what the patient is also experiencing. He must deal with the traumatic area so he can return it to the patient in a more recovered way. This obviously takes time, sometimes a very long time, in order to sufficiently work through the trauma.[16]

Final Considerations

Surely, in some cases, an analyst may not be able to dream a patient's non-dream due to personal countertransference difficulties and so is partially responsible for any possible enactment. In the present paper, however, I am concerned with situations where the analyst is involved in the chronic and acute enactment not only due to personal failings, but also, surprisingly, as a way of reaching deeply into traumatized areas.

At least seven simultaneous functions can be identified in chronic enactments:

1 Avoidance of a reliving of the trauma by freezing it and plugging up anxiety;
2 Immobilization of the analyst so that he is unable to re-traumatize the patient;
3 Use of the analyst as a protective shield against trauma;
4 Allowing deep unconscious contact between patient and analyst, making it possible to examine the traumatized areas;
5 Restoration of functions and injured parts of the mind and working through of the trauma;
6 Allowance for the necessary and adequate time for such cooperative work to take place; and
7 Use of the analyst's implicit alpha-function, of which the previous items are part.

It should be remembered, that even though we are aware of some of the factors involved, it is not known exactly how the alpha-function works (Bion, 1962b, 1992; Grotstein, 2000, 2007; Sandler, 2005, Tabak de Bianchedi, 2008). In this paper, I have emphasized its implicit action and associated it with deep unconscious communication between the members of the analytic dyad. It would seem that the patient grasps the analyst's unconscious dream, outside all explicit communication, and this fact deserves further research.[17]

But we are still struggling with an unsolved problem. Even if one acknowledges the importance of the shared implicit relationship, why must the analyst remain *unconsciously* involved in the chronic enactment? Would it not be more useful to the analytic process if the analyst freed himself from the collusion and exercised the required patience while injecting more explicit alpha-function into the dyad? In order to propose an answer for these questions, I will once more invoke the analogy with the maternal function.

A good enough mother endeavors to be at one with her baby. She experiences his suffering and traumatic situations, so she can dream them in his stead. In order for this to occur, she partially neglects her own needs (normal masochism). In a sense, something akin to an enactment is created with the mother suffering along with her baby and yet not fully aware of it. Her lack of awareness allows the mother to sustain her suffering for as long as is necessary. If that negation is prematurely shattered, there is the risk that the mother will not be able to bear her identification with the baby's suffering and traumatically detach herself from him.

In extreme situations, parents may even be willing to die in order to save their children's lives. This is possible only when there is a deep identification with the children, through which the parents feel the children as parts of themselves, beyond explicit reason. Similarly, the analyst's participation in an enactment is necessary not only by virtue of the seven functions described above, but also because the analyst, like the mother of the baby, must temporarily deny his masochism, in order to suffer with his patient (at-one-ment).

Notes

1 Among the countless authors who have been expanding these ideas of Bion are: Meltzer 1978, 1983; Segal, 1991; Ferro, 1992, 1996, 1999, 2002ab, 2006, 2009; Ogden, 1994a, 2005; Rezende, 1995; Grinberg, 1996; Symington and Symington 1996; Sandler, 1997, 2005; Tabak de Bianchedi, 1999, 2008; Caper, 1998; Green, 1998; Grotstein, 2000, 2004, 2007; Barros, 2000, 2002, 2005; Sapienza, 2001, 2008; Rezze, 2001; Junqueira Filho, 2003; Chuster, 2003; Hartke, 2008.

2 Rezze (2001) calls dreams of this type *non-dreams*, when they are dreamed at night. Grinberg (1967) and Segal (1981) refer to these same night dreams as *evacuative* or *psychotic*.

3 Grotstein (2007) refers to *mentalization* as the passage from the sensory to the image and *thinking* to the next stage, when *alpha-elements* placed in sequence give rise to narratives.

4 These observations occurred in seminars and supervisions, as well as in the author's own clinical practice.

5 During mutual idealization, what may seem to be symbiotic conceals a parasitic container/contained relationship, where both are finally destroyed (Bion, 1970). These are maniac collusions, and what seem to be alpha-elements refer to seemingly intelligible beta-elements (Sandler, 1997) and balfa-elements (Ferro, 1999) that seem to link, but involve –K.

6 See for example McLaughlin, 1991.

7 The term enactment should not be used to refer to actions carried out deliberately. The verb *to enact* is also used to describe dramatizations in general, by either patient or analyst. The trend is to reserve the noun enactment to the types of situations described in this paper, which involve both members of the analytic dyad.

8 Pioneer authors in the study of the action of pathological projective identification include Grinberg, 1957; Bion, 1961, 1962, 1974; Rosenfeld, 1965, 1987; Sandler, 1976, 1988; Grotstein, 1981; Ogden, 1982; and Joseph, 1989. Grotstein (2005), dissecting the concept, proposed the term *projective transidentification* for the situations described here.

9 Further clinical material can be found in other articles by this author, and in Yardino (2008).

10 The author's conviction that he was *non-dreaming* (reversion of perspective) during Moment M was so strong that, until his second-to-last article (Cassorla, 2008b) on the fact, he continued to use the term *non-dream* to refer to *acute enactment*, even though his arguments indicated the contrary.

11 Despite the fact that in trauma the registers of experience are not part of the symbolic net, some memories of traumatic situations may by described as fear, guilt, shame or humiliation that are dissociated but perhaps precariously symbolized (Person and Klar, 1994). However, the connection with other symbols does not take place and the trauma remains split off from the symbolic net that makes up thought. Brown (2005) suggests that non-dreamed manifestations refer to the beta screen organized in a rigid way, with defensive materialization that allows the mental apparatus a

closed-in sense of organization resulting from the reversion of the alpha-function. These are seemingly intelligible beta-elements (Sandler, 1997).

12 Obviously, these sporadic recoveries are followed by new relapses and the analytic process evolves in a spiralling forward-and-backward movement.

13 Baranger et al. (1983) show that the bastion—which I believe bears a resemblance to enactment—can be considered a foreign body that remains static as the analytic process runs its course in other areas.

14 As in the analogy of a drowning person, it is as if the rescuer (by staying alive and striving to think) persuades the traumatized person to trust the resources of the dyad in order to survive, even if they end up swallowing a lot of water when they let go of one another. They can thus separate and help (think) each other.

15 This normal masochism is similar to the mother's patience and capacity to tolerate suffering without becoming discouraged. This topic was creatively approached by Galvez (2004). Bion (1970) also uses the term *patience* to designate the suffering and the tolerance to frustration that the analyst must bear while waiting for the selected fact.

16 In this text I've privileged the study of the patient's traumatic areas, but we can't forget that they activated the analyst's complementary areas. Its working through allows the analyst to get to know himself better and identify his personal contribution to the enactment. The analyst feels grateful to his patient and to psychoanalysis. (See Levine and Friedman (2000).)

17 Stern et al. (1998) have brought forward a number of creative hypotheses concerning implicit intersubjective movements that co-exist with explicit understanding of transferential relationships. These movements result in what these authors call "moments of meeting," which occur when each participant (but particularly the analyst) manifests "something unique and authentic of himself or herself as an individual" (p. 192) beyond his or her routine therapeutic roles. These moments of meeting alter the intersubjective context and open up new space for re-arranging the defensive processes. These ideas are very close to what I presume occurs during the first stages of resolution of chronic enactment and which result in acute enactment. For this reason, I feel quite sure that "moments of meeting" are the result of the work of the alpha-function. Grotstein (2000, 2007) suggests that there is a rudimentary alpha-function in the baby that is able to send messages to its mother. The baby can also grasp the mother's resonance beyond verbal communication. Grotstein supposes that this is similar to a "deep structure" such as that which pre-determines the learning of language, according to Chomsky.

References

Baranger, M. and Baranger, W. (1961–2) The analytic situation as a dynamic field. *International Journal of Psychoanalysis*, 89:795–826, 2008 (reprinted from 1968 version).

Baranger, M., Baranger, W. and Mom, J. (1983) Process and non-process in analytic work. *International Journal of Psychoanalysis*, 64:1–15.

Barros, E. M. (2000) Affect and pictographic image: The constitution of meaning in mental life. *International Journal of Psychoanalysis*, 81:1087–99.

Barros, E. M. (2002) An essay on dreaming, psychical working out and working through. *International Journal of Psychoanalysis*, 83:1083–93.

Barros, E. M. (2005) Trauma, símbolo e significado [Trauma, symbol and meaning]. In França, M. O. A. et al. *Trauma Psíquico: Uma Leitura Psicanalítica e Filosófica da Cultura Moderna*. São Paulo: SBPSP (Acervo Psicanalítico), pp. 109–27.

Bateman, A. W. (1998) Thick and thin-skinned organisations and enactment in borderline and narcissistic disorders. *International Journal of Psychoanalysis*, 79:13–25.

Bion, W. R. (1957) Differentiation of the Psychotic from the Non-Psychotic Personalities. In *Second Thoughts—Selected Papers on Psycho-Analysis*. London: William Heinemann, 1967, pp. 43–64.

Bion, W. R. (1959), Attacks on Linking. In *Second Thoughts—Selected Papers on Psycho-Analysis. London:* William Heinemann, 1967, pp. 93–109.

Bion, W. R. (1961) *Experiences in Groups*. London: Routledge, 2001.

Bion, W. R. (1962a) A Theory of Thinking. In *Second Thoughts—Selected Papers on Psycho-Analysis*. London: Heinemann, 1967, pp. 110–19.

Bion, W. R. (1962b) *Learning from Experience*. London: Heinemann.

Bion, W. R. (1963) *Elements of Psychoanalysis*. London: Heinemann.

Bion, W. R. (1965) *Transformations*. London: Heinemann.

Bion, W. R. (1970) *Attention and Interpretation*. London: Tavistock.

Bion, W. R. (1974) *Brazilian Lectures I*. Rio: Imago.

Bion, W. R. (1977) *Two Papers: The Grid and Caesura*. Rio: Imago.

Bion, W. R. (1980) *Bion in New York and São Paulo*. F. Bion (ed.). Perthshire: Clunie Press.

Bion, W. R. (1992) *Cogitations*. F. Bion (ed.). London: Karnac.

Brown, L. (2005) The cognitive effects of trauma: reversal of alpha function and the formation of a beta screen. *Psychoanalytic Quarterly*, 74:397–420.

Caper, R. A. (1998) *A Mind of One's Own: A Kleinian View of Self and Object*. Hove: Brunner-Routledge.

Cassorla, R. M. S. (1995) Comunicação primitiva e contra-reações na situação analítica. [Primitive communication and counter-reactions in the analytical situation]. *Arquivos de Psiquiatria, Psicoterapia e Psicanálise (Porto Alegre)*, 2:11–33.

Cassorla, R. M. S. (2001) Acute enactment as resource in disclosing a collusion between the analytical dyad. *International Journal of Psychoanalysis,* 82:1155–70. (In Portuguese: *Revista Brasileira de Psicanálise* 38:521–40, 2004).

Cassorla, R. M. S. (2003) Estudo sobre a cena analítica e o conceito de "colocação em cena da dupla" ("enactment") [Study on the analytical scene and the concept of enactment]. *Revista Brasileira de Psicanálise*, 37:365–92.

Cassorla, R. M. S. (2005a) From bastion to enactment: The "non-dream" in the theatre of analysis. *International Journal of Psychoanalysis*, 86:699–719. (In French: *L'Année Psychanalytique internationale*, 4:67–86, 2006; in Portuguese: *Revista Brasileira de Psicanálise*, 41:51–68, 2007; in Italian: *L'Annata Psicoanalitica Internazionale*, 3:75–94, 2008).

Cassorla, R. M. S. (2005b) Considerações sobre o sonho-a-dois e o não-sonho a dois no teatro da análise [Thoughts about the dream-for-two and the non-dream-for-two in the theater of the analysis]. *Revista de Psicanálise da Sociedade Psicanalítica de Porto Alegre*, 12:527–52.

Cassorla, R. M. S. (2007) The analyst, his "Mourning and Melancholia," analytical technique and enactment. In Fiorini, L. G., Bokanowsky, T., Lewkowicz, S. (eds.). *On Freud's "Mourning and Melancholia."* London: IPA Publications (Contemporary Freud: Turning Points and Critical Issues Series), pp.71–89.

Cassorla, R. M. S. (2008a) The analyst's implicit alpha-function, trauma and enactment in the analysis of borderline patients. *International Journal of Psychoanalysis*, 89(1):161–80. (In German: *Internationale Psychoanalyse* :55–70, Gieben: Psychosozial-Verlag, 2009; in Spanish: *Libro Anual de Psicoanálisis* 24:55–70, 2009; in Portuguese: *Livro Anual de Psicanálise*, 24:61–78, 2010).

Cassorla, R. M. S. (2008b) Desvelando configurações emocionais da dupla analítica através de modelos inspirados no mito edípico [Unveiling emotional configurations of the analytical dyad through oedipal myth models]. *Revista Brasileira de Psicoterapia (Porto Alegre)*, 10:37–48.

Cassorla, R. M. S. (2008c) O analista, seu paciente e a psicanálise contemporânea: considerações sobre indução mútua, enactment e não-sonho-a-dois [The analyst, his patient and contemporary psychoanalysis: thoughts about mutual induction, enactment and non-dream-for-two]. *Revista Latinoamericana de Psicoanálisis*, 8:189–208.

Chuster, A. (2003) *A Psicanálise: dos Princípios Ético-Estéticos à Clínica* [Psychoanalysis: from ethic-aesthetics principles to the clinic]. Rio: Cia de Freud.

Ellman, S. J. and Moskovitz, M. (eds.) (1998) *Enactment: Toward a New Approach to the Therapeutic Relationship*. Northvale, NJ: Jason Aronson.

Ferro, A. (1992) *The Bi-Personal Field: Experiences in Child Analysis*. London: Routledge, 1999.

Ferro, A. (1996) *In the Analyst's Consulting Room*. London: Routledge, 2002.

Ferro, A. (1999) *Psychoanalysis as Therapy and Storytelling*. Hove: Routledge, 2006.

Ferro, A. (2002a) *Seeds of Illness, Seeds of Recovery. The Genesis of Suffering and the Role of Psychoanalysis*. Hove: Brunner-Routledge, 2005.

Ferro, A. (2002b) Some implications of Bion's thought: The waking dream and narrative derivatives. *International Journal of Psychoanalysis*, 83:597–607.

Ferro, A. (2006) Clinical implications of Bion thought. *International Journal of Psychoanalysis*, 87:989–1003.

Ferro, A. (2009) Transformations in dreaming and characters in the psychoanalytic field. *International Journal of Psychoanalysis*, 90:209–30.

Freud, S. (1920) Beyond the pleasure principle. *Standard Edition*, 18.

Freud, S. (1926) Inhibitions, symptoms and anxiety. *Standard Edition*, 20.

Galvez, M. J. (2004) A paciência na elaboração psicanalítica [Patience in psychoanalytical working through]. *Revista Brasileira de Psicanálise*, 38:895–914.

Green, A. (1998) The primordial mind and the work of the negative. *International Journal of Psychoanalysis*, 79:649–56.

Grinberg, L. (1957) Perturbaciones en la interpretación por la contraidentificación proyectiva [Troubles in the interpretation due to projective counteridentification]. *Revista de Psicoanálisis (Buenos Aires)* 14:23.

Grinberg, L. (1967) Función del soñar y clasificación clínica de los sueños en el proceso analítico [Dreaming functions and clinical classifications of the dreams in the analytical process]. In *Psicoanalisis-Aspectos teóricos y clinicos*. Buenos Aires: Alex Editor, 1976, pp.187–208.

Grinberg, L. (1996) *El Psicoanalisis es Cosa de Dos* [Psychoanalysis is a thing of two] Valencia: Promolibro.

Grotstein, J. S. (1981) *Splitting and Projective Identification*. New York, NY. Jason

Grotstein, J. S. (2000) *Who is the Dreamer Who Dreams the Dream ? A Study of Psychic Presences*. Hillsdale: Analytic Press.

Grotstein, J. S. (2004) The seventh servant: the implications of truth drive in Bion's theory of O. *International Journal of Psychoanalysis*, 85:1081–101.

Grotstein, J. S. (2005) Projective transidentification: An extension of the concept of projective identification. *International Journal of Psychoanalysis*, 86(4):1051–68.

Grotstein, J. S. (2007) *A Beam of Intense Darkness*. London: Karnac.

Hartke, R. (2008) A vida onírica e o trabalho analítico: entre o segredo e o mistério [The oneiric life and the analytical work: between the secret and the mystery]. Presented Donald Meltzer International Meeting, São Paulo.

Imbasciati, A. (2001) Que inconsciente ? [What unconscious?]. *Revista de Psicanálise da Sociedade Psicanalítica de Porto Alegre*, 8(1):65–88.

Jacobs, T. J. (1986) On countertransference enactments. *Journal of the American Psychoanalytical Association*, 34:289–307.

Joseph, B. (1989) *Psychic Equilibrium and Psychic Change: Selected Papers of Betty Joseph*. Feldman, M., Spillius, E. B. (eds.). London: Routledge.

Junqueira Filho, L. C. U. (2003) *Sismos e Acomodações: A Clinica Psicanalitica como Usina de Idéias* [Earthquakes and accomodations: The psychoanalytical clinic as ideas factory]. São Paulo: Rosari.

Levine, H. B. and Friedman, R. J. (2000) Intersubjectivity and interaction in the analytic relationship: a mainstream view. *Psychoanalytic Quarterly*, 69:63–92.

Levy, R. (2005) Trauma e não representação no campo analitico [Trauma and non-representation in the analytical field]. Presented International Congress of Psychoanalysis, Rio de Janeiro.

McLaughlin, J. (1991) Clinical and theoretical aspects of enactment. *Journal of the American Psychoanalytical Association*, 39:595–614.

Meltzer, D. (1978) *The Kleinian Development 3: The Clinical Significance of the Work of Bion*. Perthshire: Clunie Press.

Meltzer, D. (1983) *Dream-life: Re-examination of the Psycho-Analytical Theory and Technique*. Strath Tay: Clunie.

Ogden, T. (1982) *Projective Identification and Psychotherapeutic Technique*. New York: Jason Aronson.

Ogden, T. (1994a) *Subjects of Psychoanalysis*. London: Karnac.

Ogden, T. (1994b) The analytical third: working with intersubjective facts. *International Journal of Psychoanalysis*, 75:3–19.

Ogden, T. (2005) *This Art of Psychoanalysis: Dreaming Undreamt Dreams and Interrupted Cries*. Hove: Routledge.

Person, E. S. and Klar, H. (1994) Establishing trauma: The difficulty distinguishing between memories and fantasies. *Journal of the American Psychoanalytical Association*, 42:1055–81.

Rezende, A. M. (1995) *Wilfred R. Bion. Uma Psicanálise do Pensamento* [Wilfred R. Bion: A psychoanalysis of thought]. Campinas: Papirus.

Rezze, C. J. (2001) O sonho, o quase sonho e o não sonho [The dream, the almost dream and the non dream]. In França, M. O. A. F., Thomé, M. C. I. & Petricciani, M. (org). *Transformações e Invariâncias. Bion ↔SBPSP. Seminários Paulistas*. S.Paulo: SBPSP-Casa do Psicólogo, pp. 97–116.

Rosenfeld, H. (1965) *Psychotic States: A Psychoanalytical Approach*. New York: International University Press.

Rosenfeld, H. (1987) *Impasse and Interpretation*. London: Tavistock.

Sandler, J. (1976) Countertransference and role-responsiveness. *International Review of Psychoanalysis*, 3:43–7.

Sandler, J. (org) (1988) *Projection, Identification, Projective Identification*. London: Karnac.

Sandler, P. C. (1997) The apprehension of psychic reality: extensions in Bion's theory of alpha-function. *International Journal of Psychoanalysis*, 78:43–52.

Sandler, P. C. (2005) *The Language of Bion.* London: Karnac.

Sapienza, A. (2001) O trabalho de sonho-alfa do psicanalista na sessão: Intuição-atenção-interpretação [The analyst dream-work-alpha at the analytical session: intuition-attention-interpretation]. In França, M. O. A. F. , Thomé, M. C. I., Petricciani, M. *Transformações e Invariâncias: Bion↔SBPSP. Seminários Paulistas.* São Paulo: Casa do Psicólogo, p.17–25.

Sapienza, A. (2008) Função alfa: ansiedade catastrófica—pânico—continente com rêverie [Alpha-function: catastrophic anxiey–panic–containing with reverie]. Paper presented in Bion in Roma.

Segal, H. (1981) The function of dreams. In *The Work of Hanna Segal—A Kleinian Approach to Clinical Practice.* New York: Jason Aronson (and in Grotstein, J. S. (ed.) *Do I Dare Disturb the Universe?* Beverly Hills: Caeswa).

Segal, H. (1991) *Dream, Phantasy and Art.* London: Routledge.

Stern, D. N., Sander, L. W., Nahum, J. P., Harrison, A. M., Lyons-Ruth, K., Morgan, A. C., Bruschweilerstern, N. and Tronick, E. Z (1998) Non-interpretative mechanisms in psychoanalytic therapy: the "something more" than interpretation. *International Journal of Psychoanalysis,* 79:903–21.

Symington, N. (1983) The analyst act of freedom as agent of therapy change. *International Review of Psychoanalysis,* 10:283–91.

Symington, J. and Symington, N. (1996) *The Clinical Thinking of Wilfred Bion.* London: Routledge.

Tabak de Bianchedi, E. (org) (1999) *Bion Conocido, Desconocido* [Bion known, unknown]. B. Aires: Lugar.

Tabak de Bianchedi, E. (2008) Volviendo a pensar sobre la misteriosa funcion alfa [Second thoughts on the mysterious alpha function]. Paper presented in Bion in Roma.

Tustin, F. (1981) *Autistic States in Children.* London: Routledge.

Yardino, S. (2008) "Break point": A significant moment in the transference. *International Journal of Psychoanalysis,* 9:241–7.

Part 3

PATHOLOGICAL STATES

EDITORS' INTRODUCTION

Primitive Conscience: A Glimpse of the Primordial Mind

José Américo Junqueira de Mattos and João Carlos Braga

In his supervisions, clinical lectures and later writings, Bion postulated the existence of a "primitive conscience" or "murderous superego," which can exert a powerful and destructive unconscious force on the patient. He came to believe that this structure was rooted in a pre-natal developmental period in which the psychological and biological were still undifferentiated, this "mindless guilt" is psychically unrepresentable and without sensorial referents. Thus, while it is an aspect of the patient's ultimate reality (O) and so can "be," it remains forever outside of the dynamic unconscious and beyond symbolic/verbal organization. This is an encapsulated structure that is not subject to the processes of psychic development. It may be ameliorated or "overwritten" by more developmentally mature structures, but it can never be fully transformed to the point of being eliminated. Consequently, although its effects can be mitigated by relational experience and it may be approximated in a construction or "myth," it must forever remain beyond the reach of analysis in the classical sense of "decoding" and "uncovering" that which is hidden or disguised in the dynamic unconscious.

In a careful review of Bion's thinking, including the intimations of primitive conscience hinted at in his earliest writings, Junqueira de Mattos and Braga attempt to distinguish Bion's primitive conscience from Klein's idea of an archaic superego. The latter was believed to be built up out of experiences with a real external object that were either traumatic in themselves or were sufficiently frustrating and disappointing as to fail to counteract the innate effects of the death instinct. In contrast, Bion hypothesized—i.e. formed "an imaginary conjecture"—that primitive conscience is an aspect of the primordial mind rooted in pre-natal events that are registered at a sub-cortical level, associated with a "nameless dread" of annihilation that he called "thalamic" or "sub-thalamic fear" and which give rise to fight–flight reactions.

To Bion, this inexorable and powerfully self-destructive, self-limiting force, which only stands for and insists on what must *not* be done and never offers positive ideals or values with which to guide one's way through life, is registered in the brain, but cannot be "experienced" self-reflectively in the mind. Junqueira de Mattos and Braga argue that primitive conscience is responsible for various clinical expressions of self-hatred, unconscious guilt, suicidal and self-destructive tendencies, powerful anti-libidinal sentiments and other forms of severe, growth-limiting pathology.

While the idea of traces of pre-natal registrations of distress remains "an imaginary conjecture" for the authors, they nevertheless argue for it as a pragmatically useful hypothesis or "myth." For readers less willing to entertain the possibility of a pre-natal root of pathogenesis, we would suggest limiting their thought to the effects of massive trauma or traumatic events in the early pre-verbal period of infancy. What Bion—and Junqueira de Mattos and Braga—call our attention to is the area of the unconscious that is unformulated and not yet verbalizable. In Bion's terms, this entails a shift in our vision of the mind from the more usual sense of conscious/unconscious, neurotico-normal/psychotic, to that of a mind consisting of two parts: a limited area of psychically represented, symbolized and verbalizable contents and an infinite area of psychically unrepresented (in Freud's [1915] sense of the term), not yet verbalizable proto-elements awaiting potential transformation into psychic elements that can be represented psychically and contained within the finite mind. It also requires us to achieve a fluidity and shift in our perspective, so that we might look at the psyche from the perspective of the soma, rather than the more usual way of seeing the soma from the perspective of the mind.

Readers of this chapter will no doubt be challenged by these views. However, we think they will also be richly rewarded by its careful historical exegesis of Bion's work, the detailed clinical examples offered and the discussion of the problems encountered in attempting to contain the many clinical phenomena associated with the workings of this primitive conscience. The latter are phenomena that go beyond persecutory fears of object loss (the fear of the bad object or "no-thing") to the various forms of annihilation anxiety and loss of meaningfulness that Bion called "nameless dread" (the fear of being annihilated, engulfed by nothingness or subjected to the loss of all meaningfulness in the world).

8

PRIMITIVE CONSCIENCE

A Glimpse of the Primordial Mind

José Américo Junqueira de Mattos and João Carlos Braga

> [T]here seems to be a kind of inborn moral statement. In the way that, for example, I think that the Roman Catholic Church talks about the Original Sin. I think that that's what they mean. We are born with a feeling of guilt; we are born with that which some day turns into a kind of conscience.
>
> (Bion, 1978c)

Thirty years after his death, Bion's contributions to psychoanalysis still contain thoughts awaiting further elaboration in the mind of a thinker. One such thought was the configuration described in his 1978 Brazilian supervisions, that he called *primitive conscience*. He defined this concept as a basic feeling of guilt hiding a state of intense terror (1976b, p. 309; 1981, p. 83), and offered it as "an imaginative conjecture" (1976c, p. 318; 1981, p. 83) that would await confirmation. Unlike the classic psychoanalytic view of conscience (e.g. Freud, 1932; Klein, 1933), this configuration does not include concern and protection of the self and is not developed through introjection of parental figures. Instead, it consists only of an insistent set of prohibitions impairing personality development and emotional welfare, and is hypothesized as related to pre-natal experiences. In the clinical setting, primitive conscience may manifest itself in various forms of self-hatred (Bion, 1976c, p. 319), including suicidal thoughts and impulses, or it may be glimpsed in the precautions taken by analysands to avoid awakening severe feelings of guilt and self-punishment, in prohibitions against pleasurable sexual experiences or in impediments to the development of the self.

A closer look at Bion's writings shows that although *primitive conscience* is a concept that surfaced after 1976 when he expanded his model of the mind to include the conception of a *primordial mind*, the idea of a cruel, fundamentally critical entity can be identified throughout his work and is implicit in many different concepts and approaches. For example, the earlier concepts of *nameless dread* (Bion, 1962a, p. 116) and *catastrophic change*

(Bion, 1966) can, in retrospect, be seen to be related to this condition, as reflections of the consequence and experience of the developed mind's failure to achieve containment of terrifying feelings.

In his later writings, Bion (1976a, p. 305; 1976b, p. 309; 1976c, p. 319; 1979, p. 324) conjectured that *primitive conscience* is rooted in the thalamic and glandular records of experiences that occur before birth. He refers to such pre-natal events as producing an *inexperienced conscience* (1978a), which tends to function in a pre-emptive manner and that interferes with what may be learned from later (post-natal) experience. Thus, the prior denominations of *thalamic fear* and *sub-thalamic fear* (Bion, 1976b, p. 309; 1977–8, pp. 22, 80) draw attention to the somatic quality of primitive guilt reactions, while their innate, all-encompassing characteristics are highlighted by their analogy to *Original Sin* (Bion, 1978ac; 1977–8, p. 71).[1]

In an article where he highlighted aspects of his personal analysis with Bion (which took place from 1977–9), one of the present authors recollected in Bion's interpretations references to a conscience that only prohibits. *"Dr. Bion would point out a peculiarity of the conscience that it is always ready to say what WE SHOULD NOT do or think, but NEVER what we should"* (Junqueira de Mattos, 1980). However, it was only recently with the current study that he more fully apprehended this idea and satisfactorily grasped the meaning of what Bion had meant to convey.

Primitive Conscience: Excerpts from Two Supervisions[2]

A study of the more than one hundred recorded supervisions held by Bion in Brazil[3] in 1973, 1974, 1975 and 1978, reveals that it was in three supervisions, all of them given in April 1978, that he most extensively discussed the concept *primitive conscience.* This approach can also be observed in other supervisions, sometimes openly, at other times, implicitly. The following excerpts will illustrate Bion's discussions.

Fragments of Supervision A5[4] (Bion, 1978a)

The analysand starts the session saying that she is thinking about interrupting her analysis and also moving to a less expensive part of town. The money she would save by doing that would be given to her sister to pay for the sister's divorce. The diminution in her living condition would be significant for the analysand, and consistent with her feeling that she does not deserve to live where she now does or to be in analysis.

BION: ... if she spent her resources of time and money on herself she would be so guilty that she can't stand it. I don't think I would want to say anything of that to her, at the moment, because I'm not sure whether the patient could stand it. So, I would probably want to hear some more. But in the meantime, I would keep to myself the fact that this is a fundamental, basic guilt. To carry it a bit further: I meant that it is the kind of conscience which—if one had a religious view—one would call probably Original Sin. But from my point of view, I think that these are symptoms of a very dangerous and fundamental—basic, as I said—conscience, which is more of a liability than an asset. Now, why I would think that, why I am thinking that is because it doesn't tell her what she's to do; it only tells her what is wrong, what she mustn't do. So I would suspect that the patient would be afraid of me as being that kind of conscience.

[…] The point seems to me, to be that the two[5] are left alone with a game of primitive conscience. Now, this situation, again, seems to me to be one which crops up very frequently, in many different analyses. I could put it in these terms: that two children—two young children—need a parent, because the parent has a great deal of experience. This primitive conscience has no experience. So, that primitive conscience does not know enough to know how to look after two children. Now, the experienced mother is liable to seem very strict, because she's always saying: "Don't do that, don't do this, don't be naughty, don't … " and so on … ad infinitum. But, in fact, the experienced mother—although also frequently saying: "Don't do this, don't do that, and so on"—is much milder, much less severe than the inexperienced conscience. So, the danger of leaving two young children alone, is not only for all the naughty things that they will do, bad things, but that they will be at the mercy of a very severe, very harsh and quite inexperienced conscience. So, although it appears as if the mother was severe, in fact, the really important thing about this is that conscience will be so severe, if there's no mother there. So, the danger isn't only what naughty or wrong things the child will do, but also, what very wrong things this harsh conscience will do. Of course, at a much later stage, the danger about that kind of moral system is that it can impose a sentence of death quite unnecessarily. In other words, it's a sort of conscience which can drive a patient to suicide.

Fragments of Supervision A6 (Bion, 1978b)

The analysand is tormented and worried about his sexual conflicts. The background of the present session is that after a fight with his wife over mutual infidelity, they reconciled and had a second honeymoon.

BION: He's objecting to the fact that, if he and his wife have a honeymoon, then, his father and mother could also have a pleasurable sexual game—they could have been able to play these sexual games, enjoyable sexual games, when he wasn't allowed to, even if he learns how to get pleasure—like masturbation and so on—it is liable to be interrupted.

[...] the fact that the two people can come together and have a verbal intercourse like this, arouses reminiscences, which would mean that either he'd have to stop coming for analysis, he'd have to stop existing, or he'd have to change his views about the wickedness of his father and mother. Both being the sort of wickedness of people who do sexual things together. Something has got to happen. The trouble about killing himself is: if he kills himself, he'd be dead. If he doesn't kill himself, then ... well, he's got to do something about that conscience; if he doesn't do that, then, he ought to kill himself, because he's got no right to exist, if the parents aren't allowed to come together. If they're not allowed to have an enjoyable sexual relationship, then, that's the end of him. But, if he wants to go on existing, then he'll have to change his views about the wickedness of the parents, he'll also have to change his views about analyst and analysand, because, instead of it being just one of these stupid things, which analysts and analysands do, it actually has a result.

[...] I would have thought that the point that he needs to be aware of is the murderous quality of that conscience, which hates a happy, pleasurable and successful intercourse, verbal or otherwise. So, I think that it would be useful for him, to be aware of, so that he could make allowances for that kind of murderous moral standard, which would really mean the destruction of any creative activity.

How We Worked Through the Concept of Primitive Conscience

Classic studies on the human moral system by Freud (1912, 1923, 1930) and Klein (1933, 1957) have provided the foundation from which we have previously reflected upon guilt and its vicissitudes. We used to think that Bion's ideas in these areas derived from this same core. However, we have come to realize that with the concept of *primitive conscience*, Bion presented us with a new perspective on these issues. As a result, we have chosen to revisit our understanding of guilt and primitive mentation, to pay attention to and gather data from our own clinical experience that would converge with this idea, to trace back this concept in Bion's published work, and to re-examine it in relation to the more familiar psychoanalytic theories about morality.

From the start, we faced two problems in clinical practice. How would we be able to distinguish feelings of guilt associated with object relationships (e.g. oedipal rivalry and sadistic attacks on the breast), from this primitive guilt that masks a state of primordial terror? How to distinguish a *primitive conscience* that only prohibits from an experienced conscience that warns against unnecessary dangers? We answered the first problem by recognizing that *guilt related to object relationships might be elaborated in the emotional experience of the analytical relationship*, while guilt rooted in the primitive conscience is not. The second problem was solved by our recognition that primitive conscience does not engage in dialogues with other aspects of the personality, whereas an experienced conscience tolerates conflicts and helps one to think about them.

Taking our investigations further, we began to examine clinical situations in which growth of the personality was obstructed and creative and pleasurable experiences were interfered with. Our observations led us to agree with Bion that, indeed, evidence of primitive conscience "*crops up very frequently in many different analyses*" (1978a). Whenever we conjectured the presence of primitive conscience, we came to see that beneath the presence of guilt on a superficial level, there lay an underlying silent terror that was not tied to representations and not accessible in the symbolic dimension. Subsequently, it also became possible to identify this hidden terror in the psychic movements of analysands struggling to become themselves and accept, know and contain aspects of their proto-thoughts that had yet to be contained within their psyches.

Ultimately, we came to recognize the effects of primitive conscience in mentally disruptive states where more primitive forms of psychic functioning were eviscerated, as in psychotic breakdowns, deep depression, or in self-destructive behaviors associated with drug addiction. As a result of our efforts, we became convinced of the merit in Bion's idea of a *primitive conscience*, as a configuration that may be active in the mind, but not transformable through processes of symbolic formation, as in neurotic and psychotic phenomena. Nevertheless, his hypothesis that such a conscience is rooted in the registrations of pre-natal experience remains for us an imaginative conjecture.

The development of these ideas has changed the way that we think about some fundamental aspects of our practice:

i It heightened our awareness of the role of guilt in impeding the development of the work of analysis.
ii It led us to conclude that we were privileging movements towards knowledge at the expense of psychic movements towards not knowing. This was perhaps a consequence of our bias in attributing major importance to the theory of alpha function and *reverie*, at that time. To recognize the similar importance of not knowing opened the doors to recognize more primitive phenomena, such as those related to the hypothesis of a primordial mind.
iii It helped in the realization of a model of a multidimensional mind, in which the conscious/unconscious system (sensory data, thinking

and hallucinosis) co-exists with an inaccessible system, from which derives elements that, when expressed, do so in a disruptive manner (e.g. the feelings of *being dependent and all alone*, the *urge to exist* and a *primordial guilt*). So, the expansion of Bion's model of the mind with the inclusion of the domain of the primordial mind (which occurred during the period 1976–9), gained in consistency to us.

iv In an even more significant way, we realized that the analysand is a person battling on several internal fronts, trying first *to survive* and then *to live* his object relationships. The vicissitudes of *becoming what a person in fact is* has proved to be more demanding to the analysand than the conditions of making conscious the unconscious, reintegrating what was split off and expelled by projective identification or generating thoughts from proto-emotional experience.

v Our observation of the upsurge of certain hallucinatory patterns became more accessible. States of "non-thinking," which increasingly appeared in our offices frequently labeled as "new pathologies," became more understandable, as we were able to identify as their main features the prevalence of impulse over containment, the impoverishment of living life experiences, relationships reduced to requirements of immediate satisfaction, and the loss of moral and ethical references. Once we introduced the concept of primitive conscience in our clinical references, processes of denuding experiences of meaning and failing to discriminate between animate and inanimate objects could then be more clearly seen as reflecting the existence of a fundamental terror that interfered with the differentiation of knowing/not knowing and being/not being.

Developments in Bion's Model of the Mind between 1976 and 1979

Throughout his life, Bion maintained a monistic vision of the mind, emphasizing that its different aspects were dimensions of a single self. At first (1957–65), he envisioned within that self one psychic domain capable of thinking and performing symbolic operations, and another more primitive domain that processed somatic information and discharged via the soma the accretion of stimuli, following neuro-physiological paths. After "Transformations" (Bion, 1965), his approach became multidimensional: he created a model that can be summarized in four domains: sensorial, thinking, hallucinatory and "*being reality*."[6] He later added two more dimensions, thoughts without a thinker (Bion, 1970) and primordial mind (1976–9). It is this last domain that we want to highlight here, for which the understanding of the *primitive conscience* conjecture is the catalytic factor.

Following birth, we have a self that includes "*body or mind, and a 'mental space' for further ideas which may develop*" (Bion, 1979, p. 325). It is in the latter that fundamental developments of the personality may occur through articulations of constitutional potentialities and experiences arising from the interaction between the child and its environment. This view differs from that of the classical psychoanalytic theories of a conscious/unconscious mind, along with its tri-partite vertices (instinctual, learning from experience, and moral system), that takes this developmental moment as a starting point.

During his last years of life (1976–9), Bion stressed the disparity between mental and somatic development, between the emergence of proto-sensations and proto-emotions and the incapacities of the immature nervous system to deal with them. The non-myelinated cortex of the fetus is unable to register experiences and does not offer conditions to support a developing mind. Thalamus is the operating brain and the established nervous circuits are sub-thalamic. After birth, these primary sub-thalamic registers will remain inaccessible to the symbolic mind due to the absence of conditions to form thoughts and to think at the time the registrations occurred. To the extent that these primary sub-thalamic registrations were disturbing to the fetus, the only option that the latter would have for dealing with them would be to try to get rid of them, via mechanisms that were the precursors of projective identification. Thus, following Bion, we are proposing the existence of an area of proto-psychological "experience," a register that is "experienced" as somatic, remains forever inaccessible to the conscious/unconscious states of mind, but nonetheless, is operative and existent.

In *Taming Wild Thoughts*, Bion (1977a, p. 50) organized these ideas when he proposed a differentiation between conscious/unconscious states of mind and inaccessible proto-mental states. He describes this conjecture as follows:

> Even the foetus develops a capacity for what is later called projective identification. In other words, it has feelings or primordial ideas that it tries to deal with by evacuating them—a primitive mechanism derived maybe from the physical capacity for evacuation, literally, so that the amniotic fluid is polluted with meconium. I am suggesting that besides the conscious and unconscious states of mind, there can be another one. The nearest I can get to give it a provisional title is the *inaccessible* state of mind. It may become inaccessible because the foetus gets rid of it as soon as it can.

Thus he proposes a model of the mind that incorporates a primordial mind and *primitive conscience* and stresses the caesura of birth as a momentous event, crucial to mental life, the main focus of which comes to be the fate of the relationship between pre- and post-natal experience.

Tracking the Configuration Primitive Conscience in Bion's Work

Primitive conscience is a descriptive approach to a psychic configuration, not a causal and explanatory theory. As noted above, as a concept, it is not identical to, nor can it be fully accounted for by, the theories of Freud and Klein on the superego and death instinct. Its status is analogous to Bion's idea of the *oedipal pre-conception* (1963, p. 93), which has a different epistemological status than that of the *Oedipus complex*. Throughout Bion's work, we can find references to a violent and cruel critical activity of the personality. While some readers may think of these as being in agreement with Klein's vision of an archaic superego, a bad object integrating the set of constitutive objects of the superego, there are two fundamental novelties in Bion's approach culminating in the concept *primitive conscience* that attest to the originality of his thinking: the hypothesis of an innate morality and a model of a multidimensional mind privileging functions and not structures.

In investigating the emergence of the conscience in the child, Melanie Klein (1933) emphasized two opposite sets of functions, persecutory and protective, organized through post-natal articulation between instincts and object relationships. In Bion's formulation of a primitive conscience we only find persecutory aspects related to experiences preceding birth, nothing being said about the processes of fusion/defusion of instincts.

In Kleinian theory, the superego is formed by the re-introjection of real external objects after being invested by life and death instincts. The processes through which this occurs are present in the infant after birth, and the cruel archaic superego is tied to the splitting of frightening figures, with the death instinct not being fused with the life instinct (Klein, 1957). In contrast, Bion hypothesizes an origin prior to the genesis of the Kleinian archaic superego and emphasizes a primary form of projective identification and the absence of a suitable container for the contents of a primordial mind.

Let us now take a longitudinal approach to the steps that culminated in Bion's development of the concept *primitive conscience*. In *The Imaginary Twin* (1950), in the terrifying dream of the analysand trapped in his car while being chased by the "twin," we find features suggestive of a harsh moral activity that is alien to the part of the personality that is capable of symbolization. Subsequently, this activity is characterized as reflecting a *cruel* and *murderous superego* (Bion, 1992, pp. 32, 39, 69; Bion, 1959, p. 101). We believe that this way of thinking, present until 1962, can be assimilated to the Kleinian view of the archaic superego. It was only later, with his further investigations of the disturbances of the capacity of thinking, that Bion deepened his ideas on this primitive morality, concluding that it reflected a psychic activity contrary to the development of thoughts.

This "*internal object which is opposed to, and destructive of, all links whatsoever ...* " (Bion, 1959, p. 105), undergoes detailed examination in *Learning from Experience*, *Elements of Psychoanalysis* and *Transformations*, as an anti-thinking object. It is presented as being related to envy, as described by Klein, as a factor of the personality that is re-introjected as if it were a superego that is "*'super' to the ego* [...] *It is an envious assertion of moral superiority without any morals. In short, it is the resultant of an envious stripping or denudation of all good ...* " (Bion 1962b, p. 97).

Bion's next move (1963; 1965) was to analogize this harsh morality and its actions against the development of the personality to the myths of the Garden of Eden, the Tower of Babel, and the fate of the Sphinx in the Oedipus tale. In these passages, primitive morality takes the place of the mature superego, which, by usurping the investigative functions of reality by the ego, prevents contact of the individual with the truth. It leads to the "*starvation of the psyche and stunted growth*" as a result of "*imperfect development of the reality principle, exaltation of a 'moral' outlook and lack of respect for the truth*" (Bion, 1965 p. 38). Three chapters after this statement, in a new formulation with a higher degree of abstraction, it receives the designation of "–K".[7] A few pages later, it is presented as a "*completely immoral conscience*," whose characteristics, when personified, can be described as "*violent, greedy and envious, ruthless, murderous, and predatory, without respect for the truth, persons, or things.* [...] *This force is dominated by an envious determination to possess everything that objects that exist possess including existence itself*" (Bion, 1965, p. 102).

In *Attention and Interpretation* (1970, p. 21), Bion once again deals with the idea of a primordial moral system. In his discussion of vertices, he describes an "*extremely disturbed*" patient who "*has become better adjusted to what the psycho-analyst regards as reality.*" And he adds:

> Somewhere there is present a "superego" that is cruel, denuded of all the characteristics usually associated with the superego, and, finally, of "existence" itself. It therefore has the characteristics of "non-existence." [...] I use the term "super-ego" as a psycho-analytical intuitive theory, now with the status of a realization, which I want to reform later in terms of another intuitive theory.

Following his notational system, we might characterize this as a *minus superego,* that is, a *negative conscience* (Bion, 1962b, p. 98; 1965, p. 103).

Finally, around 1976, Bion's hypothesis of a *primitive conscience* achieves conceptual identity within the theory of a primordial mind, split off from the conscious/unconscious states of mind by birth's caesura. In the final three years of his life, this concept, is elaborated upon in Bion's written works in a descriptive, colloquial form, using models and analogies. It is a way of thinking that is always in transit, not trapped in fully finished definitions, approached and expanded through different views obtained by changes in observational vertices. This development can also be followed in the first three of the *Four Discussions with W. R. Bion* (Los Angeles, 1978d), as well as in seminars held in New York (1977–8), Rome (1977b), and São Paulo (1977–8), where there are several references to the importance of pre-natal experiences and of an activity of precocious and severe censorship of the self. However, it is in *Evidence* (1976c, pp. 318–19) that we find its most complete formulation, proposed by Bion as an *imaginative conjecture*. The context in which it appears explores the possibility of looking into the personality from two directions—the somatic and the psychic. If we observe from a somato-psychotic vertex, it is possible to highlight a type of conscience already present in the baby, with feelings of established guilt that Bion refers to as *sub-thalamic fear*. Since this is the most precise and detailed formulation present in his published work, we will cite the entire relevant excerpt:

> Let us take flight into fantasy, a kind of infancy of our own thought. I can imagine a situation in which a nearly full-term foetus could be aware of extremely unpleasant oscillations in the amniotic fluid medium before transferring to a gaseous medium—in other words, getting born. I can imagine that there is some disturbance going on—the parents on bad terms, or something of that sort. I can further imagine loud noises being made between the mother and the father—or even loud noises made by the digestive system inside the mother. Suppose this foetus is also aware of the pressures of what will one day turn into a character or a personality, aware of things like fear, hate, crude emotions of that sort. Then the foetus might omnipotently turn in hostility towards these disturbing feelings, proto-ideas, proto-feelings, at a very early stage, and split them up, destroy them, fragment them, and try to evacuate them. Suppose this caesura takes place and the infant is subjected to the trauma of birth, and the further trauma of having to adjust to a gaseous medium. I can imagine the foetus being so precocious, so premature that it tries to get rid of its personality to start off with, and then after birth—still being highly "intelligent," if that is the correct term—is able to learn all the words and phrases which people consciously use. In the very severe, very obtrusive situation such as the one I have in mind, that person learns well the difference between right and wrong; the M'Naghten Rules (the governing decision as to criminal responsibility of the insane) present no difficulty whatever. But as far as he is concerned, he may preserve a mind at the deeper level which knows nothing about that, but which might nevertheless have well-established feelings of guilt. I have been amazed to see the way in which, if you make a faintly disapproving sound to a baby, it will

> wince as if it had been subjected to an almost intolerable accusation. Has the baby a kind of well-established "conscience"? What is one to call it? I have invented terms for my own private purposes like, "sub-thalamic fear," meaning the kind of fear that one would have if no check on it at all was produced by the higher levels of the mind.

This vision is synthesized in conceptual terms in the entry "Thalamus," in *A Key to "A Memoir of the Future"* (Bion, 1981, p. 83): "There are some forms of terror which can be observed in psycho-analysis which have their origin in the developing thalamus and its 'non-myelinated nervous connections'. This, of course, is an 'imaginative conjecture' which may take years to confirm scientifically."

We can reasonably presume that it was only after 1975 that Bion developed these thoughts on precocious moral activity resulting from pre-natal experiences. We base this hypothesis primarily in an observation made by him in one of his supervisions in Brasilia (1975b) in which he attributed this primitive conscience to experiences in early post-natal life:

> I think that this internal object, the thing he calls a stomach-ache, is in fact, a very frightening conscience. Indeed, he's afraid of the analyst, as if the analyst was a sort of reincarnation of the ghost, as it were, of the mother. [. . .] But, if that is true, that's really suggesting it's extremely primitive, probably *going back to something like the earliest meals of all.* [. . .] The fact that the thing that he has eaten, has traveled right down to, wherever his stomach-ache is, it is really felt to be operating as a kind of conscience.

Still further support of this view comes from the first volume of *A Memoir of the Future* (1975a), in which Bion presents the framework of a mind with several simultaneous operational levels, including personifications of pre-natal stages of the self. Several passages[8] allow readers to glimpse the idea of a *primitive conscience.* However, it is noteworthy that Bion does not give a specific "character" to this idea, as he does to several other aspects of pre-natal life. Indirect references to it emerge in the words of the "characters" "Bion" and "Man," who possess a high degree of sophisticated thinking, as for example, in the following observation on fear:

> I have owed and shall owe my continued existence to my capacity to fear "an impending disaster". The question is not "where is one to draw the line?" but where has the line been drawn—between conscious and unconscious? by the phrenes? thalamus?
>
> (Bion, 1975a, p. 189)

A Primordial Moral System

The idea of morality as a very early human acquisition may be envisioned in myths present in many different cultures that describe man's transgression of the omnipotent will of the gods. The association between access to knowledge and punishment, which we find in the Hebrew myths of Eden and the Tower of Babel, in Greek myths of Oedipus and Prometheus, is also found in myths from cultures as diverse as the Vedic (Green, 1987) and Native American (Lévi-Strauss, 1985). This association recalls the view of Freud, who always linked the roots of our moral system to archaic events in the prehistory of humankind as well as in the individual. The murder of the father by the primitive horde—and their subsequent elevation of his memory and law as sacred—was Freud's initial hypothesis to explain the existence of fundamental feelings of guilt and persecution (1912). Later (Freud 1924, 1930, 1938), with his second theory of the instincts, the idea of a basic *unconscious feeling of guilt* was thought to reflect the presence of an undeflected residue of the death instinct in the ego. In both formulations, it is the feeling of guilt that gives rise to conscience.

Klein (1933) developed Freud's last approach and proposed a distinction between the superego, as it was already described by Freud, and an archaic superego that stands as a harsh and cruel conscience. She theorized that the latter reflected the presence of the death instinct deflected in early post-natal life, manifested throughout the virulence of sadistic impulses.

Based on Bion's writings, we can assume that he initially took these views on unconscious guilt of Freud and Klein as his own. However, after *A Theory of Thinking*, even stressing the presence in the personality of an envious superego, he linked unconscious guilt to psychological conflicts triggered by the development of the capacity to get in touch with psychic reality. Notwithstanding, it is with the concept of *primitive conscience* that Bion created a new theory about the development of the human moral system, bringing together four hypotheses:

i The fetus, despite lacking myelinated upper brain structures, is capable of experiencing sensations (proto-emotions and proto-ideas) as excitations in the thalamo-adrenal axis. These sensations give rise to proto-feelings, which will later be nominated "fear" or "hate," that could be experienced in a primordial way, mobilizing impulses to fight or to flee;

ii The experiences of swallowing and evacuating amniotic fluid could be the model for projective identification, used by the developing fetus to get rid of overwhelming or disturbing experiences of proto-emotions and proto-ideas;

iii The latter sensations are possibly experienced by the fetus as a flood of excitements that threaten annihilation. They would form a dreadful record of "noughtness" (nothingness),[9] with which, subsequent contact is to be absolutely avoided. To that end, prohibitive actions are taken ("cannot"), whose aim is to prevent that contact at all costs. Guilt ("Original Sin") would be its proper feeling;

iv Taking the birth process as a model, a caesura occurs, which renders these primordial registers inaccessible to the post-natal, symbolizing mind that will develop.

To summarize Bion's conjecture, there is a buried moral tendency that exists in the foundations of our mental life and *presses for expression*. It refers us to thoughts that are not developed from experience, that have no thinker—remnants of primeval experiences that are without registration in the cortex of the brain. Thus, the concept *primitive conscience* merges aspects of the previous Freudian and Kleinian theories on the origins of the human moral system: it is innate (although not phylogenetic) and comes about due to experiences (although these are prior to object relationships). Clinically, it is therefore possible to establish a distinction between a "mature" and a "primitive" conscience. The former includes the development of a moral system working in synergy with the functions of thinking, in a constructive manner, while the latter manifests itself in a growth-obstructing way, as prohibitions against contact with experiences that could enable the development of the personality.

These ideas are refined in Bion's final works:

> The moral system, the conscience, cannot be appreciated unless its primitive nature is recognized. Unfortunately we have to use terms like "superego" which immediately suggests something which is above everything else. It is much more likely to be underneath everything else, basic, fundamental.
>
> (1976d, p. 248)

> I don't suppose there will ever be any chance of knowing, so to speak, what a fetus thinks, but—to go on with my scientific fiction—I suggest that there is no reason why it shouldn't *feel*. I think it would be quite useful to consider that some stages of fear, of intense fear, are more easily visualized or imagined by us if we think of them as thalamic fear, or as some sort of glandular manifestation such as something to do with the adrenals, or what later on turn out to be the genital structures.
>
> (1976b, p. 309)

A Clinical Illustration

The analysand is a woman, who, despite many years of a fruitful analysis, remained submerged in intense mental suffering. She felt terribly depressed, with episodes of intense anxiety and recurring thoughts of suicide. In a hallucinatory state, she felt accused by all the "mistakes" and "sins"—real or imagined—that she might have committed. She couldn't see any good qualities in herself and had feelings of being a scoundrel and a burden to her family. Dominated by delusional feelings of shame, she imagined her husband and children discovering who she believed herself to be and as a result, losing the love and respect they nurtured for her. She described her condition as if falling into an endless abyss, possessed by intense despair, in need of tranquilizers and antidepressants. If she could not relieve her distress, the risk of suicide would be imminent.

Alerted by the conception of *primitive conscience*, the analyst started drawing her attention to the unreal, unnecessary and murderous qualities of her apparent moral standards. Slowly, a few elements evolved. Quasi-dreams[10] appeared amid terrifying dream images indistinguishable from hallucinations ("non-dreams"), detached from a background of melancholic feelings.

In time, more developed dreams appeared depicting a state of intense horror. These were taken as evidence of evolving thoughts. In the first of these dreams, she was standing before a rotted scarecrow, in which a skull-head with disheveled hair had threads hanging from its teeth. In her associations, these threads were seen as threads of hope, linking her to the world of living beings. Days later, she described two other dreams. In the first, she was walking down the street carrying her little daughter. On the opposite side, there was a huge dog, which threatened fiercely to jump a wooden fence that was constructed of sticks laid side by side. Terrified, she realized that the height of the fence had suddenly decreased, making an attack from the beast imminent. Her worst fear was that she would not be able to protect her little daughter. In a state of extreme anguish, she woke up, yet with the feeling of the threat of the terrible animal. In another dream, the patient, who was in fact at that time experiencing a cough with some secretion, dreamed that one of her lungs was divided in half. The lower half was taken by an attack of bacteria, which turned into virulent larvae, threatening to invade and eat the tissue of the healthy half.

From these dreams, it was possible to pinpoint glimpses of a murderous conscience and of the dreadful experiences of living with it. Little by little, her awareness of a mind split in two increased, with primitive elements threatening to erupt, seize her self and destroy her. The continuity of sessions showed gains in the symbolization of her frightening emotional states, but not the mitigation of the guilt. Nonetheless, it was possible for her to endure them better. She was also more able to be aware and to think about them.

We suggest that it was psychoanalytically meaningful to examine the possibility that the analysand was trapped in a fight-or-flight pattern, experiencing an invasion of foreign thoughts from an unknown and unknowable part of her (her primordial mind) into her conscious/unconscious states of mind. Stated another way, the analyst was witnessing the conflicts of a person who had to endure the risks of recognizing and becoming who she in fact was—i.e. a person with a highly active and destructive primitive conscience. Similarly, in other analyses, we were able to follow this transition from a state of mind in which the analysand is violently drawn to a non-thinking condition, to another state in which the capacity for thought is recovered, after the personality copes with recognizing and accepting the invasive primitive elements.

These views stress the discontinuity between a "somatic mind," developed before birth, and another, proto-symbolic and symbolic mind, developed afterwards.

The clinical material presented demonstrates the difficulties involved in openly dealing with primordial conditions. It highlights the futility of trying to elaborate these primordial elements, as if they were meanings *of* the analytical relationship, even as it describes the value of recognizing them as arising *from* and *within* it. While there is no "mental tissue" capable of transforming noughtness into meaningfulness, it is possible to achieve mental conditions for working on actual emotional experiences of primordial guilt and dread. These elements can be recognized as foreign ("wild thoughts") and through analytical experience and construction they can achieve representation. Identification and elaboration in words allows these proto-emotional contents to acquire significance in the domain of knowledge (K) in a multidimensional mind, as a kind of silent enemy that needs to be carefully watched. To think in these terms in a psychoanalytic process is to think in terms of personality growth, rather than conflict resolution or symbolic meanings.

Some Implications for Clinical Practice

As any other function of the mind, *primitive conscience* is an abstraction. Clinically, we can conjecture its presence in states of terror associated with disguised or openly manifested guilt that are accessible through transformations of emotional experiences of the analytical session. Being an archaic remnant ("embryonic"), it is devoid of symbolic elements when penetrating the conscious/unconscious mind. Its quality is of indiscrimination between body and psyche, and it is unresponsive to our usual psychoanalytical approaches. Bion recognized this problem for the analyst in *Evidence* (1976c, p. 319):

> Supposing we are in fact always dealing with some kind of psychosomatic condition. Is it any good talking to a highly articulate person in highly articulate terms? Is it possible that if feelings of intense fear, self-hatred, can seep up into a state of mind in which they can be translated into action, the reverse is true? Is it possible to talk to the soma in such a way that the psychosis is able to understand, or vice versa?

We also find indications from Bion on the difficulties of interpreting this condition to the analysand in his supervisions:

> I don't think I would want to say anything of that to her, at the moment, because I'm not sure whether the patient could stand it—I would probably want to hear some more. But in the meantime, I would keep to myself the fact that this is a fundamental, basic guilt.
>
> [...] Now the point about this: what should I say to the patient? What interpretation should I give? Or, shall I remain silent? Now, if I remain silent, then I am stepping into the position of being the conscience, which is no good to her; I need more information and, therefore, I'd prefer to remain silent until I heard some more. But if I were the analyst, I would not really know whether I could afford to wait, or whether it would make her more than ever, frightened of me as the unhelpful and hostile conscience.
>
> (Bion, 1978a)

And

> Of course, the problem still exists to what the analyst would say to the patient, because whatever the analyst says to the patient, is an action; he's really doing something. I would have thought that the point that he needs to be aware of is the murderous quality of that conscience, which hates a happy and pleasurable and successful intercourse, verbal or otherwise. So, I think that it would be useful for him, to be aware of, so that he could make allowances for that kind of murderous moral standard, which would really mean the destruction of any creative activity.
>
> (Bion, 1978b)

Reflections on our clinical experience lead us to emphasize five points:

i In an overall view, two perspectives should be stressed to the analyst: attention to detecting signs of a silent dread as an important means to discern the activity and presence of primordial conscience, and the importance of oscillating between the two vertices from which the analyst is able to examine the psychosomatic continuum. Both stances reduce the consequences of the split between the body and the mind. Instead of only looking at the somatic from the psychological vertex, we ought also to conjecture on the somatic origin of what later emerges as mental;

ii It is valuable to have in mind that since *Transformations*, Bion warned us that he was following a finite/infinite paradigm—and not the conscious/unconscious one anymore. It alerts us to the differences between symbolic and non-symbolic domains in dealing with thoughts, and leads beyond the dichotomy that consists only of conscious and unconscious meanings. During his final years, Bion referred to the co-existence of two states of mind: the conscious/unconscious and the inaccessible (Bion, 1977a, p. 50). The first is the classical domain of psychoanalysis; the second includes primordial sensory and emotional data of the human being as an unborn child, separated/united from the conscious/unconscious states of mind by the caesura of birth. The inaccessible state manifests itself through somatic innervations and is expressed physically through basic emotions experienced as excessive.

iii Being part of the inaccessible state of mind, *primitive conscience* can be inferred only by conjecturing it in elements that disguise a primary guilt hiding a state of terror. Since it is unresponsive to interpretations of meanings, the analyst is limited to promoting his/her approach with the conscious/unconscious system through his/her work through the emotional experiences of the session. Meltzer formulates this problem for the analyst in a different language:

> So, you are left with these patients with an unanalyzed, and I think unanalyzable, psychotic part of the personality. It doesn't mean that it couldn't develop, but it won't develop as a result of being analyzed. It can develop as a result of being nurtured, mothered, what I call the impact of the atmosphere of the consulting room. But not by interpretation or investigation.
>
> (1997)

iv Taking further this last point: on a few occasions, as in the prior clinical description, we were able to follow the working through of these conditions and observe the creation and upsurge of representations of these frightful experiences within the self, but not their "cure," their integration in the "mental tissue." In such instances, the personality grows in awareness of him/herself, but this is secondary. The main acquisition is the possibility of becoming less terrified by aspects that are part of him/herself, ceasing a kind of internal guerrilla war and allowing previously "warring" parts of the mind to "sit together to discuss the terms of a truce."

v *Primitive conscience* should be considered in those conditions clinically described as negative therapeutic reaction, non-analyzability, as well as in analyses that do not evolve, or that continue for very long periods of time, with the same or with different analysts. In such cases, it may be valuable to think that these individuals experience intense terror when struggling to make contact with sensuous or psychic reality or to become who they in fact are. When this is the case, the analysis is seen, at the same time, as a hope to escape from this deadlock and as protection against the terrifying contact. In this process, the analyst becomes an experienced and indispensable partner.

Summary

In studying supervisions given by Bion in 1978 in São Paulo, Brazil, one of the present authors (José Américo Junqueira de Mattos) identified references to a mental configuration, colloquially named by Bion as *primitive conscience.* Reviewing his articles and seminars from that period, it was possible to identify this idea in different discussions. This concept developed over Bion's last years of life (1976–9), as part of an important addition to his model of the mind. At that time, he conjectured about a primordial mind, which developed pre-natally and which would remain unchanged and active after birth. With this hypothesis, Bion drew our attention to the earliest stages of the development of the mind, to somatic imprints associated with organs (thalamus and adrenals) that are actively functioning in the body prior to birth at a time before the cerebral cortex is prepared to record and create psychic elements.

In this context, Bion conjectured that very primitive feelings of guilt, capable of triggering cruel sanctions to a fatal point, would provide the foundation for a *primitive conscience.* This conscience would not consider experience to indicate possible choices, but rather, would impose rules and prohibitions. In that way, it would nullify and oppose emotional experiences potentially capable of leading to mental growth. At different times, Bion used terms such as *nameless dread* and *sub-thalamic fear* to approach this condition. In the present chapter, we have attempted to elaborate Bion's *imaginative conjecture* into a more fully formed element of psychoanalytic theory.

Notes

1 Also in *Bion in New York and São Paulo* (1977–8).
2 The authors will refer to the term Supervision instead of Seminar, since the first was the denomination that Bion himself used on the occasions they were given.
3 Audiotape transcriptions by José Américo Junqueira de Mattos.
4 São Paulo, April 1978. Partially published in *Clinical Seminars and Other Works* as São Paulo's Supervision 18.

5 Bion's reference is to analyst and analysand.
6 In *Transformations* (1965), Bion used the terminology "being reality" (p. 145) to imply a process of becoming and we follow the same convention here.
7 In a sharper and even more abstract description, we find a new approach: supported by the Grid, it is designated as the ← ↑ psychic movement emphasizing its dynamic quality. The arrows indicate the movements towards line A (↑) and to column 1 (←) in the Grid. In more abstract description, it would be the movement toward existence from an object without existence. See *Transformations*, chapters 7 and 8.
8 I, 173; I, 180; I, 189.
9 See Bion, 1965, p. 134.
10 Following Bion (e.g. *Cogitations*, p. 40) and Rezze, C. J. (*Dreams, Quasi-dreams and Non-dreams*, 2000), we refer here to "dreams" as the symbolic elaboration, through alpha function, of emotional experiences while asleep. These experiences are useful for learning from the emotional experience when referred to in the analytical session. "Quasi-dreams" are described as "dream" by the analysand and are similar to them; however, they are not helpful in elaborating the emotional experience of the session, suggesting that they are actually transformations in an infinite domain, reflective of psychotic functioning. By "non-dreams," we mean pictorial images treated as facts suggesting the intuition of mental contents incapable of symbolic representation. They reveal attempts of the mind to get rid of non-transformable elements.

References

Bion, W. R. (1950) The imaginary twin. In W. R. Bion, *Second Thoughts*. Karnac, London, 1967, pp. 3–22.

Bion, W. R. (1959) Attacks on Linking. In *Second Thoughts*. W. Heinemann, London, 1967.

Bion, W. R. (1962a) A Theory of Thinking. In *Second Thoughts*. W. Heinemann, London, 1967.

Bion, W. R. (1962b) *Learning from Experience*. W. Heinemann, London, 1962.

Bion, W. R. (1963) *Elements of Psychoanalysis*. W. Heinemann, London, 1963.

Bion, W. R. (1965) *Transformations*. Maresfield Library, London, 1991.

Bion, W. R. (1966) Catastrophic Changes. *Bulletin of the British Psychoanalytical Society*, 5.

Bion, W. R. (1970) *Attention and Interpretation*. Maresfield Library, London, 1993.

Bion, W. R. (1975a) *A Memoir of the Future. The Dream*. Imago Editora, Rio de Janeiro, 1975.

Bion, W. R. (1975b) Supervision S17. Audiotape of supervision given at Psychoanalytic Society of Brasilia. Transcription and notation by José Américo Junqueira de Mattos.

Bion, W. R. (1976a) Emotional Turbulence. In W. R. Bion, *Clinical Seminars and Other Works*. Karnac Books, London, 1994.

Bion, W. R. (1976b) On a Quotation from Freud. In W. R. Bion, *Clinical Seminars and Other Works*. Karnac Books, London, 1994.

Bion, W. R. (1976c) Evidence. In W. R. Bion, *Clinical Seminars and Other Works*. Karnac Books, London, 1994.

Bion, W. R. (1976d) *Four Discussions with W. R. Bion*. Clunie Press, Perthshire, 1978.

Bion, W. R. (1977a) *Taming Wild Thoughts*. Bion, F. (ed.). Karnac Books, London, 1997.

Bion, W. R. (1977b) *Seminari Italiani* [Italian Seminars]. Bion, P. (ed.). Borla Ed., Rome, 1985.

Bion, W. R. (1977–8) *Bion in New York and São Paulo*. Clunie Press, Perthshire, 1980.

Bion, W. R. (1978a) Supervision A5. Audiotape of supervision given at Brazilian Psychoanalytic Society of São Paulo. Transcription and notation by José Américo Junqueira de Mattos.

Bion, W. R. (1978b) Supervision A6. Audiotape of supervision given at Brazilian Psychoanalytic Society of São Paulo. Transcription and notation by José Américo Junqueira de Mattos.

Bion, W. R. (1978c) Supervision S12. Audiotape of supervision given at Brazilian Psychoanalytic Society of São Paulo. Transcription and notation by José Américo Junqueira de Mattos.

Bion, W. R. (1978d). *Four Discussions with W. R. Bion.* Clunie Press/The Roland Harris Trust, London.

Bion, W. R. (1979) Making the Best of a Bad Job. In W.R.Bion, *Clinical Seminars and Other Works.* Karnac Books, London, 1994.

Bion, W. R. (1992) *Cogitations.* Bion, F. (ed.). Karnac Books, London, 1992.

Bion, W.R.; Bion, F. (comp.) (1981) *A Key to "A Memoir of the Future."* Clunie Press, Perthshire, 1981.

Freud, S. (1912) Totem and Taboo. *Standard Edition,* 13. Hogarth Press and Institute of Psychoanalysis, London, 1961.

Freud, S. (1915). The Unconscious. *Standard Edition,* 12.

Freud, S. (1923) The Ego and the Id. *Standard Edition,* 19. Hogarth Press and Institute of Psychoanalysis, London, 1961.

Freud, S. (1924) The Economic Problem of Masochism. *Standard Edition,* 19. Hogarth Press and Institute of Psychoanalysis, London, 1961.

Freud, S. (1930) Civilization and its Discontents. *Standard Edition,* vol. 21. Hogarth Press and Institute of Psychoanalysis, London, 1961.

Freud, S. (1932) New Introductory Lectures on Psychoanalysis. *Standard Edition,* 22. Hogarth Press and Institute of Psychoanalysis, London, 1961.

Freud, S. (1938) An Outline of Psychoanalysis. *Standard Edition,* vol. 23. Hogarth Press and Institute of Psychoanalysis, London, 1964.

Green, A. (1987) The Primordial Mind and the Work of the Negative. *The International Journal of Psychoanalysis,* 79:649–65, 1998.

Junqueira de Mattos, J. A. (1980) Impressões de Minha Análise com Dr. Bion [My Analysis with Bion: Impressions]. *Alter,* X, 3:113–27, 1980. Also in *Actualidad Psicologica* 5–6:18–21, 1997.

Klein, M. (1933) The Early Development of Conscience in the Child. In: Klein, M. *Love, Guilt and Reparation.* The Hogarth Press, London, 1975.

Klein, M. (1957) On the Development of Mental Functioning. *The International Journal of Psychoanalysis,* 39:84–90, 1958.

Lévi-Strauss, C. (1985) *A Oleira Ciumenta* [The Jealous Potter]. Edições 70, Lisboa, 1987.

Meltzer, D. (1997) Audio recorded supervision with the authors. Oxford, 1997.

Rezze, C. J. (2000) O Sonho, o Quase Sonho e o Não Sonho [Dreams, Quasi-dreams and Non-dreams]. Paper presented in a scientific meeting of Brazilian Psychoanalytical Society of São Paulo, 4/29/2000.

Wilheim, J. (2005) Síndrome do Sobrevivente da Concepção Gemelar—o Gêmeo Desaparecido. [The Twinned Conception Survival Syndrome—The Vanished Twin]. Paper presented in a scientific meeting of Brazilian Psychoanalytical Society of São Paulo, 10/6/2005.

EDITORS' INTRODUCTION

Container–Contained Inverted Relationship –(♀♂): Developments and Applications of a Very Powerful Concept of Wilfred R. Bion

Alessandro Bruni

Bruni introduces us to an aspect of Bion's thinking that has been relatively underappreciated: his concept of the *negative* or *inverted* container/contained. According to Bion, in healthy development the mother, through her **reverie**, functions as a **container** for her infant's projections of painful, unrepresented experience (the **contained**), and uses her **alpha function** to transform the projected contained into an *emotional thought* (Bion, 1962), which she can represent to the infant. This interactive process soothes the infant and, as it is introjected, enables the infant to develop an *apparatus for thinking thoughts* and to become a thinking entity with a mind of its own (Caper, 2000). Through such interactions, the infant gradually comes to possess an independent capacity for thinking that owes its origin to successful experiences with a mother who is capable of tolerating and transforming her baby's raw emotional feelings.

This process may go awry, when the mother finds her infant's projections too painful or difficult to manage. In such situations, the raw affects, which the baby looks to its mother to transform, remain unprocessed and become the basis of what the infant will feel as **nameless dread** (Bion, 1962). Thus, what should have been a positive experience of internalizing a mother, who brought emotional meaning to her baby's experiences, is instead introjected as a negative experience, that of the inverted container/contained. As a result, the infant then has within itself an experience of the mother as someone who, rather than attaching value to her child's affective life, is felt to strip away the significance of the infant's emotional world. This absence of a containing maternal presence may stir the infant's envy and, when that envy is projected, it may create an image of an enviously attacking mother, who divests her baby's emotional being of any importance.

Bruni sees this notion of an **inverted container/contained relationship**, in which the child's symbolic thinking cannot be established due to the mother's difficulties with reverie and alpha function, being on a par with Bion's (1965) description of *commensal*, *parasitic* and *symbiotic* relationships. He further expands Bion's ideas by discussing the impact of this state upon the neuropsychological dimensions of the personality, including the propensity towards somatization of experience in place of psychological representation. When the analysand is under the sway of the inverted container/contained, Bruni wisely cautions us that the analyst must be mindful of the degree to which the patient's capacity for thinking and competent psychic functioning is dependent upon the analyst's physical presence and the degree to which the patient is reactive to the physicality of the analyst's being.

9

CONTAINER–CONTAINED INVERTED RELATIONSHIP –(♀♂)

Developments and Applications of a Very Powerful Concept of Wilfred R. Bion

Alessandro Bruni

> We are trying to talk about an obscure subject, the most fundamental and primitive parts of the human mind. … Instead of trying to bring a brilliant, intelligent, knowledgeable light to bear on obscure problems, I suggest we bring to bear a diminution of the "light"—a penetrating beam of darkness: a reciprocal of the searchlight.
>
> (Bion, Sao Paulo, 1973)

Introduction: The Concept of –(♀♂)

Melanie Klein's (1946) concept of projective identification referred to the idea that the infant projects unwanted parts of the self into the mother in order to unburden its psyche. However, Klein did not attend to the effect this projection has upon the mother and it was Bion who later (1962) explored the role of the mother in making more palatable what the baby had projected into her. This was achieved by her acting as a *container* of the baby's projection, the *contained,* and through her activity of *reverie* the mother helped her child bear emotions it could not manage on its own. Bion (1962) represented the container by the symbol "♀" and used the symbol "♂" to denote the contained. The relationship of container/contained was represented by the sign "♀♂" (Bion, 1962). The sign "♀♂" may represent various psychological phenomena: the mother's capacity for reverie, the child's ability to assimilate thinking functions within himself (the apparatus for thinking), thinking containing thoughts and thoughts containing thinking, words containing things, mind containing body, the relationship between the group and the individual and so on.

In his first formulations, Bion proposed three possible manifestations of ♀♂. The first, called "*commensal*," denotes a situation of latent cohabitation between container and contained, with very little mutual interaction. The second, called "*parasitic*," describes an interaction diametrically opposed to the first, in which the ♀ threatens to destroy ♂ or vice versa. The third variation, called "*symbiotic*" (in the biological sense), represents a benign and evolutionary development in which ♀ and ♂ couple, interact, nourish each other and develop with mutual benefit that fosters the growth of symbolic thinking. In this paper, I will talk about what I consider a fourth possibility, briefly mentioned in only a few lines of *Learning from Experience*, designated by Bion as -(♀♂) (Bion, 1962). I call this manifestation "*inverted*."

This fourth kind denotes, in an abstract way, those states in which the elaboration of emotion has a negative outcome due to the child's innate inability to tolerate frustration or to the difficulty in the mother's reverie or both. In this situation, the symbolic function of thinking cannot be established in the ordinary sense and words cannot acquire the power to represent and contain affect. As a result, things and related emotions cannot be assimilated by the functions of thinking and so remain in the mind as very concrete and persecutory "*thalamic*" objects. In the effort to get rid of these objects, the subject is forced to resort to hyperbolic abuse of primitive defense mechanisms, such as splitting, evacuation and massive projective identification. In more normal development, the non-psychotic part of the personality can cope with the disappearance and absence of a real object such as the "*real breast*" by establishing a corresponding good internal object, i.e. the "*idea of breast*." This *cortical linguistic element*, allows for the permanent representation of the real objects in the internal mental world.

In contrast, in psychotic development, one cannot mentally free him/herself from the missing object. This object assumes characteristics of a persecutory presence and forces the subject to try to eliminate it through the use of primitive defense mechanisms, which generates a perverted downward mental spiral. As a consequence, the object becomes more and more intolerable and at the same time the subject weakens and loses his capacity to think in an ordinary way. The excessive use of primitive defense mechanisms, which act on persecutory objects, results in what Bion calls "*an envious force which takes existence out of objects*," represented by the graphic sign "←↑" (Bion, 1965).

The quality of the mental space created in the psyche by this kind of "*negative*" development, is a sort of "*non-place*," which is filled to the brim by "*black holes*," i.e. collapsed and encysted objects that have vanished but are capable of obscuring and annihilating mental functions. At the same time, when the analytic process intercepts these objects, they are dangerously able to ignite the patient's greed, envy and destructiveness.

Therefore, when these psychotic objects collide with the non-psychotic part of the personality, "*thinking*," in these situations, requires overcoming hallucinatory states for both patient and analyst. Bion stresses that these psychotic mechanisms are present and should be identified and analyzed even in relatively serious neurotic patients.

In order to designate the symptomatic patterns of containment that appear in these situations of inversion of the symbolic process, Bion (1962), in a few lines in *Learning from Experience*, proposes an inverse formulation of the sign which he indicates as –(♀♂). Unlike the positive ♀♂, –(♀♂) denotes a "Pseudo-Ego" situation, where meanings are impoverished, emotions are devitalized, mental growth stops and rigid moralistic superego qualities prevail. To show the usefulness of this sign in understanding clinical issues, I would like to go back to Bion's more general concept that the psychotic part of personality needs the material presence of real objects in order to be able to think.

Summarizing the concept, we could say that where there is a crack in the normal cortical ability for symbolic thought—which allows for thinking thoughts and experiencing emotions even in the absence of objects—and as a result, the subject needs the physical presence of the object and uses its perceptive gestalt as an "*inverted thalamic container*." Thus raw emotional states remain "*things-in-themselves*," which may be expressed in somatic reactions that become containers of thoughts and emotions, which otherwise could not be thought and therefore would remain split off in a devitalized state. This "*stuff for thinking*" is provided by all the sensory, motor, voluntary and involuntary nerve terminals, which connect the central nervous system (CNS) with the outside and inside of the body. When speaking about the outside, it is a question of sensory extra-ceptive patterns associated to real stimuli. When speaking about the inside, it is proprio-ceptive and intra-ceptive sensations, which are related to organic and functional symptomatic states. These can be specific organ illnesses, neuro-vegetative disorders, breathing rhythms (De Toffoli 1988), posture tensions, repetitive obsessive actions (Soavi 1988), digestive (Bollea 1990) and uro-genital (Micati 1988) disorders and perversions.

An undervalued consideration in psychoanalysis is the neuro-psychological evidence that even the soma is an "*external*" interactive environment for the CNS. Just as the whole organism is "*immersed*" in the surrounding world, so the CNS is "*immersed*" in the soma, even if clearly with less freedom of movement. While we can physically escape from a place we dislike, we cannot escape from the body we are in. However, if we consider the phenomenon of somatic anesthesia or the feeling of estrangement from the body, we can see that non-physical flights are possible. The CNS, then, has relations with two external environments: the world surrounding it and the soma.

It is important to take note that for Bion sensory organs work in two ways: through them the non-psychotic part of personality can "*receive*" information, while the psychotic part can use them, metaphorically, to "*evacuate*" beta elements, which are non-utilizable by normal thinking. The following examples illustrate the value of considering this fourth organization of the container/contained, –(♀♂).

The "Ghostbuster"

Karl Pribram relates that many years ago in the Bowery, at that time an impoverished area in New York City, police and assistance services one night received an unusually large number of phone calls from people reporting various kinds of problems: suspect noises, gas leaks, threats, illnesses. Besides being related to totally unreal impressions, most of these phone calls were concentrated at particular hours of the night. The mystery was solved when someone realized that the day before the calls, a portion of the overhead railway had been shut down. "*The calls were made at the times the trains had formerly rumbled past. The strange occurrences were, of course, the deafening silence that had replaced the expected noise*" (Pribram 1971).

In that dilapidated neighborhood, the old train had acquired, unbeknownst to all, the sedating function of "ghostbuster," which can be considered a realization of –(♀♂). People in the neighborhood had developed a primitive pre-conception that was periodically saturated and that used the deafening noise of the train as a sensory "*vehicle*" of evacuation of quantities of excitement (beta elements, Bion 1962). These elements had been condensed in the short time preceding sleep. These quantities rose up to consciousness at the customary established times even after the train was cancelled, just as they had done before. Given the absence of the expected noise as a sensory vehicle of evacuation, consciousness turned the excitement into a state of paranoid or soma-psychotic hallucinosis (Bion 1965) and caused panicked awakenings.

Drug Addicts

At the start of a therapeutic group with drug addicts in a public health service something odd happened: after the first sessions, some members of the group, one after another, started developing a fantasy, which then rapidly developed into a delusional certainty, that they were becoming afflicted by fatal illnesses. One group member even came to a meeting in a state of panicky despair showing the results of some tests suggesting that he had been affected by cancer of the liver. He did so with such certainty that even I thought it was true.

Let's assume drug addiction as a –(♀♂) support for an omnipotent fantasy used to govern reality without succumbing to the difficulties of emotional relations with the others. Now, the new fantasy of a shared fatal illness activated in the group, independent of drugs, mobilized a great anxiety due to the enormous number of things to be thought and to be emotionally experienced by all members. The group thus tried to cope with the emergence of psychic terror by making concrete the fantasy of looking for a substitutive containment at the somatic level, the fantasy of cancer, as if paradoxically that was a less threatening illness because it was tangible, physical, localized and, therefore, more capable of compressing and condensing the explosive affective pressure in the group. This fantasy seemed to express the thought: "*rather than a nameless panic, better a cancer panic!*"

Vis-à-Vis

The sign, –(♀♂), can be used to explore the widespread custom of treating psychotic patients face-to-face, at least at the beginning of analysis; or, in more general terms, the resistance that many less ill patients feel to the use of the couch. It would seem that the sensory deprivation caused by the couch, the fact of not being able to explore the analyst's real physical person and his physical surroundings, can produce in the psychotic part of the mind an unbearable decrease in the "*stuff for thinking,*" stuff which is made up mostly of those non-verbal products of the analyst that accompany interpretative activity, such as expressions of the eyes, face changes, muscular tensions and movements, voice changes, etc. In these situations, the analyst can try to be more sensitive to the –(♀♂) use the patient makes of the physical quality of the analytic relation in order to enlarge the field of "*thinkability.*"

At the end of my first consultation with a psychotic patient, I had the clear feeling that all my attempts to establish contact had miserably failed. While I was accompanying the patient towards the door, suddenly he turned his head toward the bookshelves on his right. A volume from Freud's complete works was missing! The patient looked at me with a questioning gaze. Just as suddenly, "without thinking," I answered. "The exams never end!" He smiled! He had been attracted to a sensorial vacuum (–♀♂), more than to my verbal communication. Communicating to him that I hadn't stopped studying, that I always had empty spaces, had allowed him to feel accepted.

Pauses

Along the same lines, let's consider the point of view of the psychotic part of the personality in response to weekends and holiday breaks. In these circumstances, the missing of "*stuff for thinking*" usually provided by the sessions, is not perceived directly as a "*lack of analysis*" connected with separation—something we often tend to suggest to patients with premature interpretations that only refer to separation issues. Rather, the breaks produce substitutive symptomatic "*apparitions*," whose fantastical content deserve, in my opinion, more attention and respect. They bring indeed to light those thought elements that were immobilized in the –(♀♂) self-containment provided by some underground and invisible aspects of the analytic relation itself (Bruni 1985).

I would like to suggest a rather oversimplified analogy between the ghostbuster train and the analytic session. I would say that for the poor person of the Bowery it would not be so important to know that he had a hallucination because the train no longer ran above his head, but rather, to give value to the hallucinatory "*epiphany*" and, so doing, to better understand his internal world and face his self-isolated reality. Paying attention to this "epiphany" allows the analyst to understand more fully the patient's attempt to hallucinate a meaning of the absence which is the creation of a "lie" produced by the –(♀♂) because the emotional truth of his isolation is too overpowering to be directly experienced.

–(♀♂) Capacity of Analytical Groups

Unlike the dyadic analytical setting, the analytic group conducted with Bionian method presents a constant and full audio-visual hyper-stimulation. All members, including the analyst, are synchronically exposed to the acoustic message of the speakers. At the same time, at the visual level, they share all non-verbal manifestations. This audio-visual field in which individual group members are immersed is the emotional point where "*vectors*" intersect that transport, diffuse, condense and polarize apparitions and disappearances. It can be thought of as the group's "*cytoplasm*" and as a "*thinking syncytium*" and suggests the possibility of thinking from a neurophysiological model of the "*group's mind*" as a hyper-complex system where individual apparatuses are seen as partial sub-systems or the larger group shared fantasy.

This group dimension develops a great –(♀♂) ability, whose power can often activate, demobilize and absorb the –(♀♂) configurations brought in by individuals. It is thus possible to understand how at times psychotic surges, skin disorders, panic attacks or anxious states can be absorbed and transformed, at times very quickly, after being put into the group. Obviously it is necessary that those that I would name the group's "*higher functions*" are active and awake with respect to these movements in order to foster the "*upward*" transformations from –(♀♂) to plus (♀♂). In this way, the group's proto-mental ability should not ever be overcharged and saturated. In that undesirable case the process could invert its direction: if an emptying and a transfer of "*black holes*" from the group to the individual containers happens, the risk is that one or more members of the group will develop new pathological events in the outside reality or in the soma.

Zombie Objects

A woman had an angioma on her tongue that changed color often and she was compulsively forced to check it in the mirror out of fear that it might turn into a hemorrhage, which had once actually happened. The angioma had an hereditary, autonomous etiology, but in the mind of the patient it had turned into the container of something terrifying and unknown that could kill her. Analytic work revealed that the object was her mother's nipple, torn and necrotized, but not completely dead, so that it cyclically returned like a zombie ready to impose a death sentence on the patient, who felt guilty for having torn it.

In general terms, in many cases we analysts witness heroic and painful odysseys by which patients manage to preserve their mental integrity through a powerful idealization of the mind and a self-containing barricading of themselves inside it. Often, the body, mistreated by the family environment, has been surrendered to the foe. A sort of self-cutting turns the body into a waste basket of unwanted psychic parts. In these cases, analysis must face a painful route to free the body, which for a long time had been used as a –(♀♂) jail of an internal world pervaded by dead and rotten objects. Consequently, each time we have to take care of a mistreated part of the body, we have to expect to encounter the hallucinated vision of a phantasm imprisoned in that part.

For example, a girl in analysis had been using a nasal vaso-constricting drug for about ten years and could hardly breathe without it. This addiction had emerged as a consequence of a very serious erythema, which had nearly suffocated her at age 18. Surprisingly, we also found that this symptom developed immediately after her first important sexual intercourse. With the help of analysis she decided to solve the underlying need for this addiction by having her nose cauterized. The night after this operation, she had a frightening dream of a bloody penis. She had never been to see a gynecologist and after her first such consultation, she examined herself and was convinced she felt something like a cyst—probably the entrance to the uterus. The symbolic relation of nose and penis allows for an analytical hypothesis on the emergence of the erythema: it could be considered as a –(♀♂) expression of a pseudo-phallic erection used as a bulwark against the new genital experience which had forced the female sexual identification to face the monstrous phantasms living inside and awakened by the event.

Space Phobias and Panic Attacks

I will now focus on space phobias (agoraphobia and claustrophobia) and panic attacks to demonstrate how another of Bion's brilliant intuitions, along with the use of the –(♀♂) sign, allows us to see these phenomena in a new light.

In discussing the proto-mental psychotic part of personality, which he considers an original part of the human mind, Bion noticed that psychoanalytical theory takes for granted logical and psychological precedence of the mind's establishment of Euclidean space and its related concepts of inside and outside, inclusion and expulsion, transfer and projection—that this sense of space is a given. And yet, one need only look at children playing with containers and water to suspect that such a strong interest as theirs cannot but serve to develop and build these categories of the mind before they are just taken for granted. We can easily find clinical evidence that in some primitive or pathological states the creation of space and its aggregates is not clearly established in the mind. The most striking idea that Bion presents is that mental and emotional space can be logically and epistemologically considered as antecedent to the mind's construction of a sense of physical space. Bion's idea sounds like this: "*In the beginning there is emotion! Then, the ordinary sense of space appears as the residual mental space where emotions used to be.*"

In these disorders, the construction of perceptual space seems from its very beginning to work as an inverted container –(♀♂) of unbearable feelings due to the failure of the primary environment. This spatial containment is apparently capable of absorbing, hiding and of resisting the implosive–explosive stress of the "*High Vacuum*" generated by "*black holes*" derived from original persecutory objects. The development of actual symptoms seems to signal the collapse of this original defensive structure and can generate serious problems even in subjects having a well-structured non-psychotic part.

For example, supporting the hypothesis of the original tension between space structuring and "*black holes*" emotions is the common memory of an infantile nightmare. The subject, lying in bed at night in the grip of panic, feels he has shrunken in size and the room's walls are growing taller and further apart. After awakening, he and the room slowly return to their ordinary size. According to the prevailing clustering of these objects in the various subdivisions of perceptual space, the ensuing stress can explain the various phenomenological deformation of the patients' subjective experience. Far or near, inside or outside, up or down correspond in various ways and mixes to *(acro-macri-claustro-agora-) phobic symptoms.*

In addition, instead of saying "*closed spaces make me feel air is lacking*" in claustrophobia, we could say "*a lack of air makes me feel that space is closing in*" or in more detail "*an archaic anxiety is present under the guise of lack of air and produces the feeling that space contracts, so that the walls of a closed space fearfully close in.*" We may recall that Alice (Alice in Wonderland), while falling in the hole, experienced her relative size in relation to the space around her changed along with her thoughts and emotions.

In another case, a young patient once told me about an experience he had under the effect of a psychedelic drug. He found himself sitting in front of a tree after a painful meeting with a friend and the friend's girlfriend. The couple were laughing and he immediately felt excluded and laughed at in a paranoid way. Suddenly the tree started bending its branches and he felt it would swallow him. He moved and the hallucination came to an end. After a while I realized that it wasn't the tree bending, but rather all of space that was imploding and swallowing the tree and the patient himself.

Another patient came to me because of a severe form of agoraphobia, which had become so intense it was now preventing him from conducting a "*normal*" life. This patient, when fear or another strong emotion engaged his attention, had a peculiar way of opening his eyes so wide that he resembled those who suffered from hyperthyroidism. It was as if this young man wanted to jump out of his own eye sockets in order to move as close as possible to his audience with a clear desire for attachment, incorporation and even a return to the safety of the womb. During analytical sessions, this visual tension often signaled a state of increasing anxiety and the production of mnestic and hallucinatory material.

During a crucial session of this analysis, an event occurred that seemed to define what Bion (1965) calls a "*transformation in O*," resulting in the disappearance of the patient's agoraphobia. At a certain point during the session, I felt that the patient was entering one of his typical altered states of consciousness. The patient lay motionless and rigid on the couch, his eyes in that strange, wide open state of tension and his breathing had begun to intensify to the point of his risking hyperventilation. I suspected he was entering a sort of hallucinatory stupor.

After waiting patiently, I then felt the need to say something. I do not remember what I said, but it was something intended to reconfirm my presence and closeness to him. Within a few seconds, he came out of his spiraling state and told me, "*Doctor, thank God you spoke to me! It was terrible! The space around me was expanding and the distance between objects in that space kept increasing. By the end, you were so far away in the infinite space that I was about to lose you.*" We had just breathed a sigh of relief when a similar but opposite phenomenon began to occur. Once again, the patient appeared to become paralyzed on the couch. This time, however, the sensation was that he was closing, folding in upon himself. When he was able again to speak, he said he had fallen down deep into the couch, as if he were being pulled downwards by a powerful force. The patient associated this experience to the tragic and much publicized case of Alfredino, a young boy who fell into a well, became wedged at the deep bottom, and eventually died. By the end of this analytic session, the patient was calm.

In the days that followed we noted the total disappearance of his agoraphobia. In my "*speculative imagination*," the patient was dealing with a primitive oral object, which had first appeared in nightmares involving an anxious suction-cup-like attachment to slippery surfaces. I visualized this object as a sort of "*high vacuum*," a realization of the Bion concept mentioned earlier, "*an envious force which takes existence out of objects.*" This state of mind must have in some way projected itself and then have been consolidated inside the perceptual structure of the patient's Euclidian space and as such could be responsible for the agoraphobia. In fact, when the patient was out of doors, he would feel as if the surrounding space and air were pulling him in all directions, to the point that he feared he would be dismembered.

The hallucinatory transformation that took place during the crucial session mentioned made it possible for the patient to perceive such an expansion of space that the distance between us seemed virtually infinite. With my words of reassurance the phenomenon seemed to reach its epiphany. It was at this point that the direction changed. The object in question, the "*high vacuum*," seemed to fall back and be re-introjected, re-incorporated and to finally end, having been identified and visualized.

In another case, an emotionally deprived man with serious gaps in his primal experience, used to frequent transvestites and seemed to use the perversion to "*plug*" these holes in his self. The very idea of transvestism represented, in fact, a more general metaphor of his way of relating to others: he loved to play roles, as if he were an actor, presenting himself as humbler than he really was, hoping to exorcize and hide in this way his dramatic lack of emotional experience, which made him feel inadequate and unacceptable to others.

At the beginning of his analysis, he also experienced a strange phenomenon: lying on the couch, he would suddenly arch his back and move in jerks and scream. Initially, these movements caused me to think that he felt whipped on his back and suggested thoughts related to sado-masochistic fantasies, but this idea did not go much further. On the other hand, the patient also often created in the session a drowsy atmosphere that made it very difficult for me not to fall asleep. Once in a while I was dazed by this cloud of hypnotic material, I felt a terrible undertow pulling my mind into an underlying abyss, so that I jerked awake just like the patient would do. We could then agree on the nature of the phenomenon to which he reacted: he felt his mind was all of a sudden collapsing and being swallowed up by a whirling hyperspace. It seems to me that the phenomenon took on the image of the patient sliding down holes that had opened up, because analysis had started to remove the "*transvestite prostheses*" from the real holes of his self. The phenomenon disappeared after the second year of analysis.

I think that panic attacks in their most evident manifestations (anxiety, tachycardia, lack of oxygen and panic) can be explained as an extreme ego defense, secondary and reactive to the perception of the beginning of an hallucinosis of collapse of perceptive space as a whole. It is not accidental that when describing the earliest panic symptoms, patients often recall a feeling of spatial displacement and loss of balance and control. Panic attacks, seen in the light of this model, show the terror experienced along with them. The hallucinosis of the collapse of space must be something so terrifying that I dare say it is feared more than death: a sort of pit that generates the feeling of being sucked in, or, conversely, a "*final black hole*" that prevails and sucks from inside the subject, incorporating it. This experience is absolutely unbearable and has something in common with "*thalamic terror*," the fear of a total overwhelming of the ego by the psychotic part of the personality. This is more evident when the subject does not have a capable, elastic mental apparatus that is capable of tolerating and containing the more archaic areas of the mind.

Similarly, in acrophobia or vertigo symptoms can be a defensive reaction to the feeling of being sucked into a void. In this case the object, the "*black hole*," is located at the bottom, out of the patient's perceptual spatial focus and can be seen as a force tending to annihilate and swallow gravity. This feeling is a terrible challenge that confronts every newborn. If a mother's holding is either absent or too present, a child cannot get used to this mysterious, dangerous force. Children love the game of being thrown into the air and caught by their parents and many people like roller coasters and other such thrills. These exercises provide them with an acquaintance with the mysteries of gravity.

In my experience I have found that a psychoanalytically-oriented group conducted in a Bionian way is particularly capable of allowing for the absorption of space-phobic symptoms, often within a few months' time. This is due, in my opinion, to its ability to contain, activate and transform the proto-mental state of the mind. It is a sidereal mental space strong enough to identify the "*black holes*" contained in the mind and in the body, to contain and absorb the powerful psychic stress that can ensue and bring back to life buried archaic emotions that may be dramatically enacted and subsequently undergo catharsis.

Physiological Apparatuses and Eroticisms

In general we can say that any disorder related to a physiological anatomic apparatus can be studied with the help of the sign to check if "*it was produced by*" or "*it took up the meaning of*" a need for inverted proto-mental containment. The disorders may be found on a wide range of different levels: molecular, bio-chemical, electro-physiological, histological, phantasmic, behavioral, relational and perverse. As further examples of the concept of the inverted container/contained, I shall discuss the respiratory, digestive and uro-genital apparatuses.

Often a patient's breathing catches our attention: some patients tend to breathe heavily dividing air emission in small fragments; others seem forced not to breathe unless they have finished the sentence they are saying; others have sudden coughing fits, and so on. What is the patient keeping in or letting out? What "*perverts*" his normal physiologic regulation? What value do we assign to the unknown function that is "*abusing*," in the sense of "*over-using*"?

A mother who lacks reverie may think her suffering infant daughter needs food rather than to be acknowledged and respected in her separateness. The mental "food" the mother then offers to her daughter is –(♀♂): "*it is a steak, meat, that must contain and solve the problems of growing up!*" The daughter eats her steak, but, as she is more sensible than her mother, she feels something is wrong and in the end refuses the steak, without realizing, however, that she too is using the –(♀♂) she was mentally fed. The symmetry of these two positions, the child's refusal to eat, can in extreme circumstances even prove fatal. One can try to unbind the "*anorexic knot*" by suggesting that in a paradoxical and asymmetric way there is a "*developmental intent*" to the feeding perversion, that the patient tries to realize a statement through a double negation: "*She tries to be accepted by her mother, by rejecting the mother that rejected her.*"

In a session with the male patient mentioned above who frequented prostitutes and transvestites, the following hypothesis emerged: transvestites are preferred to prostitutes because their erect penis provides evidence of a real affective involvement, whereas with prostitutes it is hard to dispel the doubt that they are just pretending. An erect penis takes up the meaning of a concrete –(♀♂) materialization that assumes in itself the existence of a feeling of affection, whose absence is feared, but cannot even risk being promoted or triggered and so cannot ever be interacted with. "*Touching to believe*" becomes "*touching instead of believing*," as the act of making the concrete touchable may foreclose forever the development of thinking, feeling and dealing with actual relationships.

Technical Approach to –(♀♂)

As concerns the interpretative approach to the clinical situations I have described, I think it is important to help the patient see the need and paradoxically the opportunity of having adopted these early defenses as a form of healing self-containment in a dangerously faulty developmental ecosystem (Funari, 1988). Only later is it appropriate and effective to point out the destructive omnipotent aspects implicit in these archaic defenses which are often characterized by pride, arrogance (rather than envy) and by a rigid, moralistic superego. It is a question of carrying out a "*reanimation of the inanimate*," by suggesting via interpretation the personification of objects and body organs. For example, it is better to say: "*Your contracted muscles seem to help you to protect yourself from the threat of your emotions*" than to say: "*You are contracting your muscles as a way of repressing your emotions.*"

It should also be kept in mind that moving from –(♀♂) → +(♀♂) necessarily implies a passage through a more or less intense hallucinosis whose products show the first signs of "*thinkability*." If the analyst can "dream" the "*stuff for thinking*" provided by the patient, he will help him "*catalyze*" this hallucinosis in order to prevent its failure and the subsequent retreat to –(♀♂). If one is careful enough, in a later phase when the process is consolidated, it will be possible with measured caution to show the patient the costs of maintaining these early and deep defensive structures which oppose development.

Acknowledgements

A special thanks to my wife Eleni, to my daughter Anna and to my son Luigi, for helping me with this English translation.

References

Bion, W. R. (1962) *Learning from Experience*. London: Karnac Books, 1984.

Bion, W. R. (1965) *Transformations*. London: Karnac Books, 1984.

Bion, W. R. (1973) *Brazilian Lectures. Sao Paulo*. London: Karnac Books, 1990.

Bollea, E. (1990) Considerazioni sul trattamento psicoanalitico dell'anoressia mentale. Presented at CPR, Italian Psychoanalytic Society, Rome.

Bruni, A. (1985) Il gruppo che non c'è: un ripensamento sulla separazione. In *Gruppo e Funzione Analitica*, anno VI—N°1. Jann–Apr 1985. Centro Ricerche di Gruppo "del Pollaiolo."

Caper, R. (2000). *Immaterial Facts*. New York: Jason Aronson.

De Toffoli, C. (1988) Trasformazioni del dolore mentale e vicissitudini del respiro in un frammento di relazione analitica, *Rivista di Psicoanalisi*, Oct–Dec 1988.

Funari, E. (1988) Organizzazioni difensive precoci e strutture fusionali. SPI Congress 1988.

Klein, M. (1946) Notes on some schizoid mechanisms. In *Envy and Gratitude*. London: Hogarth Press, 1975, pp. 1–24.

Micati, L. (1988) Sulla sessualità femminile: osservazioni sulle forze che ne ostacolano lo sviluppo e sulla loro risoluzione, *Rivista di Psicoanalisi*, Jan–Mar 1988.

Pribram, K. H. (1971) *Languages of the Brain*. Englewood Cliffs, New Jersey: Prentice Hall.

Soavi, G. C. (1988) Il mito dell'eterno ritorno e la sua importanza nella strutturazione del Sé. SPI Congress 1988.

EDITORS' INTRODUCTION

Romantic Perversion—A Pathological Organization Based on –L: Reflections on Containment and the Experience of Time

Heinz Weiss

Weiss begins with the observation that the capacity to experience time and space emerges from the capacity to tolerate separation in the mother/infant dyad. In his view, a realistic sense of time is exceedingly important if one is to tolerate frustration, because time is an essential component of the mourning process and it is only with a sense of time that one can anticipate that a frustrating situation may come to an end. Without such confidence in a world structured by time, patients may have no option but to desperately wish for a world without time, in order to prevent frightening change or avoid the acceptance of loss felt as unending and therefore too painful to bear. When the latter conditions obtain, rather than feel contained by an object, patients may feel that they are caught in a stifling or endless, claustrophobic trap.

In the analysis of patients who relate at the level of the paranoid-schizoid position, Weiss notes that the analyst may be faced with individuals in whom a stable sense of psychic time and space has not yet materialized. For such patients, there is a propensity to withdraw into "islands of timelessness" (Weiss, 2009), into which the analyst may also be pulled, becoming lost in a confused nether world, in which distinctions between past and present and self and object are blurred. When this occurs, either party may feel "imprisoned [in] ... a deadlock or a labyrinth with no possibility to escape."

To illustrate his thesis, Weiss details a wonderful clinical vignette, concerning his treatment of a woman, who had withdrawn into an ostensibly loving relationship with him, and felt as though they were encased in a magical world of loving admiration and endless time. Upon closer inspection, however, this "love" was actually an expression of what Weiss calls a "–L" link. That is, it was the opposite of realistic love and was marked by a lack of recognition of Weiss as a separate object and by his incorporation "into a near-delusional romantic system." This patient experienced herself as tightly wrapped in a timeless, idealized romantic phantasy, with her analyst as her object. However, Weiss notes that this was a kind of pseudo-containment, in that the object was not felt to be separate, the relationship failed to acknowledge time, space and reality, and therefore led only to further stasis and not to emotional growth. For Weiss, the hallmark of the latter must involve both the unfolding of mental space and the development of a realistic sense of time.

10

ROMANTIC PERVERSION—A PATHOLOGICAL ORGANIZATION BASED ON −L

Reflections on Containment and the Experience of Time

Heinz Weiss

Introduction

There is a general assumption in Bion's work that the container/contained relationship not only enables symbolization and emotional growth, but also provides the individual with a first notion of *mental space*. The latter implies the acknowledgement of a difference between container and contained, i.e. between what is being experienced "within" and what is felt to be "outside." In this contribution, I want to further suggest that the *construction of mental space is a prerequisite for the experience of time*.

In the psychoanalytic literature there have been different approaches to the origin of the concepts of space and time (see Loewald, 1972; Hartocollis, 1983; Gutwinski-Jeggle, 1992; Resnik, 1995; Green, 2002; Birksted-Breen, 2003; Perelberg, 2007). I will argue that the development of a concept of "space" depends on the previous experience of *containment*, i.e. on the transformation and re-introjection of what has been projected into a containing object (Bion, 1962), as it is provided by the earliest exchanges between mother and child (Birksted-Breen, 2009). I will try to show that this experience goes along with the withdrawal of projections and hence with the painful acceptance of separation and loss. Furthermore, I will propose, that whenever we are dealing with timeless states of mind, *the construction of mental space takes priority over the reconstruction of biographical time* (Weiss, 2009).

According to this assumption *the unfolding of a three-dimensional psychic space precedes the development of temporal experience*. It implies a gradual withdrawal of projections, so that transitions from the paranoid-schizoid to the depressive mode of psychic functioning can be made. While in the paranoid-schizoid world the past is omnipresent and the future appears as the end of all time, it is in the depressive position where transience and loss have to be faced. Therefore, I will argue, *it is not memory that makes mourning possible, but vice versa: the ability to mourn that leads to a remembering with emotion and meaning.*

This implies a *spatial model of the transference situation,* where transference is not just seen as a *displacement in time*, but as an *unfolding of mental space.* This accounts especially for patients whose basic problems do not arise from repressed memories but from a more fundamental difficulty, to differentiate past and present and to construct their mental space. Some of them retreat to what I have come to call "islands of timelessness" (Weiss, 2009, p. 89). In the transference they try to pull the analyst into their timeless world where he gets entangled with the patient's internal objects. Sometimes he may then feel seduced to respond to the patient's needs in a specific, gratifying or reassuring way (Feldman, 1993; 1998). At other times the control the patient exerts on the analyst is more palpable and he may then feel imprisoned into what appears to him as a deadlock or a labyrinth with no possibility of escape (Feldman, 2000; Weiss, 2009). To illustrate this and to discuss some of the technical problems that arise from this situation, I will briefly present clinical material from a borderline patient (Weiss, 2008).

Clinical Material

The patient, a social worker in her mid-fifties had sought therapy after a depressive breakdown. She could not cope with the idea that her husband, who now lived with a new partner, was planning to divorce her. She described in much detail the humiliations in her marriage which she had suffered without complaining, hoping that one day her husband would return. Alongside the version of her husband as cruel and disappointing, a romantic version of the relationship seemed to coexist in which certain memories and qualities, like the sound of his voice, took on great importance. Thus, while looking after her daughter and trying to deal with the demands of every-day life, the patient withdrew partially to a fantasy world characterized by unfulfilled longings and suffering.

This situation partly reflected the relationship with her father, a man with many altruistic activities and aesthetic interests, who demanded obedience and used to punish the children very cruelly. The patient spoke of him with a mixture of admiration and fear. Some of her most vivid memories concerned a religious boarding school where she had to suppress her homesickness and was often humiliated in the presence of other children. She also recalled a hiding place on her parents' farm where she used to retreat when she feared punishment or rejection. There she would bite into her arms and longingly suck the pain from her wounds.

All these details conveyed the impression that the patient was governed by a cruel internal organization, which forced her to romanticize and idealize her suffering so as not to be abandoned.

I believe that this organization can be described as operating under the influence of –L. Like the computer virus that had spread under the name "*I love you*," it impaired my internal network and seemed to obstruct any real contact and understanding. This form of love was expressed by a longing for uniqueness and infinity by which I was incorporated into a near-delusional romantic system. I think that similar convictions underlie "Golden Age" fantasies and different forms of utopian thinking (Smith, 1977; Weiss, 2010). Thus, coming to the sessions, which involved a long travel time, the patient would deny the efforts of the journey but would instead describe the beauty of the landscape, the colours of the season, etc. She would give herself a much younger appearance and speak in a melodic, girlish voice, which sometimes turned into a sort of tormented sobbing.

As long as I seemed to comply with the romantic picture she had created of my person, the therapy seemed to represent a blissful enclave (O'Shaughnessy, 1992), characterized by timelessness and an absence of disappointment, anger and conflict. She then experienced my speaking as a "revelation of truth" and would sometimes even speak of "sugar sessions."

If, however, she felt that my interpretations undermined her picture of our relationship, she would make me feel that I had done something improper, that I was trying to mock her and to get rid of her. Then the atmosphere changed, and she would submit to me as an object that would treat her in a merciless way. At those moments she evoked in me a guilt feeling of being cruelly sadistic towards her, as she would take in my interpretations with a painful hissing that seemed to be connected with her father's beatings. Mostly, however, the atmosphere of the sessions was romantic and timeless, and for this phantasy to be maintained the finite nature of the analysis had to be denied. Actually, during her analysis the patient had expressed on several occasions her wish one day to die peacefully on the couch.

The issue of timelessness was the main focus, and for long periods it seemed to be the only issue of our therapeutic work. Often I felt that recollections of her past led us nowhere, and that my interpretations were bypassed and did not really affect her. One of the mechanisms by which this was achieved, was that the patient isolated a sensual element—for example, the *sound of my voice*—from the content of what I had said. Then all that I said sounded "like music," and the only problem was to take this feeling with her for purposes of decorating her phantasy world with it and maintaining a state of mind characterized by timelessness and unseparateness.

However, if she listened to the *content* of what I had said, the atmosphere changed, and I would now be heard "as this terrible voice of a public prosecutor," full of reproach and accusation. So we would find ourselves in a situation in which there was either *love without words* or *words without love*, with only little space for thinking and constructive therapeutic work. There was some indication that, in the first case (*love without words*) the patient was relating to an idealized internal mother figure, and in the second case (*words without love*), she was submitting to a cruel father authority without allowing a relationship between her internal parents.

The pressure to re-enact this situation in different ways proved to be a recurring challenge in this analysis. I felt guilty either because I had been too cruel or because I had allowed myself to be seduced by the music of romantic idealization. The problem was how to extricate myself and resist being pulled too far in either of these two directions. Sometimes I felt that there was no way out and whatever I said, we would end in a stuck situation where cruelty was very obvious.

Sometimes however, it was possible to disentangle a bit and to observe the subtle re-enactments within the session. She would then detach herself from clinging to either an idealized or a cruel object and admit how desperate she felt when she could not control my independent thinking. Following these movements the dilemma could be *explored* instead of being acted out in the session and as a consequence her splitting lessened. This allowed a gradual understanding of the patient's complex misrepresentations. It was in such moments that intense feelings of sadness, jealousy and guilt emerged, indicating that the patient was able to give up her sensual possessiveness, to tolerate a sense of separateness and to open up a space for symbolic thinking.

However, in the beginning of her analysis, those moments were short-lived and whenever painful feelings seemed unbearable, she would quickly retreat once again into her timeless world. This was especially the case when my patient felt confronted with the reality of time and loss. Once, before a break, she gave me an interesting book, illustrating the sinking of the *Titanic*. It seemed as if she was experiencing the reality of loss like a collision with an iceberg. However, it was not quite clear whether the *Titanic* involved any idea of loss at all, because she also seemed romantically involved in a shared death phantasy with Leonardo DiCaprio, the actor in the film.

On another occasion the patient mentioned the myth of Prometheus, describing in great detail the cruel punishment he suffered from the divine eagle. At this time she experienced my interpretations as tormenting and tearing her into pieces. She also pointed out that in the end Prometheus—who triumphed over Zeus through his immortality and the endlessness of his suffering—was fused to the rock to which he was chained. This reflected a masochistic version of her timelessness as compared to the previous one, in which romantic imagination provided an illusion of endlessness, uniqueness and infinity.

As the further course of the analysis revealed, my patient was able to reconcile this masochistic scenario with her romantic version of timelessness by arguing that *if she suffered long enough, she would one day be redeemed by the love of her analyst.* This sophisticated argument seemed to be part of a complex belief system in which reality was suspended and a perverted hope was clung to in order to obstruct psychic development. Because of its obstructive quality this form of love can be described as a pathological organization operating on the basis of –L.

In describing the kinds of links between objects, Bion (1962, p. 43) discerned three basic emotional links L (love), H (hate) and K (knowledge), which can be turned into their opposites (–L, –H, –K). By analogy to his description of –K as a knowledge which is characterized by the predominant characteristic of "without-ness,"[1] this negative form of love (–L) can be understood as a possessive demand without concern for the object, as an all-embracing love without freedom, as a claim for ideality without reality, as a transfiguration without limitation.

In fact, as long as the atmosphere of the sessions was dominated by a longing for uniqueness and infinity, my interpretations could not really reach the patient. She could prevent this by extracting a sensual element from my saying, taking it into possession and incorporating it into her romantic phantasy world. Due to this romantic transformation central elements of her subjective experience were continuously abducted into a timeless sphere, thereby producing "*psychic unreality*" (Britton, 1998). In this state of mind reality was only half accepted, and separation was eliminated, by creating a "*romantic perversion of the reality of time*" (Steiner, 1993).

Whenever my patient felt confronted with the reality of loss, romantic infinity would be turned into endless suffering, which was also static, timeless and erotized. In the brief moments when she was able to give up her splitting, she felt exposed to painful feelings of hatred, mourning and guilt, which enabled her to leave her timeless universe and to face the *experience of time.* It was only when these moments could gradually be extended that she felt more able to emerge from her *psychic retreat* (Steiner, 1993) and to allow contact with difficult and frustrating aspects of reality. This gradually enabled her to resist and to feel less addicted to the false promises of a pathological organization that was based either on a romantic or a masochistic misrepresentation of the reality of time.

Discussion

For a long time my patient seemed to experience some sort of containment in her analysis. However, this was not true containment because her experience was two-dimensional and felt like an envelope or a tightly fitting skin. It did not allow separateness and therefore did not provide a space for emotion, meaning and thinking. In this state of mind she was glued to her internal objects and recollections of the past seemed to be worthless, since they were aimed at drawing me either into an idealized or into a cruel form of relationship. In the same way ordinary transference interpretations led us nowhere, because they were secretly transformed and then concretely perceived as something gratifying or dismissive.

This situation had some features in common with what Bion (1963) has described under the heading of "reversible perspective." He characterizes this phenomenon by a "lack of contact" and a "lack of ordinary conflict" (p. 52), and he goes on to emphasize that the "interpretation is accepted, but the premises have been rejected and others silently substituted" (p. 54). In that way development is obstructed and a "dynamic situation" is transformed into a "static" experience (p. 60). In the case of my patient this meant that my interpretations were experienced either as caresses or as punishments, which could go on endlessly. It was only during the brief moments when the patient could acknowledge the experience of separateness and loss that her two-dimensional world expanded and containment was now experienced as providing a space for thinking, i.e. for psychic three-dimensionality.

In order to provide an opportunity for this experience the analyst must be able to take in and digest the patient's projections. During this stage of containment parts of the patient's psyche live so to say "inside the analyst's mind"—a state that has been referred to as "marsupial space" (Rey, 1979) and which corresponds to the experience of *being understood* (Steiner, 1993, p. 132). In a second step the analyst has to compare and differentiate the patient's projections from his own internal objects and finally to re-project them in a symbolic form (Money-Kyrle, 1956). It is during this phase where *active understanding* comes into play and a state of separateness is being achieved where the patient re-gains an experience of his own mental space.

I have argued that this process is closely linked to movements towards the depressive position and hence with the acknowledgement of the oedipal situation. For my patient this meant to bring her internal parents together, to link emotion and meaning, i.e. the sensual elements and the content of what I had said. Only then containment was experienced as a three-dimensional process opening a space in which she was able to localize her emotional experiences and to think symbolically. I felt reminded of Bion's (1965, pp. 55–6) saying that, "what a developing personality […] comes to know as 'time' and […] 'space'" presupposes the "tolerance of frustration," i.e. the awareness of absence and loss.

For that reason I would say that the experience of containment must include the acknowledgment of loss, in order to achieve real development and understanding. Technically, the capacity to mourn implies the withdrawal of projections. This may be achieved by thoroughly examining the fine grain of the session, by the repeated working through of mutual enactments and by analyzing the various misrepresentations of the transference situation, which transform the here and now into a timeless atmosphere. Only then "bad infinity"—in Hegel's (1812) terms—may be transformed into what Bion calls "tolerance of doubt and tolerance of a sense of infinity" (1962, p. 94).

Perhaps Bion went a bit too far, when he equated "memory" in his late writings (Bion, 1970) with possessiveness and sensual experience. I doubt whether it makes sense to think about mental space and time *per se* as infinite, and I also would reject Bion's formulation that time has "no part" in the process of emotional growth (1970, p. 108). Instead I would say that emotional growth provides the individual with the possibility to unfold his mental space and therefore with an *experience* of time. Maybe the clinical problem is not primarily how an "ultimate reality" (*O*) can evolve by the analyst's "disciplined eschewing" of memory, desire and understanding (Bion, 1970, pp. 41 ff.), but how to make a meaningful contact with the patient in the session. It is for this reason that Bion differentiates between *memory* (which in his view is saturated with sensuous experience) and *remembering* (which he sees as a process essential to psychoanalytic work). In my patient, indeed, remembering was at first very much equated with possessiveness and sensual experience. To unfold her mental space she had to gradually give up her possessive control over the object, which was a long-lasting and often painful process in the transference and counter-transference.

Conclusion

To conclude, I would like to propose that especially for some borderline patients *the construction of mental space precedes the experience of time.* To acknowledge the "inevitability of time and ultimately death," which Money-Kyrle (1971) has described as one of the three basic facts of life, a state of separateness has to be achieved where the patient can experience his mental space as being different from the outside world and the mind of the analyst (Rey, 1979). This painful process goes along with repeated transitions from the paranoid-schizoid and borderline positions to the depressive position and is accompanied by the withdrawal of projections (Klein, 1946, Steiner, 1993). In this sense, I think, *it is not through remembering that mourning can be achieved, but vice versa that it is the capacity to mourn which enables the patient to remember with emotion and meaning.* Maybe this accounts especially for borderline patients whose *conceptions* of time and space have been distorted and misrepresented, whereas for the psychotic patient it is the *preconception of time* that has been under attack and is being fragmented.

Note

1 Bion describes the effects of –K on the container/contained relationship as resulting in "an internal object without exterior," "an alimentary canal without a body," "an envious assertion of moral superiority without any morals." He sees –K as the resultant of an envious denudation of meaning, a "stripping […] of all good," which "is itself destined to continue the process of stripping … " (Bion, 1962, p. 97).

References

Bion, W. R. (1962) *Learning from Experience*. London: Heinemann; reprinted London: Karnac, 1984.

Bion, W. R. (1963) *Elements of Psycho-Analysis*. London: Heinemann; reprinted London: Karnac, 1984

Bion, W. R. (1965) *Transformations. Change from Learning to Growth*. London: Heinemann.

Bion, W. R. (1970) *Attention and Interpretation*. London: Tavistock Publications; reprinted London: Karnac 1984.

Birksted-Breen, D. (2003) Time and the après-coup. *The International Journal of Psychoanalysis*, 84:1501–15.

Birksted-Breen, D. (2009) "Reverberation time," dreaming and the capacity to dream. *The International Journal of Psychoanalysis*, 90:35–51.

Britton, R. (1998) *Belief and Imagination: Explorations in Psychoanalysis*. London: Routledge.

Feldman, M. (1993) The dynamics of reassurance. *The International Journal of Psychoanalysis*, 74:275–85.

Feldman, M. (1998) The defensive uses of compliance. In: Feldman, M., *Doubt, Conviction and the Analytic Process*. London, New York: Routledge (pp. 177–93).

Feldman, M. (2000) Manifestations of the death instinct in the consulting room. *The International Journal of Psychoanalysis*, 81:53–65.

Green, A. (2002) *Time in Psychoanalysis. Some Contradictory Aspects*. London, New York: Free Association Books.

Gutwinski-Jeggle, J. (1992) Trauma und Zeiterleben. Theoretische Überlegungen [Trauma and the experience of time. Theoretical considerations]. *Jahrbuch der Psychoanalyse*, 29:167–214.

Hartocollis, P. (1983) *Time and Timelessness*. New York: International Universities Press.

Hegel, G. W. F. (1812) *Wissenschaft der Logik, I*. Frankfurt a. M.: Suhrkamp 1990.

Klein, M. (1946) Notes of some schizoid mechanisms. In: *The Writings of Melanie Klein, vol. 3: Envy and Gratitude and Other Works 1921–1945* (pp. 1–24). London: Hogarth Press, 1975; reprinted London: Karnac, 1993.

Loewald, H. (1972) The experience of time. *Psychoanalytic Study of the Child*, 27: 401–10.

Money-Kyrle, R. (1956) Normal counter-transference and some of its deviations. *The International Journal of Psychoanalysis*, 37:360–6.

Money-Kyrle, R. (1971) The aim of psycho-analysis. *The International Journal of Psychoanalysis*, 49:691–8. Reprinted in: *The Collected Papers of Roger Money-Kyrle* (pp. 416–33), ed. D. Meltzer and E. O'Shaughnessy. Perthshire: Clunie Press, 1978.

O'Shaughnessy, E. (1992) Enclaves and excursions. *The International Journal of Psychoanalysis*, 73:603–11.

Perelberg, R. J. (ed.) (2007) *Time and Memory*. London: Karnac.

Resnik, O. (1995) *Mental Space*. London: Karnac.

Rey, H. (1979) Schizoid phenomena in the borderline. In: *Advances in the Psychotherapy of the Borderline Patient* (pp. 448–84), ed. J. LeBoit and A. Capponi. New York: Aronson.

Smith, S. (1977) The golden fantasy: a regressive reaction to separation anxiety. *The International Journal of Psychoanalysis*, 58:311–24.

Steiner, J. (1993) *Psychic Retreats. Pathological Organisations in Psychotic, Neurotic and Borderline Patients.* London: Routledge, 1993.

Weiss, H. (2008) Romantic perversion: the role of envy in the creation of a timeless universe. In: *Envy and Gratitude Revisited* (pp. 152–67), ed. P. Roth and A. Lemma. London: International Psychoanalytic Association.

Weiss, H. (2009) *Das Labyrinth der Borderline-Kommunikation. Klinische Zugänge zum Erleben von Raum und Zeit* [The Labyrinth of Borderline-Communication. Clinical Explorations into the Experience of Time and Space]. Stuttgart: Klett-Cotta.

Weiss, H. (2010) Utopien und Dystopien als Orte des seelischen Rückzugs [Utopia and dystopia as psychic retreats] (unpublished paper, presented to the German Psychoanalytical Association, 20 November 2010).

EDITORS' INTRODUCTION

Caesura, Denial and Envy

Renato Trachtenberg

As Bion moved further into the later phases of the development of his theory, he struggled to find concepts that would express or address that which was unformed and ineffable in the human unconscious. What he was after was nothing short of a language, which he could use to describe—or at least allude to—and communicate about a dimension of human pre-psychic, proto-experience and becoming that was beyond our ability to fully render and capture in words. This dimension, which Bion called O, the "thing-in-itself," is something that we might think of as the raw, existential Experience (with a capital E) in which each of us is immersed, and which forms the substrate and basis for that part of our "experience" (with a small e) that we may ultimately come to know and feel.

The unconscious that Bion wished to address encompassed so much more than that sector of the unconscious (the dynamic unconscious) that Freud (e.g. 1900, 1915, 1923) described when he wrote so brilliantly about what was relatively saturated with meaning, verbally structured, and associatively linked but hidden, because its meanings and the anxieties they evoked were too frightening or unacceptable to be tolerated in consciousness. Bion was aware that the traditional analytic concepts and language of Freud and Klein were heavily dependent upon sense-related, empirically-derived data and that their application was dependent upon deductive thinking. In contrast, his quest moved him away from empiricism towards the inductive and the intuitive. As he did so, he needed to escape from the restrictions of the usual, technical language of psychoanalytic discourse and its limiting "penumbra of associations." He needed new vertices of observation from which to try to grasp something of this ineffable dimension and a new "language of achievement" for psychoanalysis in order to express what he grasped.

Bion's search brought him to pure mathematics and philosophy (e.g. Plato, the Neo-Platonists, Kant) from which he borrowed concepts and ideas and to the mystics, (e.g. Eckhardt and St. John of the Cross) from which he drew inspiration. It also brought him to Freud's famous quote about caesura and its implications that there may be less absolute certainty and division between seemingly absolute categories of things than we might commonly assume.

Although it has not often been written about, one of the qualities of Bion's brilliance was his capacity to see a general category or structure in a concept and apply it in an overarching way to new and unfamiliar circumstances. One gets a hint of this in *Attention and Interpretation* (Bion, 1970) when, in discussing the concepts of primitive communication and container/contained, he offers the equation, *A is to B as Container is to Contained (A/B = Container/Contained).* Once this abstraction is in mind, he can then apply it as a general principle to many different and often unexpected situations. It is this kind of movement and transformational power that Trachtenberg finds implicit in Bion's thinking in general and his use of the caesura concept in particular and that he tries to draw out in the following chapter, which readers may think of as an extended elaboration of Bion's advice to pay more attention to the link and the oscillation between what it seems to connect or divide than to the seemingly separate categories themselves.

The most important implication of this thinking is, of course, in the clinical situation. Bion believed that in order for the analyst to listen creatively to the patient's unconscious, it was essential to exercise "negative capability" and to listen without memory or desire. Trachtenberg develops the clinical implications of this view by considering the caesura, the *link*, between different states of mind or being, as an intermediate area of potential from which new and creative meanings may emerge. Thus, he explores the implications of Bion's admonition to "explore the link" rather than the categories of events on either side of any arbitrary dividing line; to use, for example, the *connection* between the conscious and unconscious as the vertex of observation, in order to maximize one's openness to encountering the new and unexpected.

Inability to assume this perspective, denial of the caesura in favor of an absolute and/or rigidly comparative perspective, is often seen as the provenance of moralistic or concrete thinking or as the result—and expression—of destructive envy. Clinical material drawn from the dreams of two patients is used to illustrate these points.

11

CAESURA, DENIAL AND ENVY

Renato Trachtenberg

Introduction

Inspired by the famous sentence of Freud (1926) in "Inhibitions, symptoms and anxiety"—there is much more continuity between intra-uterine life and earliest infancy, than the impressive caesura of the act of birth would have us believe—Bion developed the concept of "caesura" into a fundamental precept in his theory of mental functioning and the clinical encounter. In this chapter, I shall elaborate on Bion's views by examining phenomena observed in the analytic consulting room that are associated with what I have termed "caesura denial." While the patients in whom we may observe these phenomena most intensely are the ones we call "non-neurotic," caesura denial is a phenomenon that can be observed in *any* analysand. And if we remember Bion's idea that each of us contains a psychotic and non-psychotic part of our psyche, to think of this issue as a problem exclusive to more disturbed patients would be in itself an example of caesura denial.[1] Moreover, the extension of the phenomenon should include the link and, therefore, analyst and analysand. The real problem of caesura and its denial lies in the impossibility of transit, continuity and simultaneity among the different psychic dimensions kept apart by the caesuras of the human mind. When caesura denial is present, either because of excessive rigidity or excessive permeability, a series of co-sequences (both consequences and parallel sequences) is observed. Splitting and massive projective identifications may appear. But, most times, the mechanism of caesura denial is delicate and subtle, requiring a complex, spectral and undecidable observational vertex, to be detected. These ideas will be clarified below.

The different caesuras that allow human beings the possibility to live simultaneously in at least two worlds (internal/external, mental/proto-mental, conscious/unconscious, symbolic/not symbolic, etc.) as described by Bion, may be denied for several reasons. Among the latter is envy, which I shall touch on below, but is so important that it will require a separate paper to fully examine its impact. In this chapter, I will present the dreams of two patients to illustrate and contrast the difference between caesuras operating suitably in one patient and caesura denial in the other.

Caesura and Its Denial

When Bion discussed Freud's famous dictum about caesura, he included continuity itself, what unites and what separates simultaneously, as part of the concept. Bion (1977) substantially modified the implications and meaning of the Freudian sentence, as he declared: "Investigate the caesura; not the analyst; not the analysand; not the unconscious; not the conscious; not sanity; not insanity, but the caesura, the link, the synapse, the (counter)transference, the transitive-intransitive mood" (Bion, 1977, p. 56).

For Bion, then, the caesura becomes the vertex through which analyst and analysand may observe the phenomena that occur in the psychoanalytical session, and may itself become an object of observation. With fine irony, Bion said that he became impressed by the "impressive," because for Bion, caesura would only be impressive in its impossibility and to the extent to which it was denied. As Bion (1976b) said,

> I'm impressed by the fact that physical birth is so impressive ... The fact of birth certainly impresses the individual and the group. But it seems to me that it is too limiting to assume that physical birth is as impressive as many people suppose it is ... I think the lack of discussion of this point is a blind spot. Freud developed this idea of "the impressive caesura of birth," of our being too impressed by it. He didn't investigate it deeply—a great mistake from our point of view.
> (Bion, 1976b, p. 271)

It became clear to Bion that the difference and continuity, presence and absence, gain and loss, life and death, soma-psychotic and psychosomatic, etc., were only different sides of the same phenomena and that the difficulty in holding these opposites in mind at the same time reflected the human difficulty in maintaining a creative caesura.[2]

As the human mentality, better yet, the proto-mentality, needs to find a before and an after, a cause and its consequence, a definite and last origin, final solutions, etc.; caesura or undecidable boundary would be under permanent pressure to maintain itself in this spectrum of fragility and uncertainty. The idea of causality, for Bion, only makes sense in mental areas that are separate from the emotions, such as the area of morality or in the concrete world of *things*: "Some patients repeatedly state that they have some particular experience and then give the reason why—making it part and parcel of their formulation. This continued repetition suggests a state of mind, which is proper to a person who only lives in a causal world. But the only world in which causes can be said to be a prominent feature is the world of things—not the world of people, or characters, or personalities. The patient who is always telling us that he feels such-and-such 'because …' is avoiding a particular relationship which exists between one character and another" (Bion, 1977, p. 51). Thus, we seek explanations based on causality and certainty, when we lose sight of the "what," the phenomena in transit, the coexisting models of mental states. For Bion, causality means only a time sequence of facts. As Meltzer (1978) has said, Bion "helped us by slaying the dragon of causality and opened the cosmos of the mind in its infinitude of possibility for the generating of meaning" (Meltzer, 1978, p. 85).

In accord with contemporary scientific thinking—e.g. quantum physics, mathematics with Gödel's theorem, aesthetics, etc.—notions such as uncertainty, incompleteness, negativity, complexity theory, undecidability, etc., started to complement and integrate themselves in Bion's thinking. The undecidability of origins, for instance, contrary to a causal view, proposes that in each link there is a point in which one cannot decide what belongs to the subject or the object, to the mother or to the baby, to the breast or to the mouth, to the analyst or to the patient, to us or the authors we read, etc. To tolerate and sustain this undecidability requires a suitable capacity for negative capability, an expression that Bion took from a famous letter by Keats. Caesura is a link—which unites and separates—and, thus, is undecidable.

Caesura and Spectrum Perspective

Inspired by Klein, Bion highlighted the fact that we live in at least two worlds, not only internal/external, but also proto-mental/mental, finite/infinite, non-symbolic/symbolic, sensorial/imaginative, know about psychoanalysis/be a psychoanalyst, being a psychoanalyst/becoming a psychoanalyst, etc. Each pairing implies a caesura and each caesura implies the possibility of a spectrum perspective (narcissism/social-ism, in Bion's first writings, for instance). The spectrum notion helps us understand why caesura is not a place or any definite or definable spatiality. Its virtuality is what allows it to fulfill the continuity and simultaneity among/in its differences. Caesura denial prevents the recognition of this spectrum dimension and interferes with the possibility of moving from one pole to another. According to Chuster (1997, 2002), the spectral model defines itself as the indefinite and undetermined extension of phenomena from which one can extract or build an indefinite number of concepts. It is, however, a whole that can never be fully rebuilt through the sum of its parts, because the spectrum is in a permanent state of expansion and expresses the irreversibility of time. In order to be recognized and preserved, it implies the need to relinquish seeking after "answers" and implies a condition in which there is a constant creation of interpretations without reaching the finality of explaining. In the spectral configuration there is no place for causes or results.

Caesura is the most important expression of the spectral perspective. In Chuster's words:

> The creative aspects of the mind, resulting or representing the psychoanalytical function of the personality, are revealed in the radicalism … of the caesura concept. In any given moment, if we do not let ourselves be impressed by the elements of memory, desire, need of comprehension and the sensorial perception, our minds recover the plasticity of movement, moving about temporal splitting, establishing unsuspecting links, generating conjectures, exercising, in the end, imagination. Everything is metaphorable. Thus, the psychoanalyst may understand that the mental birth may free itself from the idea of physical birth and notice that, as Bion said, "*the word catastrophe* [allusive to the catastrophic change concept and transformation in O] *must be understood in the light of something that goes the opposite direction … breaking down is also very close to the metaphor breaking up.*"
>
> (Chuster, 2001, p. 106)

Caesura, Links and Anti-Links

An interesting example of caesura and its possible denial is in the investigation by Meltzer and Harris Williams (Meltzer, 1986; Meltzer and Harris Williams, 1988) of the aesthetic conflict. According to these authors, the original conflict, at the foundation of the human mind would be the primordial encounter with the mother, represented by her face and breasts, which initiates a conflict in the infant's mind between mother's known exterior beauty and the mystery of her interior. These first encounters between the baby and the mother produce a tormenting doubt, a menacing uncertainty in the baby's mind. Does the mother's outside image, her beauty, captured by the baby's sense organs correspond to the inside of the mother, trustworthy, safe in its intentions and long-lasting, with a beauty and truth only conjectured by imagination? In other words, does what I can perceptually know have correspondence with a knowledge obtained only through my imaginative conjectures? How can caesura (e.g. indeterminacy) be maintained in this encounter, which favors its denial in such a special way? How can the mystery be sustained? The capacity to tolerate this mystery will depend on one's negative capability, which opposes the negative links. To express this, Meltzer and M. Harris Williams (1988) use the poetic and spectral image that occurs at the end of Keats' "Ode on a Greecian Urn," where the poet concludes, "'Beauty is truth, truth beauty',—that is all/Ye know on earth, and all ye need to know."

With the infant's first encounter with the aesthetic object, the positive links described by Bion (1962b) (L, H, K = love, hate, knowledge), having the link among the latter as an example of caesura, would be under attack by the negative (minus) links (–L, –H, –K) resulting in a difficult tolerance to this insoluble conflict. The negative links, referred to by Meltzer and Harris Williams (Meltzer, 1986; Meltzer and Harris Williams, 1988) as anti-links, anti-emotional links, anti-life links, etc. would be an expression of envy in the aesthetic conflict. One can observe that envy does not tolerate differences and insinuates itself in the form of comparisons. The appearance of the latter indicates that caesuras are being denied. The comparative attitude is often reflected in the perception of differences, which is in itself a sign of the activity of envy. To paraphrase Bion, comparison makes sense in the world of things, not in a world of people. Comparison is a super-ego product dominated by envy in which the categories of right/wrong, better/worse, superior/inferior, etc. are used as indicators of differences. Making comparisons in this way is an expression of fanatical thinking. People cannot be compared, not even the same person can be compared to his or her self in different moments. To do so, reflects a kind of super ego-inflected moralistic thinking. On the other hand, tolerating differences requires caesuras in activity, "complex thinking" (Morin, 1999) and complex ethics (it would be of interest at another time to examine the psychoanalytical differences between ethics and morality based on these ideas).

Meltzer and Harris Williams (1988) named the negative links:

a *puritanism* (–L): opposition to pleasure and happiness in intimate relations;
b *hypocrisy* (–H): inspired by Wordsworth, when he says that hating a lie or falsehood is not the same as loving the truth, confusing hate with loving the opposite, whatever it is;
c *philistinism* (–K): opposition to any new idea just because it is new.

and described how (Meltzer, 1986), in Bion's theory of affects, conflict takes place between the emotions and the anti-emotions. As a result, this theory produced turbulence in the traditional model of conflict, where opposition was seen to be between love and hate. Bion says that, when he talks about hate, he is referring to a pole of love, since there cannot be shadow without the presence of light. The problem would no longer be, for instance, that hate was present and linked to emotions L and K, but would reside in one's hatred of the emotion of hate, itself. This would be an example of the difference between column 2 in the Grid (Bion, 1963)[3] and the need for a negative Grid: column 2 may categorize some hatred of the truth, but a love of a lie requires a negative Grid.

The influence of the factor of envy in caesura denial can be detected even in Bion's early works. Starting with "Attacks on Linking" (1959), envy as a function of a relation starts to arise as a typically Bionian idea. In *Attention and Interpretation* (1970) he wrote:

> In the parasitic relationship [of container–contained] the product of the association is something that destroys both parties to the association. The realization that approximates most closely to my formulation is the group–individual setting dominated by envy. Envy begets envy, and this self-perpetuating emotion finally destroys host and parasite alike. The envy cannot be satisfactorily ascribed to one or other part; in fact it is a function of the relationship.
>
> (Bion, 1970, p. 78)

Its location, in a link and in its spectral dimension, is undecidable. Chuster and Trachtenberg (2009) illustrates this through use of the cancer model (as Bion did in *Attention and Interpretation*) to show how a cancer-infected cell refuses to die, and, through a kind of "anti-reproductive reproduction," eliminates the death "information," destroying the organism in which it "lives," in search of perpetuation. Thus, death denial and life denial are equivalent and both are equivalent to caesura denial.

Caesura, Language and Analytical Intervention

Meltzer (1986) defines poetic capacity as "the ability of the analyst to express feelings through words in his interpretative and non-interpretative interventions, based on his own experience in finding and verbalizing his primitive emotionality" (Meltzer, 1986, p.82).

Bion wrote a lot about the problem of communication between the analyst and his patient. In "Caesura" he said:

> Can any method of communication be sufficiently "penetrating" to pass the caesura in the direction from post-natal conscious thought back to the pre-mental in which thoughts and ideas have their counterpart in "times" or "levels" of mind where they are not thoughts or ideas? That penetration has to be effective in either direction.
>
> (Bion, 1977, p. 45)

He often referred to the limitations of human language saying that our language was better suited to describe inanimate things than to express emotions. His conceptualization of the "language of achievement" (Bion, 1970), based on Keats' concept of negative capability, describes man's poetic capacity as he attempts to cross the caesura between emotion and verbalization, while attempting to preserve the vitality of feelings and the power of words. The importance of the analyst's doing so in his interventions—and the difficulty in preventing the decay of the power of language due to familiarity and repetitive use—was highlighted by Bion numerous times.

Therefore, the poetic capacity in the words of the analyst, with its expression in the language of achievement, testifies to the presence of caesura and is, at the same time, an attempt to cross it. The presence of memory, desire and the need to understand endangers such capacities, blocking the development of new ideas and may be, in this sense, an indicator of a predominance of envy and caesura denial in the analytical setting.

Caesura and Caesura Denial: About Two Dreams

Dr. B., a young doctor of about thirty, came to analysis, because of a generalized feeling of emptiness and futility, and important inhibitions in his relations with women. He wore his mother's clothes and masturbated looking into the mirror, as his fantasies oscillated between heterosexual and homosexual scenes in which he was penetrated by an older man. Afterwards, when he undressed, he looked at himself in the mirror and castigated himself, as if speaking to another person: "You are pathetic, you disgust me." Once dressed in his own clothes, he looked in the mirror again to confirm that it was he, himself, recovering his "true identity." He recalled as a very important moment in his life, the birth of a brother when he was eighteen months old. In the last months of her pregnancy, his mother had sent him to his grandparents' home and when he came back he met the new baby. He now intended to report that it was the possibility of a pregnancy that stopped him from having intercourse, but he said instead: "It is the fear I have during a pregnancy." This slip of the tongue, which we can link with the transvestite act (wish/fear of being penetrated by an older man/the father and the wish/fear to kill all internal mother's babies as if he was the only and eternal baby inside her), was very meaningful in his analysis. At the same time, he had constant doubts about his fertility, which he rationalized was due to a post-mumps orchitis that he had suffered in puberty.

In his work life, Dr. B.'s performance as a physician was very much interfered with by his fantasies, as he feared inducing severe hemorrhages every time he performed a bronchoscopy (connected with the conflicts around penetration and the mother's babies). He referred to such medical procedures as "maneuvers of people's selves."

His unconscious use of the fiber-bronchoscope as a physical device to allow contact with the inner self of the other was very pronounced, and linked to his voyeuristic fantasies (intrusive curiosity), and his transvestite activity. After we had explored some meanings of his acts and fantasies, he brought the following dream:

> I was bathing two very tiny babies, ten to twelve centimeters long, they were only head and body, they had no limbs. One was normal, but the other was made of some kind of fabric, something flaccid without any consistency, that folded all the time. The face separated from the skull as if it were a mask. With much anguish I think, "the link between the eyes and the brain will get lost and he will be blind." Suddenly, one of the eyes escapes from my hands and flies up like a moth.

Mrs. A., a woman of almost fifty, mother to three daughters, sought analysis as a result of an important marriage crisis and for the intense narcissistic pain that menopause caused her. The conflicts analyzed allowed her to enrich herself and learn from experience, resuming artistic activities (she was a pianist), which she had not pursued for many years. Her relationship with her parents, who had been long dead, had always followed a very severe, and well-established pattern. With her father, who had been a butcher, she had kept a very distant contact, repudiating him for his rough manners, his ragged, dirty and smelly clothes, and his meager cultural and intellectual ambitions. On the other hand, her mother, whom she recalled as being very sick and bed-ridden, ever since the patient's adolescence, was described not only as a very idealized person (because of her artistic and cultural talents), but was herself very idealizing of the intellectual beauty and superiority of Mrs. A., the only daughter among four sons.

Towards the end of her analysis, she brought the following dream:

> My mother takes me to an amusement park by car. Something very strange, not only because she had never driven, but, moreover, I had never gone to an amusement park, because my father was the only person who could take me and I was embarrassed to go out in his company. When I enter the hall of mirrors, I realize that they are not the usual mirrors one finds in amusement parks: instead of distorting the image, they reflected exactly what each one showed. When I look at myself, I see my husband by my side, very close to me. Suddenly, I see that it was you, who very slowly, start moving in my direction until, entering by my side, you disappear inside of me. The moment I do not see you anymore, I realize I am pregnant and that, it is certainly a boy. A great joy and excitement overwhelm me. I head for the exit, where my father has been waiting for a long time. I approach him very happily to give him the good news, and he tells me with a smile, "did I not tell you that everything would end up fine?!"

We can see that Dr. B., in his dream, shows the rigid caesura between his psychotic and non-psychotic (the normal baby) parts and, therefore, he feels terror at every moment in which the analysis threatens to produce some kind of continuity between them. The face that detaches like a mask also tells us of his pseudo-maturity and the massive/excessive projective identifications. Meltzer (1975) believes that transvestism is the best example of those kinds of identifications, for the transvestism would be a hostile caricature of the degraded and violated mother in her intimacy by these intrusive identifications. The secret act of "entering" her clothes would clinically express the violence of his projective fantasies. The babies in the dream, on the other hand, represent his penis and the fiber-bronchoscope. We can observe that the angst he feels, when he is going to introduce the fiber-bronchoscope to do biopsies, is expressed in the dream through a disconnection between the eyes and the brain (Bion's –K). The disconnection, the disjunction, depicts the impossibility of keeping the caesura; or keeping a permeable enough separation between the unconscious fantasy and the technical procedure or between the "dream" and the vigilant state. He becomes blind and can no longer see anymore the difference between himself and the internal mother in his transvestite act, between his job as physician and his enacted, transvestite sexual fantasies. Thus, his bronchoscopic procedures, "maneuvers of people's selves," are destined to sterility and death. The biopsies unconsciously symbolize and enact the envious fantasy of aborting siblings/babies that threaten his place of exclusive owner of the mother's body and mind. Such possession, in his fantasy, can then only happen if he himself becomes the mother, preventing the birth of any fertile or creative process. The eye that takes off, flying like a moth, has to do with the lost visual function of looking, a metaphor for the K link (Knowledge), and its passage to a state in which the environment is –K. The moth that destroys books and clothes (the transvestite act!) symbolizes the attempt to un-know, the philistinism ("opposition to any new idea just because it is new") that avoids the new, the babies. Without being able to differentiate fantasy from reality, this kind of paranoid terror (accusations, judgments, annulment/castration of Dr. B.'s M.D. title/penis), as a permanent mental state, was what Bion (1962a) described as a "nameless dread," which, according to Meltzer (1973), is the terror produced by unborn babies, who, like phantoms, accuse him of depriving them of their lives.

Mrs. A. describes the transformations analysis produced in her inside world, recreating a possible reality about her relationship with her parents in the dream. The bare reality of the way she saw the facts was amplified by her creative imagination allowing new possibilities of living and narrating what she once had as her "reality." Instead of making herself blind, she sees herself as she is, meaning the meeting with her own truth. We can see, in her dream, that the mental coitus requires the disappearance of the object (Klein's depressive position) so that the analytical baby conceived by that mental coitus arises as the psychoanalytical function of the personality. For the self-analysis to be made possible, her internal objects need to be rescued from their fixed places, in the only version she used to have of her story, and become reborn as protective functions, companions and revitalizers. This allows a better transferential resolution and the repetition of infantile patterns become transformed narratives, turning the past into something new, apart from what it was or would have been.

Unlike Dr. B.'s dream, Mrs. A. shows in her dream the fundamental mechanism of introjective identification (Meltzer 1967, 1973). We can observe how an internal object needs to be transformed into something else so that its functions may form part of the creative equipment of the mind. When such an object goes through the process of introjective identification, it is no longer recognizable in its own identity because it is now part of the core of the patient's self, enriching it with something that has been learned from the emotional experience. Mourning for the loss of this introjected object is the price to pay for mental growth, for the acquisition of autonomy (one's self and the other's), for the freedom of being alone without feeling lonely and for the preservation of a caesura that allows continuity among different vital dimensions (adults' and children's levels, past and present or future, etc.).

About Caesuras and "Shibboleths"

The word "shibboleth" (in Hebrew, "branch" or "cob") was used by Freud on several occasions to define and set apart who was a psychoanalyst and who was not.[4] To him, the Oedipus complex, infantile sexuality, the unconscious and his theory of the interpretation of dreams were the "shibboleths" of psychoanalysis. The Freudian "shibboleths" were used as a way to identify and recognize, theoretically, who was a "true" psychoanalyst.

For Bion, the caesura concept indicates that the psychoanalyst with his patient, in the analytic consulting room, is in a transient state of "becoming a psychoanalyst." When we use any shibboleths, in the analytical setting, to determine who is or is not a psychoanalyst, we forget that one's analytic identity is always in a state of becoming. In this sense, becoming an analyst is an indicator that the caesura is happening, like the caesura of birth, which does not allow us to claim "when" a person is born or how much of a person has not been born yet.

Now, over thirty years after Bion crossed the caesura of death, I am reminded of the line that Argentineans usually use, when they refer to the famous tango singer, Carlos Gardel, who has been dead for about seventy years: "Gardel sings better every day." Can we then not also say, "There is much more continuity between Bion's thoughts and what we can keep on creating from them, than the impressive caesura of his death would have us believe?"

Notes

1 "In analysis we are seeing a total personality who has at some time consciously or unconsciously, chosen a particular view or a particular vertex from which to see the view. This always involves inhibition of the capacity to see the views that one does not want to see. The psychotic patient may be anxious to suppress, be blind to or unaware of what the sane person is able to see … the important thing is not that a patient is a borderline psychotic, or a psychotic, or a neurotic, but that he is a total character minus … and then we have to form our own judgment of what that patient is minus, whether the person who is almost a caricature of robust common-sense and sanity is not really a character who lacks important components because he believes that a psychotic is 'mad' or 'insane,' or that someone would think him insane if it were known that he had such thoughts or ideas …" (Bion, 1977, pp. 52–3).

2 "Picasso painted a picture on a piece of glass so that it could be seen on both sides. I suggest that the same thing can be said of the caesura: it depends which way you look at it, which way you are travelling. Psycho-somatic disorders or soma-psychotic—take your choice—the picture should be recognizably the same whether you look at it from the psychosomatic position or from the soma-psychotic position" (Bion, 1976a, p. 306).

3 Bion proposed building a Grid, Mendeleiev's chemical-elements-table style, where there would be two coordinates. The vertical one would show thought evolution, from the most primitive to the most symbolic ones. The horizontal one would be formed by different uses of these thoughts. Hence, in the blank spaces formed by the encounter of each level of thought with some particular use, we would have a way to evaluate the patient's and/or analyst's formulations, some or the ones from a whole session, enabling self-supervision or better communication among psychoanalysts. The Grid could also be used as some kind of a psychoanalytical game, in which some element from an analytical session would be placed at random in any of the blank spaces; this way we could find something unexpected, surprising, that would open possibilities for new developments. Bion left a few clues and proposals that it would be necessary to build a negative Grid that would take into account the difference between pretense (written on the Grid as column 2 of the use of thoughts) and lie. It is important to remember that for Bion every formulation that aims at avoiding the angst of meeting with the unknown would be pretentious and not a lie. Therefore, in the negative Grid, all levels and uses would be placed with a minus signal (–). As in the emotional positive links (L H K) and the negative ones (–L –H –K) already referred to, the negative Grid would be useful to think an analytical session where the existing lie and envy would change the positivity of the links in their negativity. Hence, claiming that hating the truth (H) is not the same as loving a lie (–H) or that hating the emotion of hatred (or any other emotion) requires a negative Grid.

4 In the Old Testament, pronunciation of the word, "shibboleth," was used as a password and test of belonging between two warring tribes, one of which pronounced only the "s" sound and not the "sh." Thus, "shibboleth" refers now to any means of distinguishing insider from outsider, friend from foe.

References

Bion, W. R. (1959) Attacks on Linking. In *Second Thoughts*. New York: Jason Aronson, 1967.

Bion, W. R. (1962a) A Theory of Thinking. In *Second Thoughts*. New York: Jason Aronson, 1967.

Bion, W. R. (1962b) Learning from Experience. In: Bion, W. R. *Seven Servants—Four Works by Wilfred R. Bion*. New York: Jason Aronson, 1977.

Bion, W. R. (1963) Elements of Psychoanalysis. In: Bion, W. R. *Seven Servants—Four Works by Wilfred R. Bion*. New York: Jason Aronson, 1977.

Bion, W. R. (1970) Attention and Interpretation. In: Bion, W. R. *Seven Servants—Four Works by Wilfred R. Bion*. New York: Jason Aronson, 1977.

Bion, W. R. (1976a) On a Quotation from Freud. In *Clinical Seminars and Other Works*. London, Karnac Books, 2000.

Bion, W. R. (1976b) Four Discussions. In *Clinical Seminars and Other Works*. London, Karnac Books, 2000.

Bion, W. R. (1977) Caesura. In *Two Papers: The Grid and Caesura*. London, Karnac Books, 1989.

Chuster, A. (1997) A influência da ciência na psicanálise. *Revista do CEPdePA*, Porto Alegre, 6:189–202.

Chuster, A. (2001) Comentários sobre a conferência de Bion em Paris. *Revista de Psicanálise da SPPA*, Porto Alegre, V. VIII/1:103–6.

Chuster, A. (2002) *Novas Leituras: dos princípios ético-estéticos à clínica*. Rio de Janeiro: Companhia de Freud.

Chuster, A. and Trachtenberg, R. (2009). *As Sete Invejas Capitais: uma leitura psicanalítica contemporânea sobre a complexidade do mal*. Porto Alegre: Artmed.

Freud, S. (1900) The Interpretation of Dreams. *Standard Edition*, 4 and 5.

Freud, S. (1915) The unconscious. *Standard Edition*, 12.

Freud, S. (1923) The Ego and the Id. *Standard Edition*, 19.

Freud, S. (1926) Inhibición, síntoma y angustia. In *Obras completas*, v. XX. Buenos Aires: Amorrortu (ed).

Meltzer, D. (1967) *The Psycho-Analytical Process*. London: Karnac Books.

Meltzer, D. (1973) *Sexual States of Mind*. London: Karnac Books.

Meltzer, D. (1975) *Explorations in Autism*. London: Karnac Books.

Meltzer, D. (1978) *The Kleinian Development part III: The Clinical Significance of the Work of Bion*. Perthshire: Clunie Press.

Meltzer, D. (1986) *Studies in Extended Metapsychology: Clinical Applications of Bion's Ideas*. Perthshire: Clunie Press.

Meltzer, D. and Harris Williams, M. (1988). *The Apprehension of Beauty*. Perthshire: Clunie Press.

Morin, E. (1999) *O Método 3: o conhecimento do conhecimento*. Porto Alegre: Sulina.

Part 4

INFANT AND CHILD ANALYSIS

EDITORS' INTRODUCTION

Infant Observation: Catastrophic Change under a Microscope

Marianne Robinson

In recent decades, careful observations of the infant's emotional and relational growth have enriched psychoanalytic understanding of early development and have broadened our appreciation of the depth of the transference situation. From Spitz' (1945) early studies of "hospitalism," to formulations of the process of separation-individuation by Mahler (1975) and her colleagues, to the recent focus on early intersubjective patterns by Beebe et al. (2004), psychoanalysts have increasingly become aware of the immensely intricate choreography of the early mother/baby relationship. Robinson approaches this territory from the perspective of Bion's (1962ab) theories of how a baby, with the assistance of its mother, learns to manage and digest emotional experience. Her richly detailed focus on the interactions and challenges faced by an infant girl and her mother at ages 3, 16 and 40 weeks, draws the reader into the remarkable subtleties of small, but exceedingly vital, interactions that demonstrate the complexity of everyday exchanges between mother and child. In particular, she explores: "Whether that baby experiences the meeting with its postnatal reality as a crime against its previous seamless unconscious being or a bearable realization of containment" and applies Bion's ideas about how the mother helps her baby bear its emotional experiences though her capacity for containment.

Bion (1970, 1977) built upon what Freud (1926) called the "impressive caesura of the act of birth," when he noted that all change is potentially catastrophic and requires the presence, either internally or in the actual person of a containing object, of a function capable of transforming emotional turbulence into a "bearable realization of containment." Robinson illustrates how her interventions helped Mother and Baby navigate the infant's anger around feeding at 3 weeks, the transition from what had become a satisfying nursing experience to Baby learning to use the pacifier at 16 weeks, and, lastly, the painful sudden need for weaning at 40 weeks. Thus, readers accompany

Robinson, as she explores the infant's unconscious phantasies associated with the psychic pain produced by the awareness of separation, the discrepancy between phantasy and reality and the experience of loss and describes the mother's transforming reverie and alpha function in response to her infant's distress. In Robinson's view, it is the mother's capacity to make sense of this distress that ultimately fosters within her baby an evolving capacity for thought.

12

INFANT OBSERVATION

Catastrophic Change under a Microscope

Marianne Robinson

In the mid-1960s when infant observation was added to the requirements of psychoanalytic training in the British Psychoanalytical Society, Bion welcomed that development. He joked that observation of babies should be done with the same enthusiasm and curiosity that Sherlock Holmes used "when on the track of a desperate criminal" (1966, p. 576).

What is observed in infant observation is a baby building its capacity to digest experience in relation to its object world. Whether that baby experiences the meeting with its postnatal reality as a crime against its previous seamless unconscious being or a bearable realization of containment, is a matter requiring different tools than were available to Sherlock Holmes—or to us before the work of Bick (1963, 1968), Klein (1930, 1946, 1952ab), Magagna (1987), Miller (1993), Riviere (1936), Segal (1955).

In his lifelong effort to develop tools to observe and describe psychic functions, Bion used abstractions to develop what he called models that deal with the process of transformation from what is unknown on its journey to becoming known, or approximated, as I believe Bion (1963) would have put it. His aim was to develop theories that would have maximal generalizability yet not lose their grounding in the most elemental and minute aspects of the human experience.

My aim in this chapter is to illustrate how Bion's models, stated with such abstraction, are pivotal for intuiting and understanding an infant's minute-to-minute experience in its efforts to cope with the unfamiliar world outside the womb.

I referred to the baby as digesting its experiences. That is the model Bion suggested for understanding the process of learning from experience (1962a). It is incorporated in his theory of container–contained (Bion, 1962a), which expanded and deepened our understanding of projective identification, reverie, alpha function, and meaning-making that foster capacity for thought within the mother–infant bond. The currency of exchange between mother and baby in that relationship is the baby's projection of its unbearable experience into mother, who receives it in her reverie where it is transformed by her alpha function and returned to baby in tolerable portions, conveyed through her care and communication.

During development, the containing space or object is outlined, at first, in terms of physical attributes; the relationship to the uterus and to the mother's breast, and later in terms of sensual, emotional, and symbolic parameters: the relationship to the fantasized internal space of mother's body, the maternal mind and eventually to the containing function of the infant's own mind. With growth, each transformation into a new psychic container involves a painful disruption of the status quo that Bion (1976) called turbulence, or catastrophic change. It ensues when what is known is insufficient to meet present reality. Turbulence is an opportunity for growth if there is the capacity to tolerate doubt in the face of the unknown within the infant, or the capacity for holding the infant's unbearable pain within the mother. A containing relationship can then be internalized, setting in motion the infant's developmental journey; oscillating between paranoid-schizoid and depressive states, a lifelong relationship depicted by Bion as PS↔D (Bion 1977). This process culminates in the capacity for whole-object relations and the ability to orient oneself within a containing internal world.

Bion (1963, 1970) also points out that the containing relationship is vulnerable to certain dangers. These may follow the rupture of boundaries, when the container is devoured by the contained, or when the contained succeeds in puncturing the container, whether this is due to forces internal to the baby or to the mother, or as a result of an unfortunate fit between the two. The turbulence then stops psychic movement and leads to development in a different direction, namely a pull toward discontinuity, as well as actions to stop forward movement by inviting regressive distortion of the familiar, accompanied by an unconscious phantasy of returning to an earlier state.

This paper focuses on what I call "midstream" moments during emotional turbulence (Bion, 1976), the intersection of the unconscious phantasy and psychic pain in that turbulent state, with a view to following the fate of the psychic pain in relation to container–contained (Bion, 1970). In addition, I will approach the process of turbulence from the standpoint of the bi-directional caesura (Bion, 1977) within which there is oscillation—movement back and forth.

I will examine these parameters using three infant observation vignettes, each depicting moments of turbulence encountered by the infant for the first time, concretely and with compelling transparency. They show Baby, whom I observed, as she confronts the world as a separate being, and capture the following moments in the process of psychic emergence:

1 Turbulence ensuing from awareness of separateness;
2 Turbulence ensuing from awareness of discrepancy between unconscious phantasy and reality;
3 Turbulence ensuing from the experience of sudden loss.

In the narratives and subsequent discussions, I attempt to follow the state of the internal world of Baby, while inviting parallels in the reader's mind, in order to show how moments of turbulence, observed with some clarity in the developing infant, can, at a later time, serve as a compass to the analyst or therapist when confronted with the more complex picture of the adult patient whose layering of defensive fantasies has accumulated over a lifetime in the service of avoiding psychic pain, confusion and turmoil.

I. Dawning Awareness of Separateness and Dependency

The observations were made during home visits within the framework of the Tavistock method of infant observation (Bick, 1963).[1] As observer, this involved holding the baby when Mother handed her to me, talking to mother, and interacting with the baby in such a way that did not interrupt or direct its attention at the moment. In the third vignette I was confronted with a situation that prompted a spontaneous intervention on my part. In the process I departed from the traditional observational stance. In that segment I will briefly discuss my understanding of the dynamics involved at that moment without diverting from the focus of the paper.

During my observation when Baby was three weeks old, Mother said that Baby gets *angry* when she nurses. It happens on both breasts toward the end of her nursing.

The following week, Mother, as was her habit at the beginning of every observation, handed Baby to me. As we exchanged Baby, I noticed that her body did not react but that her eyes *widened* and she stared at me. I held her on my lap facing me in a half-sitting position, our bodies forming an obtuse angle (135 degrees). I saw that she would focus on something with her eyes and her body would simultaneously move toward that object as if taking it in or joining with it. She focused on my blouse with her eyes and immediately her stomach muscles contracted, her head moved forward, and she actually "power curled" herself from a half-reclining position away from me and fell into my chest. She did that three times. I was amazed at the way her eyes seemed to "pull" her body into the object they focused on.

After a few minutes she started fussing. Mother took Baby, sat down, and put her on the right breast. Baby latched on, mouth wide, eyes wide, and she took several very strong gulps, arms and hands at her side. She relaxed, she drew a big sigh, she smacked her lips against the breast several times and continued to suck strongly for a few minutes. Then she let go of the nipple, deliberately it seemed. Again she found it, very confidently. She did this a couple of times. Then started an interplay between Baby and Mother's nipple that was fascinating to watch. Baby let go of the nipple, cried for a few seconds, latched on, started to cry and let go again. She'd let go and fuss, latch on, suck, and let the milk dribble. Dribbles of milk came out of the underside of Baby's mouth and fell on mother's tights. She did this for several minutes. Let go, find the nipple, fuss, mouthed the nipple, fuss, let go, fuss. She turned her head and cried, latched on and cried. She had the nipple between her lips, crying, unable to fully take it or fully let go of it. By this time she had enough milk inside to satisfy her physical hunger and it seemed she wanted to draw away but expected the nipple to follow her. I had a sense that she was in despair because she couldn't just turn her head or do whatever she wanted and still preserve the nipple–mouth connection. I felt a paralyzing helplessness. Baby was obviously overtaken by emotional forces beyond her capacity to hold, and Mother, helpless to satisfy Baby physically, was left to suffer the agony of Baby's powerfully projected distress. After a few minutes Mother said "I can only take so much of this" and pulled down her shirt. During the nursing, I noticed that Mother looked very intently at her baby. At one point Mother said "I have to give her my attention or it doesn't work, she falls off the nipple. If I read or watch TV, she knows it immediately so I have to pay attention to her."

Discussion

I will now outline how I view the dynamics in this emotional interaction between Baby and Mother. Baby's attaching eye activity, together with her muscle reaction, which was powerful enough to cause her to fall into me, seems to enact a pull toward physical unity. Her eyes were not used for looking, but her sight seemed to function as an extension of her physical body. This appeared to be confirmed by her simultaneous open incorporating mouth and open incorporating eyes during nursing while the rest of her body was passive. Her looking would thus have been a vehicle to deny the reality of physical separateness and to achieve fusion, to join the object concretely and physically. At that moment she might be referred to as an "inside" baby whose aim is to deny the dawning perception of separateness and to return to the womb-like, preconscious unity with the object.

A process of this kind is possibly the origin of adhesion, a suggestion I have made in another paper, since it involves resisting a containing relationship on one hand while not succumbing to the agonies of separateness (Robinson, 2010).

Nursing at the breast seemed gratifying until the physical hunger was muted. However, what followed suggests a more complex and fluid developmental picture than the unidirectional pull toward physical union.

My impression was that Baby deliberately let go of the nipple and then found it again with confidence. This would suggest that her physical ability to let go and to refind the source of nurture had been brought under her conscious control. Her subsequent inability to either fully let go or fully latch on might then be linked to another issue, a psychical one. Baby's distress and protest here seem to be an expression of turbulence, as she is confronted with a situation for which her knowledge from past experience of continuous "inside" familiar unawareness is insufficient to meet a reality that her growing cognition can perceive. I believe that at the core of her turbulence is the fact of separateness as it is conveyed by the intermittent presence of the nipple for comfort and physical nurture. That nipple is now separated in an unfamiliar way from the containing presence of Mother's mind, the absence or presence of which was so powerfully reacted to by Baby. This latter statement cannot be made without including Mother and considering what she knows in her reverie ("I have to give her my attention"). Mother's awareness of her need to apply her mind, her eyes, and her attention while Baby nursed or she would "fall off the nipple" seems a clear expression of her reverie. Even her choice of the word "fall" was meaningful. Baby's "fall" was psychic, not physical. Mother knew intuitively that there was a connection between letting her baby fall out of her containing mind/attention and the baby falling off the breast that was no longer adequate to give the emotional holding that Baby's growing needs and capacity required. She translated that knowledge into a holding onto her baby with her attention.

Baby's despair appeared to be so intense that she was unable to make use of the breast, even when it was available. I think the dribbling of the milk was experienced by Baby as an act of destruction of the goodness of the physical nurturing and that this act was also related to her psychic despair. Baby's beginning awareness of the intermittent presence of the "outside" breast presented her with a discontinuity between her phantasied continuous "inside" container, the womb of unconsciousness, and the continuous "outside" container, Mother's mind.

In order to infer Baby's unconscious experience it may be illuminating to consider the confluence of experiences of the participants. There was Baby's intense distress in relation to Mother's breast, which was offered with care and the loving attention of her mind. There was Mother's helplessness and pain when her breast/mind was rejected. Her good milk was dribbled away and her loving attention insufficient to hold Baby's despair. There was also my experience of paralyzing helplessness together with an accumulating sense that something disastrous might be happening in such a way that no relief was possible. In that light, of Mother's pulling down her shirt and terminating the experience, which had turned too bad to endure, I believe it can be said that at that moment the breast, being the concrete agent of reality, seemed to be felt as an enemy/attacker whose products were felt to be poison/reality because it represented the experience of increased mental growth demanding emotional adjustment. This moment can then be described as emotional turbulence in relation to the "midstream" experience of being between the containing function of the remembered internal/uterine/unconscious state and the containing function of the mother's mind, a separate and external state. Her eyes pulled in one direction while her mouth was confronted with a different reality. There was no common sense or binocularity to serve as reference.

At the moment when Mother pulled her shirt down, the state of the Mother–Baby relationship became one in which the contained (Baby's distress) has ruptured the container (Mother's capacity to hold that distress) (Bion, 1962a, 1970).

II. Dealing with Discrepancy

The second vignette finds Baby struggling to reconcile the gap between her "breast-receptive" mouth cavity and the pacifier given her by Mother.

At 16 weeks, Baby had established a confident and rewarding nursing relationship with Mother. She was smiling, babbling, bringing her hands together while intertwining her fingers, and watching them held this way before bringing them into her mouth. She was actively inviting dialogue with the object world.

In this observation, Baby had just finished nursing and Mother put her on her blanket and gave her the pacifier, which she had only used once or twice before. Baby was alert, her eyes were open, and she was looking around as she received the pacifier into her mouth. However, instead of closing her lips around it and sucking for comfort, she kept her mouth open, her lips shaping a big *O*, her tongue receding, her mouth thus forming a cavity that was consistent with accommodating her mother's breast. Her receded tongue rhythmically prodded the pacifier in the same way it would ordinarily meet Mother's nipple in order to release milk. With such a discrepancy between her anticipating mouth cavity and the inserted pacifier, the pacifier, safety plate and all, fell into Baby's mouth. She quickly accommodated her mouth cavity to fit the teat part of the pacifier and gave a couple of sucks. Having thus secured its position in her mouth, she again formed her mouth and tongue into the "breast-receptive" cavity. At the same time she withdrew any connection to her surroundings. She seemed to close out every stimulus in order to focus all her efforts on bridging the gap between her breast-receptive mouth and the inserted pacifier. She slackened the muscles in her body and *all* of her seemed concentrated in her mouth and her eyes. Her mouth continued its activity, her tongue prodding rhythmically at the pacifier teat within the unmodified breast-receptive cavity. She *struggled* to roll her eyes upward while attempting to bring her eyelids down. She was trying to put herself to sleep! It seemed she expected that this altered mental state would make the pacifier fill her mouth cavity. Her efforts again failed and the pacifier fell into her mouth for the second time. Baby opened her eyes, spat out the pacifier and let out a sharp cry. This alerted Mother, who said "I guess she needs to nurse some more." Mother picked Baby up and quickly put her to the breast. Baby latched on and nursed contentedly until falling asleep.

Discussion

I will now discuss this vignette from the standpoint of Bion's theory of development of memory and thinking and the importance of the containing relationship in that process.

Bion (1962b) wrote that a conception is initiated by the conjunction of a preconception with a realization to form a concept. He uses a baby's *a priori* knowledge of a breast as a model. The conjunction of a preconception with a realization yields an emotional experience of satisfaction. He also states that a thought is born from the mating of a preconception with frustration and that a baby's rudimentary consciousness cannot bear the burden of realizing a no-breast. When confronted with a frustration the psychic apparatus has four options; thinking which is associated with modification and evasion, projective identification as evasion by evacuation, omniscience aimed at rejecting and escaping reality, and communication.

In an attempt to highlight and sharpen the meaning of this sequence, I will intersperse descriptions from the observation with selected quotes from Bion's writings.

Baby, when forming what I called a breast-receptive mouth cavity, suggests that she has a physical "memory" of a good breast, a concept formed from experienced physical and emotional satisfaction. This memory is also an expression of the fantasy of satisfaction with which she approaches the reality of this situation.

I set the stage with a quote by Bion describing how projective identification within a containing relationship serves the development of thinking:

> the prototype of memory appears to reside in one of the aspects of projective identification. This mechanism, employed to fulfill the duties of thought until thought takes over, appears as an interchange first between mouth and breast and then between introjected mouth and introjected breast. This I regard as reaction between container and contained seems to be the element which is nearest in this phase to memory.
>
> (Bion, 1970, p. 28)

Baby has a concept of a mouth and a breast meeting, and she signals her expectation of, and receptiveness to, that familiar interchange by shaping her mouth as a physical cavity into which only her mother's breast would fit. However, the physical shape of the pacifier introduces the beginning experience of discrepancy between Baby's phantasy and reality. Baby realizes the experience, and her tongue goes into activity to encourage a closing of the discrepant gap. The gap is too big and the pacifier falls into Baby's mouth, facing her with an undeniable no-fit. Her rudimentary memory of a satisfying breast serves as a pre-concept, which is faced with a frustration, a challenge Bion formulates as follows: "Thought means the mating of a pre-conception with frustration … no breast available for satisfaction" (Bion, 1967, p. 26).

Baby, at 16 weeks, is not capable of the thought that frustration in the face of her receptiveness would require. Instead, it seems, she reacts as if to a threatened loss and quickly takes action. She adjusts her mouth to the shape of the pacifier to prevent losing it in the process, showing her capacity, however fleetingly, to hold on to a frustrating reality. How her rudimentary apparatus will deal with that reality is still uncertain as reflected in the next quote: "The next step depends on the infant's capacity for frustration: in particular it depends on whether the decision is to evade frustration or modify it" (Bion, 1967, p. 111).

By retaining the pacifier Baby can be said to create a space that is in-between the thought of no-fit and the experience of a fit. I would call that space a not-yet-fit on one hand or a not-yet-thought on the other. Within that space, Baby was again facing frustration. The fact that she held on and did not call out to her mother at this time can be interpreted as her beginning ability to experience frustration. But what follows suggests that she was at the end of her capacity to hold herself together while being in touch with her object world. Here Bion refers to an important distinction between modifying and evading the pain of frustration. Modification is an attempt to use a relationship to lead to having a piece of knowledge to substitute for an ongoing getting-to-know relationship. Evasion on the other hand is an attempt to change the meaning of the relationship so the relationship of getting to know reality no longer represents a painful experience but a painless one. Bion: "Incapacity for tolerating frustration tips the scale in the direction of evasion of frustration" (1967, p. 112).

Baby evaded continued frustration by attempting to "fall asleep" by attempting to change her consciousness. She seemed to withdraw any orientation to the outside in order to try to hallucinate away the discrepancy, a shift she could evidently make at will. All the while, she maintained her breast-receptive cavity and her tongue prodding, making it evident that her fantasized satisfaction did not change. With the following quote Bion includes the extremes of evasion, which is destruction and even reversing the senses, that perceive frustrating reality. "Hallucination will be favored for its immediacy" (1970, p. 16) [and] "Hallucination is designed through its quality as the thing-itself to be indistinguishable from freedom" (Bion, 1967 p. 17).

However, Baby's hallucination failed to re-form the pacifier/reality into the breast/phantasy and she was hit by that realization when the pacifier fell into her mouth for the second time. The experience was too much for her and Bion describes well how the frustration becomes an internal enemy. Baby fails to modify reality. "What should be thought … becomes a bad object, indistinguishable from the thing-in-itself, fit only for evacuation … " (Bion, 1967, p. 112).

Baby's capacities for experiencing frustration on one hand, and hallucinating away frustration on the other, were exhausted. She spat out the "bad" pacifier and gave voice to her "bad" feelings. Her cry contained the unheld emotional content, and she projected it into her mother/container. Mother intuitively sensed the fantasy that Baby's mouth cavity had expressed but that only I had observed. Mother's decision to nurse gave the satisfying fit that Baby needed. With that action Mother and Baby together made a thinking couple for Baby to introject, a moment of the container–contained relationship again described with Bion's austere elegance: "projective identification … employed to fulfill the duties of thought until thought takes over, appears as an interchange first between mouth and breast and then between introjected mouth and introjected breast" (Bion, 1970, p. 28).

I was mesmerized by it all. It looked like Baby had been struggling to use all the capacities at her disposal to cope with this unfamiliar experience of a no-fit when a "remembered" fit was fantasized. I believe she used her physical concept of a nursing couple as a preconception, but when it was met with frustration the thought of a no-breast was not yet possible, leaving her with turbulence "midstream" between having an internalized concept of a (physical) nursing couple, on one hand, and internalizing a thinking (mental) couple on the other. The attempt failed and Baby alerted Mother through projective identification to metabolize and do the thinking she was not yet able to.

In the adult psychoanalytic situation the psychoanalyst's ability to follow the patient's use of the interpretation, in the same fashion that I, as the infant observer, could follow Baby's reaction to the pacifier, can be a precise instrument for sensing the patient's state of mind. I am suggesting that, for this purpose, the pacifier can be used as a metaphor for the analytic interpretation, and the baby's formed mouth cavity can be used as a metaphor for the patient's unconscious expectation of seamless satisfaction. I want to be precise about my use of this metaphor because it can be accurately said that a pacifier is a comfort substitute that gives no sustenance, while the psychoanalytic interpretation gives the nurturing that a containing relationship can provide, which makes space both for the pain of frustrated phantasies and the thought that can contain that experience. The commonality between the pacifier and the interpretation rests in the pacifier's inability to fit Baby's fantasy of the breast, and the interpretation's inability to fit the adult patient's phantasy of being perfectly understood. Experienced from the position of infantile omnipotence, the pacifier and the interpretation have the common attribute of being a discrepant object that calls for attention.

III. Baby Dealing with Loss

The third vignette, which happened at 40 weeks, needs a short introduction. When Baby was 35 weeks old, Mother, who had been her sole caregiver since birth, found full-time work. This necessitated a sudden weaning and finding of daycare for Baby. The latter was arranged with an acquaintance, Liz, who lived a forty-five-minute drive away and who had her own child, Billy, five months older than Baby. The disruption proved hard for Baby, not only because of her sudden and simultaneous loss of the breast and Mother, but also because little Billy constantly and cruelly asserted his rights to have his world all to himself. In addition, Baby had not developed an attachment to a transitional object, so there was no soothing or comfort to ease the painful loss and soften the transition. In the three weeks prior to the observation I will present, I noted evidence of Baby's plight which I summarize as follows.

Baby fell asleep as soon as she got to daycare in the morning. She stopped playing the dropping game with her keys. This was her version of the "fort … da" game so charmingly described by Freud (1914), the aim of which was to reassure that after separation there is a reunion. She stopped using her pinching capacity when picking things up. She became quiet and serious and did not seek relationships as before. She would sit in the sandbox, pick up handfuls of sand, and trickle them through her fingers, a glazed look on her face. Liz told me that Baby, who had mastered going downstairs backwards "forgot all about it and didn't remember all week." Liz also said that Baby, who was not able to hold a bottle when she first came, now "grabs it as if she's known how to all along" and "it is a blast to watch Billy give Baby the bottle because he gives it to her, then he yanks it away and then he gives it and again yanks it away." Baby often sat away from others, a blank look on her face, making no eye contact, her stillness occasionally interrupted by a furtive wave bye-bye into empty space. She babbled to herself, sometimes while playing with her lips. She pat-a-caked halfheartedly and ended it with a bit of a wave and a slow flick of the wrist. It seemed that the things she had learned in relation to her mother/object were now truncated and done as if into space. Liz said "maybe she doesn't know I'm here."

During my observation at 40 weeks, I noticed that Baby was more aggressive with her voice and much more vigorous and goal oriented compared to the more remote feel that she had conveyed in the previous three weeks. She had also developed a new behavior. Even though she was not tired, she kept burying her face in the soft couch-cushion. A number of times she used her buried face as a support point while standing up, putting all her weight into the face/cushion connection.

Liz sat down on the couch beside me, and Billy climbed into her lap. Liz rested her arm on a pink throw pillow. Billy put his head on her arm and she gave him her breast. Baby crawled over, stood up next to Liz and Billy, using the couch as support. She buried her face vigorously into the couch-cushion, saw the pink throw pillow under Liz's arm and tried to take it. She became quite insistent and Liz kept saying "no, my pillow!" Finally, I picked up a similar blue throw pillow and put it between Liz's pink pillow and Baby's face. Baby took it with delight and buried her face in it, holding it tight with her hands. She turned her back to the nursing couple and forcefully threw her "pillowed" head back onto the couch-cushion several times, babbling loudly all the while.

When Billy was finished nursing, Baby started playing with my shoe. She put the toe part of the shoe into her wide-open mouth and deliberately bit my foot inside it several times—hard. She then sat down on her haunches and started pat-a-caking in front of me. I pat-a-caked with her, putting words to the action. She became so involved in my pat-a-cake that she stood up and wanted to bring my hands together using one of her own hands, abandoning her own pat-a-cake in the process.

As if knowing that Mother was expected any minute, Baby then sat down, strangely quiet and with a faraway look in her eyes, fingering and pinching the smooth face of my watch, my rings, and my fingers.

Discussion

Baby's depression and withdrawal as a result of the sudden simultaneous loss of her mother and the breast had felt very sad for me. I also held some anger at Liz, who let her son take out his territorial sadism on this new "motherless sibling." In this observation, Baby's more energetic and active engagement with her world seemed very encouraging. Her new behavior of burying her face in the soft couch-cushion seemed to be an effort to recover the sensation of the soft breast/face contact, if not with the real object then through a substitute and by her own action. The force with which this was done, especially while Baby supported her full weight on her face, also suggested emotional pain, concretely experienced and self-inflicted, within this substitute connection.

When Billy nursed, Baby's couch-cushion contact seemingly failed to hold her, and with her newfound aggression she pursued the next best thing to the breast, the pillow that was connected to it. When she was coldly rejected, I as the observer could no longer hold what seemed a cruel deprivation so I gave a substitute pillow. The following sequence seems curious. Baby related to the pillow with excitement, as if it were not a real breast, but the ideal breast she had sought at 4 weeks, which she now controlled with her hands and that followed her wherever she threw her head. Her jabbering contained the released excitement of the experience and was in stark contrast with her silence in the previous weeks.

While positioning the pillow for Baby to find, I was very aware of its equivalence to the breast in Baby's mind. With that action I stepped outside the observer role and made a gesture more in line with a therapeutic intervention. I felt Baby was dealing with the reality of what was available in her new situation and I feared that the cruelty with which she was denied any substitute or compromise might cause her to collapse into the depression that had numbed her aliveness for the past five weeks. I believe that her subsequent idealization of the pillow/breast can be seen as holding on to (vs. numbing) the relationship of getting to know and that further incremental frustration of that idealization would hold some promise in terms of her growing ability to tolerate frustration and deal with absence.

When she bit my foot I believe that Baby let *me* feel the bite of her emotional experience rather than turning it on herself by mutilating her capacities as before, and felt as if she used me as a container for that pain. This opened a connection between us, and Baby invited dialogue with her pat-a-cake. However, that seemed to be straining her capacity to hold the experience of a substitute object, and the separateness of her pat-a-caking hands and mine became too much. I felt that she wanted to be inside my pat-a-cake. This entry into the object, by the now tired baby, seemed confirmed by her glazed eyes and sensual touching and pinching of small things, as if the skin of her fingers conveyed to this "inside" Baby a sense of being together with an object that could now be bitten and pinched. My feeling was that I had a physical baby on my lap while Baby, herself, through the sensual connection on her skin, was inside the experience/memory of Mother. This seemed a welcome contrast to Baby who had previously destroyed her acquired capacities and related into autistic-like space.

At 40 weeks Baby's defenses were complex and, until this moment, seemed to involve, in addition to the autistic-like withdrawal, infantile depression and manic reunion with an ideal breast. I think Baby's regressive forgetting was linked to an effort to recapture the lost containing relationship with Mother. and that she mutilated the capacities that on some level she perceived had caused the rupture in her life. She fell asleep when she had been awake to life. She abandoned the game of dropping and rediscovering the keys when Mother was not there to be predictably but intermittently rediscovered. She abandoned her ability to pinch in order to explore something specific when the familiar object of exploration (Mother and her body) disappeared. One can here infer a fantasy in Baby that attempts to deal with causality.

It seems what had been concealed in Baby's scattered reactions up to this point had culminated in a representation of a painful emerging into consciousness. In that sense Baby's response could or can be seen as "midstream" between the known experience of internalizing a containing relationship with a stay-at-home mother, and that of bearing a painful face-first experience of loss (no-breast) with its additional physical resonance of an also painful face-first physical entry into the world (Paul, 1980) on the other. What was yet to come was an ability to have a thought of an absent mother with its implied security of having mother's holding mind in her internal world.

The oscillation between these states is diagrammed below:

Mutilating withdrawal ↔ Manic excitement
Frustration/rage ↔ Containment within a sensually-remembered Mother

Summary

I will briefly summarize. The first vignette showed Baby at 4 weeks in emotional turbulence when she began to sense that the nipple/mouth connection was intermittent. She was "midstream" between the containing function of the remembered "inside/uterine/unconscious" state and the containing function of her mother's mind, a separate and "outside" state. In that instance Mother was unable to contain Baby's projected despair and responded in kind, signaling that *her* container was failing. In this situation what was introjected was a broken couple, a ruptured container unable to make meaning other than that the contained was too big and powerful for the container.

The second vignette showed Baby at 12 weeks confronted with a discrepancy between reality and unconscious fantasy: a pacifier when she anticipated the breast. It illustrated how Baby used her memory when meeting with a frustrating reality. As she was not yet capable of thought, she faced turbulence "midstream" between having an internalized concept of a (physical) nursing couple on one hand, and internalizing a thinking (mental) couple on the other. Her distress was received by Mother who transformed it into a containing experience, thus forming a thinking couple for Baby to introject.

The third vignette showed turbulence ensuing when Baby at 40 weeks experienced sudden loss of the breast as well as the familiar daytime care of her mother. In that situation she faced turmoil in relation to a premature rupture of the containing relationship "midstream" in the process of developing her ability to think and use symbols and internalize. At first she coped by mutilating the recently acquired capacities that related to her lost object, an unconscious effort to return to an earlier state. However, during the same observation Baby showed her active search for and experience with a substitute for the lost breast, conveying both her longing and her pain. It seems that projecting those longings and inflicting the pain on me enabled her to recover her capacity to hold herself in a suspended state, recalling the concrete sensual experience of Mother. I think with that concrete sensual experience she can be said to hold on to a remembered containing relationship.

I believe that elaborating on these moments of turbulence during Baby's first year of life has demonstrated how Bion's abstract models, stated by him with such austere beauty, enable us to approach the complexity of a baby's earliest experiences of the containing object world with an increased sense of wonder and understanding.

Note

1 Esther Bick introduced infant observation in the Tavistock Child Psychotherapy training program in 1948 (Bick, 1964) and in 1960 it became part of the curriculum of the Institute of Psycho-Analysis in London. In the decades that followed the method Bick used has come to be known as the Tavistock Method of infant observation and has taken root in training programs in many countries including the United States where I was introduced to it. The infant observation program involves visiting a baby in its environment (home or daycare) one hour per week from birth for at least its first year and documenting from memory each visit as minutely as possible. Concurrently there are weekly ninety-minute seminar meetings with three or, at most, four other infant observers for the purpose of in-depth discussion of the observations.

The observer's role is difficult since according to Bick "it involved the conceptualization of the observer's role, and also the conscious and unconscious attitudes of the observer. … The observer should feel himself sufficiently inside the family to experience the emotional impact, but not committed to act out any roles thrust upon him. … This would not seem to exclude him being helpful as a particular situation arose—by holding the baby …" (Bick, 1964, p. 558).

"The observer is confronted with a situation of intense emotional impact. In order to observe at all he must attain detachment … find a position from which to make his observation … [with] as little distortion as possible" (p. 559).

References

Beebe, B., Knoblauch, S., Rustin, J. and Sorter, D. (2004) *Forms of Intersubjectivity in Infant Research and Adult Treatment.* New York: Other Press.

Bick, E. (1963) Notes on infant observation in psychoanalytic training. *International Journal of Psycho-Analysis*, 45:558–66.

Bick, E. (1968) The experience of the skin in early object relations. *International Journal of Psycho-Analysis*, 49:484–6.

Bion, W. R. (1962a) *Learning from Experience.* New York: Basic Books; London: Maresfield.

Bion, W. R. (1962b) The psycho-analytic study of thinking. *International Journal of Psycho-Analysis*, 43:306–10.

Bion, W. R. (1963) *Elements of Psycho-Analysis.* pp. 1–104. London: Karnac.

Bion, W. R. (1966) Review of *Medical orthodoxy and the future of psycho-analysis*, by K. R. Eissler. *International Journal of Psycho-Analysis*, 47:575–79.

Bion, W. R. (1967) *Second Thoughts.* London: William Heinemann.

Bion, W. R. (1970) *Attention and Interpretation.* London: Tavistock Publications.

Bion, W. R. (1976) Emotional turbulence. In: *Clinical Seminars and Other Works*, pp. 295–305. London: Karnac Books, 1994.

Bion, W. R. (1977) *Two Papers: The Grid and Caesura.* Rio de Janeiro, Brazil: Image Editora Ltd.

Freud, S. (1914) Letter from Sigmund Freud to Sándor Ferenczi, March 11, 1914. *The Correspondence of Sigmund Freud and Sándor Ferenczi Volume 1, 1908–14*, p. 545.

Freud, S. (1926) Inhibitions, symptoms and anxiety. *Standard Edition*, 20:75–175. London: Hogarth Press.

Klein, M. (1930) The importance of symbol-formation in the development of the ego. In: *Love, Guilt and Reparation and Other Works 1921–1945*, pp. 306–43. New York: The Free Press.

Klein, M. (1946) Notes on some schizoid mechanisms. *International Journal of Psycho-Analysis*, 27:99–110.

Klein, M. (1952a) On observing the behaviour of young infants. In: *Envy and Gratitude and Other Works 1946–1963*, pp. 94–121. New York: Delacorte Press.

Klein, M. (1952b) Some theoretical conclusions about the emotional life of the infant. In: *Envy and Gratitude and Other Works 1946–1963*, pp. 61–93. New York: Delacorte Press 1975.

Magagna, J. (1987) Three years of infant observation with Mrs. Bick. *Journal of Child Psychotherapy*, 15.

Mahler, M., Pine, F. and Bergman, A. (1975) *The Psychological Birth of the Human Infant.* New York: Basic Books, Inc.

Miller, J.M. (1993). Resistance in child psychoanalysis. *Journal of Child Psychotherapy*, 19:33–45.

Paul, M. (1980) A mental atlas of the process of psychological birth. In: J Grotstein, ed. *Do I Dare Disturb the Universe? A Memorial to W. R. Bion*, pp. 551–70.

Riviere, J. (1936) On the genesis of psychical conflict in earliest infancy. In: M. Klein, P. Heimann, S. Isaacs, J. Riviere, editors. *Developments in Psychoanalysis*, pp. 37–66. London: Hogarth Press, 1952.

Robinson, M. (2010) A binocular view of adhesion: From prenatal contiguity to post-natal appetite. In: J. vanBuren, S. Alhanati, (eds.) *Primitive Mental States*, pp. 80–96. London: Routledge.

Segal, H. (1955) Notes on symbol formation. In: *The Work of Hanna Segal.* New York: Jason Aronson, 1981.

Spitz, R. A. (1945) Hospitalism – An inquiry into the genesis of psychiatric conditions in early childhood. *Psychoanalytic Study of the Child*, 1:53–74.

EDITORS' INTRODUCTION

The Threatening Character of Change: An Approach with Patients Who Experience Progress as Trauma

Angelika Staehle

While Bion elaborated the normative aspect of projective identification, as a primitive, unconscious mode of communication that predates the acquisition of language and is essential for psychic growth and development, Meltzer emphasized its sadistic-intrusive use in pathological, narcissistic relationships. Staehle briefly summarizes Meltzer's views, contrasting them with Bion's, and then uses the dialectical interplay between their formulations to explore the problems and process of treatment of patients who are difficult to reach, whose minds operate at a concrete, non-symbolic level and who are fixed in a rigid pseudo-identity. For these patients, there is a central, unconscious phantasy of simultaneously being protected and imprisoned in a place of refuge, a "claustrum" or "psychic retreat." While the latter may provide protection against paranoid-schizoid and depressive anxieties, it offers a container that no longer serves the function of understanding, processing and transforming emotional experiences in a growth-producing way.

Through her presentation of the very moving case of Alex, a deeply rejected and emotionally traumatized five-year-old boy, and the adult, Mr. C., a withdrawn, somaticizing and hypochondriacal former athlete, Staehle contrasts normal (communicative) and pathological (non-communicative) projective identification and explores the consequences of the patient's creating a self-protective and growth-paralyzing psychic retreat in the face of catastrophic, annihilating anxieties and the threat of non-being. In so doing, she illustrates Bion's assertion that impaired processes between mother and infant in the processes of container/contained "bring about non-processed, nameless dread and intolerable feelings of emptiness." It is only when the infant—or child or adult patient—can find a suitable and willingly penetrable psychic container that it can begin to develop a competent psyche. As Staehle has so poetically put it, "we need to [psychically] inhabit the house of the mother … before we may live in a house of our own."

13

THE THREATENING CHARACTER OF CHANGE

An Approach with Patients Who Experience Progress as Trauma

Angelika Staehle

Theoretical Points of Emphasis

In this contribution I want to describe the connection between my clinical experience with analyses of children and adults who are difficult to reach because they function on a concrete, non-symbolic level and are caught up in a rigid pseudo-identity, and my theoretical conceptualizations, which have been inspired by the thinking and work of Klein, Meltzer, Ferro, and especially Bion. Meltzer's starting point was Melanie Klein's (1946) concept of projective identification, seen by her as the prototype of the aggressive object relation—an anal attack on the object, by means of which parts of the ego are forced into the object in order to appropriate its contents or to bring it under control. In 1966, he examined this combination of projective identification with anal processes in his article "The relation of anal masturbation to projective identification" and suggested the term, *intrusive identification*, to highlight the sadistic-intrusive nature of this projective movement. For Meltzer (1975, 1992) the intrusive identification is the prototype of projective identification and the central mechanism of narcissistic object relations. This differs from the conceptualization of Bion, who, in addition, saw projective identification as a primitive, unconscious mode of communication which precedes the acquisition of language and is essential for "learning from experience"—a communication mode which Bion described in the framework of his model of "container/contained."

The crucial differentiating feature between the intrusive form of projective identification and the normal, primitive, communicative type is the degree of omnipotence. With the term "claustrum" Meltzer refers to an unconscious phantasy regarding the interior of the mother's body. He bases this on developmental assumptions concerning the relation between infantile phantasies and maternal functions. According to Meltzer, the infant's initially undifferentiated image of the mother gradually acquires a specific structure, a "compartmentalization" of the mother's body, as the child gains increased experience with the mother's functions. Here, the relations between the child's orifices and the maternal care offered are of particular importance. It is in this interaction that the three areas—head/breast, genitals and rectum—that Meltzer examined are gradually integrated at the psychic level.

This compartmentalization of the internal mother is closely associated with the mental state of the paranoid-schizoid position. As soon as the infant feels that its self has intruded into the object, the infant's self experience undergoes splitting. If the actual relationship with the mother is affected by intolerable separation experiences and hence fraught with massive aggression, an integration of these maternal compartments becomes impossible. Where aggression is identified with urine and faeces, no contact with the other compartments can be allowed lest they be destroyed. In this case, experiences of gratification are so strongly associated with unpleasant states that the perception of any good object becomes blurred. This for instance would be the case in a breast-feeding situation in which the baby, while drinking the milk that assuages its hunger, meets its mother's empty or hostile gaze and is frightened. In order to survive, the baby has to eliminate this hostile gaze by, for instance, closing its eyes. In this way, while a pathological splitting (fragmentation) opens up an island of pleasure for the baby, it does so at the expense of its ability to perceive reality.

In contrast to normal part objects, one can speak here of pathological part objects, which cannot be integrated to form a whole. As a result, the infant's unconscious perception of the interior of the mother is experienced in terms of *separated compartments*, each with their own contents (and associated phantasies and mental states) and each of which may come to function as a claustrum.

- The intrusive inhabitants of the *head/breast compartment* live in the illusion of omniscience. What is important here is that the internal values attached to this maternal space undergo characteristic changes stemming from the intrusive identification with the anal mastery that adheres to it. Thus, knowledge degenerates into information, understanding becomes penetration of secrets, generosity becomes quid pro quo, receptivity becomes inveiglement.
- The characters in the *genital compartment* bear a stronger resemblance to adolescents in an eroticized state. Their essential object is the erect penis and their identity is dominated by infantile phantasies about the parental coitus, during which the irresistible femininity of the

mother produces the enormous erection of the father's penis. This phantasy forms the foundation of many perverse enactments.

- The third compartment, the *maternal rectum*, contains the most seriously disturbed inhabitants. Here, the central object is the fecal penis, a leader demanding absolute, unquestioning obedience of a kind that leads to the degradation of all values:

  > Truth is transformed into anything that cannot be disproved; justice becomes talion (retaliation) plus an increment; all the acts of intimacy change their meaning into techniques of manipulation or dissimulation; loyalty replaces devotion; obedience substitutes for trust; emotion is simulated by excitement.
  >
  > (Meltzer, 1992, p. 92)

  Survival becomes the essential value. It is in this area "where the term claustrophobia takes on its most poignant significance" (ibid.). The intrusive inhabitants of the maternal rectum most clearly feel imprisoned in a claustrophobic manner.

In Meltzer's view, because intrusive identification takes place initially between internal objects, it influences the self, the emergence of emotions, identity and character. The moment the self succeeds in intruding into the object, self experience becomes split up. The result is a dominance of identifications that demonstrate the complete spectrum of grandiosity on the one hand and which continuously oscillate with massive claustrophobic anxieties on the other. The latter are various fears of entrapment in the very space in which the self imagines itself to have intruded without invitation. Seen in this light, Meltzer's theory of the claustrum is an attempt to differentiate internal, mental places in close accordance with primary bodily experiences.[1] This expansion of the term adds to our understanding of rigid transference–countertransference situations.

Clinical Examples

The following vignettes from both an analysis of a child and of an adult illustrate how even the most minimal psychic changes may activate catastrophic anxieties. For the child as for the adult, this meant making contact again with needy parts of themselves, which had been split off and/or encapsulated. Five-year-old Alex, as I shall call him, had barricaded himself behind a wall of narcissistic omnipotence in order to protect himself from the awareness of his dependence and exposure to his over-taxed parents. This, however, prevented him from being able to learn from his experience. The thirty-year-old Mr. C. experienced having to give up his grandiosity and oedipal illusions as a collapse of his identity. In describing these cases, I hope to be able to convey something of the arduous path leading through narrow straits and along risky ridges to the development of thinking (Staehle, 2005).

From a Child Analysis: Five-year-old Alex

Alex's consultation with me had been recommended by his kindergarten teachers, who worried about his swings from irascible, aggressive behavior to complete withdrawal and back. He would retreat into the restrooms, where he spent his time producing strange noises. At night he still wore a diaper; during the day he wetted and soiled himself occasionally.

Alex was conceived when his parents were still students. The unexpected pregnancy was a catastrophe for them for psychological and external reasons. Both mother and father had lived through traumatic childhoods and their own separations from their parents during adolescence had been extremely difficult. There had been serious *pregnancy* complications due to a maternal endocrine disorder. The latter threatened a necrosis of the placental tissue and necessitated a premature emergency C-section.

From the start, Alex suffered from feeding difficulties and chronic vomiting. His mother did not breastfeed him, because she found it "disgusting." During his first year, Alex was cared for by his father, who reported that he had to force the bottle into his mouth. Alex cried for hours on end and could only be comforted by permanent bodily contact, so his father placed him on his lap when he was doing his drawings, bending over the baby without eye contact. When Alex was admitted to a day nursery, at the age of one, he started to withhold his faeces. According to his parents, he was a "precocious developer," who walked at one year and talked at two. His parents were in denial over his difficulties and initially only came for consultation because the day nursery was threatening to throw Alex out. For the parents, above all for the mother, everything was always "other people's fault."

During our *first consultation* I was worried by Alex's precocious facial expression. His motor restlessness made it difficult to make contact with him. In frantic activity, he drew one conventional picture after another. I commented: "You seem to feel under pressure to get everything absolutely right so that you won't be thrown out." He answered in a loud voice: "That's how to draw flowers. All flowers look like this." Then, however, he took another piece of paper and drew a house with no windows, no doors, which he completely covered with black bars, even the roof. After a while he added a sun and said: "It's unhappy." When I asked him: "And you?" he replied very seriously: "Me, too." I was very moved. But then he tore the drawing up. He began to produce one picture after the other in a frantic manner, every now and again dropping his pencil and running around the room.

I am inclined to think that it was our brief emotional contact when he said: "Me, too," which led me to take him into treatment—in spite of my doubts regarding his parents, who were so difficult to reach and primarily seemed to wish Alex to be magically transformed into a well-adapted, undemanding child or little adult. At the same time, I felt confident that although the acrimonious, reproachful manner of his mother and the withdrawal of his father were to test me to my limits time and again, I would be able to keep a place in my heart for the parents with their disowned hardships and massive wounds.

Initially, Alex's sessions, which took place three times per week, were extremely strenuous. He would ring the door bell frantically, bump against my private house door and come crashing into the office door. The moment I opened the door he would pull off his anorak and shoes and burst into the consulting room. This repeated behavior made me think of *a constable checking to see if the doors were strong enough*. I also felt hard pressed by his attempts to intrude into my private space, while at the same time I sensed his feelings of desperate rage. I had to make sure the doors to all the rooms except for the consulting room were locked.

In my consulting room, Alex disappeared underneath the couch and remained there in silence. I waited for a while and then began to talk as if to myself, beginning to look for him. "I don't want to be found," came a voice from underneath the couch. I continued to talk to myself, saying how hard it was for me that he didn't want to be found, but that I could understand he might feel safer under the couch. After a while he said in a very quiet voice: "You can phone me." I took the toy phone, seated myself beside the couch and tried to talk to him. I didn't get through to him. He did not pick up the receiver. After a while he said that he was tired and wanted to sleep.

Meantime, it was near the end of the session and I said—again as if talking to myself—that it seemed he wanted to stay there and sleep in my consulting room. When I said—after a few more moments—that the session was over now and we would have to stop, he raged at me, forbidding me to mention the time or the end of the session.

After he left, I wondered whether I had intervened too soon. I hadn't been sufficiently careful to respect that his need "to be found" should have remained unspoken, because it still felt so threatening for me to know this about him. His trust in a robust, reliable container was still shaky. During this phase my consulting room functioned as a constitutive element in the development of a psychical space of his own. For him I was still a piece of furniture, a couch-mother. A relationship to me as a separate object was not yet possible.

He repeated the same enactment in the following session. This time I took a toy mouse, let it approach the couch and produced a squeak. Alex remained, in silence, underneath the couch until it was time for him to leave.

In the next session he himself took the mouse, retreated underneath the couch and made it produce little squeaks. After a while I took a toy turtle and moved it in his direction. The mouse answered with a squeak and I heard myself saying: "Oh, maybe the mouse is looking for a friend." In a hard tone, he rejected my overtures: "You won't trick me!"

He repeated the same pattern in the next session with the mouse letting out little squeaks. As soon as I approached his mouse with the turtle the mouse fell silent. After a short while it squeaked again. So now the situation was that I could hear him squeaking but was not able to make contact with him. For a short moment it felt as if Alex's baby mouth was desperately searching for the nipple. But then he broke out into contemptuous laughter that sent a shiver down my spine.

In following sessions he built all kinds of caves in the consulting room, no longer the one underneath the couch, but constructions made of chairs and blankets. Step-by-step he took possession of my consulting room. But for a long time I was only allowed to contact him by phone.

The image this created in my mind was of a baby wanting to go back into the womb—to be born again. Contemplating this image, I suddenly heard him say that his cavern was surrounded by water. An invisible, drowsy crocodile was lying in ambush. The two of us should take care. I said to Alex that now, perhaps, he was able trust me to keep watch with him. For a short moment he listened to me attentively.

I think that in the beginning of our work Alex helped me sense how it feels not to be able to make contact with the other, to be confronted with a physically present, but emotionally unreachable object (projective identification as communication). There are violent emotions in him (crocodiles), which he can only cope with by shutting them in (underneath the couch) or making me enclose them (in the turtle shell). But periodically these contents, so forced into a claustrum, provoke outbreaks of rage and despair.

For the time being I decided not to share my understanding with him, because he would not be able to deal with it. It was up to me to contain and metabolize (make sense of) what was happening between us. But we now had several figures with which we could represent and name Alex's emotions and could incorporate them into a story developing in the space between us. This is the precondition for emotions and affects to be acknowledged, expressed and subsequently transformed (see Ferro, 1993).

During the following months, Alex's emotions emerged from their "prison," sometimes leading to extreme acting-out behavior during his sessions. In many sessions I had to play the part of a servant whom he bullied. For example he constructed a robot that he called Steel and that he kept ordering around. Or again, he would call me up on the play-phone, giving me orders in an extremely loud voice so that I could hardly hear myself think. I tried to find words for his mental states and spoke through the various characters I had to represent. As his servant or robot, I complained to him about the inhuman way he treated me and that I couldn't stand it any longer. At first he laughed diabolically, but sometimes he stopped and calmed down. At this stage this was the only way I could get through to him for a brief moment.

In the second year, the atmosphere in Alex's sessions changed. He liked coming to his sessions and used to pre-plan our games and stories. Most of the time, he was in control of his excretory functions and could do without a diaper (nappy) at night. I assume that it was his experience of me as someone capable of protecting him and also of protecting her own orifices/doors, which enabled him to control his bladder and bowel functions and protect himself effectively against aggressive intrusions. This was signalled by his increased tolerance of frustration regarding limits set in his sessions and in peer relations outside the sessions.

To illustrate Alex's development I would like to present a session which took place in the second half of the second year of his treatment. When his father brought him to the first session following a weekend break, he told me that the third session of the same week had to be cancelled. This triggered in Alex a vivid description of a thief in front of the window of my consulting room that had the quality of a dream-like image. He went on to construct a story about the thief robbing me of enough money to buy three houses (three sessions). I perceived this image as an expression of his rage and helplessness, which, however, had to be kept at a distance, outside in front of the window. But instead of naming these angry feelings as *his,* I suggested that maybe he was wondering whether *I* would be able to protect him and my house. He responded by asking me to play hide and seek. I had to seek him and now he wanted to be found.

Shortly before the end of the session he emptied out a basket and seated himself in it, saying: "I am going to stay in here, I live here." I felt under pressure, because we had only a few minutes left. Very soon his father would be ringing the doorbell in his usual insistent manner. So I said: "I think you want to show me how hard it is for you to leave and be shut out." After a while he emerged from the basket and said: "You have no idea how hot it is inside here." He added: "You see, my father never has time for me. As soon as we get home, he will go and sit down at his computer again and stay there. I will play with my train, on my own."

Alex had never spoken like this before. I felt deeply saddened and thought how hard it was for him to tolerate the discrepancy between the *heat* and *shelter* (the basket as a concrete container) in his relation with me and his internal object relationship with an object physically present, but emotionally unreachable. When I mention the end of the session, I am experienced as someone who wants to exclude him, who does not want him to be with her. Again and again this was enacted during the first year, when he was primarily trying to get rid of his persecutory feelings by depositing them into me. Now he shows a growing capacity to notice feelings and communicate them to me.

Several weeks later Alex reported his first, short night-time dream: "I dreamt a magician changed the door of your office into a flower." In association, he speculated about the different doors in my consultancy, where they might lead and who else came to see me. Moreover, I could enter the consulting room through the other door, he said. As a magician, I tell him, he was in control of all the doors. Maybe he would like to be able to see me whenever he wanted to and that this would be nice, like a flower. He interrupted me: "But the other kids must not come, they have to stay outside."

Over the next weeks his world, till then unimagined, began to materialize in his drawings and stories with horrifying feelings and great turbulence. In a series of pictures of planes dropping bombs, missile attacks, and air crashes with exploding planes, his emotions began to take shape and could be differentiated and labelled. There were "good" and "bad" (Nazi) planes. The "bad" ones began to lose strength, until "Hitler" was left with just a shotgun. There were forts and ambulances offering help and protection.

Alex no longer felt persecuted by the urgent need to have something instantly. Now he could use drawings and stories to express, organize and dream his desires. He could have wishes and tolerate things the way they are—both in his external reality and in his inner world. He was no longer overwhelmed by one single state of mind and he had successfully moved beyond symbolic equations (Segal, 1957) or psychic equivalences (Fonagy et al., 2002). Nevertheless, a lengthy treatment was still necessary until he became able to hold on to these achievements for longer periods of time and until he could increase his capacity to digest and "think" his emotional experiences.

In one of his last sessions he said: "You know, I would like to continue seeing you. Now I can really enjoy playing with you, but I have also made friends and so I have no time left." I was both happy for him and sad. Alex was going to school by this time and got along with his peers, though from time to time he reacted over-sensitively and got himself into trouble. I was confident, though, that he would be able to make good use of his abilities. He had joined the school choir and was taking singing lessons. Both parents were better able to see him as their son and not principally as a projection of their negative sides.

Discussion

With the help of analysis, Alex was able to resume the path of development, though the scars left by his early experiences will remain. What was hard for him and will continue to be so is to be aware of what he had missed and was still missing in his relationship to his parents.

In my view, the touchstone of child analysis is the extent to which one can retain an inner attitude as analyst in which the predicament and failure of parents is neither denied nor condemned. Little Alex lived in a "barred house," a claustrum. Since his parents had provided neither support nor appropriate limits, he had not been able to internalize an object that could "contain" him and which would enable him to understand himself and others. To give an example: at the beginning of the treatment the parents complained that Alex made noises when settling down to sleep that disturbed them. It turned out that they left their bedroom door open and claimed that it was their perfect right to do so: they couldn't sleep with the door closed. Alex would have to learn to fit in.

Initially, his emotions were so overwhelming that it was impossible for him to differentiate between feeling states, to recognize them as his own and to communicate them to others. He either had to force his affects violently into others or else encapsulate them. Feeling threatened without being able to understand what was going on inside him, he could only strike out or shut himself off. When I met him, he was on the way to despising his own feelings and withdrawing into a prison of untouchableness and autistic autarchy. In the course of his treatment, we succeeded in expressing his affects through playing together and drawing pictures and were able to name them and link them first to his needs and, later on, to his wishes.

> The feeling of being adequately contained is a precondition for the experience of being a continent container, the movements in phantasy of getting into and out of an object necessarily have a significance with regard to the conception of time.
>
> (Meltzer et al., 1975, p. 226)

For Alex, this experience, described by Meltzer in *Explorations in Autism*, became available in his analysis with me—at first on a concrete level with my doors, and later on in phantasy, too. His barred prison house turned into a house with flowers and with doors that could be opened and closed. Before this development could take place, however, he had to be allowed to inhabit = use the house of his analyst, i.e. her capacity to think and to feel.

From the Analysis of an Adult Patient: Mr. C.

Mr. C., a 29-year-old student and former competitive athlete, contacted me, because of severe panic attacks and agoraphobic, claustrophobic and hypochondriac anxieties. He presented me with a list detailing his athletic successes in the left-hand column and a remarkable number of accidents and surgical interventions in the right-hand one. He recounted his manifold physical complaints, hypochondriacal fears and phobias and said that after sporting injuries had forced him to quit his athletic career, he had then tried to resume his previously neglected studies. He had not been able to travel to my consulting rooms by himself: his grandmother had had to accompany him and was waiting for him outside in the car.

For me, the way Mr. C. described his anxieties and complaints felt very intrusive. He seemed to be pressuring me as he impressed on me that I was his last hope. In my mind's eye, I saw the image of a foundling lying in front of my door, a foundling that I must take in. His intense attempts to establish eye contact touched me, but I was only aware of this after the session. During our consultation, I mostly felt an enormous pressure somehow to restore him to his lost "winner status."

I told Mr. C. that I believed he wanted me to realize both sides of him, his triumphs as well as his anxieties and accidents, and that I sensed he was very much afraid I might not take him on and bear with him. After a pause, I added that it would be important to find out and understand how the two columns were related. He seemed to accept the first of my sentences, to relax, but my second remark obviously confused him and he said: "It is strange, but my sporting friends used to call me 'Omen,' because they were convinced that I attracted bad luck. I know certain triggers of my illness, but I cannot get through to the causes. I can't manage to break through the cycle of anxiety on my own. I am afraid to make the kind of mistake one can only make once." What he then described was a life that was only a kind of surviving, dominated by obsessive ruminating, all-night computer games, perverse phantasies and an omnipotent control of his objects. His capacity to learn from and introject new experiences was limited, and his difficulties in processing emotional experiences also impaired his ability to symbolize.

History

Mr. C. described his parents by saying: "My mother is a half-orphan, my father is an orphan." This rather strange characterization made me think that in this family any separation had to be avoided in order not to evoke an "orphaned feeling" which might touch on some originally traumatic experience, whether an experience of the parents or of their children's generation. Subsequently I learned from sparse fragments that both parents had suffered massive losses.

At the beginning of his treatment, the patient reported that his panic attacks and phobias had started after the abrupt end of his sporting career—before that, he had had no problems. Later on, however, it turned out that he had been a sickly, anxious boy, who could not use the toilet in other people's houses and suffered from obsessive hand-washing, fear of bodily contact, allergies and skin diseases. All this had been denied by himself and his family. The same denial was maintained in regard to the post-partum depression of his mother, who could neither breastfeed nor touch him. He had been handed over to a wet nurse. Traces of this experience still showed in his severe fears of bodily contact. Even a slight touching of his mouth and palatal area activated intolerable feelings of choking—"choking orgies," as he put it. At two-and-a-half he fell ill with an unknown virus. According to his mother he neither ate nor drank. After a fortnight, his parents apparently took him home, out of hospital, because of inadequate care there. He was told that he subsequently had developed a squint.

During early childhood, Mr. C. had several very dangerous accidents, as well as complicated surgical interventions at 13 and 19 years of age. During adolescence he started to do sports and turned out to have surprising talent as a bobsledder. Supported by his mother, who regularly drove him to his training in a neighboring city, he exercised very intensively and with remarkable success, in spite of his unfavorable physical endowment. His rapid improvement made him feel like the adventurer and hero of his childhood dreams. After finishing school and starting his studies, he became a successful competitive athlete until his collapse. Even during his successful phase, however, he suffered a severe accident in almost every year.

When his performance deteriorated, Mr. C. suspected intrigues against him, felt cheated of his rights, and started to drink increasing amounts of alcohol to relax. Training sessions were followed by all-night parties and heavy drinking. Then, one day he collapsed during training and developed massive panic attacks. He tried to resume his sports in the next season, but a life-threatening accident forced him to retire at age 26. In his fantasies, he took refuge in a potential relationship with an Italian woman into whom he projected all his longings. Secretly, he had always entertained the illusionary belief that his athletic successes would be rewarded with a "woman for life." When it turned out that the Italian woman preferred another man, his painfully maintained system and self-esteem collapsed. The patient returned to his parents' home, tried to resume his studies, but failed to do so.

During the first year of treatment, Mr. C. was unable to come to my office on his own. He had to be accompanied by a relative, who waited for him *in the car* in front of my office. He spent his sessions evoking his glorious career and relating heroic stories about his successes, thereby creating an atmosphere of grandiosity, expecting nothing but admiration from me.

Nevertheless his narratives made it quite plain that he was unconsciously repeating and at the same time trying to control his early infantile trauma. He said that it was only when he "offered" himself to death—"Come and get me"—that he really felt strong and alive, and that this had been a source of enormous gratification. He was constantly seeking a feeling of elation at the limits of his capability and endurance, whereas normal emotions made him feel dead and empty. Very impressively he described the thrill (pleasure in fear) he experienced when bobsledding. What I found remarkable was the concrete manner in which he had restored his internal family. I had this vision of my patient sitting together with his father, mother and grandmother in the bobsled, closely huddled together in absolute mutual dependency.

At the end of the first year of treatment, Mr. C. succeeded in finishing his studies with the help and protection of an idealizing part-object mother transference. But he could not enjoy his success. Instead, he felt terribly empty inside. A dream that he reported shortly before the first summer holiday break in treatment depicted his internal situation and the transference–countertransference situation. The patient had started the session with a lengthy description of his former breakdown. He said that he could talk about it in a purely technical manner, but he did not have any feelings associated with it. Sometimes he thought that he was perhaps dead already and just didn't notice it. In my interpretations, I tried to link his remembering that earlier breakdown to the situation of an impending break in treatment. "That's nonsense," he said—but then continued with the following dream:

> I am standing on the roof of a high-rise building and I am being attacked by one opponent after another. I keep fighting and manage to push them down off the roof, one after the other. More and more of them keep coming.

The dream reveals the extent to which he still feels threatened and persecuted. In his world, there is only one possibility: *survival*. He desperately attempts to maintain his position and sees himself as a heroic fighter. My interpretation had brought him into contact with his paranoid anxieties. What showed clearly was the way he was torn between experiencing my consulting room as a safe refuge or as a threat to his grandiosity. As a bobsledder, he had temporarily found a place of pseudo-security. Now he was trying to set up this pseudo-place again in his analysis.

When in his second year his phobic symptoms abated, the patient managed to come to analysis on his own. He had also started on a job in the immediate neighborhood of my practice and used to park his car in front of my window during his working hours. I assumed that he felt the need to deposit something concrete with me in such a way that I could not lose sight of it.

Mr. C. spent many sessions describing his bodily states, sensitivities and hypochondriacal anxieties. Lying on the couch, he monitored his pulse and kept me informed about his extra-systole. He created an atmosphere in which I could not clearly tell whose heartbeat he was referring to. Gradually I realized that he experienced me as a kind of "life-sustaining machine," which he had to control in order to defend against the terrors of non-existence. But the housing *of this machine* developed more and more openings to internal and external reality. This was revealed by another high-rise building dream:

> I was standing on the roof terrace of a high-rise building. The whole structure was swaying in the storm. I was terribly scared. N. (who was with me back then, when I broke down) was on the roof with me.

In this dream the *building* is *shaking*; he is no longer the lonely, heroic fighter but filled with fear. Somebody—the analyst—is with him. At the same time, the outward defensive shell of his identity, the heroic bobsledder façade, is cracking and about to fall into pieces. Real external events—like the collapse of a wall in his home during renovation—led to severe panic attacks and hypochondriacal anxieties. When a fire broke out in the chemical factory where he was working, the patient became paranoid. In panic, he raced away in his car. Driving at high speed provided him with a sense of security—for the time being, the car had replaced the bobsled. However, there was also now a means of contact with me: He called me by mobile phone to warn me of the danger!

When he returned to his next session (Monday) he said that he felt like a wreck. He complained of back pain and launched into a detailed description of these events. After a prolonged silence he reported the following dream:

> I was driving my car on my own. But the car did not drive as I wanted it to. I was driving along a road and kept having to swerve to avoid cars. I had no control over the car. But it wasn't as if the car was completely out of my control. Sort of a mixture. In my dream I wanted to scream all the time.

He commented: "On waking up I became aware that I had, in fact, not been screaming, because otherwise my mother and my father would have woken up and come into my room."

It was no longer necessary for him to park his *car* in front of my practice; instead, it emerges as a dream thought. But the border between dream and waking state was highly precarious.

My patient continued: "Lately, I often have dreams in which I want to scream. I have a lot of disgusting dreams, and I always want to scream." He described how "being sensible" makes him feel imprisoned. All those crazy things he used to enjoy are painful now, and the things he could do now were worthless. The feeling of elation was gone. Everything, he said, seemed unreal and stupid. He merely functioned mechanically, and he had the feeling that his old values had collapsed.

After a prolonged silence he continued: "I do not know who I am. I can't see how to reconcile things. Nowadays I am afraid of the devil of a fellow I used to be. I am afraid even to think of it. Back then, when I broke down and was scared to death I swore to myself that I would be sensible—but I hadn't the faintest idea how it feels to be sensible."

I felt for him. I said that his situation was hard to bear—not knowing who he really was, no longer believing in his former, fixed identity—and perhaps anticipating that such a fixing of identity might, in fact, be impossible. That nothing can be "for ever," that feelings change. It was the baby inside him who wanted to scream in his dream, crying for help. It was important, I said, to listen to these cries and to think about them.

This has been one of the many critical balancing acts required in Mr. C.'s treatment. Gradually, the patient was making contact with his dependent self, his frozen feelings of helplessness and loneliness. But to emerge from his terrible, grandiose and at the same time highly exciting world and enter a world which was real, but felt grey and trivial to him, was threatening him in his very existence. During this period there was a constant danger of suicide. His psychical pain and his grief over wasted time in his life were still unbearable and fuelled his relentless, destructive super-ego with an enormous power. Four more years of treatment were required during which the patient gradually developed the strength to confront himself with his internal and external reality and to acknowledge his vulnerable parts as his own.

As a result of analysis, Mr. C.'s outward life changed markedly. He is working in the pedagogic field, has married and is the father of a little son. At first, it was very difficult for him to bear the experience with a crying baby, but he learned to tolerate both his own feelings and the child's crying, to soothe his son and find words to do this.

At the end of our final session he said:

> It is only now that I am able to appreciate what you have been through and your patience in listening to me. In the beginning I only wanted to get rid of my fears and panic. But in the course of our work my whole world-view has changed, my attitude towards myself and others. The same with my bobsledding career; I can see it in a different light now. Those years weren't all good, but they also had their enjoyable moments—though in fact I wasn't a top athlete, but rather a boy eager to prove himself an all-rounder. I was craving for success and recognition. I haven't been able to get rid of my anxiety states as simply as I imagined. They keep returning from time to time, but it is different now.

Discussion

In many cases, an early infantile trauma gives rise to unconscious claustrum phantasies and their subsequent elaboration and fixation. Impaired container–contained processes between mother and infant bring about non-processed, nameless dread and intolerable feelings of emptiness. Of course, we do not know how it comes about that parts of the maternal body are intrusively cathected, leading to an impairment in the development of the symbolizing capacity. What is clear is that the infant's development is clearly dependent on the physical and even more on the psychical maternal space. Bion's container–contained model and his theory of thinking imply that we first need to inhabit the house of the mother, before we are able to live in our own house.

Mr. C. had sought analysis following the breakdown of his pathological personality organization. Filled with fear, he desperately sought analytic treatment to restore his former equilibrium and find shelter in further retreat. During his bobsledding career, the bobsled had served as a perverted container and pseudo-refuge, associated with the unconscious phantasy that when he was in the sled he had invaded and controlled the body of his internal mother. This was an active reversal of his early infantile trauma, i.e. his experience of not having found acceptance in the psychical space of the depressive mother. But the price he had to pay was his constant anxiety of being discovered and thrown out. As long as his omnipotence and grandiosity were not being challenged—that is, as long as he could somehow actualize these phantasies—the claustrophobic consequences were kept under control. The socially sanctioned role of the competitive athlete lent itself to accommodating his pathology. His various hypochondriacal fears and physical complaints—such as his choking orgies—had become sexualized, thereby acquiring a masturbatory character. The absent "good milk" turned into the present "bad saliva" producing fears of suffocation. His use of the word "orgy," points to the masturbatory nature of the process. The overall result was a sado-masochistic manner of treating his body. In this way, he converted his feelings of abandonment and inadequacy into a triumph over his persecutors. His bobsledding-part became idealized and identified with an omnipotent internal father part-object.

Because his unconscious claustrum phantasy—the occupation of a compartment of the maternal body (bobsled)—was overlaid by early oedipal and sibling rivalry of a sado-masochistic nature, successes were experienced as a triumph over dangerous rivals. But these same victories exposed him to the danger of being persecuted by his revengeful internal father and siblings. The "third" was always potentially dangerous and persecutory. In contrast to other patients, who make a transient use of projective, intrusive identification, with Mr. C. this mechanism had become rigidly fixated. His projective identification was of a permanent nature—he was actually *living* inside the cathected object, imprisoned in his *pseudo-bobsledder identity*. He became suicidal when he got in touch with his split-off feelings and archaic anxieties. Mr. C. and I had to weather this development before he was able to allow and tolerate new relationship experiences, in which he felt accepted rather than depreciated. This development, however, was a "catastrophic change" as described by Bion. "The more the person is identified with the shell, the more they feel that something terrible is happening, because the shell is cracking up and they do not know the chicken" (Bion, 1973–74).

Concluding Remarks

I would like to summarize my experiences in dealing with unconscious claustrum phantasies in analytic treatments. In my view, the analyst runs the risk of colluding with the intrusive identification of those patients and in this way producing a constellation, which one could term a mutual projective identification. What I am referring to is the analyst's unconscious acceptance of the patient's projective identifications leading to a joint acting out. When this occurs, the patient may enjoy the temporary benefit of the psychical functions previously lost by him, as long as he or she remains in actual proximity to and in a relationship with the analyst. In the treatment of Mr. C., had I followed this path, it would have required me to fulfill the caring function of a "good, containing object," focusing exclusively on the helpless boy part of him, which sought refuge. The result would have been an entanglement of mutually accepted projective identifications, that would then function as a fresh claustrum or place of psychic retreat (Steiner, 1993), which depended upon unending actual contact with the analyst.

A particular characteristic of Mr. C.'s treatment was the virtually perfect congruence and compatibility of his unconscious claustrum phantasy with the socially offered status of the competitive athlete. On this issue of socially acknowledged projective identification a great deal more could be said. But that is a topic of its own.

A further risk in these cases is that the analyst will use his or her analytic theory in order to insulate himself against those unbearable intrusive identifications—with a consequent unconscious withdrawal from the patient. Finally, analysts run the risk of adopting a judgmental and denigrating super-ego attitude towards the patient.

Meltzer's thinking about the unconscious claustrum phantasy helps us to avoid this threefold danger. His concepts also help us to understand how it feels to inhabit this isolated and mad world inside an object. The identity of these patients seems fixed in space and time. There is no concept of development. This becomes especially clear with patients like Mr. C., who experience themselves as living predominantly inside the rectum of the maternal internal object. They feel as if they are living inside a machine which they have to dominate, because a loss of control would be life-threatening to the machine and therefore to themselves.

The capacity to live separately from the object presupposes a reliably containing internal object, which gives sufficient internal support to enable the subject to tolerate his anxieties. Bion describes the "cloud of uncertainty" or the cloud of "not-knowing" as a part of real life. Intrusive identification gives rise to a confusion between self and object which precludes the development of a space to think thoughts—for which an oedipal triangular relationship is the prerequisite. For a prolonged period of time there can be no communication on a triangular level, in the sense that subject and object communicate about and reflect on a "third."

In working with these patients it is important that the analyst's attitude and language enable him to reach the patient not where he *ought to be* but where he *is*. Meltzer (1992) says that in this situation the analyst functions as a kind of *travel guide* for the patient, showing him the quality of his internal world, his anxieties and his techniques of adaptation to this situation. The guide metaphor can easily be misleading. Perhaps the term "mountain guide" would be better suited to point to the difficult paths we have to walk with the patient. What renders this path so "difficult" for the analyst is the need not to give in to the pressure of the intrusive identifications—not to enact the unconsciously assigned role, but to contain and process it and to offer descriptive interventions. To describe the world which the patient inhabits is the best the analyst can do—in the hope that the patient will gradually realize that the analyst himself does *not* live in a claustrum and that there *is* an alternative world of intimate object relations.

> The person on your couch is an absolute stranger who is not displaying his personality but only his techniques of adaptation to the claustrophobic world he inhabits. The moment an analyst can recognize the incarcerated quality and the essential struggle for survival in an unlivable situation, he sees a child who has lost his way, strayed from home, who has even forgotten the qualities of the home he once knew, perhaps in the most severe cases only the womb.
>
> (Meltzer, 1992, pp. 102–3)

Note

1 In contrast to contemporary Kleinians, Meltzer adhered strongly to the notion of a part-object relationship building on parts and functions of the maternal body. His "model of the mind" always focuses strictly on the concrete experience of the object relation and "locates" these relationships in the outside world, in the internal world and even inside whole as well as part objects. (e.g. the breast). We must not forget, however, that this "breast" is both a part of the mother's anatomy and a psycho-emotional cypher.

References

Bion, W. R. (1973–74) *Brazilian Lectures.* London: Karnac Books (1990).

Ferro, A. (1993) From hallucination to dream: From evacuation to the tolerability of pain in the analysis of a preadolescent. *Psychoanalytic Review*, 80:389–404.

Fonagy, P., Gergely, G., Jurist, E. L. and Target, M. (2002) *Affect Regulation, Mentalization and the Development of the Self.* New York: Other Press.

Klein, M. (1946) Notes on some schizoid mechanisms. In: *Envy and Gratitude and Other Works 1946–1963.* London: Virago Press 1988, 1–24.

Meltzer, D. (1975) Adhesive identification. *Contemporary Psychoanalysis*, 11:289–310.

Meltzer, D. (1992) *The Claustrum. An Investigation of Claustrophobic Phenomena.* The Roland Harris Trust Library, No. 15, Strath Tag, Perthshire, Scotland: The Clunie Press.

Meltzer, D., J. Bremner, S. Hoxter, D. Weddell, I. Wittenberg (1975) *Explorations in Autism. A Psycho-Analytical Study.* London: Karnac Books.

Segal, H. (1957) Notes on symbol formation. *International Journal of Psychoanalysis*, 38:391–7.

Staehle, A. (2005) Was Hänschen nicht lernt, lernt Hans nur schwer. Engpässe und Gratwanderungen auf dem Weg zur Entwicklung der Denkfähigkeit in der psychoanalytischen Behandlung eines 5-jährigen Jungen und eines 30-jährigen Mannes. In: Kremp-Ottenheym, H., Juszczak, M., Schmidt, M., *Heilung und Stagnation in psychoanalytischen Behandlungen. Arbeitstagung der Deutschen Psychoanalytischen Vereinigung in Bad Homburg*, pp. 59–77.

Steiner, J. (1993) *Psychic Retreats. Pathological Organisations in Psychotic, Neurotic and Borderline Patients.* London, New York: Routledge.

Part 5

APPLIED STUDIES

EDITORS' INTRODUCTION

Meaning and Form: The Containing Function of Art

Margot Waddell

Waddell explores the *aesthetic dimension* of Bion's thinking, an aspect of his theory that has not received as much attention as other of his important contributions. She observes that after the 1962 publication of *Learning from Experience*, his writing took a decidedly different turn away from "his tendency to work within the medical model [as he] embedded his thinking, rather, in the arts and humanities more generally." This aesthetic dimension is especially relevant to Bion's concept of the container/contained, which, among other features, offers an account of how thinking and symbol formation arise within the context of early mother/infant interactions. It is through the to-and-fro process of mutual projections and introjections in that relationship, together with maternal reverie, that an "aesthetic reciprocity" (Meltzer, 1988) develops. In this shared encounter, affective experience that previously was without form and meaning slowly acquires emotional significance. Waddell asserts that just as the mother and her infant together give meaning to infantile happenings, so art has an analogous function in its capacity to represent previously unsymbolized emotional experience.

Waddell notes that emotional growth in the container/contained inevitably involves a certain amount of disruption in the status quo of the mother/infant dyad: new emotional experiences impact the couple, stirring turbulence that may spur further development or threaten *catastrophic change* (Bion, 1965). She likens this pattern of disruption and consequent meaning making to the experience of "the viewer, the listener or reader of the art object," whose unconscious is affected by the artistic work. The artistic production is itself an expression of the artist's unconscious rendering of a previously unmetabolized mental state and it is the latter which finds resonance in the unconscious worlds of the receiving audience. Having been affected by the artist's expression, the artist's audience then unconsciously sets about giving personal meaning to the affects evoked in them by the particular work of art. Thus, the connection between artist and audience becomes an intersubjective event in the manner of the container/contained relationship.

In addition, Waddell describes how the art object embodies the process by which the artist has turned his inner emotional turbulence into an aesthetic creation and thus may offer the viewer a pathway for the transformation of *his* internal unrest. She also highlights how artistic constructions may unconsciously guide the observer "to repair and to integrate what has been threatened, scattered or destroyed." Indeed, artistic creations themselves are partly acts of destruction, followed by reparations achieved through new ways of representing what has been attacked and damaged. Waddell beautifully illustrates these points through her analysis of poetry, a discussion of Bion's later work and a description of analytic work with a patient's dreams.

14

MEANING AND FORM

The Containing Function of Art

Margot Waddell

I am going to begin my exploration of the containing function of art in 1962 when, as Donald Meltzer (1978) notes, the mathematical and scientific scaffolding of Bion's thinking thitherto fell away, initiating an engagement with a different model of mind—one in which the aesthetic, the creative, even the mystical held sway.

For it was with Bion's (1962a) paper on the growth of the mind—"A Theory of Thinking"—and, in the same year, his book *Learning from Experience* (1962b) that, as far as psychoanalytic thinking was concerned, a new era dawned; for Bion, one of immense significance in terms of freeing himself from his tendency to work within the medical model and embedding his thinking, rather, in the arts and humanities more generally. My interest is in tracing some congruences between the aesthetic in art and the aesthetic dimension of inter- and intra-psychic processes—two different registers for exploring the world of the mind. This means that I shall be focusing on parallels rather than suggesting a so-called psychoanalytic explanation of artistic form. Central to my exploration is a model of immense conceptual potency, that of "container–contained," first mooted in that same 1962 paper.

Bion invokes the mother/infant relationship, the container and the contained, as a model for the mental holding, the sustaining, and thus the learning from emotional experiences. For in this relationship, in reasonably good circumstances, adverse emotional experiences can be rendered bearable and eventually thinkable rather than being merely destructive and incapacitating. He describes the turbulence that lies in the ever-recurring internal struggles with the "dark and formless infinite" ("Paradise Lost"), the boundlessness and shapelessness of inchoate, chaotic, disturbing internal and external psychic events to which, from infancy to extreme old age, human nature is prey.

In the container/contained model, he gives an account of what he regards as the intuitive process of unconscious symbol formation being a function that a good mother needs to be able to provide for her baby. In a state of "reverie," as he puts it, she is able to take in the emotional communications about which the infant is not yet able to think. Hopefully, a reciprocity of projection and introjection becomes established, what Meltzer (1988) later called "an aesthetic reciprocity," lodged in the inter-related rhythms of heart meeting young heart and mind the beginnings of mind. In *The Apprehension of Beauty* he elaborates on what could be described as a mother and baby's unconscious intuitive capacities for the traffic of powerful feeling, and on the beauty and harmony of such an exchange, infused as it is with passion and with love.

According to this picture, the growth of the infant's mind depends, initially, on the loving mother's containing capacity, on her being able, in a state of reverie, to be receptive to and thus in touch with the incipient meaning to be gleaned from what Bion refers to as the "raw sensa" of infantile chaotic physical and emotional experiences. Over time, these experiences can be rendered manageable, and "sensible," in terms of the dawning of an ordinary understanding of self—the basis for Bion's notion of "common-sense." In so doing the mother/carer can enable the infant, in turn, slowly to acquire the internal resources, the emotional and functional capacities, to begin to get to know the nature of different registers of being, and so, slowly, to make sense of who he or she is, and what he or she can bear. For it is in the course of this active, "worked on" process that experience becomes meaningful. The joys, pains, anxieties and losses of all ordinary daily life can be lovingly held in mind and mentally digested rather than denied or enacted; can be contained, by virtue of the fact that they have been shared, have been mutually, reciprocally, intuitively apprehended, even understood.

Over time, it became clear that in Bion's thinking, turbulence and growth are inseparable concepts. To his mind, growth depends on turbulence; on the turbulence involved in what he later called "catastrophic change," that is, the necessary and repeated internal sea-changes that lie at the heart of a person's capacity to develop. The key to whether that to-and-fro, that integrating and disintegrating process, is possible lay in the container/contained model. The concept of catastrophic change indicated the importance of the courage to undergo, at least partially, the dismantling of familiar, and therefore relatively comfortable, routine modes of a person's thinking, in order to allow growth to occur. What looks like the turbulence of breakdown may be a necessary component of a growth-promoting breakthrough.

It is not so difficult to see how this model provides a template of sorts for all relationships of intensity, passion and meaning—perhaps especially that between analyst and analysand. But what of the relationship between the viewer, the listener or reader of the art object—of a sculpture, a painting, a play, a sequence of poems (for example the *Four Quartets* by T. S. Eliot) or a piece of music? Here too, there occurs an unconscious engagement of the containing process with the inherent, worked-on form, be that in sculpted, painterly, musical or poetic terms. The art historian, Adrian Stokes, speaks of "the sense of fusion" combined with "otherness" that lies at the heart of the aesthetic experience. He writes (1963) of,

> the carver's reverence for the stone he consults so long: he elicits meaning from a substance, precious for itself, whose subsequent forms made by the chisel were felt to be pre-existent and potential. Similarly in painting there is the canvas, the rectangular surface and the whiteness to fructify, a pre-existent minimum structure that not only will be gradually affirmed but vastly enriched by the coalescence with other meanings.
>
> (p. 218)

Time is of the essence for the sculpting process. So, too, is time of the essence for the profoundly painful and complex inner work of a patient's struggle towards a more truthful understanding of the self. Much internal work has to be done, of which the culmination may, in the world of the artist, be an external "worked on" symbolic representation. The art object thus becomes the container of the meaning of that process which it incorporates, and this can have an important restorative and reparative function for the viewer. Indeed, Stokes also speaks of the broad compulsion to repair and to integrate what has been threatened, scattered or destroyed, of the degree of the aesthetic (by which here he means integrative) driving force involved. He feels the meaning, plasticity, rhythm, weight, mass and design of the art object as being employed to make clearer its self-sufficiency. It is an expression of the work of the interior, the artist's work, and also a thing of its own—of both fusion and otherness.

Donald Meltzer (1988), in conversation with Stokes, takes things a step further than the classical Kleinian aesthetic theory of the perpetual to-and-fro of the integration/disintegration, ingestion/expulsion axes. In Meltzer's words, "if we say that the artist performs acts of reparation through his creativity we must recognise that in the creative process itself, phases of attack and phases of reparation exist in some kind of rhythmical relationship" (p. 209). The contemporary poet Carol Satyamurti (2003) also talks about the significance of "destruction": not as a prior event for which reparation needs to be made, as in classical Kleinian aesthetics, but as inherent in the creative process itself. For, as she says,

> When one thinks about the workings of the natural world, or about human endeavour, creation and destruction are inseparable. The same Hindu deity represents both .... One has to have a sense of *when*

> it is the right time to mobilise critical judgement—*when* (to use the analogy with sculpture) the essential poem must be recovered from the mass of "spurious and unwanted matter" (Mandlestam, 1975, p. 225) within which it is hidden.
>
> (p. 42)

The wresting of form from chaos is essential to the "making."

Satyamurti draws on the compact and highly wrought energy of James Merrill's poem, "The Broken Bowl" to emphasize the relationship between aesthetic form and psychic process—the tight distillation of what goes on in an art work. The beautiful bowl has fallen and smashed.

> ... its loyal blaze undone,
> All spilt, its glass integrity no more ...
> No lucid, self-containing artifice
> At last, but fire, ice,
> A world in jeopardy. What lets the bowl
> Nonetheless triumph by inconsequence
> And wrestle harmony from dissonance
> And with the fragments build another, whole,
> Inside us, which we feel
> Can never break, or grow less bountiful?
> Love does that.
>
> (Merrill, 1996, p. 8)

Satyamurti dwells on the use of "love" here—"perhaps a surprising word to use," she says, "with such seriousness, of a glass bowl .... His use of this word is an indication that more than a shattered artefact is at stake here. The bowl is an internalised good object—a 'bountiful' object that 'seemed to cup the sun ...'" (p. 34).

The art object, then, promotes and expands existing mental capacities by offering a shape and a containing structure for the transformation of emotional experience into recognizable symbolic form. It is thus that the art object could be described as performing a containing function—that is, potentially, of becoming a container of meaning so that emotionality, impulse-life, fragmentary raw sensations may be held together, located, named and thereby rendered amenable to thinking and to psychic growth. As the music of the lines of my epigraph makes so clear, the writing of poetry is also a "making" process—the word "poetry" derives from the Greek word to do or to make. And the making involves here, rhythm, beat, weight, silence, space, light and so on. The artist, as Satyamurti (2003) says, is "finding form for what was formless, something coherent which now exists at some distance from oneself, outside in the world as well as inside in one's head" (p. 36). Such is the compelling and sustaining nature of great art.

In his commentary on "The Imaginary Twin" in *Second Thoughts*, Bion (1967) reflects, 17 years later, on his original membership paper given to the British Psycho-Analytical Society. He makes explicit the extent of the development of his own thinking since giving this memorable presentation. The congruences he finds between the psychoanalyst, as intuitive, creative interpreter, and aspects of the artistic process are striking. He criticizes his early formulations for not clarifying the extent to which,

> the reader is to suppose that the account is a direct intuition of what was taking place and how much a report of selected facts. In psycho-analysis the psycho-analyst must discern the underlying pattern by a process of discrimination and selection. If the account given is a selection made to demonstrate the correctness of the original selection it is utterly worthless.
>
> (p. 133)

Later on, he speaks of the "artistic representation" necessary to an approximation of a truthful report of a session which is possible if one assumes, he says, rather challengingly,

> the requisite degree of artistic capacity in the psycho-analyst which can bring about, a transformation during which selection and ordering of the material take place. The interpretation given the patient is a formulation intended to display an underlying pattern. It is therefore itself similar to the mathematical formula described by Poincaré (*Science and Method,* Dover Books, p. 30). It is also similar to some aspects of a painting, sculpture or musical composition. At their best these formulations make us aware of a coherence and order where, without them, incoherence and disorder would reign.
>
> (p. 131)

In effect, he is exploring, as so often, the limitations of the psychoanalytic interpretive model, the limitation of this particular form. His expression of the quandary is a powerful one:

> These words I write are supposed to "contain" meaning: the verbal expression can be so formalised, so rigid, so filled with already existing ideas that the idea I want to express can have all the life squeezed out of it. On the other hand, the meaning I wish to express may have such force and vitality, relative to the verbal formulation in which I would strive to contain it, that it destroys the verbal container .... Psychoanalysis itself provides an outstanding example of such a force, idea or individual in tension with its container, verbal formulation, or society.
>
> (p. 141)

Bion never ceases to tussle with this quandary: in effect, how can the psycho-analytic interpretive mode expand rather than limit the complex sensuality of emotional experience; how can it free rather than imprison embryonic thought?

His elaborations on how to capture and express so intuitive a process as the incremental growth of meaning are scattered throughout his later work. He returns to the significance of determining an "underlying pattern" in his final trilogy, *A Memoir of the Future* (1990). The nature of this pattern has been definitively described by Meg Harris Williams (1983/2010). The trilogy focuses on the kind of catastrophic anxiety already alluded to, one which attends any move forward in life's psychic journey, an anxiety which shadows all transitions of the differently weighted and freighted developmental passages across the life cycle from pre-birth to death itself. Liminal, or threshold, states of mind and body are what we are having to confront and to manage all the time. At all points of that journey people have to be able not just to feel the pain but to suffer it—an important distinction of Bion's. For those who, like Ophelia, are "incapable of their own distress," madness lies, ultimately the death of both mind and, finally, body.

It often happens that after many weeks, even months of steady analytic work, something revelatory or mutative may occur, often, like Poincaré, in a dream, or in a single session (Waddell, 2010), as a consequence of which, thereafter, the lights and shadows of the mind "must always fall with a certain difference" (Eliot, 1872). Such emotional events can, and do, come about, as Bion suggests, not so much through the interpretive method as such, but through something akin to a trapping of light between analyst and analysand which precedes the experience of the known, that is articulable, meaning in external terms. In using the metaphor "trapping of light" I am drawing on the language with which Bion, in the *Memoir*, describes how a sculpture works: "Imagine a piece of sculpture which it is easier to comprehend if this structure is intended to act as a trap for light. The meaning is reversed by the pattern formed by the light thus trapped—not by the structure, the carved work itself" (pp. 189–90). Bion often sought metaphors for alternative ways of seeing and knowing, ones that involved eschewing familiar thought processes (memories and desires, even supposed understanding). In a passage in the *Brazilian Lectures* (1990), he traces the shift from watching a game of tennis to focusing down "with a beam of darkness," as Freud put it, so that:

> the only important thing visible to us is a lot of holes which are collected together in a net. Similarly, we might look at a pair of socks and be able to see a mass of holes which have been knitted together. We should reconsider this domain of thought because as psychoanalysts

> we must be able to see that it is a pair of socks or a game of tennis, and at the same minute be able to turn down the light, turn off this brilliant intuition, and see these holes, including the fact that they have been knitted, or netted, together.
>
> (p. 21)

Bion is saying that the form of art, like the analytic encounter, captures meaning which lies outside its own boundaries—the concrete form can evoke quite other forms in a realm beyond.

Something akin to "the trapping of the light" can be seen with particular clarity to be functioning in the dreamworld, be it that of the waking or of the sleeping dream. Something may be happening between patient and analyst that is much more than the sum of the interpretive statements that can be offered in relation to, say, the dream content or to the here and now transference (Waddell, 2010). Similarly, as Meg Harris Williams (1983) points out, in poetry the

> penumbra of significance beyond the lexical connotations of words begins to impinge on the observer as he ceases to be a mere observer …. Feeling himself to be drawn into the aesthetic object, and responding to the psychic tensions captured by its formal qualities, his own inner mental structure is inevitably qualified.
>
> (p. 182)

Something of this process seemed to be occurring in the dream material of thirty-four-year-old Steven, whose analysis, as I've described elsewhere (1998), took its course over a number of years. A successful young academic, he had always used intellectuality as an effective defense against a range of infantile anxieties, above all, against the pain of intimacy. Knowledge as a form of power rather than as a source of understanding had long provided a serviceable carapace—this knowledge gradually including the latest psychoanalytic theory, particularly those aspects that he thought (rightly) most interested his analyst. His quest for knowledge had a quality which was more in tune with a desire to possess and to occupy than to understand; to know "about" rather than genuinely to explore and to identify, internally, with the functions of his objects in the quest for the meaning of his own experience.

This earlier state of mind is well caught in a brief dream a year or so into his analysis. The contrast to another dream some three years later, striking for drawing on similar images, measured a long period of intense struggle with his competitive, conformist self. The different use of the same image in each dream encapsulates the nature of the developmental process which I am describing here—risking the serviceable, safe and familiar for the unknown.

In the early dream,

> There were beautiful glass spheres, contained each in their own concave cup—spheres which I smashed with a heavy ball-bearing, gathering the broken pieces into a mixing bowl and putting the ball-bearing on top, with a rather complacent air of "what a good boy am I."

In this caricature of analytic work, the superior, self-congratulatory "good boy" Steven was able to deceive himself as to the cup-filling confection—as if, for him, it constituted an actual cake/breast, with its ball-bearing nipple, rather than a mockery of the psychoanalytic method, in terms of the container/contained model.

After three more years of hard analytic work, an external event occurred, aptly described by Steven as a "bombshell," for it introduced a mode of perception and a quality of feeling the capacity for which had rarely surfaced before. The eruption of a long-quiescent skin condition, eczema, coincided with a visit to his home in Ireland during the weekend when the eldest of his three younger sisters was due to give birth. Tormented over this weekend by his infantile feelings of failure and also of distress, among other things, at the recurrence of the very symptom which had originated at the birth of this same sister thirty-two years earlier, he had the following dream.

> I resided in the place where children are before being born—existing as protoplasmic blobs, suspended in a bluish pink atmosphere above cups—themselves seemingly attached, as if by a line of some sort, to a lily pad on the surface of the water. The children were talking together. One conversation was distinct, between me and an unborn girl. We were discussing my fear of death: "If you are born you have to die;" I said, "and that feels too terrifying." The girl disagreed—"The real courage lies in allowing yourself to be born in the first place. Once you've done that you've already taken care of the fear of death. Death doesn't seem anything like so bad afterwards. What you do is meet the cup, get down into it and be born. Then you can bear the rest." With that, she did get down into the cup and went ahead, leaving me lingering behind, fearful, and yet somehow infused with courage and expectancy.

This dream seemed to me to be a rather remarkable representation of the potential birth of the mind—of the hitherto unborn parts of Steven's personality, of the bluish pink dawning of the "thinking principle." Perhaps the "bluish pink" is suggestive of the male/female symbols of Bion's container/contained—his notion of the mother's love for the father, and his for her, being central to her capacity for reverie. Gone is the ambitious, defensive, "good boy" Steven and instead there is the fear and pain of the fetal-self feeling encouraged to proceed by the capacity to hold a dialogue with a quite other part of the self. So reminiscent of the pre-birth characters' conversation in Bion's *The Dawn of Oblivion*, this more evolved self knew that the cup constituted a safe internal container—in touch both with Steven's internal world and also his external, by way of the lily pad/umbilical cord/transference link.

Held in that container, Steven could allow himself to consider being born, to think for himself in the sense that I have been discussing—engaging, that is, with the cup of life, with the internal alpha-function mother. He was thereby enabled to proceed with his development. The cup had now become a genuinely containing object, the contents of which he was not tempted to smash up, nor on which to make major, so-called, "improvements." It was one, rather, in which his mind might be fledged and set on a course of self-discovery. We may speculate that this shift was a consequence of his early and rather disturbed, or delayed, emotional development now unconsciously having become more meaningful to him, and therefore representable in the dream image, and finally articulable and communicable in the session.

The shift in Steven was marked (not brought about) by the "bombshell" of the birth a new baby, of his nephew; "marked" because that event occurred in a psyche which seemed already prepared to be born as a result of the psychoanalytic risks he had been taking over the previous three years. It was, indeed, a *psychic* bombshell, but it constituted, true to Bion's notion of catastrophic change, "a breakthrough, and not a breakdown." The ugly, pseudo-aesthetic avoidance of turbulence in the earlier dream yielded, in the later one, to a much more fearful, yet harmonious possibility of genuine psychic growth. What this latter dream indicated was the all-important capacity in Steven to begin to face aspects of his personality which his manic smashing and pseudo-integrating activities of the past had defended him from properly knowing about, or taking responsibility for. He is now able to be in identification with a modest sense of a sister who has gone before him into parenthood rather than the traumatizing one whose birth gave him eczema. One might surmise that at the time the eczema was an expression of the breakdown of the ordinary containing function of the skin. The birth of his sister tested his young capacities beyond what he could manage and the integrating and holding function of his psychic skin, so vividly described by Esther Bick (1968) physically abandoned him. Intrapsychically, he could now release himself from his restrictive, hide-bound ways, and move outside the usual casual and contractual forms of mental corralling. This involved his being able, metaphorically, to face death itself. Life and death were as completely inter-related as turbulence and growth. What had enabled this expansion of emotional experience was an aesthetic analytical experience involving the equivalent of a "trapping of light."

For Bion, development was all—the vicissitudes of states of becoming. Development entails "thinking," thinking, that is, in the very particular way that he was struggling to express, less a cognitive than an emotional matter. The unconscious emotional experiences that lay at the heart of development were, in his terms, the essential elements of the wherewithal of the mind's expansion, and of the internal resistances to that expansion. He was exquisitely aware of the intense internal opposition to what he called "the birth of an idea," to, in Keats's terms, "the dawning of the thinking principle."

One can see how the *visual* sense, the pictograms or pictographs of which Bion so often spoke, lay, as Glover (2009) suggests, "at the core of unconscious phantasy" and how "he describes the psychoanalytical encounter more and more in terms of visual and aesthetic analogies" (p. 127)—"'the trapping of light' in all 'good,' even 'great' art." In terms of the congruences mentioned earlier, both in the analytic encounter at its best, and in the work of art, emotional experience can not only be contained but be expanded, and a development towards deeper truthfulness can occur as the sleeping images of things, to borrow from the poet Dryden, are moved towards the light.

References

Bick, E. (1968) The Experience of the Skin in Early Object Relations. *International Journal of Psycho-Analysis,* 45:484–6.

Bion, W. R. (1962a) A Theory of Thinking. *International Journal of Psycho-Analysis,* 43:306–10. Reprinted in, Bion, W. R. (1967) *Second Thoughts,* London: Heinemann.

Bion, W. R. (1962b) *Learning from Experience.* London: Heinemann.

Bion, W.R. (1965) *Transformations.* London: Heinemann.

Bion, W. R. (1967) Commentary on "The Imaginary Twin." In *Second Thoughts,* London: Heinemann

Bion, W. R. (1990) *Brazilian Lectures.* London: Karnac Books.

Bion, W. R. (1991) The Dawn of Oblivion. In *A Memoir of the Future.* London: Karnac (pp. 427–576).

Eliot, G. (1872) *Middlemarch.* Reprinted: Harmondsworth: Penguin.

Eliot, T.S. (1963) *Four Quartets.* London: Faber & Faber.

Glover, N. (2009) *Psychoanalytic Aesthetics: An Introduction to the British School.* London: Karnac Books.

Meltzer, D. (1978) *The Kleinian Development.* Strath Tay, Perthshire: Clunie Press.

Meltzer, D. (1988) *The Apprehension of Beauty: The Role of Aesthetic Conflict in Development, Art and Violence.* Strath Tay, Perthshire: Clunie Press.

Merrill, J. (1996) *Selected Poems.* Manchester: Carcanet Press.

Satyamurti, C. (2003) "First Time Ever": Writing the Poem in Potential Space. In: Canham, H. and Satyamurti, C. (eds). *Acquainted with the Night: Psychoanalysis and the Poetic Imagination.* London: Karnac Books.

Stokes, A. (1963) *Painting and the Inner World.* London: Tavistock. In: *Critical Writings of Adrian Stokes, Volume III.* London: Thames & Hudson, 1978.

Waddell, M. J. (1998) *Inside Lives: Psychoanalysis and the Growth of the Personality.* London: Karnac Books, 2002.

Waddell, M. J. (2010) "From Resemblance to Identity": The Internal Narrative of a 50 Minute Hour. In: Mawson, C. (ed.) *Bion Today.* London: Routledge.

Williams, M. H. (1983) "Underlying Pattern" in Bion's *Memoir of the Future*: *International Review of Psychoanalysis*, 10(75):75–86. Reprinted in C. Mawson (ed.), *Bion Today*, London: Routledge, 2010.

EDITORS' INTRODUCTION

The Power of Form: The Shoah in Contemporary Hebrew Literature

Beatriz Priel

While Susanne Langer (1953) proposed that feeling and emotions are central to aesthetic experience and the illumination of otherwise unknown aspects of reality, Adorno (1962) has famously declared that the magnitude of the horrors of the Holocaust are such that they defy translation into artistic creations. In this chapter, Priel offers a close reading of Israeli author Aharon Appelfeld's novel, *Badenheim 1939*, to illustrate that even in the face of such monstrous events as the Shoah, there is the possibility of creating works of literature in which unspeakable horror may be contained; i.e. transformed in ways that allow for thinking and symbolization to evolve in the reading process.

Using Bion's model of container/contained, Priel demonstrates how a literary creation may offer readers an experience, which can generate a unique containing function in the elaboration of thoughts about man-made massive trauma, furnishing shape and secure boundaries for otherwise chaotic, unthinkable contents. In so doing, Priel reveals how the experience of a work of art, as a form of human, symbolic, inner-emotional truth, can "contain the horror and allow for its transformation in the experience of the reader." The mechanisms of that transformation—containment, representation and symbolization within an aesthetic literary form—imply psychic representation and the binding of inchoate feelings, give voice and name to the heretofore silent and unnamable and, as new meanings are generated and contained, may allow readers to experience a transformative return of meaningfulness to a previously shattered world.

15

THE POWER OF FORM

The Shoah in Contemporary Hebrew Literature

Beatriz Priel

Since antiquity, art has fulfilled the important function of creating a shared space to contain the group's unconscious fantasies that might otherwise be inexpressible. Studies of ancient Greek theater (e.g. Britton, 1995; Freud, 1908; Lear, 1992; Snaevarr, 2005) have already noted the important effects that emotions raised by artistic creations have on their audiences. However the mere possibility of literature, or art in general, in the context of the Shoah has been questioned, as in Adorno's often quoted indictment that, "to write poetry after Auschwitz is barbaric" (1962, p. 312). The question of a fictional literature on the Shoah elicited strong emotional reactions during the first years after World War II, as if the facts of the horrific events resisted any displacement and transformation through art. However, Adorno later qualified his statement, affirming that "literature must resist this verdict." And, he added, "it is now virtually in art alone that suffering can find its own voice, consolation, without being immediately betrayed by it" (1962, p. 313).

Literary creations may play a unique containing function in the elaboration of man-made massive trauma. They may provide shape and secure boundaries for otherwise chaotic contents. Specifically, it is my contention that there are works of contemporary Hebrew literature in which the unspeakable horror is contained, i.e. transformed in ways that allow for thinking and symbolization to evolve in the reading process. I center here on the beholder's experience and in art's ability to arouse and communicate affect. Freud already referred to the effects of art on the beholder in *Creative Writers and Daydreaming* (1908), where he wondered how creative writers' materials "*make such an impression on us … and arouse in us emotions of which, perhaps, we have not even thought ourselves capable*" (p. 143). More recently Kristeva (1984) maintained that the religious function of giving shape to otherwise disquieting, formless and ineffable psychic contents has been recovered in the twentieth century by great contemporary poets and dramatists.

Art as Containment

In Susanne Langer's theory of art (1953), symbolism is key to the understanding of how the human mind transforms the primal need to express oneself. Langer defined art as the creation of "forms symbolic of human feeling." In this theory, the focus is not on the creative process itself, but rather on art's significance for the audience, reader or viewer. From Langer's perspective, phenomena resistant to expression in language, like dreams and feelings, are dealt with through the use of presentational symbols such as music, art and myth-making. These are ways of bringing meaning to a realm that would otherwise be "unspeakable." Thus, this perspective points to the central role of *feeling* in aesthetic experiences and proposes that, through feeling, art illuminates otherwise unknown aspects of reality.

It is important to note that, from Langer's perspective, artists are not seen as conveying their own actual or personal feelings. Artists express "ideas of feeling," that is, formulations and representations of emotions, moods and mental tensions. According to Langer, every work of art involves abstraction, plasticity and expressiveness. By its *abstraction* (i.e. being removed) from actuality, the work of art becomes mere semblance; artists create virtual objects, illusions, appearances of events, persons, emotional reactions, places, etc. as "poetic semblances." Works of art always entail *plasticity* and, therefore, these works can be manipulated in the interests of expression. Finally, works of art are *expressive*, so that their inherent symbolism becomes clear and evident.

Abstraction, plasticity and expressiveness may be seen as means that allow for the containing function of art—the creation of the artistic form that makes possible the containment of the anxieties raised by the represented contents. Intuition is seen as the link between the symbolic qualities of the work of art and the significance of the work for the observer. Thus, the aesthetic form may facilitate the creation of a new coordinate in the individual's inner space, a third dimension that is both liberating and self-reflective (Grotstein, 2000).

This conceptualization of the experience of a work of art as a form of human, symbolic, inner-emotional truth provides a coherent context for the assumed function of art as a container to hitherto inchoate psychic contents. From a Bionian vantage point, this symbolization implies the binding of inchoate feelings by the aesthetic literary form, conferring its unique naming, and allowing for a transformative internalization of new meanings. Bion expressed his belief in the importance of literature's input, especially poetry, for the search of truth when he said that, "Homer and Milton were not writing 'poetry,' they were writing 'seriously.' They wrote poetry because it was the most serious way of writing" (Harris-Williams, 2005).

In *Cogitations* (1958), Bion writes about the artist and art's effects on its audience or readership, saying that:

> [the artist] is someone who is able to digest facts, i.e., sense data, and then to present the digested facts, my alpha elements, in a way that makes it possible for the weak assimilators to go from there. Thus, the artist helps the non-artist to digest …
>
> (p. 143)

We can see here a concept of aesthetics that reaches beyond an understanding of the creative processes themselves, with implications for the other, the one at whom the art is aimed, that is, the effect of art on the viewer, audience, or reader. In addition, Bion's three-volume novel *A Memoir of the Future* (1993) dramatizes this author's belief that artistic fiction can communicate something beyond rational modes of thought, and that the experience of truth may sometimes be found in fictional rather than theoretical writing. Moreover, some of Bion's basic psychoanalytic concepts are elaborations of ideas from the realm of art and aesthetics.

For instance, following Keats, Bion adopted the concept of negative capability (Bion, 1970). Keats defined "negative capability" as the capability "of being in uncertainties, mysteries, doubts, without any irritable reaching after fact and reason" (Rollins, 1958, p. 193). Keats not only contrasted negative capability with "irritable reaching after fact and reason," but also emphasized the contribution of unrestrained imagination to the acquisition of new knowledge (Leavy, 1970; Goellnicht, 1989). Negative capability points to the capacity to bear novelty and surprise, to intuitively reach for truth that is otherwise obscured by conventional assumptions and habit. We can thus say that negative capability does not imply an ability to decipher a dream or a text, but rather an ability to *follow* a patient's discourse or a written story (i.e. the capability to let oneself get "trapped" in the discourse or story).

Another profoundly artistic Bionian concept is the idea of "catastrophic change," a concept rooted in literature and denoting the moment of knowledge in a dramatic work, the turning point in a drama at which there is a total change in perspective, the moment of truth. Moreover, Bion's crucial conception of Truth has important aesthetic dimensions, probably following Keats's poetic claim that "Beauty is truth, truth beauty".

Hebrew Prose on the Shoah

The first literary works to address the Shoah were mainly documentary in nature, reflecting a strict adherence to facts, and were determined to convey "the whole truth." Any departure from the actual events was regarded as sinful. In the immediate aftermath of the disaster, written work concerning the Shoah was reactive and presented most of the characteristics typical of the initial reactions of survivors of extreme trauma: utter conventionality and concreteness, repetition and rigidity; symbolic capacities that seemed compromised. This early testimonial writing succeeded in bringing the horror of the Shoah into the public discourse, but the transformative and containing function of art was absent. This absence speaks to the difference between artistic containment and concrete transmission of the horror.

But, art did not keep silent, and we have witnessed a journey from the meticulous and excruciating description of the Jewish external reality in occupied Europe, to literary fiction that symbolizes feelings and links external and internal realities. These are creative narratives of trauma as both the encounter with death and the ongoing experience of having survived. These fictional works correspond to recent definitions of *serious fiction* (Harrison, 2007) as fiction that offers the reader knowledge *of* reality, as opposed to knowledge *about* reality; in this case, the knowledge *of* the Shoah.

Aharon Appelfeld's stories are paradigmatic of this process. He was born in 1932 and came to Israel at the age of fourteen, as a child survivor who had spent three years wandering in post-war Europe, most of the time by himself. His mother was murdered by the Nazis when he was eight, and he eventually rejoined his father in Israel after many years of separation.

Appelfeld sees himself, and is seen by his readers, as a witness. That is, he is someone responsible for telling what happened but, in his own words, it is not enough to cry out about the events; "you must find *a form* for that crying out" (Appelfeld, 1979, p. 49). In his aesthetic search—the search for a form for that cry—Appelfeld created a style that is minimalist and paradoxical, restrained and highly suggestive. His characters are neither mute nor articulate; they generally display painful stuttering and have a permanent need to travel in endless circles.

Analysis of Appelfeld's work uncovers a particular relationship between a self-contained, very reserved, and restrained manner of storytelling and the threatening horror of the content evoked in these stories. Moreover, Appelfeld presents a testimony of the Shoah as experienced in the characters' *internal* reality. The physical, external events are only hinted at, as most of his stories take place before or after the Shoah.

Appelfeld's creation illuminates the power of the form to contain the horror and allow for its transformation in the experience of the reader. In what follows I shall look closely at one of Appelfeld's well-known novellas, translated into English as *Badenheim 1939* (1975).[1] This work is paradigmatic of literature's function as a container of collective extreme traumatic experiences.

The year is 1939 and a group of Austrian Jewish vacationers have gathered in the resort town of Badenheim. Two events that are to happen in the near future create a unique atmosphere of both expectancy and threat in Badenheim in the year 1939: the annual spring music festival that has attracted the vacationers to the resort, and an unexpected inspection to be carried out by the Sanitation Department. The public has been informed that the Sanitation Department will carry out independent investigations, and that vacationers are required to register with the authorities.

The truth is that the so-called Sanitation Department planned and carried out the vacationers' deportation to Poland, while presenting itself as a well-organized and very efficient service provider, a sort of travel agency. The truth of deportation and death is consciously evaded, hidden behind images of a pleasant trip to Poland and the almost mythic scenes of the spring festival in the exclusive resort. We read, for instance:

> The inspectors of the Sanitation Department were now spread all over the town. They took measurements, put up fences, and planted flags. Porters unloaded rolls of barbed wire, cement pillars, and all kinds of appliances suggestive of preparations for public celebrations. (p. 15)

The Sanitation Department was comfortably appointed even at night, so that guests "could sit on an armchair, listen to music, leaf through a journal, and dream of Poland. The remote, alien Poland began to seem an idyllic, pastoral place" (p. 31). The posters put up by the Sanitation Department are deceiving and conspicuously unsettling: "The development areas need you," "The air in Poland is fresher," "Sail on the Vistula" (pp. 29, 30). After a few days, the vacationers begin to refer to the deportation as emigration, a journey, or even a homecoming. All of these terms evade the coercion defining the deportation to which they are being subjected.

As ordered, everybody compliantly registered with the Sanitation Department and Poland gradually became the "right" place to go. However, all over the text, we see indications and signs left unexplained of something strange, secret, and alien that is happening. We read: "There was a different quality in the air, a sharp quality which did not come from the local forests" (p. 37). "Both cafes remained open and the band played every night, but it still seemed that some other time, some other place, had invaded the town and was silently establishing itself" (p. 38).

The novella depicts Badenheim's rapid transition from an exclusive resort to a detention camp, as the visitors delude themselves, blind to the multiple signs of the coming storm. After a few days, people were not allowed to leave the town and were banned from the pool. Later on, the post office was closed. The festival's impresario, Dr. Pappenheim, saw even in these events the possibility of something positive as he said, "we'll have time to study" (p. 47).

Then, strangers arrived in Badenheim, Jews who had been in their own homes until days before, when everything had been taken from them as they were deported. The newcomers did ask questions and were calmed by good "old words" (p. 99), such as "right procedures" and "court of law." The strange new situation was seen as a misunderstanding: "It is not a question of crime, but of a misunderstanding" (pp. 98–9). As days went by in Badenheim, even food became scarce. But, Dr. Pappenheim kept speaking eloquently about "people going gladly to Poland. They were happy, looking forward to it eagerly" (p. 107). In the last page of the book, this relentless tragic metamorphosis is summarized in a rather hellish scene:

> An engine, coupled to four filthy freight cars, emerged from the hulls and stopped at the station. Its appearance was as sudden as if it has risen from a pit in the ground. "Get in!" yelled invisible voices. And the people were sucked in. Even those who were standing with a bottle of lemonade in their hands, a bar of chocolate, the headwaiter with his dog—they were all sucked in as easily as grains of wheat poured into a funnel. Nevertheless, Dr. Pappenheim found time to make the following remark: "If the coaches are so dirty, it must mean that we have not far to go."
>
> (pp. 147–8)

There are no scenes of murder or concrete destruction, the novella consists of a slow and relentless depiction of the fabrication of lies and the methodic destruction of thinking. The victimizers *consciously* direct their lies to the victims and succeed in denuding the true feelings of both their own minds and others' minds. The parasitic container–contained relationship that characterizes lies, appears here in all its destructiveness. The fabrication of lies may symbolize the all-encompassing effects of human destructiveness. An attitude of omniscience substitutes for doubt, for the intuition of truth, and for discrimination between truth and lie (Bion, 1962). Consequently, truth disappears from the self and from the other's mind.

The restrained and suggestive depiction of the devastating power of lies as the background to the pending disaster creates a reading experience of profound sadness and perplexity. This novella is built upon the tension between seeming and being—characters remain within the domain of the seeming, while the reader combines seeming and being, and is aware of the real implications of the journey.

This reading experience and the sense of impending tragedy are reinforced through themes that are only hinted at, or appear to be unrelated to the plot. As in the interpretation of dreams, the absent and the seemingly irrelevant may be sources of truth. For instance, the narrative forcefully evokes the theme of the plague. The themes of sanitation, purification, and isolation from sources of contamination function as premonitions of disaster—the ghost of a plague hides in almost every page, in descriptions of the atmosphere of "intoxication" (p. 13) and "isolation" (pp. 14, 70) in the town. And, even more explicitly in statements like the following one: "The town was in quarantine … Is there an epidemic? A Jewish epidemic" (p. 71).

The epidemic is a recurring theme in the history of Western literature, representing severe moral crisis and the compulsive expansion of violence. These are explained as responses to the invisible threats of contamination or loss of boundaries, and death (Boothby, 1996; Weinstein, 2003). These archaic anxieties characterize sanctioned massacres aimed at the total elimination of those defined as sources of contamination, onto whom the threat has been projected. Their dehumanization is unavoidable (Priel, 2007). We see metaphorical plagues used as models for the social dissolution of basic moral codes in *One Hundred Years of Solitude* by Garcia Marquez, Sophocles's *Oedipus King*, Camus's *The Plague*, and Saramago's *Blindness*. The shadow of the plague also falls on Appelfeld's *Badenheim 1939*.

Violence enters Appelfeld's story also surreptitiously, in seemingly marginal scenes. For example, new Cambium fish were brought for the beautiful aquarium and, after a few days, these fish were "massacred" (p. 51) by all of the other fish in the aquarium, and the floor was covered with corpses. The metaphor of the closed aquarium with different kinds of fish and the tragic consequences of these differences accompanies Badenheim's metamorphosis.

While Appelfeld's restrained style has a powerful moderating effect, forestalling melodrama, we witness here the cumulative tension between the concealment of the horror in the story-as-reporting, and the revelation of the horror in the story-as-performance, that is, in the effect of the story on the reader (Rimmon Kenan, 1987). There is a unique tension in *Badenheim 1939* between the form as a clearly delineated, but flexible container and its appalling and rather unspeakable content. In the reading experience, we follow the theme of the text, but are also, at least part of the time, captivated by its form. We dwell in the aesthetic experience as a poetic space that allows us to come back to the thematic course of the text. It is as if, in this instance, truth may dwell more flexibly in fictional rather than realistic writing.

The narration of the fabrication of lies as well as the hints to plague and massacre dramatize symbolization not as static but as an incessant process that enacts Lyotard's (1990) famous indictment that "[a]rt does not say the unsayable, but says that it cannot say it" (p. 47). Appelfeld's story succeeds in transmitting the unspeakable without distorting it, thus dramatizing a most basic aspect of containment.

The unique relationship between fiction and reality that characterizes narratives of the Shoah has been poignantly described by Aharon Appelfeld himself, in one of his critical essays:

> When it comes to describing reality, art always demands certain intensification. However, that is not the case with the Holocaust for many and various reasons. Everything in it "seems thoroughly unreal." Thence comes the need to bring it down to the human realm. That is not a mechanical problem, but an essential one. When I say "to bring it down" I do not mean to simplify, to attenuate, or to sweeten the horror, but to make the event speak through the individual and in his language.
>
> (Appelfeld, 1988, p. 92)

Appelfeld's statement, "to bring it down to the human realm" means, in the language of this chapter, to contain the horror, to make the horror digestible. The inversion of the relation between the fictional and the real, between art and life, constitutes a main containing device for experiences that are well beyond the limits of human imagination. This inversion or "bringing down" produces an emotional experience in the reader that he or she can be aware of, without avoiding it or being overwhelmed by it.

Badenheim 1939 does not say the unsayable, but is steadfastly faithful to it.

Note

1 Extracts from *Badenheim 1939* by Aharon Appelfeld, translated from the Hebrew by Dalya Bilu. Reprinted by permission of David R. Godine, Publisher, Inc. Copyright 1980 by Aharon Appelfeld. Translation copyright by Dalya Bilu 1980. All rights reserved.

References

Adorno, T. (1962) Commitment. In: *The Essential Frankfurt School Reader*, A. Arato and E. Gebhart (eds.). New York: Continuum, 1982.

Appelfeld, A. (1979) *Masot beguf rishon* (Essays in the first person). Jerusalem: Hasifrya Hatzionit.

Appelfeld, A. (1980) *Badenheim 1939.* (Dalya Bilu, trans.). Boston: D.R. Godine.

Appelfeld, A. (1988) After the Holocaust. In B. Lang (ed.). *Writing and the Holocaust.* Teaneck, NJ: Homes & Meier.

Bion, W. R. (1958) *Cogitations.* London: Karnac.

Bion, W. R. (1962) *Learning from Experience.* London: Karnac.

Bion, W. R. (1970) *Attention and Interpretation.* London: Heinemann.

Bion, W. R. (1993) *A Memoir of the Future.* London: Karnac.

Boothby, R. (1996) Alter-Egos: Psychoanalysis and the theory of sacrifice. *Journal for the Psychoanalysis of Culture and Society*, 1:47–61.

Britton, R. (1995) Reality and unreality in phantasy and fiction. In: *On Freud's "Creative Writers and Day Dreaming": Turning Points and Critical Issues.* E. Spector Person, P. Fonagy, S. Figueira (eds.). New Haven: Yale University Press (pp. 82–106).

Freud, S. (1908) Creative Writers and Day Dreaming. *Standard Edition*, 9:142–53. London: Hogarth Press, 1960.

Goellnicht, D. C. (1989) Keats on reading: "Delicious diligent indolence." *Journal of English Germanic Philology* April: 190–210.

Grotstein, J. S. (2000). *Who is the Dreamer who Understands the Dream: The Study of Psychic Presences.* Hillsdale, NJ: Analytic Press.

Harrison, B. (2007) Aharon Appelfeld and Holocaust fiction. In *A Sense of the World* (pp. 67–88). New York: Routledge.

Harris-Williams, M. (2005) *The Vale of Soulmaking: The Post-Kleinian Model of the Mind and its Poetic Origins.* London: Karnac.

Keats, J. (1884) Ode on a Grecian Urn. In: *The Poetical Works of John Keats.* London: Macmillan; Bartleby.com, 1999 (p. 41).

Kristeva, J. (1984) *Revolution in Poetic Language.* (Roudiez, L., trans.) New York: Columbia University Press (original work published in 1974).

Langer, S. K. (1953) *Feeling and Form.* New York: Charles Scribner & Sons.

Lear, J. (1992) Katharsis. In: A. Oksenberg Rorty (ed.) *Essays on Aristotle's Poetics.* Princeton University Press, Princeton, New Jersey (pp. 315–40).

Leavy, S. A. (1970) John Keat's psychology of creative imagination. *Psychoanalytical Inquiry*, 39:173–97.

Lyotard, J. F. (1990) *Heidegger and "the Jews"* (Michel, A. and Robert, M., trans.) Minneapolis, MN: University of Minnesota Press.

Priel, B. (2007) Thinking extreme social violence: The model of the literary plague. *International Journal of Psychoanalysis*, 88:1–15.

Rimmon Kenan, S. (1987) *Discourse in Psychoanalysis and Literature.* London: Methuen.

Rollins, H. E., (ed.) (1958) *The Letters of John Keats, 1814–1821.* Cambridge, MA: Cambridge University Press.

Snaevarr, S. (2005) Poetics and maieutics: Literature and tacit knowledge of emotions. *Contemporary Aesthetics*, 5:1–21.

Weinstein, A. (2003) Afterword: Infection as metaphor. *Literature and Medicine*, 22:102–15.

Part 6

FINAL THOUGHTS

16

LOOKING BACK, LOOKING AHEAD

Howard B. Levine

As the contributors to this volume have demonstrated, Bion's concept of container/contained has proven to be a highly creative stimulus for psychoanalytic exploration and thinking in a wide range of areas and directions. Their chapters attest to the fact that when viewed through the lens of container/contained, growth and turbulence, development and stasis appear in a kaleidoscopic, dialectical relationship in a multitude of situations: clinical, theoretical, cultural, aesthetic. Readers will be left with much to consider and to further explore in regard to such topics as the dialogic, intersubjective, processes of dream-work and dreaming, enactment and therapeutic action; the perils and vicissitudes of reverse projective identification, primitive conscience, caesura denial, pseudo-process and stasis; the role of the object and alpha function in the development of the psyche; the traumatic nature of reality, the ineffability of both raw, unprocessed, concrete experience (O) and the unconscious and the ways in which the ineffable influences the processes of aesthetic creation and aesthetic response.

What is it about Bion and his writing that has had such a profound and varied influence on the field of psychoanalysis? Why have his thoughts taken hold in so many different psychoanalytic schools and cultures and why, after Freud, is he perhaps the most cited author in our literature?

I think that Bion's work speaks to so many different analysts, in part because he placed such great store on the uniqueness and value of individual, subjective experience and believed that bearing the truth of personal experience, no matter how idiosyncratic or painful, was essential for the growth of the psyche. We hear echoes of this belief in the titles that he chose for his books—*Learning from Experience*, *Attention and Interpretation*—and in his explanation to audiences that he would tell them something about how he thought that *he* did analysis in the hope that it might help them to understand something about how *they* did analysis.

Bion tried to lead readers and listeners away from the expectation that he would reveal some new and pre-existing universal truth. Instead, he preferred to encourage them to risk giving up the comfort of holding on to what was already known and familiar and attempted to help prepare their minds to encounter some unexpected and not yet known aspect of emerging experience. While his writings certainly added specific "facts to our understanding of human psychology, he also taught us to be wary, perhaps even distrustful, of the defensive use to which "facts" and "knowledge" (in the static sense) could be put. He cautioned that clinging to the familiarity of the known can obscure what was disturbing, unfamiliar, urgent and central at any given moment. So, too, he warned of the tendencies within the group to reject truth and oppose new knowledge, if it threatened to destabilize the comfortable investments and assumptions of the status quo.

Rather than seeking to create "Bionians,"—acolytes, disciples and adherents—Bion sought to kindle a creative spark in others that would lead to new and unexpected discoveries. This attitude towards students and colleagues was consistent with his understanding and practice of psychoanalysis and his view of the unconscious. He described the former as a probe that expands the very field it seeks to explore and viewed the latter as an ever expanding and infinite domain. He believed that the frontiers of what must be explored and what remained to be understood would be limitless and inexhaustible. Thus, he emphasized process over content, *Transformations* (another choice for a book title) over "facts" and urged us to pay as much if not more attention to the links and relations between things than to the things themselves.

If Freud's genius led him to the discovery and exploration of the realm of organized, structured but repressed mental contents and mechanisms that we call *the dynamic unconscious*, a realm which holds the key to interpreting dreams and understanding neurosis, Bion, following the implications of the later Freud, who directed our attention to the seething cauldron of the id, the problem of reality sense and all of the complications of mental life "beyond the pleasure principle," has led us into the depths of *the non-dynamic unconscious*: an ever expanding, infinite realm of emotional turbulence, catastrophic dread, annihilation anxiety, infinitizing pressures towards chaos, fragmentation and boundless dissolution. But this is also a realm of pure potential and possibility, the well spring of vitality and aliveness, if its chaotic, threatening and traumatic turbulences can be contained, suffered and transformed into the elements of thought (♂) and the tools with which to think them (♀).

Bion moved beyond Freud's theory of the dream as wish fulfillment and guardian of sleep to focus on the development of those capacities (alpha function; the apparatus for dreaming dreams; the apparatus for thinking thoughts) required to begin to dream and upon how dream-work, including the dream-work of waking life, personalizes and subjectifies internal and external experience and transforms it into something that is suitable to think with and think about. For Bion, the dream-work, which is essential to the creation of the psyche, assimilates reality and defends the psyche against the inherent traumaticity of raw, existential reality (Civitarese, 2011). From this perspective, the mind—its alpha function and mechanisms of PS↔D and container (♀)/contained (♂)—may be seen as our best chance to shield ourselves from this inescapable onslaught.

Given Bion's view of reality, the challenge that the analytic situation presents for both analyst and analysand is how to maintain composure and a competent, functioning psyche (how to "continue to think") in the face of an adverse, painful and a potentially traumatic (overwhelming, mind numbing or fragmenting) reality ("catastrophic change;" terror; "nameless dread"). How to come into contact with and continue to face ("suffer") the truth of one's existence (O), while keeping intact one's capacity to think and allowing oneself to experience enough of that "Experience"[1] so that one may learn from it and one's psyche may grow. How to keep the relationship between mind (♀) on the one hand and thought, feeling and/or perception on the other (♂) salutary and productive in the face of contents (potential experiences and psychic "facts") that may be painfully unbearable and threaten to become disruptive and even destructive to the mind that must try to contain them.

Practicing what he preached, Bion had the courage to re-examine, interrogate and revise his own early theories and conclusions—e.g. *Second Thoughts*. He had the ability to hold multiple perspectives and therefore greater complexity in mind and the remarkable capacity to shift his vertex of observation so that new configurations and relationships could emerge and be recognized in the midst of familiar constellations. These capacities enabled him to see beyond Klein's initial description of projective identification as a mechanism of defense and describe its *communicative* value, a discovery which was essential to his formulation of alpha function and the creation of his theory of thinking, and to recognize in Klein's description of the paranoid-schizoid and depressive positions a more general theory of psychic oscillation from chaos to form and from integration to disintegration to new integration and back again, a movement that he summarized by the notation PS↔D.

Bion also knew that as much as we are dependent upon language for communication, it is an inconstant ally, subject to distortion ("lies") and debased by repetitive use, the accumulation of commonplace connotations (a "penumbra of associations") around specific words and a tendency to distort observation in order to have it accommodate to what is expected and familiar. At the same time, his awareness that "Experience" (O) was inherently traumatic and could never be fully known or captured by words (K) led him to tolerate, and even to find a vertex from which he would valorize "myths" (Row C of his Grid) and even self-deception ("lies"), which he recognized was sometimes inevitable to protect ourselves from the traumatic onslaught of unprocessed Experience.

In *Elements of Psychoanalysis* (Bion, 1963), for example, when describing the essential place occupied by the analyst's statements of "personal myth" in the process of psychoanalytic interpretation, he wrote that while such statements were:

> akin to the type of statement that philosophers contemptuously dismiss as mythologies when they use the term pejoratively to describe bad theories [he] *require[d] as part of analytical scientific procedure and equipment statements of this kind.* They are not statements of observed fact, or formulations of a theory intended to represent a realization: they are statements of a personal myth.
>
> (p. 12, italics added)

He further asserted in no uncertain terms that: "Unless the experience of the psycho-analytical object is accompanied by a formulation by the psycho-analyst of a statement that has this type of component it lacks a necessary dimension" (p. 12).

Most surely, it was the inherently inexact, paradoxical and polysemic nature of words and the often impossible uses to which they could or had to be put—"making the best of a bad lot"—that led him to try to state psychoanalytic truths in novel, abstract, almost mathematical terms. What he sought was a purity of thought that would allow for the greatest possible freedom to observe and conceptualize things and the relationships (links) that existed between them. One culmination of this search was his assertion of the equation that "A is to B as container is to contained" [A/B=♀/♂]. This formulation, which underlies so much of his late writing, opened up the realm of application of this basic metaphor to untold and unforeseen areas of experience and lies at the heart of the chapters contained in this volume.

Bion's writing, increasingly in his later period, already emerging in the notebooks that would be posthumously published as "Cogitations" (Bion, 1992), has thus served as a launching pad for many different currents of psychoanalytic thought. As exemplified in this volume, these range from imaginative extensions of the contemporary Kleinian mainstream (e.g. Weiss, Staehle, Robinson) to novel theoretical iterations, such as Grotstein's reconceptualization of the function of dreaming, Ferro's narratologically-based conceptualization of therapeutic action, Cassorla's "dreams and non-dreams for two," Hartke's application of transformations in O to what were previously called the "non-specific therapeutic factors" in analysis, Junqueira de Matto and Braga's and

Bruni's explorations of primitive conscience, Trachtenberg's reflections on caesura denial, and Waddell's and Priel's application of the container/contained paradigm to aesthetic creation and the psychology of aesthetic response. At the heart of each of these contributions also lies Bion's assertion that external reality is essentially traumatic, a realization that emerged so painfully from his experience in World War I (Szykierski) and that remained central to his thinking, even on the battleground of psychoanalytic politics (Aguayo).

At the conclusion of Bion's Italian seminars (2005), Francesco Corrao, noted the "hate and love, truth and falsehood ... [that is inevitable in the human encounter and that is] violent, hard to bear and hard to transform" (p. 103) and expressed his gratitude to Bion by saying that in the face of such forces:

> we need the support and guidance of a way of thinking and a method that is problematic and unifying at one at the same time .... Dr. Bion has supplied us with this way of thinking and that he himself represents a strength in the here-and-now, because he embodies the strength of thought—its function, its use and its communication.
>
> (pp. 103–4)

Bion thanked Corrao for these remarks, noted that the direction taken by his own contributions could not have been foreseen—"like a leaf falling off a tree—one never knows which side up it will land" (p. 104)—and concluded with a final observation and a challenge that we would like to pass on to our readers, as they take what they have learned or been stimulated to discover about themselves and their patients back to their consulting rooms and analytic societies: "What is this group likely to give birth to? What thought or idea or action? And what relationship is likely to occur between it and some other group? Love or hate? Fight or flight? Dependence or freedom?" (p. 104).

The answer lies in the future. It is in the hands of our readers. The exploration and discovery, the work of analysis, continues. It is on-going and continually expanding. We shall see what develops.

Note

1 I have attempted here to distinguish raw, existential Experience of a kind that extends beyond the capacity to be fully known by writing that word with a capital "E." This is to contrast it with the kind of felt or known part of that Experience, which we colloquially refer to as "experience" and which I write with a small "e." To further illustrate the distinction, I offer that "Experience is to experience as O is to K."

References

Bion, W. R. (1962) *Learning from Experience.* London: Heinemann.
Bion, W. R. (1963) Elements of psycho-analysis. In: Bion, W. R., *Seven Servants. Four Works by Wilfred* R. *Bion.* New York: Jason Aronson, 1977.
Bion W. R. (1965) *Transformations.* London: Heinemann.
Bion W. R. (1967) *Second Thoughts: Selected Papers on Psycho-analysis.* London: Heinemann.
Bion W. R. (1970) *Attention and Interpretation.* London: Heinemann.
Bion, W. R. (1992) *Cogitations.* London: Karnac.
Bion, W. R. (2005) *The Italian Seminars.* London: Karnac.
Civitarese, G. (2011) Personal communication.

INDEX